Poverty Theory and Policy

The Johns Hopkins Studies in Development
Vernon W. Ruttan and T. Paul Schultz,
Consulting Editors

Poverty Theory and Policy

A Study of Panama

Gian Singh Sahota

The Johns Hopkins University Press
Baltimore and London

This book has been brought to publication with the generous assistance of the
Harvard Institute for International Development,
with which the author is affiliated.

The Johns Hopkins University Press, 701 West 40th Street, Baltimore,
Maryland 21211
The Johns Hopkins Press Ltd., London

The paper used in this book meets the minimum requirements of American
National Standard for Information Species—Permanence of Paper for Printed
Library Materials, ANSI Z39.48-1984.

Library of Congress Cataloging-in-Publication Data

Sahota, Gian S.
Poverty theory and policy: a study of Panama/Gian Singh Sahota.
p.   cm.—(The Johns Hopkins studies in development)
Includes bibliographical references.
ISBN 0-8018-3892-4
1. Poor—Panama.   2. Income—Panama.   I. Title. II. Series.
HC147.Z9P623 1990   89-37685 CIP

TO *Darshan, Hardyal, Nitya, Tuffail, Miko, and all those compatriots who could not bloom because of poverty*

Contents

Illustrations

Tables

Acknowledgments

This study arose out of research done in my capacity as the chief technical adviser to the United Nations for its technical aid project PAN/81/006: Critical Poverty in the Republic of Panama, 1983–85.

Permission for the publication of this work was formally given by the government of the Republic of Panama and the United Nations Department of Technical Cooperation Development. I thank both agencies for the opportunity, facilities, and resources they provided.

The study was done with the assistance of a team of national experts from the Ministry of Planning and Economic Policy, including Jośe Acosta, Ricardo Arosemena-Alvarado, Leda Arrue, Camilo Broce, Maria del Carmen de Cedeno, Giovanni Ciniglio, Viedma Luzcando, Ana Monge, Antonio Olivita, Maria Cristina de Pastor, and Armando Villarreal, as well as expatriate associate experts Hugue DeLannoy and Jean Lapeze. I received administrative and organizational help and comments on periodic drafts from Ana H. de Pitti, Aurora de Correa, and Rosa Elena de De La Cruz, who were national directors of the project, one after the other, during the course of the research. Logistical support and general leadership in advancing the project research came from economists Hector Alexander, minister of planning, and Juan Luis Moreno Villalaz, director of planning. In the later phase of the project Ricuarte Vasquez replaced Hector Alexander as minister of planning, and he authorized the publication of this research.

Several programmers from the Controller General's Office provided computational services; special mention must be made of Abel A. Mitil. The brain behind the formulation and execution of the National Socioeconomic Survey, 1983, was Maria Teresa de De Leon, and that behind programming and tabulation was Omar Rivera. Both of them worked very closely with me and my research team.

Special thanks go to Ricardo Arosemena-Alvarado (graduate student at UCLA and later Vanderbilt University), whose expert input ran from supervision of the survey, constant interaction with programmers, data processing, and correcting errors of survey data to commenting on my drafts. But for his dedicated assistance, this study would not be what it is.

With a view to increasing the rigor of the analysis, I invited several academic consultants for periods of two weeks to three months to help me in their areas of specialization. These included Jerold Bauch, Richard

Burkhauser, Robert Evenson, James Heckman, Samuel Morley, Sherwin Rosen, Chander Sahota, Larry Sjaastad, and Anthony Tang. They made substantive contributions to the quality of this research. Although I could not include all their contributions in this book, from my association and interaction with them I gained several methodological insights that I used or further developed in my own research. Due acknowledgment of their reports is made at relevant places. The conceptual approach used, the scope of the study demarcated, the analysis done, the policy implications derived, and the opinions expressed here, as well as any errors and weaknesses, however, are my sole responsibility.

This is also an occasion to thank Vanderbilt University for granting me generous leave to complete the two-year research for this project.

Thanks are also due to the Harvard Institute for International Development, Harvard University, for financial and intellectual support after I became affiliated with it starting in July 1987.

Finally, I owe gratitude to my wife, Kanta, and my son Vivek: to Kanta for undertaking the responsibilities of both mother and father while carrying the heavy load of her own professional career; to Vivek for meeting the challenge of my absence, despite his tender age, in a very creditable and mature way. Without their support, I could not have undertaken this study.

PART ONE

Conceptual Aspects

O N E

Introduction

From low-income India to affluent America, great leaders and representative governments have set goals to reduce poverty. Prime Minister Indira Gandhi repeatedly won general elections during the 1960s and the 1970s on the platform *Gharibi Hatao* (eradicate poverty). President Lyndon Johnson started the Great Society's historic War on Poverty in the 1960s. But despite some fluctuations over the years, poverty still exists in India and the United States, as it does in other free-enterprise countries. On the intellectual plane, the lack of a theory of poverty is recognized but rarely bemoaned, and in some circles it is even justified by the argument that poverty is hardly germane to any behavioral economic analysis. Why does poverty defy solutions and stymie theorizing about itself? This book demonstrates that the absence of a unified theory of poverty and, consequently, the lack of proper economic analysis and appropriate economic policies are in part to blame for discouraging practical results.

SOME DEPARTURES FROM MAINSTREAM STUDIES

This book develops a general theory of poverty and applies it to an in-depth analysis of poverty in the Republic of Panama. It assesses existing Panamanian policies from the viewpoint of poverty and designs new ones suggested by the analysis.

A number of poverty studies have been done for developed countries (DCs) and less developed countries (LDCs) in recent years. This book benefits from their approaches, but it also breaks substantial new ground and departs from the mainstream studies of poverty in theory, methodology, scope, and antipoverty policy design.

Theory

A widespread impression has prevailed among poverty experts that no theory of poverty has been developed. Consequently most existing studies are limited to quantifying poverty situations and characterizing the poor by cross-tabulating associations among variables. The poor are treated as an analytical category separate from other household groups and their behavior patterns. For instance, according to a World Bank study, "In the present state of our understanding of the poverty syndrome, there is no theoretical framework within which poverty can be satisfactorily explained in its entirety" (Altimir 1982, 5). It is argued that neither the prevailing neoclassical theory of functional income distribution nor the Marxian explanation of the misery of the industrial reserve army treats the poor as a separate analytical category, because in these models the poor are grouped together with low-income wage earners (neoclassicism) or exploited workers (Marxism). Similar intersection rather than correspondence with poverty is considered to exist in the Malthusian theory of population growth, which is the theory of entire populations; in Myrdal's theory of extreme underdevelopment situations (Myrdal 1959), which is essentially a theory of underdevelopment; in Streeten's framework of basic needs (Streeten 1978), which is largely a normative concept; in the Keynesian theory of unemployment, which explains transitory hardships of an otherwise mostly nonpoor working class; and in the "informal sector" concepts of urban poverty which are essentially descriptive terms. According to these mainstream studies, income distribution (by which I mean personal income distribution) and poverty are in general "neither equivalent nor mutually inclusive" (Altimir 1982, 5; see also Bienfed 1975).

I will show here that theories already exist and can be synthesized to develop a unified theory of poverty and personal income distribution (chap. 2). To see this, we can define poverty alternatively in absolute terms or relative terms. *Absolute* poverty is measured by some normatively specified minimum levels of food, supplemented by similarly specified minimum levels of clothing, shelter, and medical services necessary for human subsistence. *Relative* poverty is defined with respect to other income groups, usually the first or second quintiles of population, depending upon the levels of living of a society, or households with less than half of the median household income, or similar normative measures. Both represent states of deprivation, which are always felt in relation to others.

Even absolute poverty refers to a society's conventional style of living. Absolute poverty's content changes over time and across countries. Relative poverty has an absolute dimension as regards human dignity; absolute poverty has a relative dimension as regards average levels of welfare in a given society (Sen 1981). The two concepts are congruent rather than conflicting. In general, most theories of the one concept can be fruitfully used for the other concept. Doubtless both relative poverty and absolute poverty are associated with critical shortages of human capital, which may not be entirely exogenous. Poverty is a continuous variable. For instance, if an absolute poverty line occurs at 40 percent of median income, it would be naive to categorize a household with 39 percent of median household income as being beyond the purview of an income distribution theory and one with 41 percent of median income as germane to theoretical analysis. The causes of poverty lie in the same process that affects income inequalities. Its mitigation requires similar transformation. The poor, too, endeavor to optimize their welfare by maximizing their income, but they have meager endowments or sources of income whose different components overlap one another, shading one income level into another as a continuum.

In theoretical analysis, therefore, income inequalities and relative poverty may be treated synonymously. Obviously the theories of relative poverty can be usefully employed to enhance our understanding of absolute poverty. The integrated theory is developed in chapter 2.

Methodology

Consistent with the shift of emphasis from description (mere measurement of existing poverty) to analysis (determining the sources of long-term poverty) and from associations (based largely on cross-tabulations of variables) to behavioral relationships (stochastic analysis), solutions to poverty must focus more on creating earning capacity (by augmenting both human and nonhuman capital of the poor and potential poor) and less on transferring consumption to the poor. Self-reliance is preferable to dependence upon society. The problem is viewed here in terms of incorporating the poor into the growth process instead of bypassing them in the hope that the trickle-down effect or the dole will take care of them.

Lest my emphasis on creating earning capacity among low-productivity workers (the supply of skills and other resources) lead readers to infer that I am ignoring demand (the market), let me immediately mention that I shall also carry out an extensive analysis of the demand side. For instance, there is a thorough analysis of unemployment and poverty. The behavioral model is extended, à la Tinbergen (1976), to include both the supply of and the demand for skills. A rigorous analysis of possible segmentation of labor markets is carried out, among other subjects.

With a view to uncovering the sources of poverty and deriving useful policy implications, this book reflects a persistent tendency to look at various aspects of poverty from different angles by breaking the poverty problem into pieces, examining each aspect minutely, then reassembling the parts to see the whole. Accordingly, its scope is considerably larger than that of traditional poverty studies.

Scope

The development of a formal theory of poverty is one extension of the study. I carried out the empirical analysis for a number of aspects of poverty. Viewed in alternative facets, the analysis covers the life cycle dimension of poverty—fertility, infancy, childhood, adolescence, marriage, working life, and old age; the sectoral dimension—rural, urban, relatively inaccessible, and Indian areas; the policy dimension—major micro- and macro- policies bearing on poverty, including the republic's budget (taxes, tariffs, public expenditures, and tax expenditures); institutions (such as the social security system); parastatals; controls; regulations; public research; employment policy; public investment policy; incentive schemes; and so forth. It includes explorations into possible relations between poverty and employment policies, poverty and unemployment, marriage and poverty, schooling and poverty, and labor markets and poverty, both by cross-tabulations and by econometric analysis.

Income Concept

The income concept used here is more comprehensive than in traditional studies of poverty. Not only were the data on in-kind income and self-consumption carefully generated, but values were imputed to owner-occupied homes and undistributed (and largely unreported) profits and other property income. Unreported undistributed profits and interest income were estimated from sources extraneous to the main socioeconomic survey and imputed to individual households. I consider these components of income critical to measuring both absolute and relative poverty. Certain adjustments were also made to screen out transitory income. The indicated refinements and adjustments are explained in Chapter 4.

Nature and Quality of Data

Most studies use one of the following sources as the data base: the census, annual household surveys of employment and wages, or special surveys of limited areas. The first two typically generate only monetary incomes and are therefore not satisfactory for poverty analysis. Limited-area surveys aimed at removing this deficiency are in general too specific to particular econographic areas to serve as representative samples and thus too narrow to cover all the target groups of the population. For this study we carried out a special multisectoral socioeconomic survey for the entire country, including a separate subsample for Indians in an exclusively Indian territory.

Neither household surveys nor census reports can generate data on prices, undistributed profits, and similar market categories. Even the rental value of homes is not easy to determine by questionnaire. These variables were thus injected at the individual household level from outside sources (see chap. 4). Futhermore, traditional studies rarely analyze national policies not specifically directed to reducing poverty. Since policy analysis is an essential part of this study, we assembled and analyzed a number of additional sets of data series, mostly from unpublished public and institutional sources. Some of these data appear in summary form in various parts of the book. The master magnetic tape containing all these data series, preceded by proper documentation (manual to extract the data), is available at the Ministry of Planning and Economic Policy, Republic of Panama (MIPPE).

Survey of Earlier Studies and Prevailing Antipoverty Policies in Panama

In the World Bank documents, Panama is classified as an upper-middle-income developing country. But attaining this status has not solved the problem of poverty in this Central American nation. Concern with poverty increased during the 1970s and early 1980s, reminiscent of the heightened concern during this period in other LDCs. The national goal concerning poverty was spelled out in the preamble of the National Development Plan for 1976–80: "The Revolutionary Government has established as one of the priorities in this Development Plan to continue perfecting the policies of distribution and participation whose main objective is to attack the causes and manifestations of poverty in the country and to give all Panamanians equal opportunities and levels of material comfort more in tune with human dignity and social justice" (Panama, MIPPE 1975).

Various directives of national development for the present decade have reaffirmed the development and antipoverty objectives set in the 1970s. Thus one of the most pertinent objectives of the working paper *"National Development Project for Panama: Strategy for the Year 2000"* was to mitigate economic and social disparities: "The problem goes beyond increasing production of goods and services and is tied up . . . to reduce disparities of welfare, guarantee the satisfaction of basic necessities, directly attacking social marginalization, promoting income distribution, and harmonizing increase of sectorial productivity" (Panama, MIPPE 1979, 3).

In the mid-1970s the minister of planning, Ardito Berletta (subsequently the elected president of the Republic of Panama, 1984–85), invited Larry Sjaastad as a consultant economist to help do the first poverty study for the country (Panama, MIPPE 1977). The study was based on the 1970 census data and a limited household survey of incomes done in 1971.

Unlike the traditional studies of poverty, this study did not draw poverty lines and did not count the poor below specified income levels. It looked at income distribution and characterized families and persons by quintiles. According to this study, in 1970 the bottom 20 percent of the population had only 1.57 percent of total income. The bottom 40 percent had 11.76 percent of total income, while the top 20 percent enjoyed 59.91 percent of total income. Major policy recommendations included action on subsistence agriculture, since most of the poor lived in rural areas. For reducing inequalities in general, the focus was on functional distribution. Thus, one of the policy recommendations of the study was to require public enterprises to run on commercial lines and to establish a workers' fund out of their profits that would at once benefit workers as a whole, turn workers into fledgling capitalists, and (an objective not explicitly stated but implicit enough) rid the country of the nationalized sector.

A few years before that study, in 1971, Charles McLure was invited to analyze the distributional effects of taxes (McLure 1972, 1974). The following year, I was invited to estimate the distributional effects of public expenditures (Sahota 1972b, 1977). In both studies, Panama's budget was found to be mildly pro-poor. In my study the investment budget came out more pro-poor than the current budget.

A few years later another poverty study was done for western Panama by Eighmy (1977). Its data base was an unpublished, limited household expenditure survey for 1975. Using $150 per capita income as a rule-of-thumb poverty line, Eighmy found that 48 percent of the rural population of this region was poor in 1970. This study analyzed regional disparities by poverty maps based on different characteristics of the poor.

At the turn of the decade, a major nutrition survey was done by the Ministry of Health and processed by Sigma One Corporation of North Carolina in Charlotte. The minimum food basket was prepared by the Ministry of Health and costed by the Ministry of Planning and Economic Policy (Panama, MIPPE 1985). The same figures are employed in this study to determine poverty lines. Among the studies based on this survey, see those by Parillon (1983) and De Gordon (1984); both estimate malnutrition of children by district.

Poverty studies done for Latin America by CEPAL (Economic Commission for Latin America) include estimates of poverty for Panama. Using $127 for 1970 as the indigency line and applying it to the data of the 1971 household survey of incomes for the year 1970, these studies report indigency of 21 percent in Panama. Among these, see Lavados (1980), Molina (1982), and Altimir (1981, 1982). Lavados only reports a set of tables and presents very little analysis. The last two authors compare and analyze the results of poverty studies for different Latin American and Central American countries. I should also mention two poverty-related studies done at MIPPE that characterize Panama's children (Panama, MIPPE 1980d, and 1983a).

These studies were to a large extent an intellectual adjunct to a massive program of antipoverty policies put in operation under the regime described in *Comandante de los pobres,* a biography of General Torrijos (Centro de Estudios Torrijista 1984). As will be apparent in the course of this study, most of these policies met with only partial success; some defeated their own purpose, and others seem to have run their course. Nevertheless, a concerted effort was made at uplifting the poor, both in production (for instance, giving land, low-interest credit, and low-rent machinery to poor farmers in newly collectivized farms and credit and some market concessions to cooperative farms) and in consumption (especially by increasing social services). Judging from the results of its social policies, Panama now ranks near the top among developing countries in low infant mortality, high literacy, high life expectancy, low incidence of disease among the poor, high primary-school enrollment, improved sanitary conditions, increased percentage of homes with potable water supply, and similar social indicators.

The nationalized sector increased rapidly. For instance, Panama has nearly four dozen relatively large public enterprises, some of which enjoy monopoly power. Partly because of the social-service orientation of these enterprises and partly for other well-known reasons—not least the notorious inefficiency of public enterprises owing to bureaucratic interference in the operations of the enterprise, the absence of profit incentives and of the threat of bankruptcy to managers (since losses are underwritten by the government), and lack of incentives to workers because of the security of civil service and because promotion is not necessarily based on merit— most of these enterprises, including specifically a majority of private-goods enterprises, have run perennial budget deficits. A revolutionary agrarian reform was put in place in which more than 16 percent of Panama's land is estimated to have changed hands. By 1976 nearly 7,000 poor families were settled on 279 agrarian reform settlements or state farms, called *asentamientos,* which, in addition to augmented land area, were provided with subsidized credit, farm machinery at a subsidized rental, low-income housing, and technical assistance. Unfortunately, the early 1970s structure of these settlements could not cope with the high energy prices and high interest rates of the later period. The early 1980s debt crisis exacerbated the credit position of asentamientos. These conditions, coupled with poor management practices and other weaknesses, have put asentamientos into financial trouble. Encouragement was given to cooperative farms. The country borrowed heavily abroad to invest in infrastructure, social services, and public enterprises, in which the interests of the poor were given due recognition. To reduce unemployment, caused largely by the global recession and other outside events, government expanded public employment without creating conterminous productive work and thus without adequate regard for efficiency.

With the soaring interest in poverty at both the professional and policy levels, and in the light of the enunciation and repeated reaffirmations of the objective of reducing poverty in Panama, the present research project was born and christened the Critical Poverty Project. It was viewed as a means to better understand the problems of characterizing and treating poverty as well as the design and execution of policies to increase the satisfaction of basic necessities among the alienated segments of the Panamanian population. Funds for the project were provided by the United Nations.

STATE OF THE PANAMANIAN ECONOMY AT THE
TIME OF THE RESEARCH

At the time of this research the world was emerging from a prolonged period of stagflation, and Panama was still passing through a deep recessionary phase. Having experienced a mean growth rate of approximately 7 percent in the 1960s (7.1 percent during 1956–71) and approximately 5 percent in the 1970s (4.2 percent during 1972–82), the economy slid to a near-zero 0.2 percent rate of growth of aggregate gross domestic product and a negative 2.4 percent rate of growth of per capita income in the reference year of this study, 1983. The private sector experienced a negative growth rate of 9.1 percent in 1983 after two years of zero growth rate. Only the direct effect of the effort by the public sector, especially the autonomous sector, prevented the overall aggregate growth rate from becoming negative. As a result of this trend, the private sector's share in GDP fell from 75.7 percent in 1978 to 63.4 percent in 1983. Panama's private sector shrank at a rather alarming rate during the current recession.

In 1983 the banking sector, which during the 1970s had risen from almost nothing to an estimated 6 percent of the world banking business, was in serious trouble, as suggested by changes in total international banking assets (Lessard 1984). The two-digit rate of unemployment was the highest since the Great Depression. Tourism, which expanded simultaneously with the banking industry, declined drastically, causing a high proportion of family shops to go out of business. Cheap credit was no longer available to finance public investment. Public-sector deficits had reached unmanageable proportions. The ratio of public debt (foreign and domestic) to gross national product had reached unity. The ratio of public debt to central government revenue stood at 324 percent, and interest payments on public debt had risen to nearly a third of the total revenue. Out of a projected $4.5 billion GNP in 1985, $800 million was due to be paid to service the public debt in that year but was rescheduled over a longer period. According to the *World Bank Report, 1983* (table 16), Panama was one of the nine debt-crisis countries of that year. The supposedly growth-oriented policy of import substitution, pro-worker labor legislation, farm support prices, and the redistributional practices of public enterprises, whatever the rationale for them, seemed to have run its course. These approaches were under active review at the Ministry of Planning and Economic Policy during the first half of the 1980s.

Viewed in the context of the global situation, neither the early 1980s recovery of the United States nor the mid-1980s recovery of developing countries in general affected Panama perceptibly. Panama's fortunes seem to be tied more closely to its southern neighbors than to the United States, with whom it has common currency and shares the Panama Canal (a major direct-plus-indirect source of Panama's GNP). The southern neighbors too continued to be plagued by heavy foreign debts, staggering budget deficits, and persistent stagflation in general.

The poor of the world had a setback in the early 1980s. Thus, according to a state of the world report for the year 1983 by the president of the World Bank, A. W. Clausen, "Until recently, the proportion of people in poverty has been declining in all regions of the developing world except Sub-Saharan Africa. But during the last few years that proportion has gone up again—as a result of the deepest global recession in a good many decades" (Clausen 1985). The world recession had, fortunately, bottomed out in that year, and the world economy picked up in 1984. By 1985 even African countries experienced a real growth rate of GDP of 2.1 percent, after a worrisome decline for five years; but Panama experienced hardly any growth at all.

THE CHAPTER SCHEME

The book consists of fourteen chapters subdivided into five parts, as follows: part 1, conceptual aspects of the study; part 2, measurement of poverty and income distribution; part 3, characterization of the poor; part 4, behavioral analysis; part 5, policy analysis.

The remainder of part 1 consists of two chapters. Chapter 2 develops a general theory of poverty and income distribution, departing from the mainstream pragmatic approaches to studying poverty. Chapter 3 focuses on the recent history of the changes in the fate of Panamanian low-income groups of families. More precisely, it presents an empirical analysis of why both poorman's food and poorman's produce have stagnated in Panama in the past quarter-century.

Part 2 consists of three chapters. Chapter 4 describes the data base, the national multisectoral socioeconomic survey especially prepared for this study. It also explains the refinements that were made to generate comprehensive family incomes. Various measures of personal income distribution are discussed in chapter 5 and those of the incidence and intensity of poverty in chapter 6, which is the core of the descriptive presentation of poverty and provides the basis for subsequent analysis.

In part 3 I characterize the poor with a view to learning about their profiles and to identifying target groups in different sectors and regions. Various cross-tabulations by income, education, health, housing, age, family size and composition, unemployment, underemployment, labor force participation by sex, sector, province, and other dimensions, and so forth suggest some of the factors that might explain poverty. Chapter 7 is devoted to the entire country, chapter 8 to a separate characterization of Indians, and chapter 9 to the unemployment characteristics of various types of workers by poverty stratum and the extent to which the poor are affected by unemployment and traditional employment-creation policies.

An exploration of the behavior patterns of the poor and the nonpoor concerning earnings, as well as other factors that might influence earnings and poverty—for instance, fertility, labor force participation of married and unmarried persons, production by sector, education, and similar aspects—is carried out in the four analytical chapters of part 4, which contains the main econometric work done in the context of the poverty theory developed in chapter 2. The analysis was done, in part, in collaboration with some of the leading scholars working at the frontiers of the respective topics, including Sherwin Rosen on family structure and poverty (chap. 11) and Robert Evenson on fertility and poverty (chap. 12).

Part 5 consists of one final, rather long chapter. In this chapter I analyze the effects of prevailing policies on poverty under the following topics: Who benefits from Panama's social security system? Who bears the burden of Panama's taxes? Who benefits from Panama's public enterprises? Who benefits from current public expenditures? Who benefits from public investment? Who are the present and potential beneficiaries of Panama's current and proposed agricultural research policy? Who benefits from Panama's various investment incentives and price policies?

TWO

Theory of Personal Income Distribution and Poverty

Personal income distribution is distinguished from functional income distribution in at least three important ways: (1) It pertains to the income of *persons* rather than the income from *factors* of production (traditionally, labor, capital, land, and entrepreneurship; alternatively, human and nonhuman capital). (2) Personal income is a *comprehensive* measure and may consist of incomes from one or more factors at the disposal of an income unit. (3) It is a *micro* concept and focuses on the welfare of persons or families, whereas functional distribution of income is a *macro* category and relates to output produced by and distributed to aggregate classes of workers, capitalists, renters, and organizers.

Several clues to appropriate theorizing on personal income distribution follow from these characteristics. First, in today's world persons (and their families) could be well-off or poor whether they are renters, capitalists, or workers (or nonworkers, economically active or inactive, employed or unemployed), or even when they derive income from all sources. Accordingly, income from all endowments (acquired through self-effort and hard work or bought or inherited from family, society, or nature, human capital or nonhuman capital) must be analyzed, including income due to the effects of possible interactions among endowments and their externalities. Second, since this is a study of the behavior of micro units, applying the basic methodological techniques of microeconomic analysis—namely, optimization and equilibrium, given the usual constraints of endowments and individual characteristics—is a natural and fruitful choice. Third, the hallmark of an income theory is to identify the sources of the ownership of factors of production. As discussed at length in my survey article (Sahota 1978), the sources that measure one's capacity to earn income must include inherited human capital, inherited nonhuman capital, acquired human capital, and acquired nonhuman capital. Four stochastic elements, that is, luck, as well as public policy variables, in particular taxes and public expenditures, are pertinent to personal fortunes and so to a theory of personal income distribution. Last, a study of job characteristics and the structure of factor markets, that is, the demand side of factor employment and macro factors, is essential to understanding not only the distribution of personal income but also absolute poverty. The theory presented here follows these guidelines in attempting to use relevant income concepts, an appropriate methodology, the genesis of the inherited and acquired sources of income, stochastic elements, public policy, and markets.

In developing a common general theory of both distribution and poverty, several myths concerning poverty need to be set aside at the outset. Many poverty specialists appear to be mistaken in assuming that poverty is essentially a macro problem; that the poor do not strive to maximize their income; that there is no theoretical framework within which poverty can be explained; that the poor must therefore be treated as a separate analytical category; that the removal of unemployment will eliminate poverty; and that industrialization is an automatic remedy for poverty.

Theories of personal income distribution have abounded (though several of them are partial and unsatisfactory), but poverty has so far been studied almost without theory, mainly in a macro context, being treated as an analytical category separate from other income classes. Thus empirical studies on poverty have been confined mostly to characterizing the poor. Here I bring poverty into the behavioral framework of earnings. The poor, too, struggle to maximize their income, but they have meager endowments and an unfavorable environment. A search for the genesis of endowments and conductive environment leads not only to an integration of the rival theories of distribution, but also a common theory of distribution and poverty.

Postwar developments in the theories of personal income distribution fall into two epochs: the pre-1980 theories, with configuration in the 1960s, when the basic models of the Cambridge school (as enunciated by Nobel laureate Meade [1964]) and the Chicago school (as propounded by Becker in his celebrated Woytinsky Lecture [1967]) were published; and the 1980s theories (in the main that by Becker and Tomes 1979). The income distribution theories of both the Chicago school and the Cambridge school emphasize the supply side of income determination. A supply-and-demand theory of distribution is developed by the Netherlands school, whose latest version appeared in the mid-1970s (Tinbergen 1976). The pre-1980 theories, including in particular the inheritance theory of intergenerational distribution formulated by Meade and the human capital theory of intragenerational distribution developed by Becker, were partial, divergent, and incomplete, even in combination, whereas the 1980s theories are more complete, general, and mutually convergent toward consensus.[1] The theory developed here is a synthesis of the theoretical developments of the 1980s and the supply-and-demand theory of the Netherlands school of thought.

---

1. For a comprehensive survey of the pre-1980 theories of distribution, see Sahota (1978). For an updated survey that includes the theoretical developments of the 1980s and my own earlier synthetic theory of income distribution, see Sahota and Rocca (1985).

The core of the theory of distribution and poverty is a human investment model (consisting of half a dozen equations), which is developed in detail. Some of its theoretical implications are deduced by symbol manipulation. From there on its integration with the income function is only a small step.

In the theory developed here, an individual's income (Y) is a function of his or her personal characteristics, in particular, human capital (H), nonhuman capital (M), and the markets or the system (S), in which one earns and consumes one's income,

$$Y = Y(H, M, S), \tag{1}$$

where H includes traits both inherited and acquired through hard work—genetic elements, formal and informal education, acquired and inherited health and dexterity, measured ability (such as the IQ), unmeasured abilities (such as endurance, self-discipline, doggedness, drive, dynamism, determination), the efficiency with which one uses all one's resources, the capacity to migrate, and other traits that are embodied in one's body and mind. The variable M is straightforward material wealth, whether inherited through bequests or accumulated by saving out of one's own earnings. The symbol S is a catchall variable representing the overall ecology of work, such as the level of technology, job characteristics, segmented versus integrated labor markets, discrimination versus competitiveness in employment and in the acquisition of human capital, social contacts, and other environmental variables.

Eq (1) is a general function that is relevant at all levels of income. Poverty (affluence) is caused by, among other things, limited (or copious) endowments of material resources M, such as land, means of production, housing, and so on; low (high) levels of human capital H; and poverty-prone (congenial) environments S, including access to public services, in particular schooling and health services. Like all economic agents, the poor act in their own best interest, but under more severe constraints than the nonpoor, imposed upon them by nature and society as well as by themselves and the legacy of their parents. The nonpoor have more of the endowments H and M and favorable S; the poor have meager quantities of M and H and unfavorable S.

We live in an age in which public policies can make a critical difference to the growth of income and especially to its distribution. Accordingly, to be useful, a theoretical-empirical study ought, if possible, to throw light on and lead to policy implications. Given that poverty, however defined, exists in both poor countries and rich countries (though to significantly different degrees), and keeping our eyes on the feasibility of antipoverty and redistribution policies in the context of the noncommunist world, in this model the acquisition of human capital is viewed as a key to breaking the cycle of permanent poverty of families across generations.[2] The core of the theory of poverty formulated here, therefore, is a generalized human capital function. The overall theory, however, gives full recognition to the acquired and endowed components of fortunes (both human and material) as well as to family and societal environment and stochastic variables.

The Variable *H*

Recognizing the role of inheritance entails specifying a multigenerational model. The present model is developed for two generations but can be generalized to more. In this model the utility of parents (*U*) is assumed to depend upon their present household consumption (*C*) and investment in their children, whether by parental input or by the children's own effort. Using the average value of investment for all children (*I*), the ordinal utility function may be written as

$$U = F[U(C, I_{+1})], \tag{2}$$

where the variables with the subscript $+1$ pertain to children's (future) generation and the variables without this subscript relate to parents' (present) generation.

Investment in children may take two forms: investment in their overall human capital H_{+1} and investment in their material wealth M_{+1}. Accordingly, the production function for *I* is

$$I_{+1} = I(H_{+1}, M_{+1}). \tag{3}$$

Research indicates, though inconclusively, that inherited human capital has two effects. One is a direct increase in the level of ability (Bloom 1964; Watts 1975), which is a source of higher marginal product irrespective of further investment in oneself (Taubman 1975). Such an effect is, however, disputed by human capitalists in general (Mincer 1974; Griliches 1976). The other effect is that inherited human capital enters the acquired human investment function (Liebowitz 1972; Becker 1967; Griliches 1976).[3] For the sake of simplicity, investment in education is assumed to represent all human investment (*H*). Accordingly, the basic human-capital equation is of the following form:

$$H_{+1} = H(\tilde{E}_{+1}, E_{+1}), \tag{4}$$

2. That is not to say short-term poverty is less abhorrent, whether due to life cycle factors, economic or population fluctuations, physical or mental handicaps, or other reasons. Much of what is theorized about long-term poverty across generations also applies to short-term poverty. Economic policies appropriate to cope with short-term poverty may, however, be different.

3. According to Bloom, "cognitive entry behaviors," that is, prerequisites for learning in schools, "can account for up to one-half of the variance of achievement" in education (Bloom 1976, 167).

where $\tilde{E}_{+1}$ is inherited human capital and E_{+1} is acquired human capital (a behavioral variable). In this study, inherited human capital is assumed to be a function of home resources devoted to children's human-capital formation—which are proxied by mother's time (T_h^m) and father's time (T_h^f) devoted to children's nurture—average human capital in society indexed by average level of education ($\overline{E}$), exogenously given genetic inheritance (Γ), and human capital inheritance luck, u_1,

$$\tilde{E}_{+1} = \tilde{E}(T_h^m, T_h^f, \overline{E}, \Gamma, u_1) \quad \text{(human capital inherited} \quad (5)$$
from nature and nurture).

Individual behavioral investment in human capital (E_{+1}) is a function of the rate of return on human investment (v); market resources devoted to human investment (education), which in turn depend upon parents' income (Y) or wealth (M); public expenditure on (supply of) education (G^e); inherited human capital, that is, children's endowment of ability ($\tilde{E}_{+1}$); the level of efficiency of different parents in embodying educational capital in their children (ϵ_h); and school luck (u_3) in being in the right school, at the right age, with the right peers, and in the right city:

$$E_{+1} = E(\tilde{E}_{+1}, Y_h, v, G^e, \epsilon_h, u_3) \quad \text{human capital acquired} \quad (6)$$
by individual choice).

Evidently there is an upper limit on E_{+1} (and H_{+1}, for that matter) owing to increasing costs in terms of income forgone, declining life cycle return from education in the finite working life, and the fixed size of body and brain.

Inserting eqs (5) and (6) into (4), we obtain

$$H_{+1} = H(T_h^m, \overline{E}, Y_h, v, G^e, \Gamma, \epsilon_h, u_4) \quad \text{(overall human} \quad (7)$$
capital),

which is an empirically verifiable equation, except that in the cross-section samples usually employed for empirical estimates, few data are available on any measure of genetic intelligence (Γ). The stochastic term u_4 captures the luck components of u_1 and u_3.

THE VARIABLE M

Nonhuman capital (M_{+1}) depends upon inherited nonhuman capital ($\tilde{M}_{+1}$), one's own accumulated savings (M^*_{+1}), and capital market luck (u_5'). Accumulated savings, in turn, are a function of one's current property income, which is related to one's material wealth (which to avoid lagged-period variables in our two-generation model may be represented by inherited wealth), and individualized rate of return (r) one can earn. The rate of return (r), following Meade, is made a rising function of $\tilde{M}_{+1}$, owing to scale economies and other factors discussed earlier. Finally, material inheritance (M) depends upon predictable resources, such as parents' expected propensity to bequeath material wealth, which in turn depends upon parents' wealth (M) or income (Y); parents' efficiency in allocating heritable resources (ϵ_m); and unpredictable resources, for example, the demise of an uncle without issue, which will be denoted nonhuman inheritance luck (u_5'').

$$M = M(\tilde{M}_{+1}, M_{+1}^*, u_5') \tag{8.1}$$

$$M_{+1}^* = M^*(\tilde{M}_{+1}, r_{+1} \tag{8.2}$$

$$r_{+1} = r(\tilde{M}_{+1}) \tag{8.3}$$

$$\tilde{M}_{+1} = \tilde{M}(Y, \epsilon_m, u_5''). \tag{8.4}$$

The reduced form of 8.1–8.4 is

$$M_{+1} = M(Y, \epsilon_m, u_5) \quad \text{(the equation for material} \atop \text{inheritance).} \tag{8}$$

Bequests are negative when children inherit parents' indebtedness. In general, parents tend to invest more the higher the expected productivity of investment. For example, parents may be induced to send a child who is precocious to a private school; if one is a promising tennis player, they may be motivated to provide superior coaching and training facilities. On the other hand, when children are less talented than their siblings, parents tend to bequeath them relatively more material resources. There is thus likely to exist a negative covariance (insofar as Hicksian substitution effect is concerned) between M_{+1} and H_{+1}.

The covariance of H and M, that is, the interaction between human and nonhuman capital, is likely to be high. This will exacerbate inequalities. Another factor that has not received attention so far is "information," which is both income determining and income determined, in that it serves as a built-in feedback to generate inequalities. These factors make econometric estimation of earnings difficult, but no additional variables are needed.

THE SOLUTION OF THE SUPPLY-SIDE MODEL OF H AND M

Written in terms of the variables that enter parents' utility function, the budget equation is

$$Y = C + \pi_1 I_{+1}, \tag{9}$$

where the consumption C is used as the numeraire, that is, $\pi_c - 1$.

The household maximizes its utility function (2) subject to the budget constraint (9) and the three home production functions (3), (7), and (8).

For the derivation of the theoretical relations in the present section, it is assumed that the utility function and all production functions specified above are linearly homogeneous. This property ensures that all inputs are complementary to one another, that individually they are subject to diminishing returns, and that the availability of one resource increases the marginal product of other resources. Accordingly, the following demand equations hold:[4]

$$\dot{I}_{+1} = \eta \dot{Y} - (\kappa_i \eta + (1 - \kappa_i)\sigma_{ic})\dot{\pi}_{i+1} + (1 - \kappa_i)(\sigma_{ic} - \eta)\dot{\pi}_c$$

(the demand function for I_{+1} as derived by Allen [1938, 373] to which income effect $\eta \dot{Y}$ has been added),   (10)

$$\dot{I}_{+1} = a_1 \dot{H}_{+1} + a_2 \dot{M}_{+1} \quad \text{(adding-up property), and}$$ (11)

$$\dot{\pi}_{i+1} = \alpha_1 \dot{\pi}_{h+1} + \alpha_2 \dot{\pi}_{m+1'} \quad \text{(the duality property),}$$ (12)

where π_{i+1}, π_{h+1}, and π_{m+1} are per-unit "rents" for the stocks of I_{+1}, H_{+1}, and M_{+1}, respectively; the a's are the respective output elasticities ($a_1 + a_2 - 1$); the α's are cost shares ($\alpha_1 + \alpha_2 - 1$); σ_{ic} is the Allen-Hicks elasticity of substitution between I_{+1} and C for the production of U; κ_i is the share of full income spent on I_{+1}; and η is the income (wealth) elasticity of the demand for I_{+1}. The dots on variables indicate proportionate changes.

Next let the total cost of H_{+1} in eq. (7) be defined as

$$TC_{h+1} - C(\pi_h^m T_h^m, \pi_h^f T_h^f, \overline{E}, Y_h, G^e, v, \epsilon_h),$$ (13)

where π_h^m and π_h^f, respectively, are unit cost prices (e.g., wage rates) of mother's and fathers's times T_h^m and T_h^f, respectively, devoted to children's nurture. The remaining terms of (13) act as shift variables. For instance, the main autonomous supply variable, G^e, has a negative effect on TC. The same is in general true for superior environment ($\overline{E}$), which increases the productivity of family's schooling resources or reduces the cost of a given quantity and quality of education.[5] Market resources devoted to a child's schooling (Y_h) and the price of parents' time ($\pi_h^{m,f}$) are assumed to be related directly to family income. Parents' time devoted to children's weaning is assumed to be influenced by parents' education. Accordingly, the following relations exist:

---

4. These equations are derived by Allen (1938, 373, 504); a general equilibrium model of home production based on Allen's derivations has been used by De Tray (1973).

5. The coefficient v is the return to the cost of investment in a year of schooling as distinguished from Becker's (1967) definition of the return to investment of a dollar in schooling. The present measure is employed to use the data in the form in which they are available.

$$\pi_h^{m,f} = f_1(Y),$$

$$Y_h = f_2(Y), \text{ and} \tag{14}$$

$$T_h = f_3(Y).$$

Government expenditure on education (G^e) is financed by taxes on earnings, namely social security taxes (t_w) and income taxes (t_y), which reduce the net value of v. Subsequent equations, therefore, include these taxes.

Given the assumption of linear homogeneity, equilibrium price π_{h+1} is determined at the minimum average cost where marginal cost of H_{+1} equals its average cost. Taking the total derivatives of eq. (13) after substituting for the values of π_h, Y_h, and T_h from eq. (13), and expressing them in proportionate changes (denoted by dots), we obtain

$$\dot{\pi}_{h+1} = \beta_1 \dot{T}^m + \beta_2 \dot{T}^f + \beta_3 \dot{\overline{E}} + B_4 \dot{Y} + \beta_5 \dot{v} + \beta_6 \dot{G}^e + \beta_7 \dot{\epsilon}_h + \tag{15}$$
$$\beta_8 \dot{t}_w + \beta_9 \dot{t}_y + \beta_{12} \dot{\Gamma} + u_6 \quad \text{(price equation for } H_{+1}).$$

Similarly,

$$\dot{\pi}_{m+1} = \beta_{10} \dot{Y} + \beta_{11} \dot{\epsilon}_m + u_7 \quad \text{(price equation for } M_{+1}), \tag{16}$$

and

$$\dot{\pi}_c = 0 \quad \text{(price equation for the numeraire)}, \tag{17}$$

where β's are the respective cost elasticities. For example,

$$\beta_1 = (\partial \pi_{h+1}/\pi_{h+1})/(\alpha \pi_h^m/\pi_h^m), \quad \beta_2 = (\partial \pi_{h+1}/\pi_{h+1})/(\partial \pi_h^f/\pi_h^f),$$

$$\beta_3 = (\partial \pi_{h+1}/\pi_{h+1})/\partial \overline{E}/E, \text{ etc.}$$

To ease the reader's task, luck terms are redefined here:

u_1 = human capital inheritance luck
u_2 = employment market luck (see a few pages below)
u_3 = school luck
u_4 = overall human capital luck (joint effect of u_1 and u_3)
u_5 = material inheritance luck
u_6 = a derivative of human capital luck, u_l
u_7 = a derivative of material capital luck, u_5.

Let the elasticity of substitution between H_{+1} and M_{+1} inputs for the production of I be defined, following Allen (1938, 504), as

$$\sigma_{hm} = \frac{\dot{M}_{+1} - \dot{H}_{+1}}{\dot{\pi}_{h+1} - \dot{\pi}_{m+1}} \quad \begin{array}{l} \text{(elasticity of substitution between } H_{+1} \\ \text{and } M_{+1} \text{ in the production of } I_{+1}). \end{array} \tag{18}$$

Rewriting (8) in terms of M_{+1}, (18) in terms of $\dot{H}_{+1}$, substituting for $\dot{M}_{+1}$ in the thus rewritten eq. (18), and collecting similar terms, we get

$$\dot{H}_{+1} = \dot{I}_{+1} - (a_2\sigma_{hm})\dot{\pi}_{h+1} + (a_2\sigma_{hm})\dot{\pi}_{m+1}. \tag{19}$$

Substituting eqs. (12) and (17) for π_{h+1} and π_c in eq. (10) and then substituting eqs. (10), (15), and (16) for $\dot{I}_{+1}$, $\dot{\pi}_{h+1}$, and $\dot{\pi}_{m+1}$ in Eq. (19), we get the following reduced form for $\dot{H}_{+1}$:

$$
\begin{aligned}
\dot{H}_{+1} = {} & (\eta - a_2\sigma_{hm}\beta_4 + a_2\sigma_{hm}\beta_{10} - \alpha_1\beta_4\Omega - \alpha_2\beta_{10}\Omega)\dot{Y} \\
& - (a_2\sigma_{hm}\beta_1 + \alpha_1\beta_1\Omega)\dot{H}^m \\
& - (a_2\sigma_{hm}\beta_2 + \alpha_1\beta_2\Omega)\dot{H}^f \\
& - (a_2\sigma_{hm}\beta_3 + \alpha_1\beta_3\Omega)\dot{\bar{E}} \\
& - (a_2\sigma_{hm}\beta_5 + \alpha_1\beta_5\Omega)\dot{v} \\
& - (a_2\sigma_{hm}\beta_6 + \alpha_1\beta_6\Omega)\dot{G}^e \\
& + (a_2\sigma_{hm}\beta_8 + \alpha_1\beta_8\Omega)\dot{t}_w \\
& + (a_2\sigma_{hm}\beta_9 + \alpha_1\beta_9\Omega)\dot{t}_y + (a_2\sigma_{hm}\beta_{12} + \alpha_1\beta_{12}\Omega)\dot{\Gamma} \\
& + ((a_2\sigma_{hm} - \alpha_2\beta_{11}\Omega)\dot{\epsilon}_m - (a_2\sigma_{hm}\beta_7 + \alpha_1\beta_7\Omega)\dot{\epsilon}_h) \\
& + (a_2\sigma_{hm} - \alpha_2\Omega)\dot{u}_6 - (a_2\sigma_{hm} + \alpha_1\Omega)\dot{u}_7),
\end{aligned}
\tag{20}
$$

where $\Omega = \kappa_l\eta + (1 - \kappa_i)\sigma_{ic}$. Eq. (20) contains two efficiency variables ($\dot{\epsilon}_h$ and $\dot{\epsilon}_m$) for which no proxies are available (except perhaps parents' education [H], which is already in the equation). It also includes two unsystematic luck variables (u_6 and u_7). Evidently a regression equation cannot determine their separate influences. Therefore we collapse these two two-variable sets into mongrels of one variable each, namely ϵ and u. The effect of ϵ is expected to be picked up by the intercept term γ_0 in the regression equation (eq. 21) and that of u by the random term. Note that T^m and T^f have been replaced by H^m and H^f, respectively, for data problems. The regression equation is

$$
\begin{aligned}
\dot{H}_{+1} = {} & \gamma_0' + \gamma_1'\dot{Y} + \gamma_2'\dot{H}^m + \gamma_3'\dot{H}^f + \gamma_4'\dot{\bar{E}} + \gamma_5'\dot{v} + \gamma_6'\dot{G}^c + \\
& \gamma_7't_w + \gamma_8't_y + \gamma_9'\dot{\Gamma} + u',
\end{aligned}
\tag{21}
$$

where the γ's stand for the compound coefficients of eq. (20).

The Variable S and the Demand Side

The theoretical discussion so far has covered personal characteristics, that is, the supply of nonhuman capital and labor with varying levels of human capital. The symbol S in eq. (1) stands for job characteristics or the demand for persons with various skills and other endowments. The resource demands depend upon a host of factors: the dynamics of technology and productivity; the form of the production function; the degree of relative heterogeneity within various classes of factors; the degree of complementarity/substitutability between different classes of factors; the nature and structure of factor markets (segmented or integrated, competitive or monopolistic, etc.); the level of overall employment; the pace of economic activity; macro policies; labor codes; tax schedules; and similar factors. In this study I have chosen to focus on one key factor that bears on the demand for low-productivity labor—namely, the nature of changing technology. The latter change becomes more crucial when unskilled labor is found to be anticomplementary with skilled labor.

THE CORE OF TINBERGEN'S MODEL

The main implication of Tinbergen's theoretical analysis is that if technology advances at a faster pace than education, inequalities will increase, and vice versa. Theoretical underpinnings of Tinbergen's approach are also supported by a strong capital-skill complementarity found in the study by Griliches (1969); the principle of comparative advantage, in which performances by heterogenous skills are spread out in more technical and difficult jobs whereas they are concentrated in easy jobs (suggesting a tendency toward equalization), as advanced by Roy (1951) and its self-selection process by Rosen (1974); the homogeneous-labor and heterogeneous-capital model, in which scrapping of capital could occur with a decline in the labor force, by Robert Solow; and the heterogeneous-labor and homogeneous-capital model, in which an expansion in capital could reduce structural unemployment, by Akerlof (1969). All these models have implications for functional as well as personal income distribution. Tinbergen's main empirical finding is that in this century the race between education and technological development has been won by education, thereby causing a decline in inequality of earnings.

A great virtue of this model lies in highlighting the inequalities that can arise both from the supply side—personal characteristics—and the demand side—job characteristics and labor markets. By implication, the redistribution policies may be addressed to either side or both: to influence the job characteristics (technology) so as to create more demand for low-paid labor or let its demand fall at a slower rate than the rate of increase in the supply of qualified labor, or to influence personal characteristics (in particular education) with a view to expanding the supply of more qualified manpower so as to overtake the pace of technology, thereby raising the marginal products and wage rates of low-productivity workers.

THE CONSEQUENCES OF POSSIBLE ANTICOMPLEMENTARITY OF UNSKILLED LABOR WITH SKILLED LABOR AND CAPITAL

The main asset of the poor and the workers at the lower end of the income scale is their raw labor. A point of inquiry, therefore, is how the earnings of unskilled labor, relative to those of skilled labor, are affected by changing technology and economic fluctuations.

On the supply side of skills, if an economy is characterized largely by skilled workers, that is, if the mean level of skill is relatively high, incomes will be more equally distributed among skilled workers, and the distribution will tend to be skewed to the left (the small proportion of low-productivity workers will be very poor). On the other hand, if an economy is made up largely of unskilled labor, that is, if the mean skill level is relatively low, the hump will lie toward low incomes and the skew will be toward the right (the small proportion of workers with high skills will be found to be earning very high salaries).

On the demand side of skills, let me first note that in general productive factors are complementary. That is, the marginal product of a factor goes up when cooperant factors expand. Both theoretical logic and empirical estimates suggest a strong complementarity between capital and skills (Griliches 1969). A corollary of this finding is that the more advanced the level of technology a vintage of equipment may embody, the higher will be the demand for skilled labor to work with that equipment. Contrariwise, an anticomplementarity relationship may exist between modern capital and unskilled labor, and by implication between skilled and unskilled labor.[6] That is, the marginal product, and pari passu the wage rate, of unskilled labor will tend to go down with the expansion of capital-intensive technology.

In the absence of the relevant data on the demand for different skills in any country, the noted relationship comes handy to test the Tinbergen hypothesis, as has been done by Sattinger (1980). In this study, therefore, instead of fitting demand and supply functions separately, I estimate their reduced form.

The demand function for skills is given by

$$v = f(H, k), \tag{22}$$

6. See, however, Bowles and Gintis (1977), who think that the elasticities of substitution among labor categories are high.

where $k - K/L$ is the capital/labor ratio. (Alternative measures of the level of technology will also be tested.) Solving appropriately differentiated (22) and (21) simultaneously and inserting the resulting reduced form in the correspondingly differentiated eq. (1), we obtain

$$\dot{Y}_{+i} = \gamma_0 + \gamma_1\dot{Y} + \gamma_2\dot{H}^m + \gamma_3\dot{H}^f + \gamma_4\overline{\dot{E}} + \gamma_5\dot{k} + \gamma_6\dot{G}^e + \gamma_7\dot{t}_w \quad (23)$$
$$+ \gamma_8\dot{t}_y + \gamma_9\dot{\Gamma} + u',$$

where, as before, M has been subsumed in Y.[7]

As is apparent from the discussion of earlier sections, all nonstochastic structural coefficients are predicted to be positive. The reduced form (20) or (21) is an analytical rather than a descriptive equation, since it is derived from the system of supply and demand equations. Unfortunately, the numerical values of the structural coefficients cannot be easily recovered from eq. (20), since the structural equations (3–6) are underidentified and the reduced form coefficients of eq. (20) are rather large compounds of structural coefficients. Despite its intricate appearance, however, eq. (20) or eq. (21) is not really difficult to interpret. Note, for instance, that $\kappa \geq 0$ (positive share of input I in the utility function); a's ≥ 0 (positive contributions to output I by inputs H_{+1} and M_{+1}); $\eta \geq 0$ (assuming H and M are normal goods); α's ≥ 0 (cost shares); $\sigma_{ic} \geq 0$ and $\sigma_{hm} \geq 0$ (because when the choice set consists of only two goods they are necessarily substitutes and not complements); and therefore $\Omega \geq 0$. The signs of β coefficients, other than those attaching to luck variables (u's) and tax variables (t's), are predicted to be positive. In short, the ambiguity of signs of the reduced-form coefficients is caused not by the unpredictability of the signs of the structural coefficients but by the fact that the signs of most of the γ's of eq. (21) depend upon the relative magnitudes of various ($a\sigma$) and ($\alpha\beta\Omega$) terms. Since there is little basis for speculating on the magnitudes of various a's, α's, β's, and σ's, few a priori conclusions can be derived about parents' investment in their children's human wealth.[8] Nevertheless, weighing the most plausible values of individual a's, α's, σ's, and other coefficients in relation to one another, and using a priori reasoning about possible relationships between various variables, the following predictions are made:

7. For a more formal derivation of the specification of the capital-intensity variable as a proxy for the demand for skills, see Sattinger (1980).

8. Broadly speaking, intergenerational theories focus largely on distribution of ownership of factor quantities, whereas intragenerational theories tend to emphasize factor prices. As an analytical convenience, stocks are usually employed as a relevant concept for the former analysis and flows for the latter. These are matters of convenience and abstraction and do not make the two versions segmented theories. Each subsumes the other, and they purport to explain the same phenomenon of income inequality. There is essentially only one theory.

$$\begin{array}{ll}
\gamma_1 > 0 & \gamma_5 > 0 \\
\gamma_2 > 0 & \gamma_6 > 0 \\
\gamma_3 > 0 & \gamma_7 < 0 \\
\gamma_4 > 0 & \gamma_8 < 0 \\
& \gamma_9 > 0.
\end{array} \tag{24}$$

Eq. (23) is an earnings or income function, which not only embodies the general theory of personal income distribution but is also empirically estimable. Since the data for genetic ability are not easily available in household surveys, the genetic inheritance variable Γ will be omitted. Its effect is therefore likely to be picked up by γ_2 and γ_3.

THREE

Recent History of Poverty in Panama

The concern of the government of Panama with poverty and some of the antipoverty policies the Republic has followed in the past couple of decades were documented in chapter 1. During the same period, several other epochal changes have taken place, which might or might not be influenced, favorably or unfavorably, by government policies. To put the study in proper perspective, therefore, before taking up the analysis of poverty based on the National Socioeconomic Survey, 1983, a brief review of the recent history of poverty is in order. This chapter looks at recent changes in the main indicators of poverty in Panama from both the results side and the input side. In particular, I analyze the trends in two pertinent socio-demographic variables, namely food staples (here denoted *poorman's food*) and products of some of the rural cottage industries (which possibly form secondary if not primary sources of income of the poor and the Indians, and which I label *poorman's produce*). Possible causes of the observed trends are discussed, and some are subjected to in-depth analysis in subsequent chapters.

SOCIOECONOMIC INDICATORS

The main social indicators of poverty are given in part A of table 3.1, and the main economic indicators in part B. The decennial statistics of this table suggest that the changes in Panama's social services have been demonstrably pro-poor. In the health area, the crude birthrate and mortality rate have declined, while hospital birth ratios and life expectancy have increased. A spectacular decline in mortality due to poorman's diseases has been recorded. In the educational field, enrollment ratios have risen at the primary and secondary levels. The increase in retention to the final year of primary education is a broad indication that the achievement levels of the children of low-income and poor families have improved. Progress has also been recorded in housing. Thus, houses constructed that did not satisfy basic necessities fell from 34 percent in 1960 to 28 percent in 1970 (PREALC 1983, table 25). Finally, significant progress has been registered in sanitary conditions and the percentage of homes with a potable water supply. All these indicators reflect an improvement in the economic lot of low-income households in general. Whether these gains have reached the critically poor remains to be verified.

26

Whereas social services are apparently pro-poor, economic changes on the whole seem to have had the opposite effect. An encouraging outcome of the decade is a 2 percent annual increase in per capita real income, despite the global economic woes of the decade.The effect on the poor of the noted respectable rise in mean national per capita income remains to be analyzed. Major negative changes from the viewpoint of the poor are the downward-sloping trends in the production and consumption of poorman's food,[1] the output of poorman's produce,[2] and employment. Panama's food prices continue to be considerably higher than border prices; the domestic production of staple food (except rice) has fallen in absolute quantities; cottage industries from which the poor supplement their market incomes have declined; and unemployment (in urban areas) and underemployment (especially in rural areas) have increased. Thus the adverse economic changes seem to have offset, to an as-yet-unmeasured extent, the gains to the poor from social services. Between 1970 and 1979, labor force participation declined nearly four percentage points, from 61.3 percent to 57.6 percent, while unemployment increased from 7.1 percent to 8.8 percent, all of it in metropolitan areas (Correa 1984). Underemployment (a major source of poverty) is, in general, an increasing function of open unemployment.[3] Other things being equal, therefore, the poor are likely to have suffered relatively more than other classes owing to the global recession and unemployment of the recent past. An analysis of unemployment and underemployment appears in chapters 7–13, in particular chapters 7–9.

STAGNATION OF POORMAN'S FOOD AND POORMAN'S PRODUCE

Rice, maize, and beans are poorman's food, while maize, in addition, is the poor animal's (pig's) feed.[4] Between 1968–70 and 1977–79, the total domestic output of rice, maize, and beans declined in absolute quantities by 3 percent, 25 percent, and 35 percent, respectively (see table 3.2 and fig. 3.1). Aggregate production of rice and corn has picked up a bit in the

---

1. Rice, maize, and beans are termed "poorman's food" here, not because only the poor use these staples, but because the poor eat mainly or only these cereals as their daily food.

2. Strictly speaking, the products of cottage industries are not necessarily produced predominantly by the poor. However, these are practically the only things that the poor can, and probably do, produce to augment their paltry market incomes.

3. As calculated from various tables given in PREALC/ILO (1982).

4. Small farms (those cultivating between 0.5 and 1.9 hectares of land) that in the 1970 agricultural census reported agriculture as their main occupation and that accounted for a quarter of all farms raised, on the average, nearly one pig per farm compared with nearly two on other farms, whereas they had only 0.4 head of cattle per farm against 17.7 head on other farms (as calculated by Tang 1983, table 1). On this score, the pig is indeed a poorman's animal. Interestingly, the production of pigs has increased at a high rate.

Table 3.1 Main Indicators of Changes in Poverty in Panama

	1970			1980		
Indicators	Urban	Rural	Total	Urban	Rural	Total
A. *Social indicators*						
Health						
Life expectancy (years)	—	—	65.0	—	—	70.0
Number of physicians per 10,000 population	—	—	6.3	16.5	1.8	9.4
Child mortality (children less than one year) (%)	29.8	48.0	40.5	19.4	23.9	21.7
Adult mortality (%)	5.5	8.4	7.1	4.1	4.2	4.1
Hospital births as % of total births	97.3	39.7	65.0	98.8	61.2	79.5
Crude birthrate per 1,000 fertile women	36.0	38.1	37.1	25.1	28.9	27.1
Mortality rates owing to poorman's diseases						
Infectious and parasitic diseases	—	—	125.1	—	—	24.8
Infectious intestinal diseases	—	—	47.3	—	—	10.2
Tuberculosis	—	—	19.4	—	—	8.1
Whooping cough	—	—	4.9	—	—	0.8
Tetanus	—	—	11.6	—	—	0.2
Measles	—	—	21.1	—	—	0.1
Nutritional deficiencies	—	—	9.0	—	—	2.5
Maternal mortality	—	—	13.5	—	—	6.0
Education						
Literacy rate for population ten years old or older (%)	93.9	64.5	79.3	95.0	75.5	85.8
Primary enrollment ratio	—	—	78.8	—	—	94.8
Primary education (rates of retention to final year)	—	—	55.0 (1976)	—	—	60.0 (1982)
Secondary enrollment ratio	—	—	59.9	—	—	69.3
Number of students in university	—	—	421.0	—	—	2,506.0
Housing						
Houses without potable water (%)	—	—	35.7	—	—	20.3
Houses without sanitary services (%)	—	—	28.3	—	—	12.0
Population with access to potable water (%)	100.0	41.1	70.5	100.0	60.7	82.0

Table 3.1   Continued.

Indicators	1970			1980		
	Urban	Rural	Total	Urban	Rural	Total
B. Economic indicators						
Per capita GNP in 1980 prices ($)	—	—	1,353	—	—	1,779
Gini coefficient	—	—	0.56	0.47[b]	0.55[c]	0.55[c]
Unemployment[a]	9.8	4.2	7.1	11.9	4.3	8.0[d]

Sources: Child mortality: 1970, *Panama en Cifras*, November 1974, p. 41, table 212.01; 1980, *Panama en Cifras*, November 1982, p. 54, table 221.01.

Mortality rate: 1970, *Estadísticas Vitales*, ser. B, Controller General, p. 67; 1980, *Panama en Cifras*, November 1982, p. 54, table 221.01.

Hospital births as a percentage of total births: 1970, *Estadísticas Vitales*, 1970, p. 20; 1980, *Panama en Cifras*, November 1982, p. 55, table 221.02.

Crude birthrate: 1970, *Panama en Cifras*, November 1974, p. 40, table 212.01; 1980, *Panama en Cifras*, November 1982, p. 54, table 221.01.

Education: Data are available in unpublished form in Human Resources Department of the MIPPE.

Employment: 1970, *Estadística del Trabajo*, ser. O for 1971, Controller General, p. 11, table 1; 1979, *Situación Social, Estadística del Trabajo*, 1979, sec. 441; *Trabajo y Salario*, Controller General, p. 27, table 441.09.

Number of physicians per 10,000 inhabitants: *Situación Social, Asistencia Social*, 1980, Controller General, sec. 431, p. 8, table 431.05.

Life expectancy: *Health Bulletin*, 1980, Controller General, no. 903, p. 3.

Growth of per capita income: *Panama en Cifras* (annual).

[a] Unemployment data pertain to metropolitan areas noted in the "urban" column and the rest of the country noted in the "rural" column, except for 1983, for which year it is for urban and rural areas as traditionally defined in Panama.

[b] For 1980.

[c] For 1983.

[d] Unemployment for 1983 was 9.7 percent.

1980s, but hardly perceptibly. Per capita output fell from 70, 22, and 5 kilograms, respectively, in 1970 to 48, 19, and 4 kilograms in 1979 for the three crops (see fig. 3.2).[5] Per capita apparent consumption shows even sharper declines, as we see from table 3.3 and figure 3.3. The drop in production has been sharper in less developed provinces (Darién, Herrera, and Veraguas) than in others. The fertile-land provinces (in particular Chiriquí) registered an increase in output, but not sufficient to offset the decline in poor areas.

Even greater has been the stagnation in cottage industries that have

5. Between 1960 and 1970 apparent production per capita of maize, beans, potatoes, raw sugar loaves, and molasses fell by 35 percent, 29 percent, 13 percent, 55 percent and 53 percent, respectively, while the production per capita of rice increased by 5 percent. Between

Table 3.2 Area Cultivated and Quantity Produced (Thousands of Quintals) of Rice, Maize, and Beans, 1968–1979

Year	Unhusked Rice			Maize in Grain			Beans in Dry Grain		
	Hectares	Produced	Index	Hectares	Produced	Index	Hectares	Produced	Index
1968	128,600	3,594.4	—	100,300	1,846.1	—	17,200	119.4	—
1969	125,700	3,643.0	—	102,500	1,929.1	—	17,500	116.1	—
1970	93,100	2,891.5	—	64,900	1,243.8	—	13,600	72.9	—
1971	95,600	3,002.1	—	63,100	1,192.2	—	12,000	72.9	—
1972	105,200	2,760.6	—	65,700	977.7	—	10,300	68.8	—
1973	105,300	3,573.3	—	67,600	1,208.0	—	12,100	77.1	—
1974	112,200	3,932.4	100[a]	75,500	1,308.7	100[a]	16,100	89.4	100[a]
1975	115,400	4,074.0	104	74,300	1,437.7	110	16,600	92.5	104
1976	122,350	3,184.9	81	83,150	1,410.3	108	15,560	72.7	81
1977	109,980	4,105.6	104	82,780	1,757.0	134	14,850	88.9	99
1978	99,110	3,579.9	91	68,600	1,421.8	109	11,770	72.0	81
1979	98,530	3,539.4	90	69,570	1,395.9	107	10,950	81.9	92
1980	—	—	96	—	—	91	—	—	61
1981	—	—	109	—	—	96	—	—	82
1982	—	—	99	—	—	104	—	—	49
1983	—	—	112	—	—	116	—	—	81
Per capita, 1968	—	2.66	—	—	1.36	—	—	0.09	—
Per capita, 1979	—	1.95	—	—	0.78	—	—	0.05	—
Production in 1978–79 as % of that in 1968–69	—	97.0	—	—	75.0	—	—	65.0	—

Source: Panama, Controller General, *Situación económica sección 312—Producción agropecuaria, superficie semorada de arroz, maíz y frijol de bejuco, ano agrícola, 1979–1980,* pp. 4, 16, 25.
[a]Index of the quantity produced for rice, maize, and beans, from the latest estimates published in *Panama en Cifras, Anos 1979–1983* (Panama: Controller General, November 1984), pp. 20–21.

Aggregate quantities produced

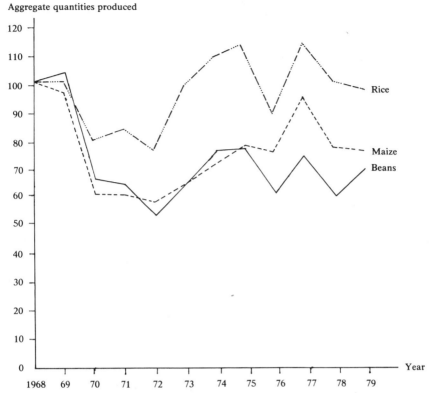

Figure 3.1   Aggregate quantities (thousands of quintals) of rice, maize, and beans produced, 1968–1979. Data from table 3.2.

traditionally formed the cash products of the rural poor, as we see from table 3.3.

The trend in the production of maize and beans was downward even during the 1960s. Thus for the past two decades the poor seem to have lost both as producers and as consumers. Why have poorman's (and poor animal's) food and poorman's produce declined in absolute quantities, not to speak of per capita quantities?

To answer these questions, we must first determine whether the fall in production and apparent consumption of staple food implies a correspond-

1960 and 1978, the changes in per capita production were as follows: maize, −50.7 percent; beans, −51.7 percent; potatoes, −18.2 percent; raw sugar loaves (*panelas*), −72.5 percent; and molasses (*miel de caña*), −64.2 percent. During the more recent quinquennium, 1975–80, the rates of growth for almost all food products were negative, while those for almost all cash crops, especially export crops, were positive (Dirección de Estadística y Censo, as reported in PREALC/ILO 1983, table 23).

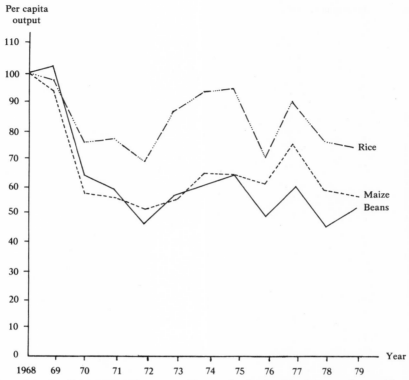

Figure 3.2   Decline of per capita output (thousands of quintals) of rice, maize, and beans, 1968–1979. Data from table 3.2.

ing fall in the consumption of overall food. Might the poor not have substituted other grains for rice, maize, and beans? Neither the available data on substitutes nor observational evidence provides any indication that they did. The sources of the noted decline must be found elsewhere. For the drop in cottage industries, there could be three reasons, among others: (a) Low-income households have voluntarily found alternative, more remunerative vocations, in which case they ought to be better off. (b) Cottage industries have been mechanized, which not only put home producers and artisans out of business, but also reduced the appeal and consequently the overall demand for these home-produced articles. (c) Demand for these products has fallen without there being a shift to mechanization. In the last two cases, the poor would suffer. Unfortunately, that is what seems to have happened. In view of the deterioration in the job situation over the reference period, the first explanation is highly improbable. The decline

Table 3.3 Apparent Consumption (Kilograms per Person) of Poorman's Food and Output of Poorman's Produce, 1969–1982

| | Food: Apparent Consumption | | | | Poorman's Produce: Output | | |
| | | Maize | | | | | |
Year	Rice	Grain	Deriva-tives	Beans	Molasses	Raw Sugar Loaves	Hats
1960	—	—	—	—	5.0	3.9	218,000
1969	73.6	30.7	0.6	4.4	1.7	2.2	—
1970	70.1	22.2	0.9	4.0	2.5	1.8	142,000
1971	66.5	23.2	0.8	4.1	2.1	1.4	NA[a]
1972	51.3	16.1	1.2	3.4	2.0	1.4	NA
1973	56.6	20.5	1.0	2.9	1.9	1.3	NA
1974	74.9	28.9	1.1	4.2	2.2	1.2	NA
1975	79.5	18.4	1.2	3.5	1.7	0.9	NA
1976	55.5	18.0	0.9	3.1	1.5	0.9	NA
1977	63.7	22.2	1.3	3.0	1.5	0.8	NA
1978	52.9	16.7	1.3	2.8	1.9	1.1	NA
1979	48.2	17.1	1.3	2.7	1.9	1.0	NA
1980	55.5	17.7	1.6	2.7	1.8	1.0	NA
1981	55.3	11.2	1.8	3.0	1.5	0.9	NA
1982	55.9	21.2	2.4	2.9	1.2	0.9	NA

Sources: Panama en Cifras, annual, esp. 1971, p. 148; 1980, p. 174; 1983, p. 179. For 1960 (converted into kilograms): *Censo Agropecuario,* 1970, vol. 1, table 24, p. 212. The data in the *Panama en Cifras* are defined as *abastecimiento annual por habitante* in kilograms, which I translate here as apparent consumption.
[a]NA = data not available.

in the demand for cottage products warrants analysis, but probably not a separate one, in that it likely is caused in part by the same economic and policy variables that might be responsible for the fall in food agriculture. Let us therefore analyze the causes of that stagnation.

An investigation into the decline in food agriculture opens up the gamut of problems of agricultural development and the government's policy toward agriculture. This is the subject matter that will be analyzed in depth in the chapter on agricultural poverty. At this stage I shall mainly raise issues and discuss only the bare bones of possible reasons for the malady of Panama's agriculture. These reasons may be assembled under two heads as follows:

Structural aspects
    Land tenure and tenancy
    Distribution of land and other productive assets

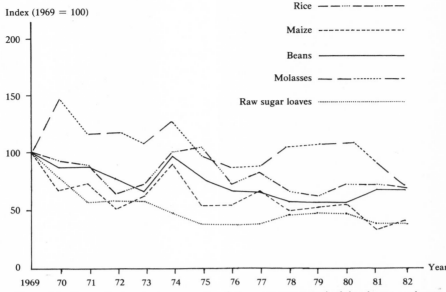

Figure 3.3   Per capita apparent consumption (kilograms per person) of rice, beans, molasses, and raw sugar loaves, 1969–1982. Data from table 3.3.

Agricultural policies
   The asentamientos
   Export agriculture
   Protection of food crops
   Price supports
   Concessional imports of agricultural inputs
   Agricultural credit policy
   Agricultural labor policy
   Agricultural research policy

STRUCTURAL ASPECTS

Land Tenure and Tenancy

Legal irregularities abound in Panama's agricultural sector. About 70 percent of the farm households having less than 50 hectares per farm do not hold legal title to the land they cultivate. Lack of legal title is more serious among small landholders. At the upper end, farms having 200 hectares or more improved their legal holdings of land during the 1970s. At the turn of the decade they held title to over 80 percent of their land (Panama, MIDA 1980). For cultivation the lack of legal entitlement may not be an impediment, for few ordinarily are deprived of the possession of land. But it creates a problem when a farmer needs credit, which is not easy to get, especially by small landholders, since land without legal title is not acceptable as collateral. Because of their low savings capacity and meager market surplus, small landholders are the ones who need credit more but get less. Small farmers in general have abundant labor but scarce and less fertile land and little capital. Therefore their optimizing behavior amounts to maximizing yield per hectare from their land. Large farmers, on the other hand, are short of labor and, by definition, have abundant land. Faced with high-cost agricultural labor (see below) in relation to subsidized capital, the profit-maximizing large producers tend to use capital-intensive techniques (e.g., tractors) and raise laborsaving farm products (e.g., cattle). Traveling through the countryside, one is struck by the spectacle of crops grown on small hillside lots and animal farms situated on level, apparently fertile land in the plains, especially along roads. The existing land tenure system of Panama thus tends to be biased toward cash crops and cattle farms and against food crops.

Distribution of Land and Other Productive Assets

Panama's land distribution, with a Gini coefficient of 0.75, is among the most skewed in Central and South America. The area of large farms has been steadily increasing since 1960, as the data below reveal.

	Total	Size in Hectares			
		0.5–9.9	10–99.9	100–999.9	1,000–Higher
1960					
Farms	100	65	33	2.5	0.095
Area	100	12	46	26.0	15.74
1970					
Farms	100	60	37	3.2	0.117
Area	100	8	46	30.0	16.27

Source: PREALC/ILO (1983, table 7).

In Asian countries where distribution is less skewed and differences in the fertility of land between small landholders and big landowners are much smaller than in Panama, the yield per unit of land decreases as farm size increases. This is not the case in Panama, where yield is higher on big farms.[6] It is known in Panama, however, that *minifundistas* cultivate much

6. The yield of rice was practically the same on small and large farms in 1959–60. Since then rice productivity on small farms has declined, whereas that on large rice farms increased by 160 percent between 1959–60 and 1978–79, all attributed to mechanization and associated practices (PREALC/ILO 1983, tables 12 and 13).

poorer land than *latifundistas*. Moreover, the alternative to the tractor in Panama is the digging stick, the *chuzo*, which may reduce land erosion (since the land is never loosened by plowing), but which lowers the yield to about one-third of that on mechanized farms. Nevertheless, after a big jump in the rice yield on large farms, the differences tapered off in the 1970s. The ratio for farms of 20 hectares or more to farms having less than 20 hectares in the province of Chiriquí was 1.63 in 1971 or 1.56 during 1971–74 but declined to 1.44 in 1979 (or 1.445 during 1976–79). Furthermore, the ratio of land in crops declines sharply as farm size increases. The result is that less land is devoted to the production of the poorman's food (rice, maize, and beans) and more to the production of the food of the nonpoor (the noted staples and meat, milk, and tomatoes) than would be the case were land more equally distributed. Another reason for the decline in land use for staple food crops is the retirement of poor land from these crops owing to a fall in their real prices in the late 1970s and a rise in the price of inputs such as fertilizer.

The substitution of capital and land for labor in large farms reduces private costs (and thus increases the producer's profits) but increases social costs, since the abundant factor of rural areas—labor—is used less intensively than scarce factors. An additional reason for large farm holders to prefer cattle ranching is the lack of high-quality schools and other amenities in rural areas. They live in cities where their children can get a good education. Cattle farms require less supervision, which suits absentee landlords.

The distribution of other productive assets generally correlates with the distribution of land. The distortions due to the skewed distribution of assets other than land can be rectified, to some extent, without altering ownership patterns, for example, by giving small landholders easy access to credit, fertilizer, new production techniques, schooling, agricultural education, and other means of production. The government has had these programs for some time, but so far they seem to have made only a marginal impact. Most credit has gone to big farmers.

AGRICULTURAL POLICIES

Government intervention in agriculture increased sharply during the 1970s. Today *quantity controls* apply to almost all agricultural exports and imports. All products and factor *prices*, including the prices of imported agricultural inputs, are supported, controlled, or subsidized. Stringent labor codes and minimum wages are operative in rural areas. Subsidized credit is provided to promote specific commodities. Concessional services and subsidized machinery are supplied to certain groups of producers. In addition, the government directly intervenes in agricultural input and output *markets*. To carry out these policies, a network of institutions has been created. The Banco de Desarrollo Agropecuario (BDA) provides subsidized credit to small producers, and the Ministry of Agriculture does so for organized low-income associations, such as *asentamientos* (collective farms). The Empresa Nacional de Maquinaria supplies subsidized services of machinery. The Empresa Nacional de Semillas provides seeds (mostly imported) at concessional prices. The Instituto de Seguro Agropecuario provides insurance service of certain types to agriculture, a rare service in developing countries. Exportable sugar is the monopoly of sugar complexes of the public sector. Asentamientos, which make up over 5 percent of rural households, are supported by government through subsidized services. Finally, the multimonopolist IMA (Instituto de Mercadeo Agropecuario) administers agricultural pricing policies, buys surplus produce, maintains public warehouses, and is the sole exporter and importer of agricultural products. The agricultural market is thus almost castrated.

All these policies are well coordinated, compatible and complementary in the sense that all focus on the same goals: self-sufficiency in food and betterment of the rural poor. There is hardly any desirable agricultural policy ever recommended by agroeconomic experts and experimented with by policymakers, from the price-support policy of the United States to the land-to-the-tiller policy of Israel (short of land redistribution) that the Panamanian government has not tried. Many of these policies have, according to the objectives set in the particular circumstances, been successful in other countries—for example, price supports that have made America the granary of the world and the land distribution policy that has made Taiwan, one of the most thickly populated countries in the world, brim with surplus rice. The irony of events is that, concerning the agricultural poor, nothing seems to work in Panama! Let us look briefly at Panama's various agricultural policies to find out what went wrong.

The Asentamientos

The asentamientos constitute a bold experiment with pockets of socialism in a capitalistic setting. In Panama the government not only has the traditional power of eminent domain but also has held virtual title to much farmland, insofar as even today over two-fifths of agricultural land is held by private parties without title. The land to which the government has held title, however, is of relatively low fertility, since by the time it started organizing asentamientos, for instance, fertile land had already been occupied by private owners, with or without legal title. The asentamientos largely came into existence during the first three years of the Torrijos government. Part of the land carved out for the asentamientos belonged either to private farms or to government but had been occupied (mostly illegally) by *campesinos* (peasants). It was therefore a clever policy to make the best of the given difficult situation as well as a type of land reform.

The Panamanian government has provided subsidized credit, machinery services, and other facilities to the asentamientos, opened accessible primary schools and health posts for them, and assisted them in managing common property. Because largely poor households were collected on relatively inferior land, the asentamientos have become permanently dependent upon public assistance. Recent government austerity measures necessitated by the present financial crunch—caused by prolonged recession, mushrooming foreign debt service, an unmanageable central government budget deficit, a perennially rising foreign trade deficit, high interest rates, and the drying up of Latin American markets for Panama's entrepôt trade—have led to serious problems for asentamientos.

Representing approximately 7,000 rural families or 5 percent of rural households and considerably less than 1 percent of cultivated land, as of 1983 asentamientos form about 50 percent of all organized agricultural groups that receive subsidized public facilities, as follows:

Asentamientos	216
Agrarian councils	48
Marketing councils	17
Agricultural cooperatives	85
Incorporated enterprises	4
Associations	74
Others (including parastatals, private enterprises, and multinationals)	13
Total	457

With public assistance, the agricultural practices of the asentamientos have moved from the *chuzo*—the metal-tipped digging stick used to make a small hole in soil to plant a grain of seed—to machinery, thus skipping the use of all labor-intensive, intermediate techniques such as animal power. Since the mid-1970s, however, the asentamientos, and almost all organized groups, have shown signs of weakness. Their proportion in mechanized farms fell from 3.5 percent of the total farms in 1975 to 0.9 percent in 1981, as follows:

	1975 (%)	1981 (%)
Private producer, mechanized	10.8	36.6
Organized producers	3.5	0.9
Parastatals	0.0	0.6
Traditional (chuzo) producers	85.7	61.9

The movement from mechanization to the chuzo has caused reduction in yield of the affected farms. Many asentamientos have repeatedly failed to repay their loans. Many of the campesinos who used to cultivate their own small plots before the formation of asentamientos are known to be disenchanted with common-property production, even though they now have more land per capita and evidently reap some economies of scale. The latter purposes could perhaps have been equally well served by cooperatives, in which, unlike the asentamientos, private incentives are not stifled, though production (as distinguished from marketing) co-ops have not in general been very successful either. The problems were aggravated by the recession and unemployment and the resulting deterioration of the government's budgetary position. The effect of these bad times has been particularly heavy on the poor.

One wonders why the Israeli kibbutz has done so well and the Panamanian asentamiento tends to do so poorly. One of the explanations seems to be that the asentamientos are the collectives of the poor—the very poor—whereas the kibbutzim were started by semiskilled, semieducated, lower-middle-income farmers. The bold Panamanian experiment has run into rough waters. Current policymakers seem to be disillusioned by it. It remains to be verified whether small, independent farmers have fared better than the campesinos in the asentamientos. In any case, the success or failure of the asentamientos in the long run (not perhaps during the present hard times) will provide useful lessons for other countries.

The asentamientos engage largely in subsistence cultivation, mainly rice. As such their emergence might to some extent have mitigated the effect of the general trend away from food crops. On the other hand, a typical *latifundista* (big landlord), being less sure of the timely availability of labor now than when some poor households cultivated small pieces of land on or near his *hacienda* (farm) but looked for additional employment on the big farm for their main livelihood, might have substituted capital-intensive cash crops and thus more than offset the positive effect on food production in the asentamientos. Moreover, since—as shown by the array of numbers in the preceding paragraph—the asentamientos have largely reverted to the chuzo, owing to the difficulty of renting machinery, food production in these farms must have suffered. The yield from the chuzo cultivation is no more than one-fourth to one-third of that in mechanized farms.

Export Agriculture

Subsistence agriculture cannot earn badly need foreign exchange; thus, export crops may tend to receive preferential treatment. Faced with foreign-exchange shortages, the government of Panama provided several incentives for exports, even though the erstwhile import-substitution policy is still operative. Where the country has natural comparative advantage, export incentives may be unnecessary, but export producers have enjoyed various advantages anyway. Panama is not unique in this respect. In fact, it has perhaps not provided as much inducement for exports as many other countries. Other counties award "export medals" (India), give export subsidies (Brazil), and provide various other incentives to exporters.

Nevertheless, exporters in Panama do enjoy certain differential facilities. Apart from numerous tax concessions, almost all plantation regions are well connected by roads to the seaports and the capital cities of provinces, whereas large tracts of traditional agriculture are still relatively inaccessible. Emphasis is being put on export crops to earn foreign exchange—the traditional exports of bananas, coffee, and sugar and the "nontraditional" exports of citrus fruits, cacao, and tomatoes (Panama, MIDA 1980). Export crops generally use more productive land (example: Chiriquí Land Company in Panama), leaving less fertile land for subsistence crops. Multinational agribusiness firms, such as the United Fruit Company, are extensively involved in producing export crops. Although the modern technology they use may be expected to seep out, to some extent, to food agriculture in general, this has unfortunately not happened so far in Panama. In African countries backwash effects have been observed more commonly than spread effects. Some investigators have found that productivity in food agriculture is inversely related to the importance of export crops.

Panama's experience seems somewhat mixed: the absolute yield of rice in Panama is estimated to be no higher than a quarter of the yield in East Asian countries (Tang 1983). It increased at a perceptible though not impressive rate of a little over 3 percent a year between the late 1960s and the mid-1970s, remained static during the mid-1970s, and has picked up again in the 1980s. The yield of beans has not changed at all. The yield of maize was static till the late 1970s but has been showing signs of improvement.

Nothing I have said here implies that promoting export agriculture is a bad policy. That these products—bananas, sugar, and so on—compete favorably in international markets means they have comparative advantage and therefore merit encouragement. Several other crops deserve promotion to earn scarce foreign resources. I have only noted a possible dual nature of Panama's agriculture, between the modern, large-scale, capital-intensive export agriculture produced largely in plantations, estates, and large commercial farms and the traditional small-scale, labor-intensive, food agriculture based largely on the chuzo technology. The duality, combined with the investment bias in favor of export crops relative to food crops, might in part explain the stagnation of staple food in Panama.

Protection of Food Crops

Food agriculture is a protected infant industry that has shown no signs of growing up. Only the IMA can import food products, including maize, beans, onions, and milk, which it sells at much higher prices than the CIF (cost, insurance, and freight) import prices. As data for 1976 indicate, food prices in Panama are from 150 percent to 500 percent higher than border prices expressed in U.S. dollars per metric ton, as we see from table 3.4.

Almost every country of the world follows the policy of attaining self-sufficiency in food. Why not Panama? Food is such a critical necessity that no country wants to depend for its food on other countries. England, France, Germany, Japan, and many other countries have protected their agriculture steadfastly through quantity quotas, tariffs, subsidized inputs, and support prices to domestic agriculture. Apparently, therefore, there is nothing wrong with Panama's protection of its staple food products.

An economic case for protection is based on the infant industry argument. The industry is given protection from outside competition so that in the long run, when scale and other economies have been fully realized and proper technology has been learned and adopted, the infant will grow up and be able to compete with imports. In the case of agriculture, the self-sufficiency argument reigns supreme. However, unless through research and other means new seeds and improved agricultural practices are developed and adopted and the availability and access of water, fertilizer, and other modern resources is increased with the objective of raising domestic productivity, protection may simply lead to high-cost agriculture. For behind tariff and quota walls, inefficient producers and unsuitable lands will continue to remain in operation while efficient farms will be under no pressure to search for innovations. Because of high-cost food agriculture, accompanied by high support and retail prices, overproduction and underconsumption of agricultural output may persist side by side. Rice is probably such a case in Panama. As we saw in table 3.3, the output of rice has not increased significantly, and per capita consumption has declined, even though the income elasticity of demand for rice is calculated to be 0.046 in urban areas and 0.26 in rural areas. Yet IMA's warehouses have been inundated with surplus rice. Some people attribute the discrepancy

Table 3.4 Ratios of Agricultural Commodity Prices in Panama to Those in the United States

Product	1970–73	1975–78	1980–83
Corn	1.54	1.95	2.40
Sorghum	3.24	2.75	2.41
Rice	0.71	1.05	1.33
Potatoes	2.24	2.76	3.54
Tomatoes	5.89	5.53	9.04
Tobacco	0.61	0.60	0.78
Beef	0.53	0.61	0.64
Milk	1.39	1.22	1.14
Eggs	1.39	1.27	1.84
Chicken meat	3.01	2.72	3.67

Source: Willis Peterson, "Panama Agriculture: Production, Prices, and Policy Recommendations" (mimeographed, MIPPE, March 1984), table 5.

to cheaper contraband rice from Costa Rica, but little is known about magnitude. The high price of rice is another possible reason. In any case, protection does not seem to be an apt long-term cure for static agriculture. An alternative is to devote resources to research to develop techniques that increase the yield of food crops per hectare—for example, the seed-fertilizer technology so successfully exploited in some parts of Southeast Asia.

Price Supports

Price supports, a successful agricultural policy elsewhere, have not delivered the goods in Panama. The government of Panama supports the prices of practically all agricultural products. Price supports play two main roles: they reduce risk to the farmer by ensuring stable prices, which as a rule are announced in advance of the sowing season, and thus they provide "partial insurance" for farm incomes against fluctuations in harvest prices.[7] Because of low elasticities of demand for primary products, without price supports bumper crops may drastically reduce rather than increase farmers' incomes. Therefore, without assured prices farmers cannot plan their planting efficiently. This policy is a key factor in explaining the success of United States agriculture. Why has this policy not succeeded in Panama?

Part of the explanation seems to lie in the wide coverage of Panama's price support policy. When all the prices in the entire agricultural sector

7. Income insurance is partial, insofar as prices but not quantities produced are guaranteed. At supported prices, bumper crops will bring high incomes to producers; lean crops will reduce them. If crops are destroyed by flood or drought or pests, the price support policy by itself provides no relief to farmers.

are fixed, the role of the market in confronting the producer with shifts in the demands of different products is eliminated. This may lead to distortions and inefficiencies. It is true that for social cost minimization, a distortion in one market requires distortions in related markets too. In the absence of the market, or at least a giant computer and comprehensive general equilibrium model that can simultaneously solve all the relevant equations (which Panama lacks), autonomously determined distortions in all product markets may not turn out to be in the right directions or the right relative proportions. For instance, various indicators reflect (see table 3.4) that producer prices for food crops (rice, maize, beans, and sugarcane) in Panama are too high, while those for beef, tobacco, milk, and other locally consumed cash crops are on the low side.

Apart from regulated prices, quantity controls exist on almost all imports and exports of food products. These controls exacerbate the distortions due to price controls. High producer prices and restrictions on competitive imports protect the inefficient producer, which means a high average cost of production. Efficient producers cannot expand because inefficient producers are not weeded out of the available land and because demand does not expand (see below). Price supports not only cause social costs but also create budgetary problems for the government. If supported prices happen to be the equilibrium prices (which can at best be only by a fluke), they are redundant; if they are above the equilibrium prices (which is the objective of price supports), the government must run a deficit budget. In Panama, the deficit on supported prices is made up by charging higher prices for imported food products (corn, beans, milk, etc.). On both counts—high-cost domestic agriculture and profit margins on imported products—consumers thus have to pay high prices despite subsidies on domestically produced food products. Contraction of domestic demand owing to high prices stifles domestic supply and induces the import of contraband rice through the open borders of Costa Rica.

Not only have food prices been high in Panama relative to border prices, but their effect on the very poor (those with less than $100 per month family income in 1972) has been mildly higher than on the very rich (those with monthly family incomes exceeding $2,000). Besides, during the decade of the 1970s, the prices of poorman's food items rose by higher percentages than prices of the nonpoor's food items.

Finally, while price supports may keep small-scale farmers in production, the real beneficiaries are the large producers who have the surplus to market. A high price of a subsistence crop is unlikely to benefit the subsistence producer either relative to large farmers or even in absolute terms unless it is accompanied by productivity-increasing investment, which unfortunately has not occurred in Panama compared with several other developing countries, such as East Asian nations.

Concessional Imports of Agricultural Inputs

In a policy that is well intentioned but ill suited to the Panamian economy, according to Law 62 of 1974, all agricultural inputs can be imported tax free. This policy is consistent with the domestic price support policy, since it widens the profit margins of producers. Combined with concessional interest rates and high labor costs (see below), however, this measure provides an incentive to capital-intensive and foreign exchange-intensive production methods. For instance, the ratios of imported inputs to total cost are 12 percent and 60 percent, respectively, for traditional (chuzo) and mechanized farms for maize and 9 percent and 63 percent, respectively, for rice.[8] Rice seeds, as well as other high-yield varieties of seeds, are imported, since there are no conditions to produce high-yield seeds locally. Because of noted adverse effects, therefore, this policy is neither allocationally nor distributionally appropriate.

Agricultural Credit Policy

Cheap credit is a policy with mixed blessings. The government of Panama's policy of providing cheap credit to agriculture is carried out by the Banco de Desarrollo Agropecuario (BDA), which charges agricultural borrowers 3 percent less than the market rate (which is financed by a surcharge of 1 percent on nonagricultural loans). Credit is essential for producers, especially those who have few savings of their own. Rural credit, however, typically does not go to the worthy—that is, the needy producer—rather, it goes to the credit worthy. Panama has perhaps not done badly in this respect, since the asentamientos have received credit and other assistance liberally from the MIDA. This organization, however, accounts for only 1 percent of rural land. The bulk of medium and small farmers are left out, for BDA, with its operating costs of approximately 6 percent of its

8. Not only are the yield differences rather large, so are the differences in the foreign-exchange components of inputs, as the following data bear out:

	Maize	Rice
Yield (qq/ha)		
Chuzo	15	18
Mechanized	65	68
Foreign exchange components of inputs (%)		
Chuzo	12	9
Mechanized	60	63

Source: Data supplied by Dirección Nacional de Planificación Sectorial, MIDA (Panama, MIDA 1983a).

loans and a discount of 3 percent on the market interest rate, can hardly cope with the demand from those who have practically no collateral to offer. The problem relating to agricultural credit in Panama, however, is not so much the allocation of credit among borrowers as its effects on factor proportions. When the labor force as a whole suffers because of capital-intensive methods of production, so do poor households. Not only do the latifundistas substitute capital for labor, even the asentamientos prefer to rent machinery for cultivation (which is laborsaving) rather than using labor-intensive means such as bullock power, presumably because machinery is *available* to them from the Empresa Nacional de Maquinaria at subsidized rents.

Agricultural Labor Policy

Contrary to the popular view, the problem of labor policy arises not as much from the equity/efficiency trade-off as from supply-and-demand forces. In a free-enterprise economy, a policymaker is often faced with a choice between higher remuneration to low-paid labor and expansion of employment. There is in general a trade-off between high minimum wage and high demand for low-productivity labor. On equity grounds, the relevant comparisons are those between the labor share as a whole and the nonlabor share; between the earnings of those who are employed at the floor remuneration level or minimum wage and the incomes of those who are independently and comfortably above these floors; and between those who are lucky enough to retain their jobs despite minimum wages and others who are not.

Insofar as absolute poverty is concerned, it is the last-mentioned labor/labor inequity that really matters. This inequity evidently results from the forces of supply and demand. Very low or subsistence wages are bad enough for human dignity, but incessant unemployment is a curse of the first degree. It may be that without a minimum wage all or most low-paid workers would be poor because of miserably low levels of free-market wages, but evidently not as critically poor as those who lose jobs altogether owing to the minimum wage policy, unless the unemployed are taken care of by the society, which is not the case in Panama.

When the noted labor/labor distortion is added on to the earlier-discussed capital/labor distortion, the poor are doubly hurt. In Panama, on the one hand, capital is cheapened by concessional credit, subsidies to machinery and equipment, tax concessions on imported capital inputs, and investment incentives of various kinds. On the other hand, rural labor is made costly by three policy measures, among others: a minimum rural wage (of $4.50 per day as of fall 1980) that is believed to be significantly higher than the equilibrium wage rate for the reference category of labor;

labor laws that put several restrictions on employers, making labor less attractive to them; and social security contributions that currently cost the employer about *11 percent* of the wage bill. All these measures were intended for the benefit and dignity of labor. Some of them are common in all democratic countries of Europe and North America. In the developed countries, however, the unemployed are taken care of by the state, whereas developing countries as yet can ill afford this service. The irony of the matter is that while these labor laws are beneficial to those who have jobs, they discourage the employment of more low-productivity workers. Besides, they induce the substitution of nonlabor methods of production for labor-intensive methods. In the process, food production suffers, because it is labor intensive relative to cash crop and export agriculture, which is in general capital- and skill-intensive.

Agricultural Research Policy

In agricultural research priorities are hard to determine, the gestation period is inordinately long, and the outcome is typically uncertain. In 1980 and 1981 the agricultural research institute (Instituto de Investigación Agropecuaria de Panama, IDIAP) spent a little over $3 million (or about 0.01 of GNP) annually on current account and about half of that on capital account for agricultural research. This includes $6 million in aid by the USAID (to be used over a period of five years) to strengthen the technical capacity and physical facilities of the institute. Less than $100,000, or 6 percent of the total, was allocated to research on agriculture. The rest went to institutional development (75 percent), livestock research (14 percent), and the production (as distinguished from development) of seeds (5 percent) (Panama, IDIAP 1981, 11). In several areas, total factor productivity growth has been respectable, for example, sugarcane, tomatoes, and livestock. A modest total factor productivity growth has also been experienced in rice. Nevertheless, the results lag far behind those in several other developing countries, especially in food crops. For instance, for corn and beans total factor productivity has actually declined.

    Given Panama's rather weak performance in increasing the yield of its staple crops during the past fifteen years, when several developing countries experienced green revolutions, the top priority for research should perhaps go to developing high-yield varieties of seeds, especially for unirrigated areas. The research so far done by the young IDIAP appears to be of the extension type (usually expected to yield quick though feeble results), and relatively low priority seems to be given to developing innovations in agricultural practices and high-yield varieties of seeds (the payoff from which is usually high but is uncertain and generally slow). Up to the appearance of asentamientos, extension service was fairly well developed. In fact, since not much investment in agricultural research was made, the expanded extension services amounted to putting the cart before the horse. Since the agrarian reform, however, extension services have almost evaporated. It is apparent that as soon as some innovations are developed, extension services will be needed to disseminate them.

In this area there is need to reconsider priorities. Since, despite some productivity gains in recent years, the rice yield in Panama is only a fraction of that attained in other rice-producing nations, such as the East Asian countries, a major payoff should be expected from research in high-yield varieties of rice seeds.

CONCLUSIONS

The poor have gained from Panama's social services but have been hurt by the exogenous economic changes. The economic policies of the 1970s have not borne the expected fruit. Instead they are causing some losses to the poor. The benefits to the poor from social services have increased, whether measured by inputs (resources devoted to these services) or by results (such as the increase in life expectancy, literacy, and hospital births, the reduction in child mortality, and similar improvements in quality of life). The poor have, however, lost ground in all three basic areas of private welfare: their food, their produce, and their only resource (labor). During the two decades from 1960 to 1980, they suffered with respect to food because aggregate quantities of maize and beans produced fell substantially. The output of rice has recently increased, but only moderately, and per capita production and apparent consumption have fallen for all three crops. During the two decades, the production of the most important cottage industries of the poor, namely, molasses, raw sugar loaves, and hats, shrank in absolute terms. Finally, the demand for the sole resource the poor are endowed with—labor—has fallen because of the increase in unemployment and probably also underemployment.

Apart from those factors that in today's integrated world are at best only partially under any government's control, especially in an open economy like Panama's, the causes of the stagnation of Panama's food agriculture can be traced, to a significant extent, to the country's public policies and certain structural aspects of its agricultural economy. Panama's food agriculture is replete with price and quantity distortions, which need to be rationalized to put agriculture on the right track. In particular, mechanization and credit are highly subsidized, while labor is made more costly by (the otherwise well-intentioned) policies of rural minimum wage, the employer's social security contributions, and the labor code. This has led to capital-intensive techniques of production and the substitution of laborsaving products, such as cattle, for labor-using products such as crops.

Also, supported prices are too high, and so are consumer prices relative to border prices. This policy has necessitated quantity controls on imports and exports and complicated systems of tariffs and concessions on tariffs, for example, to agricultural inputs. The protection of food agriculture has not been accompanied by the necessary amount of complementary research on the development of new seeds and improved production practices suitable to Panama's rather infertile land. As a matter of fact, the hallmark of Panama's egalitarian policy has been redistribution through price distortions to the exclusion of alterations in resource ownership and resource productivity.

What is needed perhaps is a dismantling or rationalization of the multiple layers of subsidies and price and quantity controls on both product and factor sides. Obviously this cannot be done in one stroke. An economy is geared to certain institutions of production and consumption; it takes time to get accustomed to new conditions and to undertake retooling and readjustment. Eventually supported prices will need to be brought down so that inefficient producers are weeded out, efficient producers have opportunity to expand, relatively fertile land is reallocated to food agriculture, the cost of production is lowered, and producer and consumer prices are brought into line with each other without intervening subsidies.

A final point emerges from the analysis of this chapter: self-sufficiency in food is not sacrosanct, but it is highly desirable for a land-abundant country like Panama. A food embargo by foreign suppliers, which is not uncommon these days, may cause a disaster of great magnitude. To achieve self-sufficiency, however, the domestic consumer must be willing to meet the domestic production cost. If the poor cannot pay that price for food, the remedy is to modernize agriculture with a view to lowering the production costs or to remove poverty by direct means rather than supporting high-cost agriculture and sustaining poverty by price subsidies for food. There are more efficient methods of reducing poverty than interfering with prices. A number of them will suggest themselves in the course of this research.

PART TWO

Measurement of Poverty and Income Distribution

F O U R

The National Socioeconomic Survey, 1983

The basic source of data for this study is the National Socioeconomic Survey, done in 1983. It is a stratified random survey of 8,399 households, about 2 percent of the nation's households. The percentage surveyed, however, varies from province to province. For the number of households surveyed by province, the expansion factors, and related statistics, see appendix 4A to this chapter. A separate survey was done of 105 Guaymi Indian households, forming approximately 1.2 percent of the total. Both surveys contain the following information by household:

1. Location

2. Condition of home and amenities

3. Demographic characteristics

4. Education of household members

5. Expenditure patterns

6. Statistics on health and child mortality

7. Occupational patterns of the head of household and his or her parents and working sons and daughters

8. Socioeconomic characteristics of individual members of households in the nonagricultural sector, such as employment, income (wages, rents, interest, dividends, transfers, in-kind income and self-consumption), and income of the self-employed

9. Socioeconomic characteristics of households in the agricultural sector, such as sales and self-consumption of crops; stocks, sales, and purchases of poultry, dairy, and other products; costs, tenancy, and land tenure; access to technology; fixed assets; off-farm employment; and wages from labor

10. Data on unemployment and underemployment

11. Opinion questions

Given the 2 percent coverage and the average of about 1,000 households per province or approximately 150 households per district in a country with fewer than 2 million people, 12 percent of the size of Mexico City (with an estimated population of 16 million in 1983), I consider that the data

51

are probably reliable not only at the province level but also for a majority of the fifty-nine (out of sixty-five) districts covered in the survey. This chapter describes a few conceptual and measurement aspects of income and other key variables tabulated in this report.

SOME STATISTICAL PROPERTIES OF THE NATIONAL SOCIOECONOMIC SURVEY

The sample used to collect the data for the National Socioeconomic Survey is framed within the design of the national multipurpose sample of households (master sample) used by the Statistics and Census Office (SCO) for its permanent program of household surveys begun in 1963. This sample is revised every ten years, after the population and housing censuses. The latest revision has been in force since August 1983.

Income Concepts

Income as a measure of welfare should be comprehensive and, to the extent possible, permanent. Comprehensiveness requires that no component of the actual or potential flow of purchasing power and self-consumption be omitted. As a practical measure of its permanent flow, income should include the appropriate aspects of such potential components as the social security fund, undistributed profits, owner-occupied homes, changes in the number of livestock, and similar components.

As is commonly known, incomes compiled in the decennial population censuses of almost all the countries of the world, including the United States, are limited to pretax monetary measures. Household surveys in general rectify the census income deficiency by generating data on in-kind and self-consumed income. Yet rarely has a household survey been found to exceed two-thirds of personal income in national accounts. With a view to reducing the bias introduced by the understatement or omission of certain components of income in household surveys, we made several corrections in the present survey data. A summary of these corrections and adjustments follows.

Imputation of rental value to owner-occupied homes.   Rental value of owner-occupied homes was estimated by generating rent/income ratios from the 1980 demographic census, adjusting them to comprehensive income classes, and updating to 1983.

Adjustments for undistributed profits and underreported dividends and interest income.   Purchasing power is realistically measured by current consumption and by accretions to net worth, which can result from voluntary or involuntary savings as well as from accrued capital gains. Measurable and, by and large, foreseeable capital gains arise largely from undistributed profits. Estimates of inequalities and relative poverty will therefore be understated if undistributed profits are not added to income. In this study, therefore, undistributed profits are duly accounted for.

The omission of retained profits in traditional studies of income distribution and poverty is not due to disagreement with the definition of income given above. Rather, it results from the lack of data. The problem does not end there. Not only is information about the ownership of capital stock lacking, but dividends and interest income are notoriously underreported in household surveys.

Corrections are made here for underreported property income and the absence of undistributed profits in household surveys. These corrections consist of adding the undistributed part of net-of-tax profits to distributed profits and reconciling the appropriately blown-up amounts of reported profits with total profits in national accounts as estimated from the Treasury Department's tax records and from reported interest income with the corresponding category in national accounts as calculated from the Banking Commission's interest data. For the detailed procedure, see appendix 4B.

Treatment of social security funds. Social security contributions conform to neither straightforward income tax nor savings and accumulation of equity. Social security benefits may accrue, in the short run and medium run, in the form of medical services, work-related injury payments, and similar benefits, and in the long run as old-age pensions. The system is not fully funded. Current benefits to past workers—for instance, to current retirees—are paid almost entirely out of current contributions by today's workers. The relation between contributions and benefits is thus somewhat tenuous. It nevertheless exists and is more or less direct. For instance, pensions are related to one's years of contributions and to one's last few years' salary before retirement.

In view of this, social security contributions and benefits may be treated in either of two ways: Contributions may be seen as long-term savings, hence a part of disposable income. In this case benefit payments, except insofar as they represent the interest on accumulated social security funds, will have to be ignored to avoid double counting. Contributions may be considered payroll taxes, in which case disposable income will be net of social security taxes and gross of social security benefits. In this study the latter treatment—"income received"—was employed as a more appropriate measure of income for measuring poverty. The former treatment—"income produced"—was used as a more relevant measure of earnings capacity for analyzing sources of poverty (e.g., for earnings functions).

Salaries and wages reported in the questionnaire are gross of the employee's share and net of the employer's share of social security contributions. Accordingly, it is necessary to raise payroll taxes paid by employees by the employer's share of social security taxes. In the year 1983 the noted shares were as follows: employer = 10.75 percent and employee = 9.25 percent of wages (including thirteenth-month payments), or a total of 20 percent of wages. The participating self-employed pay the entire share of 20 percent. Incomes reported by them in the National Socioeconomic Survey are gross of these contributions.

Generating prices for self-consumption and in-kind income.   Household surveys rarely collect prices, which therefore have to be injected from outside sources. In this study agricultural prices were developed from within the survey, by using the data on quantities and values of sales of different products. For those areas where sales of particular agricultural products were zero, national prices of the respective crops were injected, since the prices of neighboring geographic units were found difficult to program. National prices are given in appendix 4C. For lack of data for two consecutive years and for separate estimates of home-produced and purchased feed, livestock and poultry products were treated in the same manner as crop produce—only their self-consumption and sales were used as the flow of annual income. In-kind income in the nonagricultural sector was valued at mean prices of the respective commodities, such as meals.

Depreciation.   Corresponding to in-kind income, there is in-kind cost of owner's depreciable resources, such as owned farm machinery, silos, and transport equipment. A stylized depreciation rate of 8 percent was applied to the capital cost of owned machinery and equipment to arrive at capital consumption in the production of agricultural crops.

Correcting for transitory ups and downs of income.   In the reference period of the survey, Panama experienced a drought, which started in the last two months of 1982 and lasted till April 1983, a period that coincided with Panama's so-called dry season (*la estación seca*). A large number of animals are known to have died from the drought in Veraguas. With a view to eliminating possible transitory dips in agricultural incomes, data were collected for two periods: the calendar year 1982 and a ten-month period in 1983, from January through October, since the survey was carried out from October 17 to November 13, 1983. In search of the normal-year output, a number of tests and adjustments were planned. Contrary to apprehensions, however, the 1983 crop output turned out to be significantly higher than that for 1982. Consequently the data for the year 1983 were used without any adjustments for the drought and the crop output data for 1982 were ignored. The values of livestock, poultry, and so forth, were collected for the year 1982 only; since the hump in these sales usually comes toward the end of the calendar year, the period of 1983 that was the "future" at the time of the survey. The same estimates were used for 1983 with appropriate adjustments for price increases. For the agricultural sector, the income from pigs and other livestock was generated by summing net changes in inventory (in 1982) and sales.

Disposable income.   The estimates of the distribution of the benefits of social services and other public services have to be based on data extraneous to the household survey. These will be treated as adjustments to the survey-based disposable incomes to calculate net personal incomes. Estimating the benefits of public expenditure and extrabudgetary policies is a complex problem that will be dealt with in a separate chapter. In setting poverty lines, only direct transfer payments were included in disposable income.

In the survey data, personal income tax and social security taxes (the employee's part) are explicitly reported. Corporation income tax does not appear in the survey, since reported dividends are net of both the progressive corporation tax of Panama and the 10 percent dividend tax that is deducted at the source. However, in imputing the ownership of undistributed profits to owners, corporation and dividend taxes were deducted. In the national accounts tradition, disposable income is defined net of all four income taxes: corporation tax, dividends tax, personal (and education security) income tax, and social security tax. The same definition is employed here, except insofar as the definition of pretax income is different, for example, to the extent that undistributed profits and the rental value of owner-occupied homes are included in the concept of personal incomes used here.

The main concepts.   The main concepts and the corresponding measures of income calculated from the National Socioeconomic Survey are the following:

YI = Census type of monetary income

YII = National accounts type of personal income

$YIII$ = Reported income

YIV = Disposable comprehensive income

YV = Per capita disposable comprehensive income

The income concept used in this study is YIV (aggregate) and YV (per capita). It is important to note that this concept does not correspond exactly to any of the national accounts categories. Rather, it lies in between disposable, personal, and national income, because none of the noted three national accounts categories is as appropriate for poverty and income distribution analysis as the measure used here, *YIV*. This measure is net of direct taxes (personal and education security income tax, corporation tax, social security tax, and dividends tax) but gross of undistributed profits as well as gross of imputed rental of owner-occupied homes and transfers.

In short, the concept of income used here differs from national income in that, among other things, it is net of direct taxes and treats social security contributions as taxes; it differs from personal income in that it excludes direct taxes and includes undistributed profits; and it differs from disposable income in that it includes undistributed profits and the imputed rental value of owner-occupied homes. For lack of a better nomenclature, therefore, I denote this measure of income variously as modified disposable income (*MDY*), disposable comprehensive income (*DCY*), or simply income (*YIV*, aggregate; *YV*, per capita).

A number of other concepts and measures of income are analyzed, including the main components of income. Special mention may be made of an even more comprehensive concept of income or welfare in which the benefits of public services and the burdens of taxes are superimposed on the indicated incomes.

Matching household income with the corresponding category of income in national accounts.   The main poverty lines for this study are drawn with respect to income. Consequently, poverty measures can be highly biased and misleading if household income does not match the corresponding category of income in national accounts, since no measure of aggregate income is considered more reliable than national accounts. When the income of the National Socioeconomic Survey—duly adjusted for imputed, unreported, undistributed, and other components of income—is blown up for the entire population, the resulting figure is 29.7 percent short of the corresponding category of national accounts. That, however, is not unusual. Rarely has the blown-up income of household surveys in the whole world ever been found to exceed about two-thirds of national income. Accordingly, in this study all incomes were adjusted upward by 29.7 percent.

Adjusting the census (monetary) income to conform to the comprehensive income of the National Socioeconomic Survey.   For comparison and certain other purposes as well as sensitivity analysis, the 1980 census data also came in handy. Accordingly, the relevant adjustment factors were developed to generate self-consumption, in-kind income, rental values of owner-occupied homes, undistributed profits, and other categories missing in the

1980 census income to make them conformable to the household comprehensive income. The procedure is explained in appendix 4C. The adjusted census income should, however, be treated as rough and ready and used with caution.

Income Unit

The income unit employed for the main analysis of this study is *per capita family income*. The reason for analyzing per capita family income rather than overall family income is the search for an appropriate index of family welfare and proper comparisons, since family sizes vary widely both laterally (for same family income groups) and vertically (across income classes). For certain purposes, income per adult-equivalent person may be preferable, and we do compute such measures too. Income per person, however, is more objective and nonarbitrary and is easily understood by the layman.

Ranking

Overall income distribution, as well as the distribution within the poor, within the nonpoor, and by province, is classified mainly according to deciles. For this purpose households were ranked on the basis of per capita family income at the national and provincial levels.

Index of Educational Achievement

A statistic developed from the survey that will appear more than once in the empirical part also needs to be explained here—the index of educational achievement by children aged seven through eighteen of different families. For certain purposes, such as schooling intensity of children in a family, this mean index of achievement is handier to analyze than schooling levels of individuals. The index is derived in appendix 4D.

INTERACTION BETWEEN THE DATA-GENERATING AND DATA-USING STAFF

A novelty of the data-generating process of this survey, usually lacking in household surveys in general, is the intensive, constant feedback between the research team committed to analyzing the data and the experienced statisticians and programmers of the Census Bureau of the Statistics Department, Controller General, Government of Panama, who carried out the survey. The research team was involved in preparing the questionnaire; it participated in the pilot survey, got actively involved in observing the completion of the questionnaires and traveling with the interviewers to far

Table 4.1 Adjustment to Monetary Income of 1980 Census to Generate Comprehensive Income, 1980[a]

Serial Number (1)	Monthly Monetary Income Class, 1980 Value ($) (2)	Monthly Comprehensive National Income Class, 1980 ($) (3)	Adjustment Factor (4)	Mean Annual Comprehensive Income per Household ($) (5)	(Column 5) 1.29 = Adjustment to National Income Per Household ($) (6)	Share in Total (Ratio) (7)	(Column 5) 1.16 = Adjustment to Personal Income in National Accounts per Household ($) (8)	Households Number (9)	Households Share (10)	Column 7/ Column 10 (11)	Decile (12)	Income Developed according to the Procedure of Preceding Columns from Micro Data by Decile Per Capita Income (13)
1	75	—	1.521	1,138	1,468	0.0350	1,320	62,778	0.1716	—	1	286
2	75–99	<187	1.292	1,348	1,739	0.0115	1,564	17,500	0.0479	—	2	475
3	100–124	—	1.170	1,573	2,029	0.0180	1,825	23,368	0.0639	0.12	3	611
4	125–174	188–253	1.129	2,025	2,612	0.0351	2,349	35,501	0.0971	0.36	4	768
5	175–249	254–354	1.106	2,813	3,628	0.0680	3,264	49,441	0.1352	0.50	5	961
6	250–399	355–560	1.090	4,246	5,477	0.1287	4,925	62,026	0.1696	0.76	6	1,201
7	400–599	561–843	1.093	7,028	9,066	0.1568	6,907	47,161	0.1290	1.22	7	1,578
8	600–799	844–1,119	1.088	9,131	11,779	0.1085	10,502	24,305	0.0665	1.63	8	1,990
9	800–999	1,120–1,664	1.089	12,459	16,072	0.0861	14,452	14,489	0.0396	2.17	9	2,814
10	1,000–1,499	1,665–3,411	1.293	19,386	25,008	0.1935	22,488	20,420	0.0558	3.47	10	6,582
11	1,500	3,411	1.767	37,102	47,861	0.1588	43,038	8,751	0.0238	6.67	—	—
		Total	1.232	5,593	7,215	1.0000	6,488	365,740	1.0000	1.00	—	1.728

[a]Because of discrete jumps in the adjustment factors, it is natural for slight discrepancies to arise between the cutoff points of income classes. They were therefore smoothed out. The brackets for the first three classes came very close to one another. Hence they were collected in one class. The Gini coefficient of this series is 0.4678. The incomes of this table should be considered approximate. Wherever the incomes of the National Socioeconomic Survey, 1983, can be used, they should be preferred to those developed in this table.

Table 4.2 Derivation of the Relationship between the Income Generated for This Study and the Corresponding Categories in National Accounts (Dollar Figures in Millions)

	1980	1981	1982	1983
1 National accounts categories from standard sources:				
2 National income at market prices	3,211	3,551	3,882	4,091
3 National income at factor cost	3,039	3,317	3,666	
4 Estimated personal income[a]	2,889	3,158	3,468	
5 As % of national income	(90.0)	(88.9)	(89.6)	
6 Social security contributions	228	241	284	
7 Corporation tax revenue	93.8	119.1	119.8	139.7
8 Corporation effective tax rate	0.33	0.33	0.33	
9 Personal income tax revenue	130	162	178	
10 Net-of-tax profits (line 7/line 8 − line 7)	187.6	238.3	239.6	279.4
11 Reported dividends as % of net-of-tax profits (approx.)	—	—	—	2
12 Undistributed profits (line 10) (1− 02)	184	233	235	274
13 Pensions and other transfers by business and social security system to persons	69.5	84.1	93.8	
14 Income concept used for the census-based data (MPY)[b]	2,959	3,256	3,572	
15 As % of NY	(92.2)	(92.2)	(92.0)	
16 MDY relevant for the socioeconomic survey[b]	2,829	3,094	3,394	
17 As % of NY	(88.1)	(87.1)	(87.4)	

[a] As an illustration, the calculations for the year 1982 are as follows: $PY = NY − U_2 − T_c − T_{ss1} + TR = 3,882 − 235 − 120 − 153 + 94 = 3,468$.
[b] Calculations for 1982 are described below:

$MPY = NY − T_c − T_{ss1} + T_{ss2} + TR = 3,882 − 120 − 284 + 94 = 3,572$
(relevant for the census-based income, part 1).
$MDY = MPY − T_p + TR_g = 3,572 − 178 + 0 = 3,394$
(relevant for the survey-based income, part 2).
At the time of this study, the data for 1983 were not available.
For definitions of symbols, see the General Appendix.

corners of the country, provided detailed programming guidelines on the conceptual and measurements aspects of critical variables, and actively collaborated in coding and cleaning up the data and in the overall tabulation process. Such an interaction between data-generating personnel and data-using researchers greatly improves the quality and the relevance of the information collected and classified. Consequently, subject to the caveats mentioned above and depending on how correctly respondents supplied (and interviewers induced) information, this socioeconomic survey is expected to emerge as one of the best done in the LDCs.

Appendix 4A

Number of Households Surveyed by Sector and Province, National Socioeconomic Survey, 1983

| | National Total | | Selected for Analysis after Cleaning Up | | | | | Expansion Factors | | | Indians | | |
| | | | | Rural | | Urban | | | | | Surveyed | | National Total of Persons |
Province	Households	Persons	Total Surveyed	Total Subtotal	Inaccessible Areas[a]	Subtotal	Marginal Areas[b]	Urban	Rural	Areas of Difficult Access	Households	Persons	
Bocas	11,922	47,135	330	329	133	4	196	14	29.0692	43.9533	131.8599	30	193	17,468
Coclé	31,946	153,488	981	976	725	21	251	13	33.0965	30.7421	92.2263	—	—	—
Colón	34,776	149,420	487	485	205	21	280	178	70.7075	60.5347	181.6041	—	—	27,588[c]
Chiriquí	61,784	295,453	1,200	1,199	178	0	421	156	53.3774	50.3992	—	64	435	30,862
Darién	4,590	22,023	248	248	233	15	15	0	22.9846	16.1125	48.3375	—	—	8,924
Herrera	22,404	94,987	818	817	276	7	341	0	29.8673	24.8376	74.5128	—	—	—
Los Santos	21,766	79,334	783	782	674	6	108	6	28.4169	27.2105	81.6315	—	—	—
Panamá	205,255	902,824	2,599	2,595	567	0	2,028	20	79.7428	76.8542	—	—	—	2,294
Veraguas	38,369	189,333	953	950	744	39	206	49	39.9990	36.6003	109.8009	11	62	5,955
Total	432,812	1,933,997	8,399	8,381	4,535	113	3,846	436	—	—	—	105	690	93,091

Sources: Panama, Controller General, Department of Statistics, National Socioeconomic Survey, 1983.

[a]Inaccessible areas are rural areas of difficult access as defined by the Controller General. The communities of these territories are not linked with market towns. Goods for marketing are moved largely on foot. These areas have never been included in the annual household surveys.

[b]This subset of households is neither exhaustive of all households in urban marginal areas nor necessarily confined to shantytowns, working-class residential areas, or known poor areas. The selection depended in part on convenience, but as far as possible it conformed to the definition used by the Controller General. The definition of marginal areas, however, is not precise, since the survey tracts are not demarcated to separate out such areas. Because of these caveats, the subsample may not be representative of what are real marginal areas or shantytowns with unplanned temporary shelters and scanty public services or communities not integrated with the main urban areas.

[c]In the Cuna Indian reservation of (Comarca de) San Blas.

Appendix 4B
Treatment of Undistributed Profits

Two corrections were made to the dividends and interest reported in the survey: one for the undistributed part of profits net of corporation taxes, the second for the well-known tendency by recipients of unearned income to underreport property income. To test the latter impression, all observations reporting this income were pulled out and traced through location codes to the respective residential areas (after expunging the names of subjects). In Panama the rich can be broadly identified by the areas they reside in—they tend to live in easily identifiable wealthy residential areas. Surprisingly, or rather predictably, almost none in the above subsample turned out to be from the known wealthy areas of Panama City. A large fraction belonged to the capital city of an interior state, Los Santos.

Accordingly, the reported dividends and interest (a paltry 0.1 percent of national income) were added to the respective recipients as is. The magnitudes of these components in national accounts, however, are over seventy-eight times as high. Thus the estimates obtained from the corporation tax statistics and the interest data from the Banking Commission for the year 1982 (the latest year for which data were available at the time of the study) give interest income of $185 million and dividends of $71 million. Estimated undistributed profits come to $164 million. After assigning roughly half of these amounts to foreigners, this source comes to $210 million, or about 6 percent of national income. No change in these magnitudes was assumed for 1983. Following McLure (1974) and Sahota (1972b, and 1977), this figure was allocated to the top two deciles according to the relatives worked out from the 1971 income survey. This adjustment raises the overall incomes of the ninth and tenth deciles by 7.99 percent and 7.37 percent, respectively.

The basis for allocating half the profits (about 3 percent of national income) to foreigners cannot be easily defended—it could be more, it could be less. Alternative estimates of this component are not going to affect the incidence of poverty, as measured here by the basic food basket. They may, however, make the upper tail fatter or thinner. Without marshaling all the evidence and summarizing the opinions of knowledgeable persons on the topic, two leading foreign-participation sectors may be noted: the Chiriquí Land Company, a subsidiary of the United Fruit Company, with annual contribution of approximately 2 percent to GDP, is almost entirely foreign owned; and the banking sector has the characteristics shown below.

Measure	Millions of Dollars, 1983
Panama's national income	4,000[a]
Number of banks	
National	14
Foreign	107
Total banking assets	42,875
Domestic assets	5,326
Capital and reserves of all foreign banks	1,374
Estimated international banking system's expenditure	
Direct	113
Direct and indirect	197
Foreign currency liabilities	43,000
Share of offshore and transborder banks in terms of loans in Panama's banking system (%)	67
World market share of Panama's banking system (%)	6

Source: Data from the records of the Banking Commission as collected by Lessard and Tschoegl (1984).
[a]Approximate.

Appendix 4C
Adjusted 1980 Census Income

Before the National Socioeconomic Survey, 1983, there was only one survey of comprehensive incomes in Panama, the Household (Incomes) Survey (1971) for incomes in 1970. The population census of Panama, like censuses all over the world, collects only monetary income, which is not a satisfactory measure of economic well-being for poverty analysis. Accordingly, monetary income of the *Population Census, 1980* was adjusted for in-kind income (such as self-consumption and nonmonetary benefits paid by employers, co-ops, etc.) and for undistributed and unreported profits. It was supplemented by some information from the *Household Survey, 1982*.

The ratios of in-kind income to monetary income by income classes derived from the *Income Survey, 1970* were used to adjust the 1980 census incomes to develop comprehensive incomes. This procedure was available. Equally important is the adjustment for undistributed profits, which represent an income (or forced saving) of the same sort for rich stockholders as social security contributions represent for wage earners. The dividends reported in the *Income Survey, 1970* for the cities of Panamá and Colón came to only 0.07 percent of personal income, whereas aggregate profits form approximately 6 percent of national income. The reported profits of individual families were therefore adjusted to the level of true profits. A result of this adjustment is that the reported incomes of the upper bracket go up by 44 percent, from approximately $21,000 per annum to $37,000. The resulting distribution appears in table 4.1, column 5.

The purpose of these adjustments is to arrive at disposable national income at market prices, that is, national income minus net current transfers abroad. This concept of income is more appropriate for distribution analysis than that of either gross personal income, to which the incomes of the census and household surveys are approximations, or disposable personal income as in national accounts. For relative and absolute poverty analysis, I calculate national income net of personal, corporation, and social security taxes. In a subsequent chapter, the benefits of the expenditures of these taxes will be appropriately added to private incomes. Any shortfall of the resulting income (blown up to arrive at its national aggregate) from disposable national income is then assumed to be due to a uniform understatement of incomes by households across all income classes, which in this case comes to 29 percent. Final incomes adjusted to remove this shortfall appear in column 6 of table 4.1. For certain purposes, however—for instance, when no account can be taken of tax burden and expenditure benefits and when data on undistributed profits are not available—personal income is also appropriate. Accordingly, this series was also calculated and is reported in table 4.1, column 8.

A simplified algebraic model with actual calculations for several categories of aggregate incomes follows.

Let the variables be defined as follows:

W_1 = Wages received in monetary form

W_2 = Wages received in kind

V_1 = Monetary income in owner-occupied vocations

V_2 = In-kind income in owner-occupied vocations

U_1 = Profits and interest distributed

U_2 = Profits and interest not distributed

R = Rents

TR = Transfers to persons from government, relatives, and private business (including social security)

T_c = Corporation tax

T_p = Personal income tax, education security tax, and dividend tax

T_b = Indirect business taxes

T_{ss1} = Social security taxes paid by business and government

T_{ss2} = Social security taxes paid by persons

PY = Personal income in Panama's national accounts

NY = National income in Panama's national accounts

MPY = Modified personal income of this study

MDY = Modified disposable income of this study

T = Revenue of the central government other than social security taxes

The distinction between personal and disposable income in national accounts and an intermediate concept of the two categories estimated here is brought out in the following equations:

$$W_1 + W_2 + V_1 + V_2 + U_1 + U_2 + R = NY$$

$$NY - U_2 - T_c - T_{ss1} + TR = PY$$

$$PY - T_p - T_{ss2} = DY$$

$$NY - T_c - (T_{ss1} + T_{ss2}) + TR = MPY \text{ used for census income}$$

$MPY - T_p = MPY1$ used for socio-economic survey: incomes received

$NY - T_c - T_p = MDY2$ used for socio-economic survey: incomes produced

The calculations of PY, MPY, and MDY are given in table 4.2. The three years' average of the percentages of MDY (the concept of income generated in the National Socioeconomic Survey) to the national income reported in national accounts is 88.

Appendix 4D
Calculating the Index of Educational Achievement of Children Aged Seven through Eighteen

Since a family may have more than one school-age child aged seven through eighteen, an average index of educational achievement by children of a family is convenient to use for certain behavioral functions. To calculate this, let the symbols be defined as follows:

Age in years $= A$

Number of years to date for
which a child ought ordinarily $= A - 6$
to be in school

The number of school years
already completed $\quad = E$

Sum of maximum school years of i
number of children in a household $\quad = \sum_{i=1}^{I}(A_i - 6) = \sum_{i=1}^{I}A_i - 6I$

Sum of school years completed $\quad = \sum_{i=1}^{I}E_i$

Index of educational achievement
of the school-age children of
a household $\quad = S = \dfrac{\sum\limits_{i=1}^{I}E_i}{\sum\limits_{i=1}^{I}A_i - 6I}, A \geq 7,$

where ordinarily $0 \leq S \leq 1$, but S may exceed unity, when a child skips a grade or has gone to preprimary school. Since the minimum age to enter primary school in Panama is six years, we force A to exceed 6 for the present relation.

FIVE

Income Distribution

The first survey of incomes in Panama was made in 1971 for data from the year 1970. That survey collected income from practically all sources but omitted those categories of income that have to be imputed. It also suffered from a lack of conceptual refinements; for example, it double counted both social security contributions by the employee and social security pensions. Before that year, only data for wages were available, collected in the annual household surveys of employment and wages. The 1960 census did not generate data on incomes other than wages for metropolitan areas. In line with the annual household surveys, the 1970 census too collected data only for monetary wages. The 1980 census extended the census income concept to include all monetary income, as have recent annual household surveys. The 1983 National Socioeconomic Survey is the first source that has generated comprehensive incomes from all sources.

CHANGES IN DISTRIBUTION SINCE 1970

The Gini coefficients based on these scattered sources are given in table 5.1, and income shares by deciles are given in table 5.2. Because the data from these sources are not comparable, caution is needed in drawing conclusions from the calculated changes in income inequalities over time.

In the 1970s, three estimates of the Gini coefficient—McLure (1974) Sahota (1972b), and Panama, Controller General (1975)—are close to one another (table 5.1), in the upper fifties. The Gini coefficients for the period 1980–83 are also close to one another, in the mid-forties with respect to households. The two sets are not comparable, however, since the earlier estimates are for persons while the latter are for households. The Gini coefficient from the National Socioeconomic Survey is 0.44 for households and 0.55 for persons, which I consider more reliable than others. The doubtful comparability of the data for different years apart, the computed Gini coefficients for these two periods provide little evidence that inequalities of private incomes in Panama declined significantly during the 1970s. One may, however, infer that inequalities have not increased. It is expected that when social services are superimposed upon private incomes, income distribution will show some improvement.

Table 5.2 brings out some aspects of the internal structure of the changes in distribution. The top ten deciles seem to have lost to the lower-middle and bottom deciles. This result persists even when the 1980 and 1983 deciles are converted into population (instead of household) deciles. Thus, unlike several other Central and Latin American countries, Panama seems to have improved its income distribution during the past fifteen years. There is little more that can be inferred from the available data, as summarized in tables 5.1 and 5.2, about changes in income distribution over time. We therefore turn to the static analysis of income inequalities in the 1983 National Socioeconomic Survey.

PROVINCIAL INCOMES

The province of Panamá produces 63 percent of the nation's income and pays 79 percent of the nation's personal income tax. Chiriquí produces another 13 percent, and the rest of the country brings in less than a quarter of national income. Chiriquí, the granary of Panama, produces nearly a quarter of Panama's agricultural income. The province of Panamá produces one-fifth, and Los Santos and Herrera are bracketed third with approximately 13 percent each. On the whole, among provinces agricultural production is not as concentrated as nonagricultural production. The largest concentration of the latter, as expected, is in the district of Panamá, which accounts for 42 percent of national income. (Panama City comprises thirteen of the nineteen *corregimientos* of the district.)

The range of per capita family income extends from $692, $744, and $830, respectively, for the low-income provinces of Darién, Veraguas, and Coclé, to a high of $2,377 for Panamá. Annual per capita incomes of middle-income provinces—Colón ($1,533), Chiriquí ($1,471), Herrera ($1,469), Bocas del Toro ($1,444), and Los Santos ($1,449)—are close to one another and lie between 79 percent and 87 percent of the national per capita income ($1,766). In terms of mean per capita provincial income, therefore, Darién, Veraguas, and Coclé are poor relative to other provinces. The first impression one gets is that their poor are poorer than those of other provinces even in absolute income, since the average family in all three provinces lies below the national poverty line. It is, however, probable that the averages conceal more than they reveal, for it does not follow that a larger proportion of the families of these provinces are necessarily poor. Nor does it follow that they are poorer in absolute terms than the poor of other provinces. For that knowledge, we must turn to within province income distribution.

Per capita income in Los Santos rises from 54 percent of that of Colón and 66 percent of that of Bocas del Toro, according to the 1980 census monetary income, to 95 percent and 100 percent, respectively, according to the comprehensive income of the National Socioeconomic Survey (table 5.3). The result is also supported by independent socioeconomic indicators

Table 5.1 Gini Coefficients over Past Quarter-Century

Year of Estimates	Sources of Data	Reference	Nature of Estimates	Gini Coefficient
1960	Population Census, 1960	ECLA[a] (1969) as reported in Shail (1975)	Based on wages only for two cities, Panamá and Colón	0.5002
1969	Annual Household Survey, 1969	McLure (1974)	Based on wages only	0.5567
1970	Combined data from Population Census, 1970, Agricultural Census, 1970, and Household Survey, 1969	Sahota (1972b)	Nonwage income derived from censuses combined with wage income from Household Survey	0.5975
1970	Population Census, 1970	ECLA[a] (1974) as reported in Shail (1975)	Nonmonetary income also included, but no adjustments for imputed components	0.4483
1970	Income Survey, 1971	Panama, Controller General (1975)	Nonmonetary income also included, but no adjustments for imputed components	0.5634
1980	Population Census, 1980	Arosemena-Alvarado (1980)	Unadjusted for nonmonetary income	0.4414[b]
1980	Population Census, 1980	This study	Adjusted for self-consumption, in-kind income, and undistributed profits	0.4678[b]
1983	National Socioeconomic Survey, 1983	This study	Comprehensive income	0.4654[b] 0.5537[c]

Note: It is evident that all the Gini coefficients with magnitudes in the fifties are with respect to persons and all those with magnitudes in the forties are with respect to households.

[a]ECLA = Economic Commission for Latin America; also written as CEPAL = Comisão Economico para America Latina.

[b]With respect to households.

[c]With respect to persons.

Table 5.2 Decile Shares of Income, 1970, 1980, and 1983

Decile	(1970) (1)	1980 (2)	(2) − (1) (3)	1983 (4)	(4) − (2) (5)	(4) − (1) (6)
1	0.6	0.9	0.3	0.7	−0.2	0.1
2	1.2	2.6	1.4	2.2	0.4	1.0
3	2.0	2.9	0.9	3.7	0.8	1.7
4	3.3	3.9	0.6	5.3	1.4	2.0
5	4.8	5.0	0.2	6.9	1.9	2.1
6	6.5	7.2	0.7	8.1	0.9	1.6
7	8.6	8.8	0.2	10.4	1.6	1.8
8	11.8	11.7	−0.1	12.3	0.6	0.5
9	17.8	17.6	−0.2	17.0	−0.6	−0.8
10	43.4	39.4	−4.0	33.4	−6.0	−9.9
Gini	0.57	0.49	−0.08	0.46	−0.03	−0.03

Sources: See table 5.1 of Household Survey, 1971, for estimates for 1970; Population Census, 1980, adjusted, for estimates for 1980; and the National Socioeconomic Survey, 1983, for estimates for 1983.

from other data sources. Possible explanations of this result include various migrations and other resource movements and structural changes in agriculture. In particular, Los Santos is steadily becoming a modern livestock-raising province. It seems to be on its way to winning against traditional crop-farm provinces and even plantation provinces. Similar factors may explain the calculated improvement in the economic status of other agricultural provinces relative to the banana economies (particularly Bocas del Toro) and the commercial economies (specifically Colón).

RELATIVE SHARE OF THE SOURCES OF INCOME BY PROVINCE

Although many products of Panama are produced in both the modern sector and the traditional sector (which may distinguish low-income producers from high-income producers), and though there are nonpoor and poor recipients of income from the same sources, to some extent differences in the economic status of people in different geographic areas can be gauged by the relative shares of different sources in total income. The statistics for provincial incomes by sources (not reported in detail here) indicate that the two top per capita income provinces, Panamá and Colón, derive no more than 2.4 percent and 5.3 percent, respectively, of their incomes from agriculture. The poorest of all provinces, Darién, depends on agriculture for over 35 percent of its income. The agricultural income shares of several other provinces, however, do not reflect their true economic status. The high share of Bocas del Toro, for instance, signifies its highly advanced techniques of banana production. Very little information about

Table 5.3 Comparison of Census Incomes and National Socioeconomic Survey Incomes by Province, 1983

Province	National Socioeconomic Survey, 1983[a]						Census-Type per Capita Income			Demographic Census, 1980[b]		Median Monetary Income		
	Mean per Capita Annual Income	Index with Panama = 100	Share in Income	Share in Population	Number of Persons (000)	Mean Persons per Household	($)	Rank	Index	Persons (000)	Mean Persons per Household	Per Capita ($)	Index	Rank
Panamá	2,377	100	62.73	46.68	3	4.40	2,134	1	100	790	4.5	917	100	1
Colón	1,533	64	6.69	7.73	149	4.30	1,418	2	66	129	4.1	723	79	2
Chiriquí	1,471	62	12.72	15.28	296	4.78	1,262	3	59	252	4.9	468	51	4
Herrera	1,469	61	4.06	4.91	95	4.24	1,070	6	50	81	4.5	421	46	5
Los Santos	1,449	61	4.40	4.10	79	3.64	1,201	5	47	70	3.9	394	43	6
Bocas del Toro	1,444	60	2.01	2.44	47	3.96	1,257	4	59	35	4.6	595	65	3
Coclé	830	35	3.78	7.94	154	4.80	675	7	32	139	5.2	314	34	8
Veraguas	744	32	4.20	9.79	189	4.93	598	8	28	165	5.0	252	27	9
Darién	692	29	0.45	1.14	22	4.80	500	9	23	17	4.5	392	43	7

Sources: Census estimates from Panama, Controller General, Censos nacionales de 1980, vol. 1, tables H5 and H12. Annual income per median person was calculated from the corresponding values for median families.

[a]Excludes Indians.

[b]Excludes collective households and Indians.

[c]One need not be too concerned with the low values of income in the census relative to those in the National Socioeconomic Survey, since apart from being partial income estimates, median incomes (as given in the census report) are necessarily lower than mean incomes (as in the National Socioeconomic Survey) of a skewed distribution. What are more relevant in the present context are relative magnitudes.

inequalities is revealed by relative shares of property income, own-account income, and in-kind income in different provinces. Property income is likely to play a more significant role in determining interfamily inequalities (table 5.4) than interprovince inequalities. Implicit income from the ownership of homes tends to lessen the skewness of explicit income from nonresidential property.

The share of labor in nonagricultural income (computed by attributing 50 percent of self-employed people's income to labor) is about 62 percent for the nation as a whole. It is highest in the more modern economy of Panamá (67 percent) and lowest in Los Santos, one of the leading agricultural states of the country (35 percent). It is also low in the low-income provinces of Darién (42 percent), Veraguas (50 percent), and, somewhat surprisingly, Chiriquí (50 percent). In a subsequent table in this chapter, we will see that income inequalities are lower in more developed provinces than in less developed ones. These results suggest (though it is premature to draw this conclusion) a direct relation between development and reduction in inequalities. Finally, as expected, the proportion of income paid in direct taxes is substantially higher in metropolitan provinces (and in the commercialized banana economy of Bocas del Toro) than in other provinces. This result is consistent with the alternatively computed high values of Panama's tax progression presented in a subsequent chapter.

INCOME BY COMPONENTS

The bulk of nonagricultural income (when half of own-account income is assigned to work) is due to labor. It comes to 61.6 percent of national income. The precise share of labor income from agriculture is not known, since the income produced or consumed by unpaid family workers is not shown separately. Total disposable income of the agricultural sector is 8.87 percent of national income, of which about 2 percent goes to paid employees (who earn a paltry 0.02 percent from off-farm employment). The rest is attributable to land, capital, unpaid family labor, and other resources.

Assuming half the income from self-employment in both agricultural and nonagricultural sectors goes to labor, the overall share of property in national income is about 19 percent. Transfer income from all sources is a whopping 12 percent of national income, approximately half from government.

The data just reported pertain to income received or used. More light will be thrown on this topic by the analysis of income produced by different factors of production, taken up in a subsequent chapter.

INCOME DISTRIBUTION BY COMPONENTS

Per capita income by about two dozen components and by deciles is presented in table 5.4. The column percentages of different deciles (not reported in table, but easily verified) indicate that the first and second deciles derive roughly 58 percent and 40 percent of their incomes from agriculture as against 4 to 7 percent in the upper two deciles, suggesting that the poor are concentrated in rural areas. This finding is further supported by the ratios of lines 2 and 12, which indicate that the poorest two deciles are very low in wages in the nonagricultural sector but relatively high in the agricultural sector.

As may be verified from table 5.4, 37 percent of all nonagricultural employment income is accounted for by the tenth decile as against a trifling 0.2 percent by the bottom decile and 3.3 percent by the second decile. The situation in agriculture is the reverse. That seems to be the sector where functional and personal distributions of income reflect each other. For instance, over one-third of employment income in agriculture (even without including the income of unpaid family members) goes to the bottom 20 percent of families (lines 12 and 13). Only 11 percent goes to the top 20 percent of families. As expected, property income is skewed, as is the income from wages and salaries of the nonagricultural sector. Recall, however, that property income includes the imputed value of owner-occupied homes. Were the latter component excluded, property income would come out much more highly skewed. The bottom 40 percent of households account for 11.4 percent of disposable income as against 34.1 percent of the single top decile; that is, the income of the bottom 40 percent is only one-third that of the top 10 percent of households.

Family transfers are highly equalizing, whereas government transfers exacerbate inequalities. The poor of the bottom decile neither contribute to nor receive perceptibly from the social security system (lines 9 and 18). For all practical purposes, it does not affect them. Also, personal income tax payments are not as progressively distributed as government transfers are regressively distributed (line 9), and just as unequally distributed are reported property incomes (line 6) net of the imputed values of owner-occupied homes (line 6). The estimated income elasticity of this tax in simple logarithmic regressions comes out as follows:

With respect to overall gross income 1.26 (21.2); $r^2 = 0.98$
wages in the nonagricultural sector 0.83 (10.6); $r^2 = 0.93$
property income 1.15 (7.5); $r^2 = 0.86$
government transfers 0.68 (13.7); $r^2 = 0.95$

That is, the tax is progressive with respect to gross income and overall property income but regressive with respect to wage income and transfers from government. The former regressivity is explainable by the existence of traditional deductions, exemptions, straightforward tax-free salary components of public officers (known as *gastos de representación*), tax loopholes and underreporting of property income, and so on. The high positive elasticity of what I have defined here as transfers to families from government consists largely of retirement pensions and similar social security benefits.

The second panel of table 5.4 presents per capita income of the average family by decile. The mean per capita income from monetary wage in nonagricultural employment is $1,137 (line 2); the median is $830 (not shown in table); that in the bottom decile is $11; and that in the top decile $5,592. An average family in the bottom decile can expect $13 per head from its property income (made up solely of the imputed value of owner-occupied homes); a family in the top decile receives $1,347 per head. Thus per capita property income of the tenth decile exceeds the mean per capita income of the nation from wages and salaries by over 18 percent. This represents the economic security in life the well-off enjoy that is not available to the poor. The economic insecurity of the rainy day is a curse on the poor, for which a universal social security system is a possible remedy, but so far the system has not reached the poor of Panama.

INCOME DISTRIBUTION WITHIN PROVINCES

Provincial income distribution is given in table 5.5. Panel A of this table reports the number of persons; panel B contains similar data on aggregate incomes, panel C on the number of households, and panels D and E per capita incomes.

The following results, among others, are of interest. First we note a demographic result. Recalling that the deciles of this study are based on family income where each decile includes 10 percent of families, panels A and C indicate the trend in family size. We can see that the curves for family size decline with income almost monotonically (with a minor reverse deviation between the first and the second deciles in the case of Colón and Los Santos). The exceptions are Bocas del Toro and Panamá, where the curves are the shape of an inverted parabola. That is, in the latter two provinces, middle-class families are larger than low- and upper-income families. Why this should be so is not clear. Possibly it is due to the modernity of business, commerce, and agriculture, in which the two provinces lead.

Turning to income distribution, we can see that the ratio of the share of province income to the share of province population exceeds unity only for Panamá. With 46.7 percent of the country's population, Panamá produces and receives 62.8 percent of national income. The poor provinces, Coclé, Darién, and Veraguas, with 7.9 percent, 1.1 percent, and 9.8 per-

Table 5.4 Income Distribution by Decile and Components of Income, National Socioeconomic Survey, 1983 (Excluding Indians)

Component of Income	Total	Decile									
		1	2	3	4	5	6	7	8	9	10
		Aggregate Income ($000)									
1 *Nonagricultural income*	3,358,458	10,008	45,517	103,015	163,052	224,623	271,699	350,020	419,671	615,433	1,154,518
Employment											
2 Monetary	2,199,845	2,637	16,580	57,357	107,011	159,105	181,053	243,663	303,176	378,645	750,111
3 In kind	43,571	29	1,110	2,995	4,842	5,266	5,679	6,894	6,026	5,248	5,478
Own-account											
4 Monetary	227,921	669	6,388	10,187	14,915	15,049	23,945	30,380	23,617	42,513	60,334
5 Self-consumption	19,803	41	496	909	937	1,281	1,551	2,310	2,909	4,554	4,812
Property											
6 Reported	22,893	53	223	603	527	693	541	1,600	2,496	4,479	11,675
7 Imputed	377,161	3,017	8,297	11,692	13,955	15,463	16,972	19,612	24,892	94,290	168,968
Transfers											
8 Family	149,359	3,164	10,309	13,732	13,244	13,990	16,435	18,109	18,501	20,133	21,737
9 Government	238,308	113	806	3,143	5,614	9,731	19,892	21,427	31,499	54,446	91,633
10 Others	79,594	281	1,383	1,994	2,903	4,041	5,629	6,022	6,549	11,121	39,766
11 *Agricultural income*	302,690	14,490	31,259	27,447	23,152	22,578	17,367	19,767	17,990	32,197	96,441
Employment											
12 Monetary	65,025	5,351	12,781	11,582	7,867	8,298	4,647	4,127	3,205	4,152	3,212
13 In kind	423	19	4	6	29	0	363	0	0	0	0
14 Off farm	5,541	333	934	1,042	454	274	156	786	664	447	408

15 Market surplus	176,414	2,889	9,673	8,980	10,095	10,505	10,033	12,546	12,693	25,643	73,353
16 Self-consumption	55,285	5,896	7,865	6,036	4,665	3,500	2,166	2,307	1,427	1,953	19,465
17 Taxes paid	422,039	1,311	4,275	11,424	20,128	30,816	34,757	47,246	57,396	73,915	140,766
Social security											
18 Employee[a]	148,920	383	1,582	4,358	7,728	11,744	13,161	17,552	21,343	26,652	44,413
19 Employer	172,552	443	1,860	5,045	8,948	13,601	15,242	20,333	24,727	30,882	51,490
20 Self-employed	4,371	113	96	179	165	181	315	530	493	731	1,564
21 Personal income tax	96,196	370	766	1,841	3,286	5,289	6,037	8,830	10,832	15,641	43,298
22 Gross-of-tax income	3,838,072	25,055	78,703	135,687	196,218	260,983	304,625	390,652	462,882	679,250	1,304,012
23 Net-of-tax income	3,426,033	23,744	74,427	124,262	176,090	230,167	269,867	343,406	405,486	605,334	1,163,246
24 Households	432,812	43,270	43,270	43,270	43,270	43,270	43,270	43,270	43,270	43,270	43,362
25 Persons	1,933,997	320,266	234,368	224,780	218,823	210,502	187,889	180,872	161,871	150,473	134,153

Per Capita Income ($)

1 Nonagricultural income	1,737	43	194	458	749	1,067	1,446	1,935	2,593	4,090	8,606
Employment											
2 Monetary	1,137	11	71	257	489	756	964	1,347	1,873	2,516	5,592
3 In kind	23	0	5	13	22	25	30	38	37	35	41
Own-account											
4 Monetary	118	3	27	45	68	71	127	168	146	283	450
5 Self-consumption	10	0	2	4	4	6	8	13	18	30	36
Property											
6 Reported	12	0	1	3	2	3	3	9	15	30	87
7 Imputed	195	13	35	52	64	73	90	108	154	627	1,260

Table 5.4 Continued.

Component of Income	Total	Decile									
		1	2	3	4	5	6	7	8	9	10
						Per Capita Income ($)					
Transfers											
8 Family	77	14	44	61	61	66	87	100	114	134	162
9 Government	123	0	3	14	26	46	106	118	195	362	683
10 Others	41	1	6	8	13	19	30	33	40	74	296
11 *Agricultural income*	157	63	133	122	106	107	92	109	111	214	719
Employment											
12 Monetary	34	23	55	51	36	39	25	23	20	28	24
13 In kind	0	0	0	0	0	0	2	0	0	0	0
14 Off farm	3	1	4	5	2	1	1	4	4	3	3
15 Market surplus	91	13	41	40	46	50	53	69	78	170	547
16 Self-consumption	29	26	34	27	21	17	12	13	9	13	145
17 *Taxes paid*	218	6	18	51	92	146	185	261	355	491	1,049
Social security											
18 Employee[a]	77	2	7	19	35	56	70	97	132	177	331
19 Employer	89	2	8	22	41	65	81	112	153	205	384
20 Self-employed	2	0	0	1	1	1	2	3	3	5	12
21 Personal income tax	50	2	3	8	15	25	32	49	67	104	323
22 Gross-of-tax income	1,985	109	336	604	897	1,240	1,621	2,160	2,860	4,514	9,721
23 Net-of-tax income	1,766	103	318	553	805	1,093	1,436	1,899	2,505	4,023	8,671

[a]Social security contributions are already included in agricultural and nonagricultural incomes; therefore they are not added to totals.

Table 5.5 Province Income Distribution, National Socioeconomic Survey, 1983 (Excluding Indians)

Province	Total	\\	1	2	3	4	5	6	7	8	9	10
						Decile						

A. Total Population (Hundreds of Persons)

Province	Total	1	2	3	4	5	6	7	8	9	10
Total	19,339	2,003	2,344	2,248	2,188	2,105	1,078	1,809	1,619	1,505	1,342
Bocas del Toro	471	11	55	82	80	73	52	34	37	28	15
Coclé	1,535	391	324	231	190	128	103	73	55	24	25
Colón	1,494	125	212	108	188	219	131	170	116	66	88
Chiriquí	2,954	299	512	520	359	266	261	232	225	160	119
Darién	226	71	55	34	24	13	5	6	3	6	4
Herrera	950	219	151	110	103	72	68	68	57	49	50
Los Santos	793	96	139	114	94	76	85	63	41	52	35
Panamá	9,028	378	484	768	1,005	1,140	1,090	1,089	1,023	1,076	975
Veraguas	1,893	713	405	214	145	121	84	73	63	44	31

B. Total Income ($000)

Province	Total	1	2	3	4	5	6	7	8	9	10
Total	34,160	237	744	1,243	1,760	2,301	2,699	3,434	4,055	6,053	11,682
Bocas del Toro	681	1	19	47	65	79	74	66	93	113	124
Coclé	1,273	44	99	121	152	140	145	140	141	95	198
Colón	2,289	11	66	104	150	241	192	320	295	251	660
Chiriquí	4,346	34	165	286	289	287	371	445	567	641	1,261
Darién	153	6	16	19	19	14	7	12	6	25	27
Herrera	1,396	22	47	62	82	79	98	127	145	188	547
Los Santos	1,150	12	46	63	76	82	122	118	104	214	312
Panamá	21,463	30	157	420	813	1,248	1,569	2,068	2,546	4,350	8,255
Veraguas	1,408	78	127	116	115	132	121	139	156	179	248

Table 5.5 Continued.

Province	Total						Decile				
		1	2	3	4	5	6	7	8	9	10
					C. Households (Hundreds)						
Total	4,328	433	433	433	433	433	433	433	433	433	494
Bocas del Toro	119	5	9	13	16	16	14	10	14	14	6
Coclé	319	63	60	47	42	27	25	22	15	8	10
Colón	348	27	35	36	36	48	34	42	34	27	33
Chiriquí	618	54	83	100	69	61	62	51	55	44	40
Darién	45	12	11	7	5	3	1	1	1	2	1
Herrera	224	45	29	25	24	19	19	18	15	15	16
Los Santos	218	22	33	29	28	19	23	13	14	17	14
Panamá	2,053	83	88	130	187	214	231	250	270	272	303
Veraguas	594	120	84	47	30	26	21	18	13	12	12

D. Per Capita Income ($)

Total	1,766	103	317	552	805	1,093	1,436	1,898	2,505	4,022	8,671
Bocas del Toro	1,444	45	345	558	804	1,087	1,418	1,915	2,528	4,026	8,305
Coclé	830	113	306	545	799	1,096	1,406	1,908	2,543	4,014	7,932
Colón	1,532	90	307	579	798	1,102	1,465	1,890	2,550	3,799	7,496
Chiriquí	1,471	114	322	540	803	1,003	1,422	1,914	2,521	4,001	10,608
Darién	692	83	326	545	810	1,068	1,484	1,961	2,509	3,849	7,145
Herrera	1,469	99	305	557	799	1,090	1,442	1,869	2,555	3,848	10,903
Los Santos	1,449	124	332	552	805	1,094	1,436	1,880	2,561	4,100	9,034
Panamá	2,377	78	325	555	810	1,096	1,439	1,898	2,490	4,045	8,463
Veraguas	743	110	314	538	793	1,086	1,443	1,897	2,489	4,024	8,057

E. Index, Bocas del Toro First Decile = 1

Total	39	2	7	12	18	24	31	42	55	89	191
Bocas del Toro	32	1	8	12	18	24	31	42	56	89	183
Coclé	18	3	7	12	18	24	31	42	56	89	175
Colón	34	2	7	13	18	24	32	42	56	84	165
Chiriquí	32	3	7	12	18	24	31	42	56	88	234
Darién	15	2	7	12	18	24	33	43	55	85	158
Herrera	32	2	6	12	18	24	32	41	56	84	241
Los Santos	32	3	7	12	18	24	32	42	57	90	199
Panamá	53	2	7	12	18	24	32	42	55	89	187
Veraguas	16	2	7	12	17	24	32	42	55	89	178

cent, respectively, of the country's population, account for only 3.7 percent, 0.4 percent, and 4.1 percent, of the nation's income.

In interpreting decile incomes of different provinces, note that the basic distribution of population by deciles was done at the national level. All families of the country were ranked according to per capita family income and were divided among ten national deciles. After that each family carries its national rank even when studied by province and sectors separately. As such, it is unlikely that either the population (persons) or the families of any province or sector will turn out to be 10 percent in each decile of the respective area. Readers should therefore look at income panels in relation to, but not independent of, population and household panels. For example, the bulk of the population of Coclé, Darién, and Veraguas is concentrated in the first two national deciles, 46.6 percent, 57.4 percent, and 59.0 percent, respectively, with incomes of 11.3 percent, 15.7 percent, and 15.6 percent in the corresponding national deciles. On the upper end, the tenth deciles of the same provinces, with 3.2 percent, 1.7 percent, and 1.6 percent, respectively, of population enjoy 15.5 percent, 17.8 percent, and 17.6 percent of incomes.

We see that, across provinces, per capita income among the poor is probably more unequally distributed than per capita income among the rich. With the poorest of the poor group, those in the bottom decile of Bocas del Toro, as index = 1 (panel E), the range of the poor in other provinces goes up to 2.7 (in Los Santos) while the range of the rich lies between 158 (for Darién) and 241 (for Herrera). Interestingly, the rich of Panamá province, with an index of 187, form the median group among the rich of all provinces. From this result, it seems that the poor of the poorer provinces are not necessarily more poor in relation to the respective province's nonpoor than are the poor of the nonpoor provinces in relation to their nonpoor. Nor are the rich of the richer provinces necessarily more rich in relation to their other classes. If there is any evidence, it appears to be to the contrary. Yet the interpretation above may not be a correct one, since it is subject to a statistical illusion in the present definition of province deciles. What happens is that the bottom deciles of poor provinces bulge with the poor and thus raise the calculated mean income of this class from what it would be were only the very bottom poor picked up by this decile. Likewise, the top decile of the nonpoor provinces contains a relatively large proportion of rich families, thus lowering the calculated mean from what it would be if only the top rich formed that decile. For example, the 2 percent of bottom poor will have a lower mean income than the 20 percent of bottom poor of a given province. One should therefore interpret the results of panel E of table 5.5 with caution.

GINI COEFFICIENTS

The foregoing results are more compactly brought out by Gini coefficients, which simultaneously take account of both the numerator (income) and the denominator (population). The calculations by province yield the following values of the Gini coefficients:

Province	Gini Coefficient
Bocas del Toro	0.46
Coclé	0.55
Colón	0.51
Chiriquí	0.56
Darién	0.59
Herrera	0.64
Los Santos	0.55
Panamá	0.48
Veraguas	0.62
Republic	0.55

We can see that the three poor provinces (Darién, Veraguas, and Coclé) and the three agricultural provinces (Los Santos, Herrera, and Chiriquí) experience high inequalities of income (the index in the sixties and the upper fifties), while Panamá and the commercially oriented provinces of Bocas del Toro and Colón have relatively low inequalities (the index in the forties or low fifties). The correlation of the Gini coefficient with per capita income is -0.57. Thus there is some evidence that growth and modernity have built-in forces that reduce inequalities.

The Gini coefficient is a useful measure of inequalities because it is a simple, one-numbered index. More elaborate distribution functions are available, but they lose the simplicity of the Gini in making comparisons. A drawback of the Gini is that it is not very sensitive to minor changes in income distribution. A problem common to all inequality measures pertains to the denominator or base. For example, the distribution among persons of an area can be significantly different from that among families. For the urban and rural sectors of Panama, the Gini coefficient for households is ten percentage points lower than that for persons. The Gini coefficient for urban income is 0.47 with respect to urban persons, 0.37 for urban households, and 0.33 for urban earners.

Comparing Gini coefficients for urban and rural incomes via-à-vis nonagricultural and agricultural incomes indicates little difference between the distributions of income produced and income used. Incomes in the rural (agricultural) sector are significantly more unequally distributed than those in the urban (nonagricultural) sector. Accordingly, as time passes and the rural labor force migrates to urban-industrial-commercial centers, we may expect the distribution to improve.

The Gini coefficients of within-decile distributions are close to zero from the positive side; that is, the Lorenz curves are normal and lie close to the diagonal from below for the second through the ninth deciles. Those for the bottom and the top deciles, on the other hand, acquire negative signs, signifying that the poor (nonpoor) groups of the poor (nonpoor) provinces relative to the respective provinces' other income deciles are in general not poorer (richer) than the poor (rich) of the nonpoor (poor) provinces relative to their nonpoor (poor) classes. Although this result has the statistical caveat discussed earlier, it is supported by overall Gini coefficients by province, according to which poor provinces have higher values of the Gini coefficients than the nonpoor—for example, Veraguas 0.62 and Panamá 0.48. Even in terms of the absolute values of per capita family incomes, the tenth-decile rich (presumably, latifundista) of Herrera and Chiriquí come out over a quarter higher than the rich (largely the business and commerce magnates) of the corresponding deciles of Panamá and Colón.

EXPENDITURE PATTERNS

The Gini coefficients of the distributions of income, total expenditure, and total food expenditure among persons are 0.4823, 0.3757, and 0.2689, respectively. Their relative values are as expected.

Measured expenditure is generally considered to represent permanent income more closely than measured income at any point in time. Whether that is so is moot in the present context. What is more pertinent is that expenditure represents more accurately that concept of goods and services a person *takes out* (consumes) of the social aggregate than what one *puts into* (produces for) it. According to that approach, the distribution of economic welfare (as indexed by consumption expenditure) is by 28.4 percent more egalitarian (Gini coefficient 0.3757 as against 0.4823) than the distribution of income, although the distribution of "power" is believed to be related exponentially to income irrespective of expenditure.

CONCLUSIONS

Inequalities of private income in Panama continue to remain high. In 1983 the Gini coefficient for the country as a whole was 0.55, reflecting little change in income inequalities during the 1970s. The Gini coefficient of the distribution of expenditure is 78 percent of that based on income, and that of food expenditure is 56 percent of that for income. In general, the poorer a province or a sector, the higher the inequalities. The Gini coefficient (of income) is higher for rural areas (0.56) than for urban areas (0.47). The bottom 36 percent of the population (persons in the first three deciles of households) received only 6.3 percent of the nation's income, while the top 7 percent received 34 percent. Contrary to what is generally believed, inequalities of private income in Panama are caused as much by unequal wages and salaries and government transfers as by property income. The poor are concentrated in three traditional-agriculture, rural provinces: Darién, Coclé, and Varaguas. The Engel elasticities for food and total expenditure are 0.38 and 0.56, respectively.

SIX

Poverty

DEFINITION

In this study poverty is defined based on a minimum food basket. Three poverty levels are specified: income that cannot buy the minimum food basket, denoted the critical poverty or indigency line; income 50 percent higher than the indigency line, a number that approximately follows from the food plus nonfood cost (in the *Household Expenditure Survey, 1972*) of those whose expenditure on food just buys the minimum food basket, denoted "poverty 1.5," or the lower measure of poverty or the poverty of basic needs; and income twice the indigency level, a norm used in most poverty studies, here denoted "poverty 2.0," or the higher measure of poverty or the poverty of conventional needs. The last two measures are an attempt to take account of "basic needs" (food, shelter, clothing, medicines, etc.) in human life. In the context of each category of the poor the rest of the population is considered nonpoor. For certain analytical purposes (especially in the regression analysis), I subdivide the nonpoor into three subcategories: those whose per capita income lies between twice and three times the critical poverty line (denoted near poor); the rest of the families except those above the mean of the tenth decile, denoted nonpoor or middle class; and those above the mean of the tenth decile, denoted rich.

THE PREPARATION OF THE MINIMUM FOOD BASKET

The most recent basic food basket for Panama was developed by the Ministry of Health through a nutrition survey in 1980. Quantities of various food items required for the minimum nutrition of persons by age and sex, according to Food and Agriculture Organization (FAO) standards, were estimated for provinces and districts of Panama from the calorie (and other nutrient) contents of typical food items consumed in each place. The commodities consumed by people in different provinces and sectors of Panama that yield the specified levels of calories were costed at the Ministry of Planning and Economic Policy by Armando Villarreal (Panama, MIPPE 1985). The cost ranges between a high of $628 per year for male adolescents in Bocas del Toro and a low of $122 per year for infants below age two in Darién. The mean per capita cost (for all ages and sexes) at the national level comes to $392 per year. As we will see shortly, this is the figure that becomes the critical poverty line of this study.

The data for the cost of minimum food basket by age, sex, and province were injected into the National Socioeconomic Survey, 1983, electronic tape at the family level to develop the cost of minimum food basket for each family. The results are summarized in table 6.1.

We see from table 6.1 that the relatively poor among those provinces that depend primarily on farm agriculture have consistently lower costs of food baskets across all sizes of families. The poor are more efficient in their consumption of calories than the rich. Evidently they buy low-quality foods containing higher levels of calories. There is a perceptible decline in per capita calorie cost as family size increases. Note that this decline is not due to scale economies; they may exist, but we have not yet estimated them. The observed moderate decline is entirely due to differences in family composition. Apparently this trend results from an increase in the number of minor children, women, and old people relative to male adults and adolescents as family size expands.

The number of persons in various age groups by family size for the country as a whole is given in table 6.2. Note that though for brevity the tables in this chapter report old age groups (including all working and senior adults as one group), actual calculations used a more detailed break-down by age as well as province.

In the foregoing paragraphs we have looked at the consumption aspect of family size. Viewing from the production aspect, we can see that the ratio of male adults to total family members increases as family size declines, while the ratio of children (below age fifteen) to total members rises as family size increases. The ratio of male adults in the family goes down from 0.69 in one-member families to 0.43 in two-member families, 0.24 in five-member families and 0.19 in ten-member families. The mean is 0.26. Per capita family earnings will therefore tend to be lower and poverty incidence higher for identical adult earners as the family size gets larger.

THE INCIDENCE OF POVERTY

This section examines the *incidence* of poverty, that is, the proportion of the population that is poor according to specified poverty lines. The critical poverty estimates by province and decile are given in table 6.3, and the lower measure of poverty (1.5 times the indigency line) in table 6.4. The corresponding distribution of total population by decile and province is given in table 6.5. Remember that all deciles are based on families ranked according to per capita family income. The body of tables 6.3 to 6.5, however, deals with individuals, whose number is not expected to be 10 percent of the total (even though families are by definition). Also remember

Table 6.1 Actual Cost of Minimum Food Basket and Number of Persons by Family Size and Province as Calculated from National Socioeconomic Survey, 1983

Province	1	2	3	4	5	6	7	8	9	10	Total
						Cost ($)					
Bocas del Toro	543	477	455	438	435	457	452	454	421	475	455
Coclé	365	352	362	350	359	355	359	356	353	348	355
Colón	446	436	432	428	426	435	436	439	457	436	434
Chiriquí	372	343	338	335	334	344	341	342	341	339	340
Darién	341	322	289	291	290	293	294	283	282	286	292
Herrera	335	321	317	314	313	315	318	312	317	301	315
Los Santos	320	300	314	312	315	321	323	319	332	324	315
Panamá	447	427	427	425	431	434	437	442	439	435	432
Veraguas	391	350	356	346	349	345	349	344	347	358	350
Total											
Per person	413	393	394	391	392	392	397	396	391	385	392
Per family	413	786	1,182	1,584	1,960	2,352	2,779	3,198	3,519	3,850	1,748
						Persons					
Bocas del Toro	2,311	3,558	4,941	6,892	8,235	5,412	4,396	6,200	1,836	3,354	47,135
Coclé	2,642	7,556	13,920	18,116	22,440	25,926	20,552	13,248	12,843	16,245	153,468
Colón	3,577	9,360	17,070	26,104	26,070	20,730	16,471	12,184	6,732	11,122	149,420
Chiriquí	5,868	13,322	25,428	42,192	47,105	46,620	28,854	24,288	17,568	44,208	295,453
Darién	329	718	2,006	2,538	2,238	2,923	3,330	2,448	1,105	1,611	19,246
Herrera	1,887	6,438	10,644	17,304	20,700	15,654	7,630	4,264	3,960	6,506	94,987
Los Santos	3,226	7,552	12,258	15,524	15,220	11,832	6,538	3,736	1,467	1,981	79,334
Panamá	15,170	53,082	104,094	159,228	166,160	136,644	99,421	63,552	42,651	62,822	902,824
Veraguas	3,476	7,956	14,391	22,724	28,360	28,848	23,436	20,864	15,597	23,681	189,333
Total											
Per person	38,486	109,542	204,752	310,622	336,528	294,589	210,628	150,784	103,759	171,530	1,931,220
Per family	38,486	54,771	68,251	77,656	67,306	49,098	30,090	18,848	11,529	17,153	433,188

Family Size

Table 6.2 Number of Persons by Age Group, Family Size, and Decile, National Socioeconomic Survey, 1983

Age and Sex	Family Size by Decile										Total
	1	2	3	4	5	6	7	8	9	10	
Male	26,502	47,189	70,016	85,502	80,520	66,266	45,002	30,525	21,274	33,143	505,939
Female	11,642	51,695	74,385	92,413	84,508	69,484	46,103	30,106	19,548	35,012	514,896
Male adolescent 16–18	310	1,888	4,486	8,245	10,256	12,492	10,141	7,934	5,243	9,302	70,297
Female adolescent 16–18	80	2,137	6,308	7,001	9,311	9,460	9,328	6,695	3,796	7,211	61,327
Child 14–15	—	862	6,156	11,274	16,706	17,678	13,360	10,295	7,374	11,164	94,869
Child 12–13	—	929	3,889	11,894	19,472	19,288	15,559	10,623	7,676	11,180	100,510
Child 10–11	—	937	5,477	12,403	18,422	18,449	13,850	10,457	7,627	12,078	99,700
Child 8–9	—	878	4,272	14,611	21,724	19,187	14,839	11,662	8,406	13,455	109,034
Child 6–7	—	514	5,028	14,306	20,111	17,846	11,555	9,475	6,658	9,899	95,392
Child 4–5	—	884	6,190	16,492	20,075	16,855	10,567	8,506	6,244	10,970	96,783
Child 2–3	—	445	8,417	18,835	19,410	14,987	10,925	8,098	4,354	9,249	94,720
Child <2	—	1,310	10,489	18,064	16,320	13,046	9,849	6,720	5,624	9,108	90,530
Total	38,534	109,668	205,113	311,040	336,835	295,038	211,078	151,096	103,824	171,771	1,933,997

Table 6.3 Critically Poor Persons by Decile and Province, National Socioeconomic Survey, 1983 (Excluding Indian Areas)

Province	Number of Critically Poor Persons by Decile of Families											Total Critically Poor Families
	1	2	3	4	5	6	7	8	9	10	Total	
	Absolute Numbers											
Bocas del Toro	225	557	178	591	829	920	910	904	766	998	6,878	1,490
Coclé	6,286	6,728	7,630	6,562	5,826	5,520	6,338	5,328	5,295	4,600	60,113	10,352
Colón	1,556	3,709	3,327	2,614	2,682	3,622	3,576	4,166	3,497	3,518	32,267	6,030
Chiriquí	4,455	5,559	4,996	5,714	4,710	6,084	5,904	4,858	5,370	5,343	52,993	9,813
Darién	844	756	1,331	986	1,014	858	970	835	716	647	8,957	1,634
Herrera	2,294	3,158	3,139	3,249	3,010	2,838	2,435	3,244	3,770	2,974	30,111	5,992
Los Santos	1,073	1,601	1,382	1,541	1,582	1,772	1,245	1,350	1,649	1,403	14,678	3,385
Panamá	5,771	7,850	8,335	8,942	7,006	9,688	10,213	9,378	8,147	8,449	83,779	16,382
Veraguas	10,095	10,387	11,018	10,150	10,584	9,496	10,135	8,526	8,416	7,771	96,506	17,759
All	32,599	40,385	41,336	40,357	37,243	40,798	41,726	38,589	37,626	35,703	386,362	72,837
	Percentages											
Bocas del Toro	0.01	0.03	0.01	0.003	0.04	0.05	0.05	0.05	0.04	0.05	0.36	0.34
Coclé	0.33	0.35	0.39	0.34	0.30	0.29	0.33	0.28	0.27	0.24	3.11	2.39
Colón	0.08	0.19	0.17	0.14	0.14	0.19	0.18	0.22	0.18	0.18	1.67	1.39
Chiriquí	0.23	0.29	0.26	0.30	0.24	0.31	0.31	0.25	0.28	0.28	2.74	2.27
Darién	0.04	0.04	0.07	0.05	0.05	0.04	0.05	0.04	0.04	0.03	0.46	0.38
Herrera	0.12	0.16	0.16	0.17	0.16	0.15	0.13	0.17	0.19	0.15	1.56	1.38
Los Santos	0.06	0.09	0.07	0.08	0.08	0.09	0.06	0.07	0.09	0.07	0.76	0.78
Panamá	0.30	0.41	0.43	0.46	0.36	0.50	0.53	0.48	0.42	0.44	4.33	3.79
Veraguas	0.52	0.54	0.57	0.53	0.55	0.49	0.52	0.44	0.44	0.40	4.99	4.10
All	1.69	2.09	2.14	2.09	1.93	2.11	2.16	2.00	1.95	1.85	19.98	16.83

Table 6.4 Nonpoor Persons by Decile and Province, National Socioeconomic Survey, 1983 (Excluding Indian Areas)

Number of Nonpoor Persons by Decile of Families

Province	1	2	3	4	5	6	7	8	9	10	Total
					Absolute Numbers						
Bocas del Toro	7,067	4,911	5,458	4,499	4,523	3,345	3,423	2,583	2,166	2,282	40,257
Coclé	12,375	10,423	9,686	10,610	9,407	10,166	9,196	7,890	7,492	6,130	93,375
Colón	14,566	17,561	14,354	12,741	10,962	12,637	9,783	9,735	7,076	7,738	117,153
Chiriquí	34,977	28,460	24,766	28,050	22,996	22,116	22,686	21,802	19,284	17,323	242,460
Darién	1,639	1,404	1,371	1,427	1,518	1,407	1,411	1,105	899	885	13,066
Herrera	7,656	7,608	7,545	6,501	6,397	6,113	6,256	6,156	5,375	5,269	64,876
Los Santos	7,794	7,180	7,053	6,083	7,070	7,082	6,289	5,845	5,260	5,000	64,656
Panamá	107,809	100,121	98,800	88,000	84,963	76,062	69,401	68,857	69,027	56,005	819,045
Veraguas	12,276	9,162	9,531	10,084	10,183	9,562	8,864	8,041	8,994	6,048	92,747
All	206,159	186,830	178,564	167,997	158,019	148,490	137,309	132,014	125,573	106,680	1,547,635
					Percentages						
Bocas del Toro	0.37	0.25	0.28	0.23	0.23	0.17	0.18	0.13	0.11	0.12	2.08
Coclé	0.64	0.54	0.50	0.55	0.49	0.53	0.48	0.41	0.39	0.32	4.83
Colón	0.75	0.91	0.74	0.66	0.57	0.65	0.51	0.50	0.37	0.40	6.06
Chiriquí	1.81	1.47	1.28	1.45	1.19	1.14	1.17	1.13	1.00	0.90	12.54
Darién	0.08	0.07	0.07	0.07	0.08	0.07	0.07	0.06	0.05	0.05	0.68
Herrera	0.40	0.39	0.39	0.34	0.33	0.32	0.32	0.32	0.28	0.27	3.35
Los Santos	0.40	0.37	0.36	0.31	0.37	0.37	0.33	0.30	0.27	0.26	3.34
Panamá	5.57	5.18	5.11	4.55	4.39	3.93	3.59	3.56	3.57	2.90	42.35
Veraguas	0.63	0.47	0.49	0.52	0.53	0.49	0.46	0.42	0.47	0.31	4.80
All	10.66	9.66	9.23	8.69	8.17	7.68	7.10	6.83	6.49	5.52	80.02

Table 6.5 Overall Population by Province and Decile, National Socioeconomic Survey, 1983 (Excluding Indian Areas)

Province	\multicolumn{10}{c}{Number of Persons by Decile of Families}										Total	Total Families
	1	2	3	4	5	6	7	8	9	10		
	\multicolumn{12}{c}{Absolute Numbers}											
Bocas del Toro	5,114	7,859	5,883	6,020	5,240	4,773	3,712	3,291	2,628	2,615	47,135	11,922
Coclé	2,160	18,493	16,663	17,233	14,944	15,456	14,246	13,989	11,450	9,854	153,488	31,946
Colón	17,089	20,421	19,678	17,726	16,047	13,737	14,080	11,809	9,689	9,144	149,420	34,776
Chiriquí	33,070	38,062	36,651	29,802	33,018	27,958	24,973	27,371	23,069	21,479	295,453	61,784
Darién	2,661	2,898	2,439	1,980	2,321	2,110	2,528	2,121	1,702	1,263	22,023	4,590
Herrera	11,062	10,427	12,398	9,985	10,297	9,212	7,902	8,482	8,049	7,173	94,987	22,404
Los Santos	9,634	8,947	9,432	7,979	7,092	8,575	8,168	7,273	6,059	6,175	79,334	21,766
Panamá	105,972	117,024	106,048	104,308	93,083	86,512	78,090	74,179	74,837	62,771	902,824	205,255
Veraguas	21,829	23,316	21,559	18,995	19,404	17,453	19,683	17,793	15,251	14,050	189,333	38,369
All	227,591	247,447	230,751	214,028	201,446	185,786	173,382	166,308	152,734	134,524	1,933,997	432,812
	\multicolumn{12}{c}{Percentages}											
Bocas del Toro	0.26	0.41	0.30	0.31	0.27	0.25	0.19	0.17	0.14	0.14	2.44	2.75
Coclé	1.09	0.96	0.86	0.89	0.77	0.80	0.74	0.72	0.59	0.51	7.94	7.38
Colón	0.88	1.06	1.02	0.92	0.83	0.71	0.73	0.61	0.50	0.47	7.73	8.03
Chiriquí	1.71	1.97	1.90	1.54	1.71	1.45	1.29	1.42	1.19	1.11	15.28	14.28
Darién	0.14	0.15	0.13	0.10	0.12	0.11	0.13	0.11	0.09	0.07	1.14	1.06
Herrera	0.57	0.54	0.64	0.52	0.53	0.48	0.41	0.44	0.42	0.37	4.91	5.18
Los Santos	0.50	0.46	0.49	0.41	0.37	0.44	0.42	0.38	0.31	0.32	4.10	5.03
Panamá	5.48	6.05	5.48	5.39	4.81	4.47	4.04	3.84	3.87	3.25	46.68	47.42
Veraguas	1.13	1.21	1.11	0.98	1.00	0.90	1.02	0.92	0.79	0.73	9.79	8.87
All	11.77	12.79	11.93	11.07	10.42	9.61	8.96	8.60	7.90	6.96	100.00	100.00

that though the population analyzed here does not include Indian areas, it is possible that some Indians living outside Indian areas appear in the sample.

We can see that 19.98 percent of Panama's population (16.83 percent of families) is below the critical poverty line (table 6.3)—that is, cannot buy the minimum food basket—29.59 percent of the population (25.17 percent of families) is poor according to the lower measure of poverty— cannot afford to buy minimum food and nonfood necessities (table 6.4)— and 38.66 percent of the population (33.11 percent of families) is poor according to the conventional measure, that is, falls below twice the cost of the minimum food basket (table 6.5). The highest incidence of poverty is in Veraguas, where more than half the population is critically poor (table 6.3). A quarter of the nation's critically poor population lives in Veraguas. Darién and Coclé are next, with 40.4 percent and 39.2 percent of the population in indigency. Panamá province, with 21.7 percent of the nation's critically poor persons, has the lowest incidence of critical poverty, only 9.3 percent of the population. Bocas del Toro, Chiriquí, and Los Santos are next to Panamá, with 14.6 percent, 17.9 percent, and 18.5 percent critical poverty incidences. The poor provinces maintain their ranking in the two poverty measures. The well-off provinces, on the other hand, get reshuffled according to the higher measure of poverty (table 6.5). In this measure Los Santos (40.2 percent incidence) is second only to Panamá (24.7 percent poor), while Chiriquí (with 40.9 percent poor) jumps ahead of Bocas del Toro (with 45.9 percent poor). In other words, the ranking of provinces based on poverty is consistent with the ranking of provinces according to per capita provincial income for poor provinces but not necessarily for well-off provinces. The results are consistent with the distribution results of the preceding chapter, where we found that the rich of the relatively well-off provinces are not necessarily richer in comparison with their poor than the rich of poor provinces are compared with theirs (this is a weak inference). Here the same results appear to be suggested even in absolute terms (a strong inference).

The shares of each province in the population and the income of the country by the three measures of poverty (table 6.6) provides a slightly different perspective on poverty. We see that those who are indigent in Veraguas form 5 percent of the nation's population but receive less than half of 1 percent of income. The poorest of all the poor are those in Darién, who form 0.46 percent of the nation's population but receive only 0.03 percent of total income. The critically poor of Bocas del Toro are the richest indigents among the critically poor of all provinces, with the ratio of the share of income to the share of population of 0.167 against 0.126 for Colón, 0.122 for Panamá, and 0.105 for the nation as a whole. Bocas del Toro thus comes out better off than other provinces, no matter which

Table 6.6 Relative Shares of Income and Population of Poor and Nonpoor by Province, National Socioeconomic Survey, 1983

Share of Country's Income (%)

Province	Indigency			Poverty (1.5)			Poverty (2.0)			Total	
	Nonpoor Income	Poor		Nonpoor Income	Poor		Nonpoor Income	Poor		All	
		Popu-lation	Income		Popu-lation	Income		Popu-lation	Income	Popu-lation	Income
Bocas del Toro	1.93	0.36	0.06	1.82	0.71	0.18	1.64	1.12	0.36	2.44	1.99
Coclé	3.43	3.11	0.30	3.18	4.10	0.55	2.92	4.85	0.82	7.94	3.73
Colón	6.49	1.67	0.21	6.25	2.42	0.46	5.87	3.30	0.84	7.73	6.71
Chiriquí	12.42	2.76	0.30	11.99	4.52	0.73	14.41	6.25	1.31	15.28	12.72
Darién	0.41	0.46	0.03	0.38	0.65	0.07	0.34	0.78	0.11	1.14	0.45
Herrera	3.96	1.56	0.13	3.88	1.93	0.21	3.75	2.34	0.34	4.91	4.08
Los Santos	3.30	0.76	0.07	3.17	1.33	0.20	3.07	1.65	0.30	4.10	3.37
Panamá	62.29	4.33	0.53	61.22	7.81	1.60	59.61	11.55	3.21	46.68	62.82
Veraguas	3.67	4.99	0.45	3.39	6.13	0.73	3.16	6.82	0.97	9.79	4.12
Total	97.91	19.98	2.09	95.28	29.59	4.72	91.76	38.66	8.24	100.00	100.00
Gini	—	—	0.092	—	—	0.130	—	—	0.150	—	0.189

Table 6.7 Relative Shares of Income and Population of Poor by Decile, National Socioeconomic Survey, 1983

			Share (%)			
	Indigent		Poor (1.5)		Poor (2.0)	
Decile	Population	Income	Population	Income	Population	Income
Poor						
1	1.69	0.02	2.71	0.04	3.63	0.08
2	2.09	0.06	2.13	0.15	4.04	0.28
3	2.14	0.11	3.02	0.25	4.35	0.56
4	2.09	0.15	3.25	0.38	4.01	0.63
5	1.93	0.18	3.04	0.45	4.02	0.80
6	2.11	0.25	2.99	0.53	3.91	0.94
7	2.16	0.30	2.89	0.60	3.71	1.04
8	2.00	0.32	2.95	0.71	3.82	1.23
9	1.95	0.34	2.82	0.77	3.57	1.29
10	1.85	0.37	2.78	0.85	3.60	1.45
Total	19.98	2.09	29.59	4.72	38.66	8.24
Gini	—	0.3248	—	0.3034	—	0.3139
Nonpoor						
1	10.66	2.98	9.57	3.47	8.56	3.78
2	9.66	4.00	8.41	4.27	7.45	4.55
3	9.23	4.99	8.24	5.14	6.76	4.94
4	8.69	5.74	7.50	5.74	6.48	5.68
5	8.17	6.74	7.03	6.54	6.13	6.41
6	7.68	7.77	6.67	7.43	5.71	7.01
7	7.10	8.96	6.18	8.68	5.44	8.58
8	6.83	11.89	6.19	11.70	5.51	11.30
9	6.49	16.03	5.75	15.31	4.99	14.23
10	5.52	28.82	4.87	26.99	4.32	25.28
Total	80.02	97.91	70.41	95.28	61.34	91.76
Gini	—	0.4615	—	0.4395	—	0.4196

aspect one looks at. Recall (see table 5.1) that this province's Gini coefficient is the lowest among all provinces. This result, however, is based on the population in non-Indian areas only. Comparisons with Chiriquí and Colón are nevertheless on the same footing.

Income distribution within poverty groups (table 6.7) indicates that the bottom 40 percent among the critically poor have a quarter of the total income of the poor, while the top 9.3 percent among the critically poor have 17.7 percent of their income. In the higher poverty measure, the bottom 41.5 percent of the poor receive approximately the same share of the poor's income (18.6 percent) as the upper 9.3 percent (17.6 percent). Similar comparisons based on table 6.7 confirm this trend—that the inequalities prevail even among the poor but that the poorer a group, the

Table 6.8 Poverty Gap of Critically Poor by Decile and Province, National Socioeconomic Survey, 1983

Province	Decile										Total
	1	2	3	4	5	6	7	8	9	10	
Bocas del Toro	0.0033	0.0069	0.0022	0.0041	0.0039	0.0033	0.0024	0.0017	0.0008	0.0004	0.0289
Coclé	0.0597	0.0553	0.0565	0.0436	0.0330	0.0263	0.0240	0.0147	0.0099	0.0040	0.3271
Colón	0.0197	0.0424	0.0334	0.0217	0.0172	0.0215	0.0158	0.0146	0.0069	0.0051	0.1982
Chiriquí	0.0430	0.0434	0.0329	0.0310	0.0206	0.0205	0.0156	0.0096	0.0062	0.0024	0.2251
Darién	0.0071	0.0064	0.0099	0.0067	0.0058	0.0034	0.0028	0.0020	0.0009	0.0002	0.0452
Herrera	0.0212	0.0265	0.0229	0.0211	0.0171	0.0139	0.0095	0.0099	0.0074	0.0025	0.1517
Los Santos	0.0098	0.0131	0.0082	0.0077	0.0067	0.0035	0.0027	0.0022	0.0007	0.0007	0.0614
Panamá	0.0728	0.0935	0.0878	0.0819	0.0493	0.0529	0.0444	0.0275	0.0141	0.0051	0.5292
Veraguas	0.0937	0.0847	0.0835	0.0712	0.0638	0.0497	0.0420	0.0248	0.0157	0.0052	0.5344
Total	0.3303	0.3722	0.3371	0.2890	0.2173	0.1981	0.1600	0.1072	0.0641	0.0258	2.1011

Note: Poverty gap is expressed as percentage of total household income.

lower the inequality of income within that group. (See the Gini coefficients in tables 6.6 and 6.7.) The incomes are more equally distributed among the poor than among the rich, which is consistent with the widely observed Pareto distribution.

POVERTY GAPS

The income by which the poor fall below the poverty line, called the *poverty gap* or the *intensity* of poverty, is given in tables 6.8 (for indigency), 6.9 (for the lower measure of poverty), and 6.10 (for the higher measure of poverty). The gaps expressed as percentages of the total household income of the nation are 2.10 percent, 3.87 percent, and 8.36 percent, respectively. Since critical poverty itself is high enough (20 percent of population) for Panama to worry about, in the remainder of this chapter I shall focus mainly on the critically poor.

The distances by which different subgroups of the poor fall below the critical poverty line are given in table 6.8 by decile and province. We see that the bottom decile has a critical poverty gap of 0.33 percent of national income and the bottom 40 percent of the poor have a gap of 1.32 percent of national income. Over 50 percent of the gap exists in two provinces, Panamá and Veraguas.

A number of estimates of poverty in Panama for individual years are collected in tables 6.11 and 6.12. Because of differences in the data on incomes from different sources, it would be risky to draw conclusions about the trend in poverty over time. The least objectionable comparisons are those based on the estimates by the same author for two different points in time, since at least their methods would be conformable. Two such estimates are available, one for the years 1970 and 1980 by Molina (1982) and the other for 1980 and 1983 in this study (marked SES). These percentages are reproduced below:

	1970		1980		1983	
Molina (1982)						
Poverty incidence	39	(census)	37	(census)	—	
Poverty gap	6.8	(census)	5.7	(census)	—	
This study						
Critical poverty incidence	—		20.05	(census income adjusted)	19.98	(SES)
Critical poverty gap	—		2.80		2.10	
Poverty gap	—		9.31		8.4	

Table 6.9 Poverty Gap: Lower Estimates of Poverty (Poverty 1.5), National Socioeconomic Survey, 1983

Province	Decile										Total
	1	2	3	4	5	6	7	8	9	10	
Bocas del Toro	0.014	0.008	0.017	0.014	0.011	0.012	0.007	0.004	0.003	0.001	0.095
Coclé	0.129	0.128	0.107	0.084	0.075	0.056	0.048	0.034	0.018	0.005	0.688
Colón	0.068	0.081	0.054	0.063	0.058	0.050	0.031	0.014	0.008	0.004	0.435
Chiriquí	0.109	0.102	0.082	0.081	0.058	0.054	0.036	0.027	0.013	0.004	0.571
Darién	0.014	0.020	0.016	0.011	0.009	0.009	0.004	0.003	0.002	0.000	0.091
Herrera	0.043	0.050	0.048	0.039	0.031	0.028	0.032	0.018	0.010	0.003	0.307
Los Santos	0.031	0.026	0.024	0.020	0.017	0.012	0.008	0.007	0.004	0.002	0.156
Panamá	0.209	0.261	0.169	0.199	0.140	0.099	0.083	0.065	0.033	0.011	1.274
Veraguas	0.188	0.161	0.181	0.142	0.123	0.102	0.074	0.059	0.039	0.013	1.086
Total	0.809	0.841	0.702	0.656	0.526	0.424	0.329	0.236	0.134	0.047	4.708

Note: Poverty gap is expressed as percentage of total household income.

Table 6.10 Poverty Gap, Higher Estimates of Poverty (Poverty 2.0), National Socioeconomic Survey, 1983

Province					Decile						Total
	1	2	3	4	5	6	7	8	9	10	
Bocas del Toro	0.001	0.040	0.038	0.033	0.029	0.019	0.011	0.007	0.006	0.001	0.210
Coclé	0.211	0.220	0.167	0.143	0.119	0.098	0.080	0.055	0.032	0.012	1.139
Colón	0.128	0.131	0.120	0.129	0.102	0.050	0.047	0.048	0.029	0.009	0.792
Chiriquí	0.213	0.190	0.177	0.146	0.111	0.102	0.067	0.048	0.031	0.008	1.094
Darién	0.023	0.034	0.025	0.018	0.015	0.011	0.010	0.008	0.005	0.002	0.150
Herrera	0.076	0.081	0.078	0.060	0.057	0.061	0.038	0.025	0.015	0.006	0.496
Los Santos	0.055	0.052	0.043	0.037	0.030	0.022	0.023	0.016	0.009	0.003	0.290
Panamá	0.472	0.426	0.445	0.295	0.275	0.220	0.157	0.111	0.059	0.027	2.462
Veraguas	0.280	0.262	0.265	0.225	0.200	0.162	0.128	0.105	0.068	0.034	1.729
Total	1.459	1.435	1.357	1.087	0.937	0.744	0.562	0.424	0.254	0.102	8.361

Note: Poverty gap is expressed as percentage of total household income.

Table 6.11   Cost of Monthly Minimum Food Basket for a Five-Member Household, 1970, 1980, and 1983

Reference	Data Base	Sector	1970 ($)	1980 ($)	1983 ($)	Year of Estimate
Molina (1982)	Household Survey, 1967	Republic	46	(91)	(104)	1970
CEPAL (Consultant: Lavados, 1980)	Household Survey, 1967	Metro	53	(104)	(120)	1970
		Rest	40	(79)	(91)	
Panama, MIPPE (1980)	Household Survey, 1967	Metro	(71)	140	(161)	1980
		Rest	(60)	118	(136)	
CEPAL (1981b)	Household Survey, 1967	Republic	(65)	129	(148)	1980
Panama, Ministry of Health (1984), used as the base in this study	National Nutrition Survey, 1980	Republic	(72)	(142)	155	1983

Note: The figures in parentheses are deflated/inflated values to the base-year prices. Deflated/inflated figures are given for broad comparisons.

Subject to the caveats mentioned above, whatever inferences we can glean from the available estimates of poverty indicate that there is no evidence that poverty in Panama has either increased or decreased over time since 1970. The conclusion is consistent with the results of income distribution of chapter 5. It must, however, be noted that the conclusion is independent of the impressive expansion of social services during the 1970s, as we saw in chapter 3 (table 3.1). In contrast to that, in the Third World countries in general poverty is believed to have increased (see chap. 1). By comparison, Panama's performance in not letting its poverty worsen even during adverse times is creditable.

Given these results, a natural question that arises is how, in the face of increasing unemployment and falling per capita consumption of rice, beans, and maize (see chap. 3), poverty in Panama can avoid increasing when it has done so in other developing countries. A conservative answer would take protection under the caveat mentioned above—that the data bases are not comparable, so no conclusion is really possible. A more forthright answer would be that the observed extraordinary improvements in health, education, and welfare are not merely direct utility-increasing changes but also enhance the productive capacity of the poor. A decline in sickness would surely increase the number of days worked not only by the person concerned, but probably also by some other members of the family. An improvement in health is conducive to work effort. A decline in child mortality, which reduces fertility (see chap. 12 below) and thus saves the

Table 6.12 Existing Estimates of Poverty and Poverty Gaps, 1970 and 1980, Compared with Corresponding Estimates of This Study, 1980 and 1983

		Indigency		Poverty	
Reference	Sector	1970 (%)	1980 (%)	1970 (%)	1980 (%)
		Poverty			
CEPAL (Consultant: La-	Urban	9.3	—	22.4	—
vados, 1980)	Rural	33.5	—	49.4	—
Altimir (1981)	Republic	25.0	—	39.0	—
Molina (1982)	Republic	—	—	39.0	37.0
PREALC (1980a)	Republic	21.1	—	35.6	—
CEPAL (1981b)	Urban	14.0	—	46.7	—
	Rural	56.1	—	71.6	—
CEPAL (1982)	Republic	—	23.7	—	53.9
This study	Republic	20.05[a]	19.98[b]		
		Poverty Gaps			
CEPAL (Consultant: La-	Metro	2.3	—	3.1	—
vados, 1980): gap as %	Rest	16.0	—	3.1	—
of income of nonpoor	Republic	5.8	—	8.1	—
Altimir (1981): gap as %	Republic	—	—	8.1	—
of family income					
Molina (1982): gap as %	Republic	—	—	6.8	5.7
of GNP					
This study: gap as % of	Republic	—	2.80[a]	—	9.31[a]
family income		—	2.10[b]	—	8.4[b]

[a] From census 1980.
[b] From National Socioeconomic Survey, 1983.

mother's time for economic activities that augment measurable income is poverty reducing. A decrease in crude birthrate and fertility leads to higher per capita income. A reduction in adult mortality among the poor increases the return from investment in children and raises per capita output of the poor. An expansion of education among the poor is productivity increasing. There is no reason to believe that the will, capacity, and willingness to work go down with improvement in potable water, shelter, and sanitation. The expenditure on health, literacy, and similar social services thus is an investment in the poor that probably has a very high payoff in terms of GDP. Likewise, public assistance to poor farmers of the asentamientos, whether or not it is injurious to overall national growth, does not exacerbate poverty. One must also not forget that among the six macro policies (see chap. 14) and two economic changes (see chap. 3) analyzed in this study,

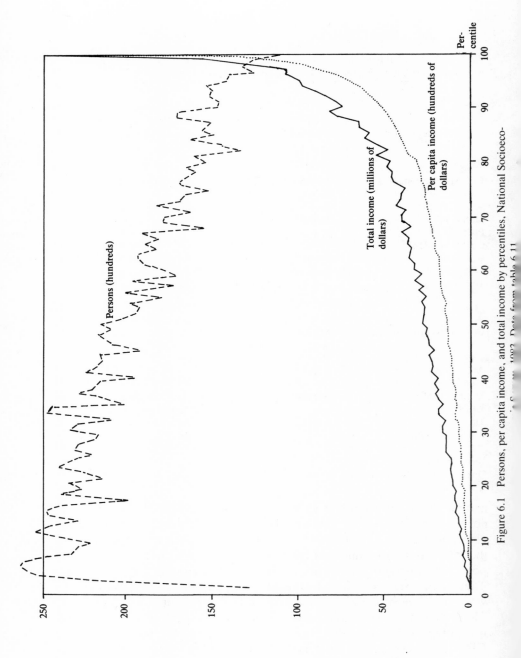

Figure 6.1 Persons, per capita income, and total income by percentiles, National Socioeco-
~~nomic Survey, 1992. Data from table 6.11~~

on the whole only three do not favor the poor—namely, incentive schemes, unemployment, and the stagnation in production of poorman's food. All other policies have been found to be pro-poor. Thus it would be a great mistake to neglect the productivity aspects of social services. Accordingly, I believe that the massive expansion of social services and its impressive results in Panama have contributed to an improvement of the economic position of the poor despite adverse global conditions. From Panama's experience it appears that social services that reach the poor are indeed growth promoting as well as income redistributing and poverty reducing.

RELATIVE POVERTY

Figure 6.1 sketches percentiles of per capita incomes, total income, and total persons. We see that the mean income of the one hundredth percentile is 1,371 times that of the second percentile. The sample median income ($1,250) is 70 percent of the sample mean income ($1,766). Using the national median to draw a *relative* poverty line, conventionally fixed at half of the median income (which is supposed to account for nonfood basic needs also), 29 percent of Panama's population is poor. This is almost exactly equal to our lower poverty measure.

A more correct measure of relative poverty, however, is provided when (half of) the median income of each province, rather than the national median, is used as the cutoff line for its population. Among the results of these calculations (not reported in table form) and their comparisons with those in table 6.3, some points are worth noting.

Those who are in relative poverty are also in absolute poverty, except for Panamá province.

The better-off a province, the closer to each other are the incidences of absolute and relative poverty (observe the zigzag lines of panels 1 and 2 for nonpoor provinces in comparison with poor provinces).

The poorer (better-off) a province, the lower (higher) its median income, that is, the lower its relative poverty line, the lower the ratio of its median income to its mean income, and the lower the ratio of the per capita income of those just above the relative poverty line to the mean income of the nonpoor.

The incidence of relative poverty is between 28.3 percent and 29.6 percent. Because of the low relative poverty line in poor provinces, the poverty gap is low. Accordingly, it will require a relatively lower amount of absolute investment to uplift a larger absolute number of the poor in poor provinces than in nonpoor provinces. From this point of view an attack on poverty in Veraguas is likely to eliminate the most poverty and make the greatest impact. For instance, the incidence of critical poverty is 15 percent higher in Veraguas (4.99 percent) than in Panamá (4.33

Table 6.13   Per Capita Income and Poverty (Indigency) of Selected Countries of the World in the Late 1970s

Country	GNP per person 1975 ($ with Kravis Adjustment)	Percentage of Population in Poverty in 1975
1 Bangladesh	200	64
2 Ethiopia	213	68
3 Burma	237	65
4 Indonesia	280	59
5 Uganda	280	55
6 Zaire	281	53
7 Sudan	281	54
8 Tanzania	297	51
9 Pakistan	299	43
10 India	300	46
11 Kenya	413	55
12 Nigeria	433	35
13 Philippines	469	33
14 Sri Lanka	471	14
15 Honduras	514[a]	45
16 Senegal	550	35
17 Egypt	561	20
18 Thailand	584	32
19 Colombia	612[a]	18
20 Ghana	628	25
21 Morocco	643	26
22 Ivory Coast	695	25
23 South Korea	797	8
24 Chile	798	6
25 Zambia	798	10
26 Turkey	914	14
27 Tunisia	992	10
28 Malaysia	1,006	12

percent; see table 6.3). The critically poor of Veraguas have 0.45 percent of the nation's income and Panamá's critically poor have 0.53 percent of it (table 6.6). Yet eliminating poverty in the two provinces requires almost exactly the same effort, an augmentation of the income of the poor by $18 million per year for either province (table 6.8).

Finally, a rough comparison of the incidence of poverty in most Third World countries is given in table 6.13. Given the noncomparability of data and procedures across countries, the incidence of poverty as well as the ranking of countries should be taken with a grain of salt. Moreover, the estimates pertain to the mid-1970s and are thus somewhat out of date. Subject to this caveat, Panama was about third highest in incidence of poverty among the Latin and Central American countries reported in the table.

Table 6.13   Continued.

Country	GNP per person 1975 ($ with Kravis Adjustment)	Percentage of Population in Poverty in 1975
29 Costa Rica	1,048[a]	6
30 Taiwan	1,075	5
31 Guatemala	1,128	10
32 Brazil	1,136	25
33 Peru	1,183	25
34 Iran	1,257	13
35 Panama	1,271[a]	25 (1970)[a]
		23 (1980)[d]
		20 (1983)[d]
36 Uruguay	1,331[a]	4[b]
37 Mexico	1,429	14
38 Yugoslavia	1,701	5
39 Argentina	1,720[a]	1
40 Venezuela	2,083	10
41 United States	7,060	14[c]

Sources:
1. Most estimates as reported in Sen (1980).
2. Altimir (1981) for Latin and Central American countries for poverty and those countries marked with superscript *a* for income.
3. The United States sources for the United States.
4. For Panama, the estimates for 1970 are from Altimir (1981). Those for 1980 are calculated from the census data and those for 1983 from this chapter, table 6.3. Comparisons between the three estimates are naturally rough.
[a] For 1977.
[b] For urban sector only.
[c] For the United States, the measure consists of poverty, not indigency. For all other countries, it is the indigency measure.
[d] These estimates are not necessarily comparable to that for 1970 or between themselves.

Conclusions

According to the estimates of this study, 20 percent of Panamanians are critically poor with respect to the basic food basket, and approximately 29 percent are poor with respect to basic needs. The incidence of critical poverty varies from 51 percent in Veraguas to 9.3 percent in Panamá province. The critical poverty gap is 2.10 percent of national income, which, coincidentally, is almost exactly equal to what the critically poor have— namely, 2.09 percent of national income. The results provide no evidence that poverty has increased in Panama since 1970. Because of their relatively low relative poverty line, it costs less to reduce poverty in poor provinces, such as Veraguas, than in relatively well-off provinces such as Panamá. If the output/capital ratio of a project that exclusively benefits the critically poor was 1:5, an investment of $90 million (or 2.65 percent of national income) in Veraguas would eliminate the critical poverty of 17,759 families. Lower values of output/capital ratio would require proportionately higher investment. The remaining chapters are devoted to identifying and analyzing the critically poor and deriving policies, projects, and programs appropriate for reducing their poverty at the minimum cost.

PART THREE

Characterization of the Poor

SEVEN

Characteristics of the Poor

The preceding two chapters analyzed the income of the poor by type, measured the incidence and the intensity of poverty, and estimated the distribution of income. In the present chapter I will characterize the poor, focusing mainly on the who, what, and where of poverty: who the poor are; where they work and live; what kind of jobs they do; what their education and health conditions are; who among the old, the young, and children are poor; and so forth. The why of poverty will be analyzed in chapters 10–13.

The chapter is divided into several sections. The first investigates the interaction of the poor with the environment they live in. More precisely, we will look at the family structure of the poor and the nonpoor, analyzing the work, earnings, and family characteristics of youths, adults, and the old. The second section analyzes certain additional characteristics of low-income elderly people, the third those of women, and the fourth those of children. Housing conditions of the poor are discussed next, followed by the educational characteristics of heads of households and their parents and children, job and occupational characteristics, and intergenerational mobility. A few general characteristics of the unemployed are then scanned. (With a view to identifying the precise nature of any links between unemployment and poverty, all of chapter 9 is given over to verifying possible relationships between the two maladies.) Finally, the last section is devoted to mapping poverty.

INCOME AND FAMILY STRUCTURE OF THE POOR

Spouse Dependency Differences

Figure 7.1 presents family structure by age classes and by deciles of male household heads.[1] We see that the relative share of spouses is perceptibly higher among the poor than among the rich. The share of spouses in the bottom decile of heads of households is 11 percent against the mean of 9.3 percent of the top three deciles. As we will see in other parts of the book,

---

1. Except where forms of marriage are studied for comparison, the term "marriage" in this study defines all relationships in which persons of opposite sexes live together as husband and wife, including formal marriage (*casamiento*), union or common-law marriage, and similar forms of living together by consent.

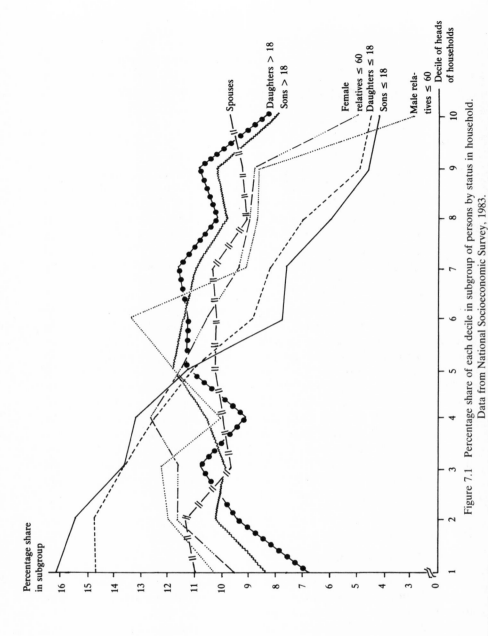

Figure 7.1 Percentage share of each decile in subgroup of persons by status in household.
Data from National Socioeconomic Survey, 1983.

108

the labor force participation rate among spouses in poor homes is substantially lower than in nonpoor homes. These two factors in combination lower the per capita income for poor families. An obvious remedy is to increase labor force participation among low-income spouses.

Child-Dependency Differences

The relative share of children up to age eighteen, both sons and daughters, is approximately 3.5 times as high among the families of the bottom (poor) decile as among those of the tenth (rich) decile. This share increases monotonically from the tenth decile to the bottom decile. The poor of the bottom decile have 15 percent of the nation's children while the rich of the tenth decile have less than 4.5 percent. As we will see in succeeding sections, a large proportion of the rich are older persons whose children have grown up and become independent, while an equally large fraction of young couples with dependent children, low starting salaries, and high incidence of unemployment are in low-income brackets. The demographic life cycle theory finds support in this study (see also below). Despite that offsetting factor, however, even when they are no longer young, the poor have large families with high dependency ratios. One clue to reducing poverty thus is to induce low-income families to reduce their fecundity, which in this Catholic country is palatable mainly if done through rhythm methods and abstinence.

The Earner/Dependents Disparity

The affluent have smaller shares of all classes of persons other than household heads—their earner/dependents ratio is substantially higher than that of other groups. Nearly one-third of the top decile's population consists of heads of households against less than one-fifth for the bottom decile. Female relatives (mostly grandmothers) show a clear bulge upward among the middle deciles. Further analysis of this issue will be presented in the next section.

In brief, the demographic pattern that emerges from the multisectoral socioeconomic survey is somewhat as follows: Old and young relatives (grandparents, adult children, and adult relatives) are looked after by (if dependent) or choose to stay with (if earners) middle-class parents. Poor families have the lion's share of young children and a moderately high share of dependent spouses. Well-off families, on the other hand, have relatively fewer dependents, old or young, and their earning children and relatives tend to stay independent. In these homes maids seem, in part, to substitute for grandparents. Alternatively stated, the dependent grandparents and siblings probably perform useful economic services (leaving aside the emotional aspects), obviating the need for baby-sitters and other service personnel. To that extent, thus, the conventional measures will overstate poverty.

Overall Dependency Ratios

Dependency ratios and a few other ratios are calculated in Table 7.1, which shows that the dependency ratio declines steadily from 4.5 in the bottom decile to 0.7 for the top decile (col. 6). The earner/dependents ratio rises correspondingly from 1.0 to 1.9 (col. 8).The ratios of both child dependency and elder-dependency declines as one moves up the income scale. In terms of the earner/dependents ratio, the middle class is roughly on a par with the upper-income class. As a result of the the dependency differences, the ratio of the income of the tenth decile to that of the bottom decile goes up from 26 per earner and 49 per family to 72 per adult-equivalent person and 84 per capita for the nation as a whole and, more or less, by corresponding multiples for urban and rural sectors. In short, the earning capacity, demand, market structure, and other economic and environmental factors cannot entirely explain poverty. The family's demographic structure is also related to poverty.

The Very Rich of Panama

Table 7.1 also subdivides the tenth bracket into low rich, middle rich (top 5 percent), and top rich (top 1 percent). For a proper perspective, it is relevant to see not only how poor the poor are, but also how rich the rich are. We see that the top 1 percent of families in the nation have an income that exceeds the income of the bottom three deciles, or approximately all the poor of Panama. Panama's top rich are indeed very rich. The poverty gap of $72 million or 72,837 critically poor families (see chap. 6) can be closed by transferring less than one-third of the $249 million income (table 7.1) of Panama's 432 richest families, or exactly one-third of the income of the 360 urban richest families.

Poverty by Age Structure of Heads of Households

Figure 7.2 provides a cursory view of the life cycle profile of incomes of heads of households by sex and three broad income classes. Without reporting elaborate tables, the following results may be noted.

Within age groups inequality is the highest among old (over sixty) female heads of households and lowest among young (under twenty-five) female heads of households. The rich women who, being old, probably have few dependent relatives living with them are a source of the low dependency ratio of the upper brackets. The highest inequality among male heads of households appears in the age group twenty-five to thirty. Since they are rather too young to receive bequests (their parents are not yet likely to be in their seventies and eighties), the widening inequality of this group is apt to reflect differences in abilities, education, and hard work. The highest poverty, too, appears among old female heads. The next poor group is formed by young (below twenty-five) heads. Here males predominate. The poorest group among male heads is the young, which is consistent with the demographic version of the life cycle theory of poverty. An implication of this theory is that most of the poor in age group twenty-five and lower are not likely to be poor in the life cycle sense.

Peaks in Life Cycle Earnings Profiles

There is no peak in the income of rich female heads—their income curve rises monotonically with age. None of the other groups follow that profile. The good fortune of this class of women is perhaps due mainly to inheritance.

The income peaks of both rich and poor as well as male and female heads of households are reached during ages forty to fifty-nine, while those of middle-class male and female heads occur near or after retirement. This result may be explainable in part by the fact that the middle class, especially in urban areas, is almost entirely covered by social security, and, as we will see in chapter 14, Panama's social security system is generous to retirees. In the reference age group, most are skilled, semiskilled, and experienced. Probably they draw their pensions and also work for additional income. A disproportionately higher number of male heads than female heads in the twenty-five and lower age group may indicate the differential opportunities in high-class jobs (such as executive and managerial) available to upper-income young men compared with young women. This may also be due in part to the accumulated experience or increasing productivity of education and training, since the middle class is in general better educated than other classes.

To sum up, the poor have more spouses than the nonpoor, and labor force participation among spouses in poor homes is significantly lower than in nonpoor homes. These two factors combined become a source of poverty. Admittedly, the remedy is not to reduce the poor's share of spouses. Spouses are not an inferior good. They are, indeed, a source of pleasure (consumption) and perennial welfare gains, objects of love and emotional satisfaction, and companions of supreme value. Rather, the remedy lies in increasing the employability of spouses and their propensity for labor force participation.

Table 7.1 Income per Family, per Capita, per Earner, and per Adult-Equivalent Person and Dependency Ratios, National Socioeconomic Survey, 1983 (Excluding Indians)

Decile	Number of Families (1)	Number of Persons (2)	Number of Earners (3)	Number of Adult-Equivalent Persons[a] (4)	Dependency Ratio (5)	Family size (6)	Earners per Family (7)	Income ($00/year)			
								Per Family (8)	Per Capita (9)	Per Earner (10)	Per Adult-Equivalent Person (11)
Country											
Total	432	1,933	731	1,717	1.6	4.5	1.7	78	17	46	19
1	43	230	42	191	4.5	5.3	1.0	5	1	5	1
2	43	234	63	200	2.7	5.4	1.5	17	3	11	3
3	43	225	70	193	2.2	5.2	1.6	28	5	17	6
4	43	219	72	191	2.0	5.1	1.7	40	8	24	9
5	43	211	74	185	1.8	4.9	1.7	53	10	30	12
6	43	188	79	171	1.4	4.4	1.8	62	14	34	19
7	43	181	80	163	1.3	4.2	1.9	79	18	42	21
8	43	162	82	148	0.9	3.8	2.0	93	25	47	27
9	43	150	86	143	0.7	3.5	2.0	139	40	70	42
10	43	22	81	130	0.7	3.1	1.9	268	86	144	80
Top 5%	17	62	39	61	0.6	3.6	1.8	336	118	181	120
Top 1%	4	11	7	12	0.5	2.3	1.6	561	233	311	223
Urban											
Total	240	1,039	448	940	1.3	4.3	1.9	109	25	58	27
1	6	22	4	19	3.8	3.8	0.8	3	1	3	1
2	8	48	13	41	2.7	5.9	1.6	19	3	12	4

3	14	81	23	70	2.4	5.8	1.7	32	5	19	6
4	20	111	34	96	2.2	5.5	1.7	44	6	26	9
5	25	150	44	115	1.9	5.2	1.8	56	10	32	12
6	28	120	54	117	1.4	4.6	1.9	65	14	65	19
7	31	136	50	121	1.3	4.4	1.9	83	16	46	21
8	33	132	60	128	0.9	3.9	2.1	97	24	47	27
9	35	126	72	121	0.8	3.6	2.1	149	40	70	42
10	38	120	71	317	0.7	3.2	1.9	273	86	144	86
Top 5%	19	55	34	55	0.6	2.9	1.8	339	117	189	117
Top 1%	4	9	6	10	0.4	2.3	1.6	548	236	319	216

Rural

Total	193	895	232	777	2.1	4.6	1.4	41	8	27	10
1	37	208	38	172	4.5	5.5	1.0	5	1	5	1
2	35	186	50	150	2.7	5.3	1.4	16	18	11	3
3	29	144	45	125	2.1	4.9	1.5	26	26	17	2
4	23	108	37	95	1.0	4.7	1.6	37	8	22	9
5	18	80	30	71	1.6	4.5	1.6	49	10	29	12
6	15	60	24	54	1.4	3.9	1.6	55	14	34	15
7	12	44	20	40	1.1	3.6	1.7	69	19	40	20
8	10	29	14	77	1.0	3.1	1.5	78	25	49	28
9	8	23	13	23	0.7	2.9	1.6	114	39	67	41
10	5	13	9	13	0.5	2.5	1.6	229	92	140	98
Top 5%	3	7	5	6	0.5	2.5	1.7	313	124	135	141
Top 1%	1	2	1	1	0.6	3.0	1.9	630	214	349	271

Note: The figures in columns 1 through 4 are in thousands. Those in columns 8 through 11 are in hundred dollars of annual income.
[a] For calculating adult-equivalent persons, the following weights were used: adult = 1.0, age 0-4 = 0.42, age 5-14 = 0.63.

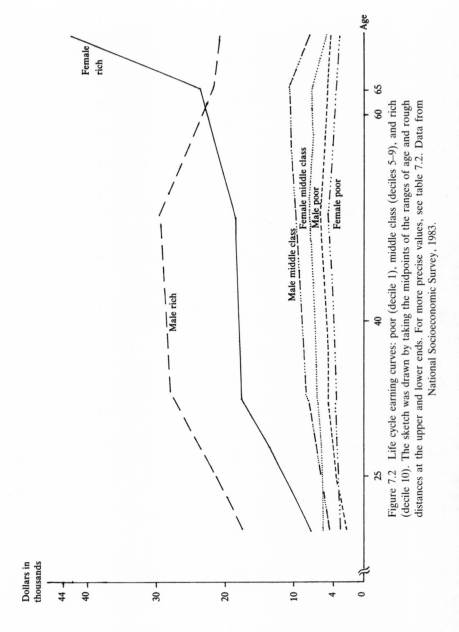

Figure 7.2 Life cycle earning curves: poor (decile 1), middle class (deciles 5–9), and rich (decile 10). The sketch was drawn by taking the midpoints of the ranges of age and rough distances at the upper and lower ends. For more precise values, see table 7.2. Data from National Socioeconomic Survey, 1983.

114

The poor also have much higher child-dependency ratios and old-age-dependency ratios than the nonpoor. The remedy for the former suggests itself—to reduce fertility among the poor. Providing health and family planning services for those who are poor is in the long run among the most potent instruments of policy for reducing family size. Once again, the child-dependency ratio could very well be due to life cycle factors.

A high old-age-dependency ratio does not necessarily increase poverty; its net effect may even be to reduce it, for the elderly of poor families would otherwise be even poorer, since there is no other old-age security for them. They have been left out by the national social security system. By living with their children's families they may reduce the family's measured per capita income, but they increase their own income over what it would be otherwise. In addition, they participate in implicit household production. Accordingly, the custom of keeping one's grandparents with the family voluntarily is beneficial to both parties and so deserves to be encouraged. A possible inducement to poor people to keep their families small is a universal system of old-age insurance. The desirability and feasibility of such a system for Panama are studied in chapter 14.

Between age groups, poverty is concentrated among old female heads of households and heads of both sexes who are under twenty-five. Not all members of the latter group are likely to be permanently poor. They also reflect a life cycle phenomenon. The observed incidence of poverty in the young group is consistent with the demographic theory of life cycle earnings. Nevertheless, the burden of poverty among the young can be lessened by taxing them at later age to subsidize them when they are young and raising children, when young wives forgo market income to engage in household production and when their experience is meager and starting salaries are low. This can be done—and is being done to some extent already—by providing play schools for children so that young mothers can work (if they desire), advising the young against early marriages so they have fewer dependents when their salaries are low, and providing subsidized vocational training and education in general to enhance their life cycle earning capacity so they pay higher taxes in later age when they earn higher incomes and have higher earner/dependents ratios.

MORE ON OLD-AGE POVERTY

Table 7.2 presents the concentration of the old plus life expectancy and child-mortality rates by province. We see that there are discernible differences in life expectancy, child mortality, and old-age-dependency ratios between provinces. Two factors seem to help explain these differences: the relative predominance of Indians in a province, and poverty incidence. Provinces in which life expectancy is relatively high tend to have lower

Table 7.2   Life Expectancy, Child Mortality, and Ratio of Old People by Province, 1980

Province	Life Expectancy			Child Mortality		Old Persons Sixty and over in One Hundred Households
	Total	Male	Female	Male	Female	
Bocas del Toro	68.17	66.21	70.22	32.53	27.67	3.4
Coclé	72.18	71.45	74.00	27.10	18.21	6.6
Colón	71.65	69.79	73.60	22.92	18.71	7.4
Chiriquí	71.81	70.71	73.53	22.44	20.23	5.7
Darién	65.39	62.70	68.21	44.52	34.83	3.8
Herrera	73.02	70.67	75.48	23.24	16.73	6.7
Los Santos	74.32	72.22	76.53	19.06	14.52	9.1
Panamá	75.88	73.58	78.29	16.15	12.23	6.4
Veraguas	69.28	67.52	71.12	28.33	23.30	5.6
Total	73.30	71.17	75.53	21.57	17.27	6.3

child mortality and a higher share of the old, though not necessarily. The highest share of the elderly goes to Los Santos, which is second only to Panamá province in life expectancy (and child mortality) but is about at the median in per capita income. Salubrious climate (preferred by the elderly), migration of young workers to neighboring Panamá province, the dynamics of job expansion, the availability of health services, and similar factors may explain the relatively low share of the elderly in Panamá province and the relatively higher share in Los Santos. The results are consistent with the analysis of income and other socioeconomic indicators for Los Santos. See chapter 5, where we also saw that family size in Los Santos is the smallest in the country. Accordingly, it is relevant at this point to look at the old by family size.

The Elderly by Family Size

Most male senior citizens in rural areas live by themselves (one-member family) or with their spouses (two-member family). The distribution curve for urban retirees, both male and female, on the other hand, tends to be U shaped: relatively more one- to three-member families and nine- to twelve-member families have persons over fifty residing with them than do four- to eight-member families.

Briefly, most male senior citizens live by themselves or with their age-mates (usually spouses). In urban areas, however, the distribution curve is U shaped; that is, relatively large fractions of one- to three-member families and families with nine or more members have elderly parents residing with them. More than half of the male retirees across all household sizes engage in market work, and a majority of the women who work are single. In general, the less well-off a province, the higher the proportion of the elderly living with below-sixty heads in low-income deciles. Whether it is out of distress or because of family attachment is a moot point. It is a bit of both. The elderly in low-income provinces therefore need more attention in any antipoverty measures in relation to their age-mates in better-off provinces. When not living by themselves, the elderly of middle-class families in nonpoor provinces are found to live predominantly with their families.

CHARACTERISTICS OF FEMALE HEADS OF HOUSEHOLDS

There is a general impression that men work more after marriage than before, or that married men work more than single men, and that women work less after marriage than before, or that married women work less than single women. Since choices about marriage, work, children, and children's schooling by and large are made voluntarily (within the usual income, natural, and other constraints), a logical question is why the welfare-maximizing agents may work differently after marriage than before. Or do they?

Welfare versus Income

Possible misrepresentation of welfare by measured income, especially present income in the sense of national accounts, has been the subject matter of economic debate, particularly in the wake of the development of the modern theory of human capital since the 1960s. For example, a newlywed couple produce a child knowing that their per capita family income will go down by one-third. There must be some benefit in having a child. Similarly, two working persons of opposite sexes get married; the wife settles down to household production and the husband specializes in market work. Their joint measured income goes down. Apparently they are not worse off by this choice, because they joined voluntarily. Household production is valuable, and there is evidently a division of labor to realize the comparative advantage for benefit by each party. To the extent that the choice of married women in poor families not to participate in market work is voluntary (not forced by the market; e.g., by lack of demand for their services), poverty measured by conventional income will be overestimated. At the same time, imputing income to household work—for example, by assigning the market wage rate of the identically qualified employed female to the nonworking housewife—may be considered arbitrary and influenced by value judgments, since married females might be considered different workers by the employer insofar as, for instance, childbearing may interrupt the continuity of work. Housewifery might be involuntary—forced by lack of demand for labor and so on. On the other hand, the national accounts concept of measured income is objective, easily understood by the expert and the nonexpert, and provides conformable comparisons across countries and over time. In view of these overriding advantages of the conventional measures of income, I chose the national accounts concept of income for this study. Women's behavior with respect to work, fertility, and schooling is viewed in that light.

The *National Survey of Fertility, 1975–76* has information on women's work behavior before and after marriage. A cross-tabulation prepared from this source by Gougain (1983) indicates that women who work in the market "only after marriage" are almost uniformly spread across all occupations and income classes. The proportion of those who worked "only before marriage" is more than three times as high for wives with less than primary education than those with ten years or more of schooling. Over 50 percent of those who worked only before marriage did so in low-status inferior jobs, while only 14.7 percent worked in high-status jobs. A large majority of those who work before marriage hold inferior jobs, fail to acquire education, and are less qualified for market jobs after marriage. Two-thirds of them work in the informal sector. Poverty is evidently both the cause and the consequence of this behavior.

This immiserizing effect of work before marriage because of childhood poverty must be distinguished from the opposite effect of premarriage productive work experience by educated persons. The latter has a positive impact on earnings, as we will see in subsequent chapters.

The analysis of labor force participation, marriage, and earnings of married and single women will be done in chapter 11. In the remainder of this chapter I report on the educational and occupational characteristics of female heads of households.

Education

There are 87,211 households in the Republic of Panama headed by women, who form about 20 percent of total household heads. While the overall distribution of heads among different levels of education is probably representative of the distribution of jobs requiring that level of education, the educational levels among the bottom three deciles are limited largely to the primary-school level. Hardly any female heads of households with university education are in the first three deciles. Between 10 and 16 percent of heads have secondary education. As in the rest of the society in general, the schooling levels of the present generation of women heads of households are substantially higher than those of their mothers and fathers.

Occupational Status

Women heads of households are, by and large, uniformly distributed across income deciles, with a moderate upward bulge in the middle. The disparities, however, show up in the distribution of heads between occupations. In general upper-decile female heads predominate in higher-status occupations, such as managerial and office work. Middle-decile heads tend to be salespersons, conductors, artisans, operators, laborers, or in kindred occupations. Agricultural and personal-service workers are concentrated in the bottom deciles. By and large the same occupational distribution prevails among male heads of households.

Schooling of Children

Finally, since the mother's interaction with a child is an important factor in that child's schooling, children's education may also be looked at in relation to women's poverty. The school enrollment data indicate that the percentages of children in age groups six to twelve and thirteen to eighteen who do not attend school is much higher among the bottom deciles, whereas practically all children in the upper deciles are in school.

CHARACTERISTICS OF CHILDREN OF POOR FAMILIES

The United Nations "Declaration of the Rights of the Child" of 1960 stated that small children should "enjoy special protection" and should be provided the means to grow in a "healthy and normal manner." The articles of the "Convention on the Rights of the Child" emphasize education, nourishment, and health care among other things. The "International Year of the Child" (1979) saw the appointment by UNICEF of a subgroup of experts of the United Nations Commission on Human Rights in Geneva to prepare documents on the rights of children. But little attention has so far been paid to these pious declarations by many individual countries. A stocktaking of children's status in Panama is in order.

In this study, statistics on children have appeared in several figures and tables. For instance, we saw in figure 7.1 that the bottom 20 percent of households (roughly but not quite conforming to the critically poor households) have 29.3 percent of the children under nineteen, whereas the top 20 percent of households have only 9.5 percent of them. In other words, approximately 30 percent of children in Panama are critically poor. The overall dependency ratio of the bottom 10 percent households is 4.5 against 0.7 in the top decile (table 7.1). In the subsample of females heads of households of the preceding section, we saw that the bottom two deciles, forming 15.6 percent of female heads, account for 22.8 percent of their children six to eighteen years old and 26.3 percent of six- to twelve-year-olds. The same two deciles have 57 percent of six- to twelve-year-olds not attending school and 34.3 percent of thirteen- to eighteen-year-olds not attending school. Thus a much larger proportion of children than of adults are critically poor. Moreover, the harm poverty does to poor children is even more serious—for example, low levels of schooling. Detailed analysis of the poverty of children and the transfer of poverty from generation to generation through children appears in chapters 10 (intergenerational transfer of human capital) and 12 (fertility and poverty). In the remainder of this section I will discuss three main characteristics of children's poverty in Panama: malnutrition by district, school dropout rate by district, and a fertility function fitted to time-series and cross-sectional data.

To begin with, note that, consonant with the general expansion of health services and the consequent improvement in overall health of the population during the past decade or two, a noticeable reduction in child mortality was also recorded. For instance, the percentage of children below fifteen who died of the major five diseases of children—enteritis and other diarrheic diseases, malignant tumors including neoplasms of the lymphatic tissues and the hematopoietic organs, pneumonia, measles, and anemia—declined from 0.645 percent in 1970 to 0.384 percent in 1976 (Panama, MIPPE 1980d, tables 5 and 65). It is important, however, to see where in the country the population of children has lagged behind in these gains.

Both malnutrition and dropout rate are closely associated with low-income districts. The highest malnutrition prevails in Veraguas, Chiriquí, and Bocas del Toro. The statistics by suffrage units (*corregimientos*, about 7.5 per district—the country is divided into sixty-five districts) indicate malnutrition exceeding 50 percent and largely between 60 to 70 percent in Indian-inhabited corregimientos. The districts with sizable populations of Indians are also considerably behind the national averages in school-enrollment: they have low enrollment (late start) at age six (the first year of school) and dropout rates exceeding a quarter of school-age children at age ten (when the national enrollment rate is nearly 98 percent) and rising to higher levels at age twelve (the final year of primary education).

Finally, a simplified regression of fertility on time trend and per capita provincial income is presented below for a taste of a much more rigorously estimated fertility function that will be presented in chapter 12 on the analysis of the fertility behavior of women in poor families.

The Indian sample
$$F1 = 8.46 - 0.00159Y + 0.0827T; \quad \text{adj. } R^2 = 0.86$$
$$(19.2) \quad (-6.3) \qquad (1.83) \quad \text{No. obs.} = 65$$
$$[6.68] \qquad [1,377] \qquad [5]$$

The non-Indian sample

$$F2 = \underset{[5.91]}{\underset{(38.20)}{9.13}} - \underset{[1,377]}{\underset{(-13.1)}{0.00138Y}} - \underset{[5]}{\underset{(-5.99)}{0.1471T}}; \quad \text{adj. } R^2 = 0.76 \\ \text{No. obs. } = 65$$

In these equations $F1$ and $F2$ stand for fertility rates for Indians and non-Indians, respectively, Y is province per capita income (data available for six provinces), and T stands for serial number of years (1966–70). The numbers in parentheses are t values, and those in brackets the mean value. (Data on fertility rates: Panama, MIPPE 1984; per capita income from this survey.)

We see that the substitution effect on fertility is stronger than the income effect (the coefficient of per capita earnings is negative and highly significant) for both Indians and non-Indians. The trend effect that may stand for changing tastes and environment and improved health and medical services (when income is held fixed) is negative (significant at the 0.5 percent level) for non-Indians but positive (significant at the 5 percent level) for Indians. One interpretation of this result is that reduced child mortality resulting from improved medical and health services lowers the fertility rate and family size in modern society, which is consistent with the results of chapter 12 from alternative sources of data where survival rate is found to reduce fecundity. Within the primitive society of Indians, on the other hand, the same health measures lead to higher fertility and family size, which is typical of developing countries in Asia and Africa.

The condition of the Indian child thus clamors for urgent attention. Medical and health facilities are good for health, but they also increase population in an almost stagnant mountain economy. Simultaneous action is needed to raise the productivity and income of Indians or to induce them to leave their barren mountains (while maintaining their legal rights to their land) and migrate to developed areas. The latter alternative is not culturally palatable and is worthwhile only when Indians are employable in other areas. To enhance their employability they need schooling. So we come full circle to the need for schooling.

In short, the *incidence* of poverty is considerably higher among children than among adults. In terms of *intensity*, too, poverty hurts children more than adults. It retards their stature. They cannot benefit from schooling. Malnutrition and school dropout rates are higher the lower the mean income of a district and the higher the proportion of Indian population. An effective remedy against the immiseration of Indians due to population explosion, on the one side, and falling productivity caused by deforestation and soil erosion in an already barren land, on the other side, is the economic development of their territories and expanded schooling to enable them to migrate and seek remunerative employment in the relatively developed areas of the country.

Table 7.3 Rent, Mortgage, Water, Sanitation, and Crowding Conditions of Homes, by Decile and Sector, National Socioeconomic Survey, 1983

Home Conditions	Total	Deciles									
		1	2	3	4	5	6	7	8	9	10
Total homes	432,812	43,270	43,270	43,270	43,270	43,270	43,270	43,270	43,270	43,270	43,270
1. Number of rooms	1,300,513	89,123	94,549	103,886	112,341	113,455	121,467	129,950	132,113	142,111	167,747
Rooms per home	3.0	2.1	2.2	2.4	2.6	2.6	2.8	3.0	3.1	3.3	3.9
2. Owner-occupied homes											
Number	311,089	38,517	36,379	34,300	32,779	29,844	28,456	27,584	25,468	26,993	30,769
% of total	71.9	89.0	84.1	79.3	75.8	69.0	65.8	63.7	58.9	62.4	71.0
3. Water tap inside home											
Number	351,368	19,309	24,128	31,322	35,037	38,069	38,513	40,235	41,310	41,401	42,044
% of total	81.2	44.6	55.8	72.4	81.0	88.0	89.0	93.0	95.5	95.7	97.0
4. Without sanitary service											
Number	36,829	14,628	8,814	4,930	2,784	2,150	909	1,081	535	576	422
% of total	8.5	33.8	20.4	11.4	6.4	5.0	2.1	2.5	1.2	1.3	1.0
5. Mean rent per month ($)	81	10	20	27	34	44	44	76	89	108	199
6. Mean mortgage per month ($)	104	15	35	58	82	92	80	110	126	179	260
7. Rent/family income ratio (%)	9.9	21.6	14.0	11.3	10.0	9.9	8.6	11.4	11.5	9.2	8.9
8. Mortgage/income ratio (%)	15.8	32.4	24.5	24.2	24.0	20.6	15.5	16.6	16.3	15.3	11.6
9. Family size (persons/family)	4.5	5.3	5.4	5.2	5.1	4.9	4.3	4.2	3.7	3.5	3.1
10. Floor unpaved (% homes)	18.9	60.6	53.6	29.6	18.9	11.1	7.6	5.0	2.8	3.0	1.9
11. Drinking water from river (% homes)	14.2	46.0	33.6	21.2	13.5	8.7	7.3	4.2	2.5	3.1	1.9
12. Has electricity (% homes)	70.8	21.5	32.3	51.5	66.6	81.2	82.9	89.1	93.0	93.8	96.1
13. Has television (% homes)	61.8	15.9	22.5	42.7	55.1	69.9	73.6	81.6	82.0	84.9	89.6
14. Has refrigerator (% homes)	51.8	10.9	12.0	23.6	39.1	53.1	62.3	70.3	77.8	80.1	88.9

HOUSING AND POVERTY

Housing conditions are classified in table 7.3. Among the 432,812 households of Panama, 50,737 (7.11 percent) own mortgaged homes, 83,115 (19.2 percent) live in rented homes, and the rest are in fully owned homes (whether decent or condemned) or homes provided by employers, churches, community, and similar agencies.

Rents and Mortgages and the Poor

The mean rent or mortgage (per mean home of three rooms) is eight times the rent and sixteen times the mortgage paid by the bottom decile, while the mean rent and mean mortgage paid by the top decile for an average home of 3.9 rooms are 2.45 times and 1.6 times, respectively, the corresponding mean values. Whereas family size declines with income (see table 7.2), size of home increases with income (row 1 of table 7.3).[2] Yet the irony of the fate of the very poor, for example, in decile 1, is that their rent/income and mortgage/income ratios, where applicable, are more than twice as high as those of the middle and top deciles. It is thus not surprising that only 11 percent of the bottom decile families live in rented or mortgaged homes. The rest own some kind of shelter, probably shacks in shantytowns or improvised or condemned homes. From this sample survey it appears that the magnitudes of rents and mortgages per home paid by different income classes are not suitable indexes for measuring the incidence of housing poverty or inequalities of home services. That a large majority of the poor neither rent nor buy homes on mortgage and so by the process of elimination get classified as owner-occupiers does not necessarily imply that the poor have accumulated equity in the form of real estate. To learn about their housing poverty, one must look at the physical amenities of the abodes of poor families, to which we turn next.

Potable Water and Electricity

Table 7.3 reports several variables that reflect the quality of homes. We see that only 37 percent (in decile 1) to 47 percent (in decile 2) of critically poor households in rural areas have drinkable tap water inside their homes. In rural areas indoor potable water is not available even to 16 percent of the top decile homes. In urban areas, on the other hand, nearly 100 percent of homes have indoor tap water. Among the urban poor, on the average, no more than 4 percent lack this amenity.

---

2. Note also that *household* size increases with income, whereas *family* size decreases (table 7.1, col. 6).

In rural areas, an indoor tap water supply may be considered a luxury. What is important for the poor of this year-round mild-weather country is the mere availability of potable water, whether indoors or outdoors. To identify those rural households that lack this basic necessity one should look at line 11 of table 7.3: households without water from an aqueduct or a sanitary well—that is, families that drink mainly river water or rain-water. While 14 percent of Panama's families depend on river water for drinking, 46 percent of the bottom decile and 34 percent of the second decile do so, compared with 2 percent in the top decile (which are evidently vacation homes). Most of the water-poor families live in mountains and inaccessible areas. Therefore they need to be provided, at least, with ap-propriate health care to protect against cholera, diarrhea, and similar water-caused diseases. They deserve these facilities and medicines free or at subsidized prices from the society (which means government), because clean water has a large consumers' surplus enjoyed by those who use it and not available to those who do not have access to it. Other public utilities have similar implications.

Interdistrict disparities of potable water and electricity are not as closely associated with income levels as are intradistrict interfamily disparities. Evidently this is because public utilities have large economies of scale and so cannot be provided efficiently without being operated as monopolies, which, because of the well-known potentially undesirable effects of private monopolies, are invariably provided by the public sector. Provision by individual homes would be prohibitively costly. Therefore only those dis-tricts that fall within the public supply sources have the public utilities under reference. However, where services cannot move, people may—they migrate and "vote with their feet" for these services. For these and other reasons, these services are positively correlated with mean district income and mean housing adequacy index (see table 7.4). Once again policy implications like those derived above emerge, namely that those areas not provided with public utility services deserve some compensation from the society in the form of subsidized or even free health services and medicines.

Sanitary Services

As in the case of tap water, sanitary services are crucial only in urban areas, in the sense that other basic necessities are more important for the rural poor. As such, the high percentage of 39 percent homes without sanitary services in the bottom decile of rural areas is not necessarily a sign of squalor. In urban areas, on the other hand, lack of sanitary facilities is an unbearable destitution. In this regard Panama has done very well. Prac-tically all urban homes enjoy sanitary facilities (table 7.3). (That sewage is drained into the ocean rather than treated, even in the capital city of Panama, is another matter—the ocean as a natural scavenger seems a free good to the narrow isthmus with vast waters around.)

The availability of electricity and the use of refrigerators and television sets are highly correlated, as are unpaved floors and drinking water from rivers and rain. Thus any of these variables could be used as an index of housing quality. Better still, a composite index of housing quality could be prepared. In this study such an index is prepared by a principal components analysis of the district-level data (see below). What is relevant to note here is that national averages are unlikely to reflect the real conditions of the poor. Thus, while 71 percent of homes nationally are supplied with electricity, only 21.5 percent of poor homes are (zero percent of poor homes in some districts, such as Cañazas and La Mesa in Veraguas).

Overcrowding, Housing Shortage, and Housing Poverty

Housing poverty is guaged not only by low quality of homes but also by their low quantity. A key factor in determining housing poverty is the shortage of housing. Three alternative measures of housing shortages are given in table 7.4. The definitions of overcrowding and housing deficiency or housing poverty as well as the procedure of calculating the absolute and relative measures are explained in the footnotes to table 7.4. We can see from this table that according to the conventional standards used for uncongested homes in Panama, 34.4 percent of the nation's homes are over-crowded. By way of a check on the housing data of the National Socioeconomic Survey, 1983, estimates based on the 1980 census are also reported (col. 1'). The latter source gives a slightly higher figure for housing shortage of 38.2 percent. Not surprisingly, the poor live in crowded homes. Those in the bottom two deciles, with a mean family size of 5.4 persons, live in homes whose average size works out to 2.15 rooms. Those in the top decile, with a mean family size of 3.1 persons, live on the average in homes with 3.9 rooms (table 7.3).

The greatest crowding occurs in Veraguas, where the overcrowding index rises to 71 percent in the district of Santa Fé, 63 in San Francisco, 51 in Calobre, and 49 percent in Cañazas. Equivalent ratings of over-crowded homes are also found in some districts of Chiriquí. The defiency of homes—that is, the percentage of additional homes needed to eliminate overcrowding, which is used here as an index of housing poverty based on the basic need for shelter, comes to 14.3 percent according to the absolute housing poverty line (between 2.5 and 3 persons per room depending on the size of home with and without kitchen) and 8.3 percent according to the relative housing poverty line (twice the mean density of persons per

Table 7.4 Housing Deficiency by District, National Socioeconomic Survey, 1983

| Province and District | Percentage of Over-crowded Homes[a] | | Deficiency of Homes According to Absolute Housing Poverty Line[c] | Deficiency of Homes According to Relative Housing Poverty Line[d] | Per Capita Income |
	According to Survey (1) (%)	According to Census (1') (%)	(2) (%)	(3) (%)	(4) ($)
Bocas del Toro					
Bocas del Toro	7.47[b]	39	2.10	3.69	1,444
Changuinola	7.77[b]	30	2.15	3.78	1,460
Coclé					
Aguadulce	23.57	23	6.20	7.16	1,430
Antón	36.85	48	14.42	9.15	720
La Pintada	41.43	52	18.64	9.78	488
Natá	28.14	38	9.38	2.98	989
Olá	56.62	59	34.23	9.30	538
Penonomé	42.46	48	19.34	4.04	664
Colón					
Colón and rest of district	35.02	46	13.93	8.64	1,845
Chagres	59.63	54	40.54	9.49	387
Donoso	68.43	59	36.99	8.38	489
Portobelo	50.00	66	16.64	10.11	733
Santa Isabel	44.40	50	23.76	5.45	315
Chiriquí					
San Félix	30.93	37	17.03	13.81	799
Alanje	27.11	43	16.39	9.05	971
Barú	33.57	42	12.62	9.61	1,080
Boquerón	34.95	33	14.17	9.49	798
Boquete	27.84	28	7.40	8.50	1,985
Bugaba	29.07	32	11.25	8.51	1,125
David	23.13	27	6.88	7.13	2,175
Dolega	30.98	30	10.16	8.50	857
Gualaca	26.75	37	13.64	8.93	1,317
Remedios	30.01	42	10.42	12.17	1,657
Renacimiento	48.55	47	27.33	10.43	1,208
Darién					
Chepigana	45.13	50	22.62	10.47	752
Pinogana	42.90	58	21.50	10.19	563
Herrera					
Chitré	7.89	15	1.88	3.59	2,747
Las Minas	44.62	56	21.82	10.76	1,985
Los Pozos	40.98	43	17.25	9.44	410
Ocú	33.64	45	13.78	9.05	674
Parita	13.87	21	4.27	5.54	1,081
Pesé	32.11	32	10.46	8.96	703
Santa María	18.18	16	6.52	7.54	814
Los Santos					
Guararé	8.86[b]	25	3.10	5.10	1,465
Las Tablas	17.63	22	4.50	6.86	1,792
Los Santos	18.43	26	6.09	7.36	1,431

Table 7.4 Continued.

| Province and District | Percentage of Overcrowded Homes[a] | | Deficiency of Homes According to Absolute Housing Poverty Line[c] | Deficiency of Homes According to Relative Housing Poverty Line[d] | Per Capita Income |
	According to Survey (1) (%)	According to Census (1') (%)	(2) (%)	(3) (%)	(4) ($)
Macaracas	34.76	34	10.67	9.92	908
Pedasí	10.45	19	2.47	5.95	1,007
Pocrí	12.21	31	2.59	4.87	1,055
Tonosí	30.93	54	11.88	11.61	1,435
Panamá					
Arraijan	31.38	38	10.37	8.66	1,802
Capira	51.72	55	28.31	10.61	525
Chame	37.56	43	17.27	10.38	1,043
Chepo	40.38	48	21.38	10.72	1,044
La Chorrera	30.80	35	9.00	7.06	1,494
Panamá and rest of district	20.44	31	5.97	7.55	3,101
San Carlos	41.15	59	30.09	11.04	479
San Miguelito	41.65	39	14.10	8.82	1,767
Veraguas					
Atalaya	28.68	44	8.72	6.54	785
Calobre	50.60	57	35.96	11.61	328
Cañazas	49.06	67	21.35	9.14	227
La Mesa	46.73	67	26.28	9.88	313
Las Palmas	58.93	76	31.04	11.35	391
Montijo	37.02	59	18.01	10.05	457
Río de Jesus	38.15	63	18.86	9.22	321
San Francisco	63.30	68	44.24	10.21	256
Santa Fé	70.61	71	50.44	10.64	237
Santiago	21.93	32	5.49	6.53	1,386
Soná	48.31	67	20.41	10.98	879
Country	34.42	38.2	14.29	8.29	1,766

Source: National Socioeconomic Survey, 1983, except column 1', which is from the Census of Population, 1980 as tabulated by the Controller General's Office.

[a] Any home with more than three persons per room (counting proper kitchen as a room) is defined as crowded.

[b] Except for the districts of Bocas del Toro and a couple of other districts, the coefficients of the two sources are more or less comparable. As noted in chapter 4, the district-level data of the survey should be used with caution, since not all variables at the district level are statistically significant. Moreover, in our estimates, the kitchen is counted as a room and the sorting is somewhat broad based, as it has to be in the absence of data on the size of rooms. Consequently, for any district where the estimates from the two sources are wide apart—as in the case of the two districts of Bocas del Toro and Guararé in Los Santos—the census-based estimates should take precedence.

[c] Absolute housing poverty index is defined by the percentage of persons in a district in excess of three per room.

[d] Relative housing poverty index is defined by the percentage of persons in excess of twice the median number of persons per room in the nation. The inference is taken from the relative poverty line as being half of the median income of the population concerned.

room). The former index rises to 50 percent in Santa Fé and 44 percent in San Francisco in Veraguas and lies in the twenties and thirties in most low-income districts.

Cost of Eliminating the Housing Shortage

What it will cost the nation to eliminate housing poverty is difficult to estimate, since physical amenities of various kinds are involved and the housing shortage calculated in this subsection measures only the number of rooms, without regard to their condition and precise location. Moreover, housing construction, urban renewal, and neighborhood development require expenditures on community facilities, public utilities, streets, commerical areas, government offices, access roads, and so on, in addition to tenements per se. Subject to these qualifications, costs were obtained from the Ministry of Housing, Republic of Panama. The MIPPE's cost estimates for a low-income home are significantly lower, about two-thirds of those of the Ministry of Housing. The cost of low-income housing estimated by USAID in connection with its project of privatization of public housing is close to that of the Ministry of Housing. According to the Ministry of Housing estimates, the capital cost of eliminating housing shortages comes to $480 million in metropolitan areas and $886 million in the country as a whole. The latter figure is approximately 26 percent of national income.

Overcrowding is not necessarily limited to poor families. But assuming that all the shortfall of housing occurs among the critically poor, their overcrowding can be eliminated by the construction of low-income homes at a cost of $537 million, net of the cost of community facilities, and so on. At a mortgage rate of 10 percent, this amounts to 75 percent of their incomes. Evidently this cost is astronomical for a poor family. Assuming that crowding extends to middle-income families also, the mortgage cost to private families is not exorbitant. The capital cost in the current state of the country's national and international indebtedness is, however, prohibitive.

In aggregate, the total income of the poor is $71.5 million, and the poverty gap is $71.7 million. Thus an annual flow of $71.7 million is needed to remove the nutritional deficiency of the critically poor and a one-time capital cost between $537 million (for home construction), and $886 million (home and public facilities and utilities) is needed to eliminate the housing poverty of all families. The mean per capita poverty gap is $186, and the mean per capita annual mortgage is between $93 and $140 (where the lower figure is two-thirds of the 10 percent of $537 divided by the critically poor population of 386,362 of table 6.3). This works out to a per capita income of $464 to $511 for food and housing needs, approximately 18 to

30 percent higher than the critical poverty line. Including clothing and medical necessities, the lower measure of poverty (1.5 times the critical poverty line; see chap. 5) thus seems to be more realistic than the upper measure (double the poverty line).

The present policy of the government of the Republic of Panama regarding public housing is to require 10 percent of the income of the allottee (in the monthly salary range of $150 to $120 in 1985) to be paid as mortgage to the National Mortgage Bank (the National Savings Bank in the case of Colón) for a period of thirty years. Evidently the subsidy embodied in this arrangement is several times the cost. This is made possible by social security funds and foreign loans in the past. For instance, 80 percent of the funds for the Don Bosco project consist of foreign loans.

These statistics concerning what is desirable may be compared with what exists. The families of the first and second deciles, with $178 and $448 per capita or $933 and $2,559 per family incomes, respectively, spend $9 and $24 on water and $33 and $96 on gas and electricity and live in homes whose imputed rental values are $42 and $226. The combined cost of all three items sums to 8.8 percent and 14.0 percent of the respective deciles' incomes, which is approximately one-sixth the cost of a low-income home estimated above and is roughly equal to what the Panamanian government currently requires low-income families living in publicly supplied homes to pay (10 percent of their incomes). This is a big order for the society to meet. In the current state of affairs, an uncrowded decent home for every Panamanian seems a remote possibility.

EDUCATIONAL CHARACTERISTICS OF THE POOR

Educational characteristics of those who are unemployed or underemployed and the related job characteristics will be studied in depth in chapter 9. Here we look at the educational characteristics of the poor whether unemployed or not.

Schooling of the Head of Household

The education of heads of households by age, sector, and decile is cross-tabulated in table 7.5. It is interesting to find that by virtue of nearly 100 percent enrollment of primary-school-age children for over a decade, there are only 2.3 percent among the "young" heads of households aged thirty-five or below who do not have primary-school education. At the same time, 10 percent of the "young" heads of the bottom decile's households have not completed any grade. Over 10 percent of the overall nation's "young"

Table 7.5   Education of Heads of Households by Poverty Strata and by Sex and Sector, 1983

Level of Education of Household Heads Aged over Thirty-five	Total	Number of Heads of Households by Decile[a]					
		1	2	3	4	5–9	10
Rural area							
Technical training	7,514	261	504	918	624	4,670	537
Total age >35	148,612	26,845	26,478	23,011	18,327	49,001	4,950
Primary	92,482	16,210	16,890	15,840	11,917	28,892	2,733
Secondary	7,743	396	166	568	844	5,085	684
Vocational	995	16	0	0	44	816	119
University	883	0	0	0	81	623	179
None	35,742	9,821	8,775	5,726	4,184	6,985	251
Technical training	10,767	402	647	877	1,257	6,600	984
Households without head	143	89	27	0	0	27	0

[a]National decile by households. The sample excludes Indian areas. The totals of various education classes of each category are likely to exceed the subtotals of each category, since vocational training and technical training may overlap formal school degrees. The levels of education classified here do not necessarily imply graduation. Rather, they mean some years of the given level from year one through its completion.

heads and over one-third of the tenth decile's "young" heads have university education, whereas only about half of 1 percent of the bottom decile's heads have college education.

For the poor, high school seems to be more important for employment and a more practical proposition than university education. High-school education is more crucial for getting out of urban poverty. The poor are very low here too. Only 8 percent of the bottom decile's "young" heads reach this level as against 95 percent among the tenth decile who finish high school, of whom 25 percent take up jobs, while the rest continue for university and technical education. Only 22 percent of "young" heads in the bottom decile and 28 percent of those in the second decile have reached high school. What is puzzling in this regard is why a quarter of the heads of the bottom two deciles who have high-school education are critically poor. A possible explanation is unemployment. As we will see in chapter 9 on unemployment/underemployment and poverty, the highest incidence of unemployment is among urban young people with completed or partial high-school education. Note, however, that those with high-school education in the bottom two deciles form only a little over 1 percent of total urban labor force. It remains to be seen whether the incidence of unemployment is high among the secondary workers of upper deciles or primary workers of lower deciles. For that analysis, see chapter 9.

In the above-thirty-five age group (which, for short, I will call the "old-ish" generation), as expected, the educational levels of the heads of poor households are lower than those of their counterparts in the "young" group. Here 34 percent of those in the bottom decile and 29 percent in the second decile of the nation as a whole have not completed any school grade. At the same time, even among the "oldish" group of Panama, 62 percent in rural areas have completed at least some years of primary school (and an additional 13 percent have gone on for higher education), and the same percentage in urban areas have completed high school or more. This is the generation that went to school before the 1960s. Thus, even before the 1970s' concerted effort for universal primary-school education, high proportions of Panamanians had completed primary-school. Secondary education is a different story. Only 1 percent of the "oldish" heads of the bottom two deciles in rural areas and 8 percent in urban areas have reached that level.

In summary, Panama has solved its primary-school problem except in inaccessible and tribal areas. What is now needed is to turn to high-school education, for in today's state of technology it is rare for anyone without high-school education to find a decent job in the modern sector.

Generation Gaps in Schooling

The estimates of the schooling of heads of households and their parents indicate that for the nation as a whole, whereas only 2 percent of the "young" heads are without any schooling, 32 percent of their fathers and 34 percent of their mothers reportedly had no schooling. The national figures for university education have gone up from 3 percent for fathers and 1 percent for mothers to 12 percent for heads. Between poor and nonpoor, in the tenth decile, secondary-education levels have gone up from 39 percent for fathers and 30 percent for mothers to approximately 61 percent for both parents, and university levels from 14 percent for fathers and 5 percent for mothers to 34 percent for the current generation's "young" heads.

In schooling, therefore, there is at least a two-generation gap between the poor and the upper income classes. The poor have made impressive progress in primary education, whereas the rich have gone beyond it and have moved en masse into high school and university education. There are no prospects for the poor to reach those levels within a generation, as judged from the past trends and the magnitude of the gaps involved, unless special national effort is made. A few statistics for male heads should substantiate the point. (See table below.)

	Bottom Decile			Top Decile		
Level of Education	Education of Parents of Heads (%)	Education of Heads Age<36 (%)	Expected Education for Children (%)	Education of Parents of Heads (%)	Education of Heads Age<36 (%)	Expected Education for Children (%)
Primary	27	77	48	28 (34)	5	2
Secondary	1	8	37	39 (30)	61	9
University	0	1	10	14 (5)	34	84

Source: Table 7.5 and data from the National Socioeconomic Survey, 1983. The figures in parentheses are for mother of the head. The statistics for "expected education for children" are from an opinion question in the National Socioeconomic Survey, not tabulated in any table of this chapter.

The progress has been impressive in both groups, but the gap between the schooling of the poor and the nonpoor has widened. Primary education, which is negatively related to fertility (see chap. 12), has expanded demonstrably among the poor, while secondary and university education, which is necessary for urban modern-sector jobs (see chap. 9), has rapidly increased among the nonpoor but has made little impact on the poor.

Although the large lack in schooling that exists among the poor is lamentable, it also offers the society an opportunity to take strides in closing the education gap and thereby possibly reducing poverty. The goal that now seems in order is high-school education for the children of the poor.

Dropouts

We have seen that the poor heads of households have low schooling, and their expectations about their children's schooling are low too. We have also seen that the school enrollment rate is almost 100 percent for ten-year-olds but that it declines from the apex at a rapid rate on both sides of age ten. A natural next step is to verify who these dropouts and late drop-ins are. The results are as expected: the droputs are mainly among poor families and districts. Of the twelve and under school-age group not attending school, 40 percent are in the bottom decile, 25 percent in the second decile, and 15 percent in the third decile—that is, the bottom 30 percent of households account for 80 percent of school-age children not attending school.

Table 7.6 reports the bottom fourteen districts on the basis of low school enrollment among ten-year-olds. By and large these are also low per capita income districts (see the last column). An exception is Boquete, where the relatively low rate of school enrollment is probably due to the high seasonal demand on coffee farms in this resort hill town. We see that the enrollment for the districts noted in table 7.6 is the highest for ten-year-olds among all age groups, but at 79 percent enrollment it is nineteen percentage points lower than the national average of 98 percent.

Dropping out is bad, but late dropping in is also bad, especially because it is one of the causes of subsequent dropout. There is ample evidence here that both late starters and dropouts are from poor families and low-income districts. The overall dropout rate among the bottom two deciles is 71 percent in the thirteen to eighteen age group and 17 percent in the six to twelve age group.

Conclusions and Implications

In summary, Panama has solved its primary-school problem except for very poor families in a few inaccessible areas. High-school education and pre-school education for the poor, however, remain neglected.

There are wide disparities between the schooling of poor and nonpoor heads of households. While more than 60 percent of the urban areas' household heads aged below thirty-six have high-school education or higher, in the bottom two deciles over two-thirds in urban areas and nearly 95 percent in rural areas have not reached that level. In education, there is at least a two-generation gap between the poor and the upper income class. The poor have made impressive progress in primary education, while the rich have gone beyond it and have moved en masse to high-school and university education. There appear to be few prospects for the poor to attain the education levels of the well-off groups of today within a generation unless something extraordinary is done about it. The education gap between the rich and the poor has widened somewhat. Primary education has been found to reduce fertility in Panama, but it is not enough to land nonpoor jobs.

Expected or desired schooling and intergenerational changes in schooling levels between the poor and the nonpoor reveal that the expected schooling of the children of poor families is no higher than that attained by the parents of nonpoor heads.[3] High rates of "wastage" (repeating

3. A rural-urban comparison indicates that the expectations or aspirations of the urban heads of the bottom decile for their children's education are close to those of the rural heads of the top decile, as is apparent from the following statistics:

	Bottom Decile Urban Heads (%)	Top Decile Rural Heads (%)
Primary	9	18
Secondary	37	37
University	42	39

Table 7.6 Proportion of Children Not Attending School, by Age, for Selected Low-Enrollment Districts, 1983

District	Percentage of Children Not Attending School by Age in Years								Per Capita Family Income ($)
	5	6	7	8	9	10	11	12	
Chiriquí Grande	0.98	0.70	0.56	0.48	0.49	0.50	0.55	0.57	NA
Barú	0.85	0.29	0.12	0.12	0.13	0.12	0.22	0.16	1,980
Boquerón	1.00	0.36	0.29	0.14	0.25	0.17	0.33	0.17	798
Boquete	0.78	0.37	0.13	0.16	0.16	0.23	0.20	0.19	1,985
Bugaba	0.94	0.34	0.12	0.21	0.14	0.10	0.20	0.19	1,125
San Félix	0.91	0.40	0.39	0.33	0.24	0.23	0.26	0.20	799
San Lorenzo	0.98	0.58	0.51	0.38	0.29	0.25	0.41	0.48	NA
Tolé	0.99	0.63	0.38	0.31	0.20	0.26	0.23	0.33	NA
Los Pozos	0.98	0.62	0.36	0.30	0.23	0.18	0.16	0.36	410
Pesé	0.93	0.44	0.28	0.18	0.19	0.16	0.13	0.21	703
Guararé	0.88	0.40	0.16	0.20	0.07	0.16	0.19	0.31	1,465
Pocrí	0.64	0.40	0.28	0.22	0.28	0.19	0.21	0.51	1,055
Chepo	0.94	0.30	0.24	0.18	0.16	0.14	0.20	0.17	1,044
San Blas	0.86	0.53	0.57	0.37	0.39	0.31	0.31	0.38	NA
Mean of districts above	0.95	0.45	0.31	0.26	0.23	0.21	0.26	0.31	1,090
National mean	0.74	0.34	0.17	0.07	0.06	0.02	0.08	0.14	1,766

Source: Tables supplied by the Ministry of Education, Republic of Panama.
Note: Indians are included. These fourteen districts account for approximately 14 percent of school-age children. NA = not available.

grades) and dropout prevail among pupils from poor families. The repetition of grades reaches 36 percent among the below-thirteen age group of the bottom decile. The peak enrollment (98 percent) occurs at age ten, implying that some children (who happen to be mostly from poor, including Indian, homes) do not start school till that age. The dropping out begins at age eleven, increases rapidly to 14 percent for twelve-year-olds, and rises exponentially through teenage years. According to the reported reasons for not attending school, about one-third of the dropouts from poor homes reflect a lack of preparedness for school. Children from poor homes have significantly lower grades than the mean (not reported in tabular form). Several pieces of evidence from the educational characteristics of the poor from this section—widespread "wastage," high dropout rates from primary through secondary schools, low grades, and less motivation than among children from nonpoor families—thus suggest that a major source of low educational achievement by poor children is the lack of *preparedness for primary school.* A possible key to closing the two-generation educational gap between the well-off and the poor, among other remedies, thus, is a head-start program for children from poor families. The productivity of preschool education in preparing and motivating children from poor families has been found to be much higher than for children from well-off families.

Preschool Education for Poor Children

As a program to break the cycle of permanent poverty and promote long-term growth,[4] preschool education shows promise. Poverty, underemployment, low-productivity occupations, high fertility and child mortality, high child- and spouse-dependency rates, and one-income families are strongly associated with low schooling levels. Over 31 percent of children are in critical poverty compared with 20 percent of persons in critical poverty. The percentage of children not attending school is much higher in poor families than in nonpoor families. We have also seen that the high dropout rate, relatively low grades, high rate of repetition of school grades, and low motivation for school among the children of poor families are largely due to poor preparedness for school, especially for primary school. One of the most effective measures for school preparedness for poor children is preschool education.

4. This policy was streamlined in collaboration with three education researchers, who wrote their reports as short-term consultants of the Critical Poverty Project of Panama, namely C. K. Sahota (1983) and Bauch and Rodriguez (1984). Sahota surveyed the research on the topic that supported my hypothesis about the most productive investment in the children of poor families. The latter two scholars worked on giving a practical shape to the policy and prepared a five-year plan for preschool education of poor children.

These results are consistent with the findings of experiments on pre-school education with control and noncontrol groups of children in other countries. For instance, in the United States the Head Start (preschool) Program for the children of poor families was started as a part of the Democratic administration's War on Poverty in the late 1960s. With a view to ensuring a high quality of preschool education and evaluating the effectiveness of the War on Poverty, eleven models were developed at various universities in America to carry out separate controlled experiments and generate panel data for analysis. In 1975 the developers of these eleven models formed the Consortium for Longitudinal Studies. The results of their experiments and analysis started coming out in 1983. They provide strong evidence that preschool education of children from poor families significantly reduces the high-school dropout rate and increases the probability of completing high school with significantly improved grades and scores. Preschool education has been found to lessen teenage pregnancy (another cause of school dropout), to diminish crime, and to increase the will and capacity of these persons to seek and hold nonpoor jobs. The groups that attended preschool were more independent and used less public assistance and welfare.

The results above are now considered more or less conclusive and are well documented. What is not yet widely known is the finding of research that school quality benefits the less able and poor children more than the more able pupils and that preschool education has considerably higher productivity for poor and less gifted children than for more able and non-poor children. Students who need the most help in preparing for school are the ones who gain the most from high-quality intervention at the pre-school level.

OCCUPATIONAL CHARACTERISTICS

Economically Active Persons and Unemployment

The mean rate of economically active persons is 44 percent. In rural areas the participation rate is eleven percentage points lower than in urban areas for those aged twenty-five to fifty-nine and significantly higher among teenagers and elderly people. The higher rate for the latter age groups reflects poverty and the absence of old-age pensions in rural areas. The lower participation rate in rural areas for the adult age groups twenty-five to fifty-nine reflects the preponderance of home production by women. To the extent that home production substitutes for market or field work, real incomes in rural areas, and pari passu real incomes of the poor, are understated.

The rate of unemployment comes out to 9.7 percent. An interesting phenomenon of unemployment by age is that in the age groups ten to fourteen and fifteen to nineteen, 21.7 percent and 35.7 percent, respectively, in the urban sector are unemployed against 14.7 percent and 20.6 percent in the rural sector. The rural unemployment rate is significantly lower than that in the urban sector, despite the fact that a much higher proportion of rural teenagers become economically active. In the age group ten to fourteen, however, percentages are somewhat misleading: fewer than 400 urban youngsters report being unemployed, whereas in rural areas, with 42.86 percent of the nation's economically active persons, nearly 1,000 are unemployed. In the age group fifteen to nineteen, the number of unemployed in urban areas outstrips the corresponding number in rural areas. The highest age-specific unemployment rate prevails in age group fifteen to nineteen in urban areas (35.7 percent) and the next highest in age group twenty to twenty-four (22.4 percent), also in urban areas. The relative differences are even higher among new entrants in the labor force. Two provisional conclusions following from these calculations are worth noting: unemployment is less a problem of poor (rural) areas than of nonpoor (urban) areas; and since unemployment is low in age groups twenty-five to fifty-nine, most of the unemployed are probably not primary workers (heads of households) but rather are secondary workers (spouses, young children, and others without dependents who can themselves depend upon family when not employed). This analysis is pushed further in chapter 9.

Place of Work

The agricultural sector, with 8.3 percent of disposable income (see table 5.3), provides jobs to 27.2 percent of the work force. Over 93 percent of the bottom decile's and 74 percent of the second decile's labor force depends for subsistence on agriculture. As against this, only 4 percent of the tenth decile's work force is in agriculture, and 96 percent is in the nonagricultural sector.[5]

Between 4 percent (in the agricultural sector) and 8 percent (in the nonagricultural sector) of workers engage in economic activities on the streets (as vendors, peddlers, casual laborers, shoe shiners, lottery-ticket agents, car washers, and similar categories). Some of these workers make good middle-class incomes; others can hardly make ends meet. A fifth of the work force of the nonagricultural sector's bottom two deciles works

5. Recall that these are national deciles—that is, the decile cutoff lines are based on national mean per capita incomes of each decile without adjustment for unequal sectoral mean incomes, public services, community facilities, cost-of-living indexes, and other differences. Thus 30.6 percent and 25.4 percent of the agricultural sector's labor force are in the first and second deciles, respectively, as against a paltry 0.8 percent and 3.4 percent of the nonagricultural sector's labor force.

Table 7.7 Principal Activities of Economically Active Persons by Sex, 1983

Economic Activity	Total	Decile 1	2	3	4	5–9	10
Total							
Absolute	610,598	54,394	57,656	53,231	56,079	318,639	70,509
%	—	100.0	100.0	100.0	100.0	100.0	100.0
Sundry activities	1,882	0.2	0.3	0.7	0.7	0.2	0.1
Agriculture	181,315	91.7	74.4	48.0	30.7	13.1	5.8
Mining	738	0.0	0.0	0.2	0.1	0.1	0.3
Manufacturing	54,968	1.7	4.2	9.2	11.2	11.2	6.8
Electricity	11,424	0.0	0.2	1.2	2.3	2.4	2.5
Construction	36,125	0.6	3.6	8.0	8.5	6.8	4.6
Commerce	84,135	1.3	5.9	12.3	13.4	17.7	13.4
Transport and communications	35,120	0.8	1.5	3.5	5.5	7.5	6.9
Financial establishments	22,064	0.1	0.4	0.7	1.8	3.9	11.2
Services	179,505	3.6	9.4	16.2	25.7	36.4	47.1
Canal Area	3,232	0.0	0.1	0.0	0.1	0.7	1.3
Male							
Absolute	338,984	33,688	35,127	32,236	34,690	167,744	35,499
%	—	100.0	100.0	100.0	100.0	100.0	100.0
Sundry activities	502	0.3	0.0	0.2	0.3	0.1	0.0
Agriculture	113,511	91.6	73.6	50.1	29.3	16.4	8.5
Mining	511	0.0	0.1	0.3	0.0	0.1	0.6
Manufacturing	31,486	1.5	4.7	10.9	11.7	11.3	8.1
Electricity	7,167	0.0	0.1	1.1	3.0	3.0	1.9
Construction	24,355	0.6	4.7	8.7	11.0	8.2	6.0
Commerce	42,354	0.8	5.5	10.1	11.4	16.6	14.5
Transport and communications	21,249	0.7	1.7	3.7	6.6	8.4	7.8
Financial establishments	11,869	0.2	0.6	0.8	1.6	3.8	13.6
Services	83,269	4.3	8.8	14.1	24.9	31.0	38.1
Canal Area	2,711	0.0	0.2	0.0	0.2	1.1	1.9
Female							
Absolute	271,614	20,706	22,529	20,995	21,389	150,895	35,100
%	—	100.0	100.0	100.0	100.0	100.0	100.0
Sundry activities	1,380	0.0	0.7	1.5	1.4	0.4	0.0
Agriculture	67,804	91.8	75.7	44.4	32.9	9.5	3.0
Mining	227	0.0	0.0	0.0	0.2	0.1	0.0
Manufacturing	23,482	2.2	3.4	7.0	10.2	11.0	5.5
Electricity	4,257	0.0	0.3	1.3	1.2	1.7	3.1
Construction	11,860	0.6	1.9	7.0	4.5	5.2	3.3
Commerce	41,781	2.1	6.6	15.7	16.8	19.0	12.4
Transport and communications	13,871	0.9	1.2	3.3	3.7	6.5	6.1
Financial establishments	10,195	0.0	0.0	0.6	2.0	4.1	9.8
Services	96,236	2.4	10.2	0.0	27.1	42.3	56.2
Canal Area	521	0.0	0.0	0.0	0.0	0.2	0.7

138

on the streets. The mean for the nation is 7.1 percent. This percentage declines as incomes rise and is less than 4 percent for the top decile (see column percentages). The rural sector's street workers form only 4 percent of the total rural work force and depict an inverted parabolic curve. In urban areas the result seems to support the typical migration pattern, according to which new migrants, along with local unskilled laborers, are unable to find regular employment and end up in large numbers as street workers. Most of them are among the critically poor of the urban sector. In rural areas, on the other hand, there is probably very little street work for the very poor, although there are relatively more jobs for those who have some capital (e.g., tools) or are young and hardy enough with their machetes to make rural middle-decile incomes. In general, the more primitive an economy, the more economic value muscle power commands. Rural poverty is thus likely to strike the old and the weak more mercilessly than does urban poverty. This phenomenon reflects upon one more aspect of the life cycle theory, inasmuch as the noted parabolic shape of the street work across deciles is similar to the shape of the muscle power in one's life, remembering that the well-off at the top deciles have little need to work on the streets.

Household work depicts little variation among deciles in rural areas. In urban areas it follows a trend similar to that for street work. In the upper-half deciles, household work is practically extinct, indicating the prevalence of two-income families. One-income families are found mainly in the bottom two deciles, a phenomenon that will also find support from an alternative analysis in chapter 10.

Principal Activities

The participation of the poor in principal activities occurs in agriculture, as may be seen from table 7.7. For all practical purposes, the poor are absent from the top-ranked economic activities: Canal Area, financial establishments, electricity, mining, and transport and communications. The very well-off (top decile) economically active cluster in services but also have more than their fair share in financial establishments and commerce. The poor too have a perceptible presence in services (though barely in commerce), indicating that the service sector is a patchwork of low-status jobs and upper-status jobs. Note that since different activities have widely disparate shares of the labor force, the relevant comparisons of shares are between different deciles in a given activity. The most important result of this brief analysis, which is corroborated by other analyses, is that an increase in the productivity of poor workers is practically synonymous with increasing the productivity of agriculture. This topic—productivity-increasing innovations in agriculture—will, accordingly, deserve our special attention in the policy chapter (chap. 14).

The same picture emerges when workers are cross-classified according to principal occupation instead of principal activity (industry), except that in urban areas personal services contain multitudes of poor workers. In the nation as a whole, agriculture and personal services together account for 42 percent of the overall labor force. Indeed, 94.8 percent, 81.9 percent, and 58.8 percent, respectively, of the first, second, and third deciles' manpower are in the stated two occupations.

Small Business

A very high majority of low-productivity, poor-family workers in urban areas are found in small establishments. A possible program that can create nonpoor jobs in the urban sector is the expansion and technological improvement of small business, where the bulk of low-paid personal services are provided. Small business is thus the third major area, along with productivity-increasing agricultural research and preschool education, that receives special attention in the dozen or so antipoverty policies recommended in this study.

Occupational Mobility

For a family to be poor in one generation is unfortunate enough. For it to be poor generation after generation is a disaster of high magnitude. In studies of poverty and income distribution, therefore, it is useful to measure the degree of mobility in a given society. The present survey uses two types of data for this purpose: data on incomes for two generations, namely, earnings of working children eighteen or older by earnings of parents, and data on occupations of three generations, namely, occupations of the head, the head's father and mother, and the head's working children eighteen and older. Certain additional statistics, such as those on education across three generations, serve as explanatory variables. In this section I do a brief analysis of cross-tabulations. An econometric analysis will be done in chapter 10.

In table 7.8, occupations are arranged from high rank (in terms of a weighted index of wage rate and education) to low rank. The table is a cross-classification of heads of households (columns) against their fathers (rows). We see from the last column and the last two rows that the children (the present-generation heads) of 32.3 percent of fathers have moved up from low-rank occupations to higher-rank occupations in comparison with their fathers, while the children of 14.1 percent of fathers have moved down. These are gross percentages. There is a net upward movement of

18.2 percent during one generation. It is possible, however, that some occupations have been upgraded or that higher-rank occupations have expanded in relation to lower-rank occupations. Upward mobility is meaningful all the same, because upgrading of an occupation in all likelihood signifies higher wages. It may, for instance, be seen that the work force of managers and administrators has risen from 1.5 percent (fathers) to 5.25 percent (children), office employees from 0.74 percent to 4.75 percent, and salesmen from 4.12 percent to 5.23 percent. On the other hand, the farm work force has been reduced by more than 50 percent in one generation,[6] and, surprisingly, professional and technical personnel have been so categorized that their share has fallen from 19.95 percent (fathers) to 7.85 percent (sons), apparently because of reclassification or error in declared professional/technical occupations.

Looked at from a different angle, only 4 percent of total managers and administrators among the present heads of households are found to be the children of managers and administrators compared with 36 percent of total professionals whose fathers were also professionals. Those heads of households who are classified as managers and administrators have expanded by 350 percent and employers by 640 percent, while (recalling a possible reclassification or error in declaration of their occupation) professionals have shrunk to 39 percent. Only 40 percent of the present heads of households in agriculture are sons of farmers, and they form 87 percent of all farm households. Thus the fraction of those in agriculture who do not come from farm families is very small.

The mobility ratios dwindle as one moves up toward top-ranked occupations, evidently because as one approaches the top of the ladder one finds it more and more difficult to climb higher. Nevertheless, the calculations reveal clear-cut evidence for high upward mobility from low-rank economic activities. It is not certain, however, whether the movement from low-productivity occupations involves mainly high-paid workers of those occupations or applies across the board to all levels.

A conclusion of this section is that there is a high degree of interoccupational mobility in Panama. In relative terms, low-productivity occupations are shrinking and high-productivity occupations are expanding, and, low-productivity workers are probably moving to jobs in higher-paid economic areas. That is a good result insofar as permanent poverty is concerned.

---

6. Note that the numerical artifact of the cross-tabulation in which fathers exactly equal the heads of households is not of any significance. Each male head of household was asked about his own occupation and his father's. A father who has more than one child will be reported by all of them. That double-counting of fathers does not vitiate the results of occupational mobility.

Table 7.8 Intergenerational Mobility: Male Heads of Households and Their Fathers, 1983

Occupation of Father of Head of Household	Occupation of Head of Household												
	Not Specified	Not Working	Managerial and Administrative	Professional	Office Employment	Transport Workers	Salespersons	Artisans and Operatives	Services	Other Artisans and Operatives	Casual Workers	Agricultural and Related Workers	Total
	Absolute Numbers												
Not specified and not working	0	210	0	80	80	80	71	196	80	0	0	0	791
Managerial and administrative workers	0	1,313	921	1,199	778	198	657	870	378	36	50	106	6,506
Workers in occupations not identified	0	80	0	80	79	61	0	160	0	0	0	0	560
Professional, technical, and related workers	1,542	24,062	6,379	12,242	5,716	4,855	3,661	10,688	6,392	1,136	2,039	7,614	86,226
Office employees	0	704	302	670	681	80	156	173	282	79	80	0	3,207
Transport workers	141	2,614	921	1,282	1,315	2,470	963	1,566	1,096	291	287	192	13,140
Salespersons	293	3,154	2,765	2,407	1,139	757	2,752	1,630	1,443	189	193	1,125	17,843
Artisans, operatives, and related workers	383	8,788	3,439	4,226	2,765	1,851	2,671	8,422	3,005	342	666	1,496	38,054
Workers in personal services	133	4,589	1,808	2,698	1,311	1,650	1,068	3,873	2,608	489	912	2,029	23,168
Other artisans and operatives	0	1,256	345	569	458	401	224	1,348	765	314	172	265	6,117
Casual workers	103	1,876	545	253	643	450	221	1,002	712	156	587	124	6,672
Agricultural and related workers	1,720	49,941	5,278	8,258	5,596	7,910	10,213	20,836	18,492	4,424	5,558	92,298	230,524
	Percentage												
Not specified and not working	0	0.05	0.00	0.20	0.02	0.02	0.02	0.05	0.02	0.00	0.00	0.00	0.18
Managerial and admin...													

	not identified	Professional, technical, and related workers	Office workers	Transport workers	Salespersons	Artisans and operatives	Workers in personal services	Other artisans and operatives	Casual workers			Agricultural and related workers	%
not identified	0.00	0.02	0.00	0.02	0.02	0.01	0.00	0.04	0.00	0.00	0.00	0.00	0.11
Professional, technical, and related workers	1.47	5.56	2.83	1.32	1.12	0.85	2.47	1.48	0.26	0.47	1.76		19.95
Office workers	0.07	0.16	0.15	0.16	0.02	0.04	0.04	0.07	0.02	0.02	0.00		0.74
Transport workers	0.21	0.60	0.30	0.30	0.57	0.22	0.36	0.25	0.07	0.07	0.04		3.04
Salespersons	0.64	0.73	0.56	0.26	0.17	0.64	0.38	0.33	0.04	0.04	0.26		4.12
Artisans and operatives	0.79	2.03	0.98	0.64	0.43	0.62	1.95	0.69	0.08	0.15	0.35		8.29
Workers in personal services	0.42	1.06	0.62	0.30	0.38	0.25	0.89	0.60	0.11	0.21	0.47		5.35
Other artisans and operatives	0.08	0.29	0.13	0.11	0.09	0.05	0.31	0.18	0.07	0.04	0.06		1.41
Casual workers	0.13	0.43	0.04	0.15	0.10	0.05	0.23	0.16	0.04	0.14	0.03		1.54
Agricultural and related workers	0.40	11.54	1.22	1.91	1.29	1.83	1.36	4.81	4.27	1.02	1.28	21.33	5.35
Total	0.40	11.54	1.22	1.91	1.29	1.83	1.36	4.81	4.27	1.02	1.28	21.33	53.26
Number	4,305	98,585	22,703	33,964	20,561	20,763	22,657	50,764	35,253	7,456	10,544	105,253	432,812
%	0.99	22.78	5.25	7.85	4.75	4.80	5.23	11.73	8.15	1.72	2.44	24.32	100.00

Mobility Ratios

Diagonal/column total = proportion of fathers whose children stayed in ancestral occupations	0.14	0.14	0.21	0.19	0.16	0.22	0.11	0.05	0.09	0.40	—
Diagonal/row total = proportion of children who stayed in ancestral occupations	0.04	0.36	0.03	0.12	0.12	0.17	0.07	0.04	0.06	0.87	—
Row total/column total = ratio of children to that of fathers	3.50	0.39	6.40	1.60	1.30	1.30	1.50	1.20	1.60	0.46	—
Column of SW triangle/column total = proportion of fathers whose children moved up	0.00	0.07	0.30	0.27	0.40	0.39	0.53	0.67	0.60	0.38	0.323
Columns of NE triangle/column total = proportion of fathers whose children moved down	0.82	0.69	0.34	0.16	0.25	0.15	0.14	0.07	0.02	0.00	0.141

CHARACTERISTICS OF THE UNEMPLOYED

An intensive microeconomic analysis of possible interrelation between unemployment, underemployment, and poverty is done in chapter 9. Here
I will note some macro characteristics of unemployment for the year 1979,
estimated from the 1979 household survey by Correa (1984):

36 percent of unemployed men and 46 percent of unemployed women
are new entrants to the labor force;

66 percent of unemployed men and 63 percent of unemployed women
are below age twenty-five;

33 percent of unemployed men and 19 percent of unemployed women
are heads of households;

81 percent of unemployed men and 97 percent of unemployed women
are in the employee category;

6.7 percent of men and 13.5 percent of women are unemployed;

26 percent of unemployed men work in construction or commerce, and
54 percent of unemployed women work in commerce or services;

25 percent of unemployed men work as artisans or operators, while 48
percent of unemployed women work in personal services;

mean years of secondary school completed by unemployed men and
women are 1.4 and 2.0, respectively;

65 percent of unemployed men have searched for jobs for less than six
months, whereas 52 percent of unemployed women have searched for
one year or more.

In summary, the incidence of unemployment falls heavily on young
persons without experience who are not yet heads of households; on those
with mean education of one to two years of high school; and on women
more than men. About half of the unemployed women list personal services
as their occupations, and over a third of unemployed men are categorized
as artisans or operators. While the unemployed in personal services and
probably also in the artisan and operator category are likely to be in the
informal sector, there is little to indicate that unemployment hurts the
poor, at least not relatively more than the nonpoor. In chapter 9 we will
delve deeper into this aspect of unemployment to understand who the
unemployed really are; what relation, if any, exists between unemployment, underemployment, and poverty; and what associations are discernible between unemployed and employed primary workers and unemployed
and employed secondary workers.

SPATIAL CHARACTERISTICS OF THE POOR

Spatial poverty is more easily identified than interfamily poverty. Regional development programs and antipoverty projects are also easier to target than programs addressed to chosen classes. Usually a high degree of spill-ins and spillovers of regional development processes is also recognized. Interprovince poverty has been characterized in the preceding sections. Here I present district-level poverty maps. As I stated earlier, data are available for fifty-nine of the sixty-six districts of the country.

Poverty Maps

Maps, in a way, are a relief from drab tables, charts, and other arrays of numbers. Poverty maps present a spatial ordering of various indicators of poverty, leading to insights that often cannot be gained from numbers and graphs without mental strain. They can also depict the quality and intensity of linkages, development processes, and so on. Essentially, maps are a way of characterizing regions, adding a spatial dimension.

Maps have their limitations too. They cannot represent information by social strata. The eye view (as the primary organ of perception of mapped information) fares unfavorably with the mental view in terms of handling a number of strata. Traditionally, maps use no more than five symbols to show five classes or values of indexes. Above that number the eye tends to lose perspective. Maps are not the right instruments to deduce rela-tionships between the information of one map and that of another. Nor do they reveal why some districts are different from others. In brief, they are to some extent a substitute for cross-tabulations but not for econometric work.

Maps are employed to bring out implications or suggestions for reme-dying poverty through specific sectoral and regional programs (schools, health clinics, roads, off-farm jobs, etc.) instead of programs aimed at persons of different income classes. The conceptual base for the mapping methodology is the so-called central place theory, whose tools of analysis consist of urban-rural linkages, growth centers, and service or market towns. The focus or bias of central place theorists in general is—but does not have to be—toward investment in industrial-urban centers as growth or service nodes to provide markets for goods and factors of the hinterland. The development of the hinterland as such is seen largely through the trickle-down effect of the expansion and efficiency of markets for goods and factors in urban-industrial centers, along with physical linkages through roads and other means of communication, and leads to a general neglect of direct investment in technology and human capital in the hinterland. I will not present poverty maps here but will report the results of the maps

Table 7.9 Principal Components Analysis: Mean Values and Standard Deviations of Thirty-seven Poverty Indexes, National Socioeconomic Survey, 1983

Variable	Definition	Mean	Standard Deviation
FWT	Farms without title (%)	82.67	10.46
OFFS	Farms without off-farm income (%)	52.07	16.10
IPTS	Medical attention index	25.85	19.61
IVID	Life index	49.56	14.55
IVIV	Housing index	59.54	17.85
ISSOC	Social security index	20.92	20.23
IURBA	Urbanization index	26.15	17.50
TC	Rate of population growth during 1970–80	1.64	2.05
IPND	Density of population (per square mile)	37.68	27.04
PNA	Nonagricultural population (% share)	43.91	24.12
XMORINF	Infant mortality rate	75.78	12.63
INST	Medical institutions (number)	19.45	19.84
DEFCM	Deaths with medical certificate (% of total deaths)	58.13	22.18
NAP	Births with medical attention	63.75	27.69
IMED	Medical doctors (number per 1,000 population)	24.14	25.10
IODO	Dentists (number per 1,000 population)	29.66	22.55
IENF	Nurses (number per 1,000 population)	23.88	27.49
IPAR	Paramedics (number per 1,000 population)	26.17	25.71
DCXS	Road density (km per 100 km^2)	13.52	14.70
LE	Life expectancy (years)	53.31	12.85
NFUT	Number of firms using tractors (%)	25.10	34.63
IAPTA	Irrigated area (%)	1.03	2.45
XGINI	Gini coefficient (index)	27.17	14.13
XDESN	Child malnutrition (% of children)	79.26	10.67
XHCRITI	Number of critically poor (%)	63.86	21.78
MEDUC	Mean education level of community	4.46	1.74
XEMPR	Employment rate in rural areas	93.43	6.23
XEMPU	Employment rate in urban areas	84.21	9.24
XEMPT	Employment rate total	90.72	10.43
XSHARE	Share of agricultural income (%)	74.67	20.69
FARMS	Households receiving technical assistance (%)	5.03	6.48
TAXES	Taxes paid as % of income	0.99	0.83
CARS	Automobiles per 100 households	9.38	8.80
MARKET	Ratio of agricultural sales to total	74.25	21.64
XOLD	Ratio of old-age population to total	92.24	2.84
FERTIL	Fertilizer per hectare	20.40	27.41
XPHOC	Shortage of homes (%)	64.67	14.90

Note: Thirty-seven variables, fifty-eight observations.

of per capita income. They are based on five categories of per capita income: the top category with income exceeding \$2,000, or 13 percent above the national per capita income or mean income; the next to the top, between the mean income and the top category's cutoff line; the middle category, between the mean and half of the mean; the next between half and a quarter of the mean (almost equal to the critical poverty line); and the bottom category, below a quarter of the mean income (below the critical poverty line). Only three districts, all growth centers, fall in the top category, but they account for one-third of the population. In the second category fall Colón, Boquete, Las Tablas, Arraiján, and San Miguelito, which are either growth centers or market towns. Combined with the top category, they account for 46 percent of the population. Seven districts, all in the bottom-income province, Veraguas, fall below the national critical poverty line and have 4.5 percent of the country's population.

Let me point out that since district mean incomes are aggregates, they conceal within-district poverty in that the mean incomes of the hinterland are invariably lower the poorer the center-hinterland linkages.

Principal Components Analysis of Poverty Indicators

A number of poverty maps based on different indicators were prepared, but they are closely correlated, and the patterns of most are similar. Therefore, instead of presenting maps one could either use one or two key maps to convey the information or, preferably, use a weighted index of all relevant indicators of poverty. A scientific method of weighting individual indicators to obtain a single composite index is the principal components procedure, which I have employed in this study. The results obtained here summarize over three dozen poverty indicators, defined such that high values indicate being well-off or low poverty or a desirable state, and low values reflect worse poverty or an undesirable state. For consistency, therefore, the following variables were redefined as described: XMORINF—100-MORINF; XMCRITI—100-MCRITI; XUEMPU—100-UEMPO; XPHOC—100-PHCC; XGINI—100-GINI; XUEMPL—100-UEMPL; XSHARE—100-SHARE; XDESN—100-DESN; XUEMPR—100-UEMPR; XOLD—100-OLD, where the symbols are as defined in table 7.9.

The results of the principal components analysis also show how these variables interact across districts. Each component is a linear combination of original variables, with coefficients equal to the eigenvectors of the correlation matrix. The eigenvectors are customarily taken with unit norm. When this is done, the first principal component has the largest variance of any unit-length linear combination of the observed variables. In the context of this chapter, the first principal component accounts for the

Table 7.10 Principal Components Analysis: Eigenvalues and Standardized Variances of Thirty-seven Principal Components, District Data, 1983

Principal Component	Eigenvalue	Difference	Proportion	Cumulative
PRIN1	14.0350	10.5709	0.3793	0.3793
PRIN2	3.4641	0.9525	0.0936	0.4729
PRIN3	2.5116	0.5193	0.0678	0.5408
PRIN4	1.9920	0.1046	0.0538	0.5946
PRIN5	1.8875	0.2553	0.0510	0.6456
PRIN6	1.6322	0.0441	0.0441	0.6898
PRIN7	1.5881	0.3039	0.0429	0.7327
PRIN8	1.2842	0.2304	0.0347	0.7674
PRIN9	1.0537	0.1368	0.0284	0.7959
PRIN10	0.9169	0.1255	0.0247	0.8207
PRIN11	0.7913	0.0612	0.0213	0.8420
PRIN12	0.7301	0.0597	0.0197	0.8618
PRIN13	0.6704	0.0749	0.0181	0.8799
PRIN14	0.5955	0.0878	0.0160	0.8960
PRIN15	0.5076	0.4860	0.0137	0.9097
PRIN16	0.4589	0.0461	0.0124	0.9221
PRIN17	0.4128	0.0354	0.0111	0.9333
PRIN18	0.3773	0.0497	0.0102	0.9435
PRIN19	0.3276	0.0766	0.0088	0.9523
PRIN20	0.2509	0.0131	0.0067	0.9591
PRIN21	0.2378	0.0429	0.0064	0.9655
PRIN22	0.1948	0.0073	0.0052	0.9708
PRIN23	0.1874	0.0412	0.0050	0.9759
PRIN24	0.1461	0.0039	0.0039	0.9798
PRIN25	0.1421	0.0244	0.0038	0.9837
PRIN26	0.1177	0.0069	0.0031	0.9868
PRIN27	0.1107	0.0228	0.0029	0.9898
PRIN28	0.0879	0.0170	0.0023	0.9922
PRIN29	0.0709	0.0103	0.0019	0.9941
PRIN30	0.0605	0.0092	0.0016	0.9958
PRIN31	0.0513	0.0137	0.0013	0.9972
PRIN32	0.0375	0.0146	0.0010	0.9982
PRIN33	0.0229	0.0061	0.0006	0.9988
PRIN34	0.0167	0.0047	0.0004	0.9992
PRIN35	0.0120	0.0016	0.0003	0.9996
PRIN36	0.0104	0.0064	0.0002	0.9998
PRIN37	0.0039	—	0.0001	1.0000

maximum amount of variability among the poverty indicators across districts. The second principal component squeezes out maximum remaining variability once the effect of the first component has been removed. There are as many components as the number of variables in the model. The last principal component has the smallest variance of any linear combination of the poverty indicators (explains the least variability). The component scores are the objective positions of individual districts on the component. By virtue of the arrangement described above, the component score with the lowest value indicates the most critically poor district.[7]

For this purpose, I have used thirty-seven poverty indicators, some from the National Socioeconomic Survey, others from diverse sources. The variables defined as indexes, with their mean values and standard deviations, are listed in table 7.9. Note that I have not included the per capita income variable in the set of poverty indicators. (The district income variable was reported in table 7.4 above.) We are interested in seeing how observable variables other than income identify regional poverty.

Table 7.10 presents eigenvalues and the standardized variance accounted for by each of the thirty-seven components of the study. We see that the first principal component explains 38 percent of the standardized variance, three components account for 54 percent, and nine components explain 80 percent. The thirty-seventh component accounts for only 0.0001 percent of the standardized variance.

Table 7.11 reports eigenvectors for the thirty-seven variables of the model for the first seven principal components. Recalling that the variables were defined so that the higher the value of a variable the worse the poverty, high positive values of coefficients, called "loadings" or "scores," indicate being well-off and negative or low positive loadings indicate poverty. Accordingly, the eigenvector of the first principal component has low loadings (indicating poverty) on land without title (FWT), growth rate of population (TC), infant survival rate (XMORINF), employment (XEMPU), absence of underemployment in rural areas (XEMPR), and low indexes of the inequalities of income (XGINI). High positive values of loadings (implying being well-off) are found on quality housing (IVIV), social security coverage (ISSOC), urbanization (IURBA), share of nonagricultural population (PNA), mean education level in community (MEDUC), cars per one-

7. The principal components technique arranges and weights the included variables or indicators of poverty in a concise form. Principal *components* are composite indicators of poverty calculated by linear combinations of poverty indicators, so as to maximize the sum of squared correlations of indicators with a component, called *loadings* or *scores*. *Eigenvalues* are sums of squared loadings for each component converted to the percentage of total variability in the correlation matrix with each component. *Eigenvectors* are sets of eigenvalues. The *first component* or principal component extracts or explains as much variability of poverty as possible. *Subsequent components* extract maximum residual variability.

Table 7.11 Principal Components Analysis: Eigenvectors for First Seven Principal Components

Variable[a]	PRIN1	PRIN2	PRIN3	PRIN4	PRIN5	PRIN6	PRIN7
FWT	−0.14	0.21	−0.11	−0.10	0.10	0.28	−0.21
OFFS	−0.01	0.33	−0.14	0.11	−0.12	0.16	0.16
IPTS	0.20	0.12	0.32	−0.22	0.04	0.02	0.01
IVID	0.21	0.03	0.03	0.16	−0.16	0.08	−0.06
IVIV	0.25	−0.03	−0.02	0.01	−0.07	−0.01	−0.08
ISSOC	0.22	0.12	−0.01	0.08	0.03	−0.11	−0.08
IURBA	0.23	0.15	−0.02	0.13	−0.02	−0.01	−0.04
TC	0.07	0.26	−0.27	0.04	0.10	−0.19	0.07
IPND	0.24	0.08	0.02	0.19	−0.03	0.03	0.01
PNA	0.22	0.06	−0.07	0.07	−0.14	−0.01	−0.11
XMORINF	0.02	−0.13	0.31	0.36	−0.21	0.08	−0.01
INST	0.14	0.25	0.07	0.20	0.15	0.23	−0.24
DEFCM	0.22	0.07	−0.11	0.10	0.10	0.04	−0.04
NAP	0.22	−0.14	0.01	0.21	−0.01	0.02	0.06
IMED	0.20	0.15	0.26	−0.14	0.03	0.15	0.05
IODO	0.14	−0.04	0.29	−0.17	0.01	−0.26	0.14
IENF	0.17	0.24	0.23	−0.16	0.11	0.13	−0.02
IPAR	0.18	0.11	0.30	−0.28	0.03	0.10	0.02
DCXS	0.16	−0.10	0.01	0.12	−0.27	−0.08	0.16
LE	0.08	0.01	−0.23	0.14	−0.07	0.35	0.27
NFUT	0.10	−0.24	0.07	0.24	0.24	0.02	−0.07
IAPTA	0.08	−0.18	−0.07	0.18	0.01	−0.01	−0.09
XGINI	−0.10	−0.02	0.08	−0.18	−0.13	0.38	0.31
XDESN	0.16	−0.14	−0.08	0.03	−0.05	0.05	0.14
XHCRITI	0.20	−0.07	−0.21	−0.16	0.20	0.02	0.13
MEDUC	0.19	0.10	−0.21	−0.18	0.10	0.04	0.04
XEMPR	−0.06	0.15	0.27	0.25	0.06	−0.17	0.36
XEMPU	−0.07	0.14	0.14	0.19	0.39	−0.19	−0.21
XEMPT	0.07	−0.01	−0.16	−0.20	0.30	−0.17	0.30
XSHARE	0.16	0.04	−0.18	−0.10	−0.10	−0.30	−0.31
FARMS	0.04	−0.32	0.02	−0.02	0.37	0.17	−0.07
TAXES	0.18	0.14	−0.12	0.01	−0.06	−0.16	−0.03
CARS	0.19	−0.16	−0.03	−0.04	−0.07	−0.10	0.19
MARKET	0.14	−0.19	−0.17	−0.12	0.06	0.26	−0.02
XOLD	−0.04	0.21	−0.06	0.26	0.33	−0.08	0.39
FERTIL	0.09	−0.28	0.10	0.18	0.32	0.15	−0.02
XPHOC	0.19	−0.20	0.04	−0.15	−0.03	−0.21	0.07

[a] For definitions, see table 7.9.

hundred households (CARS), and so on. This principal component shows approximately equal loadings on the index of the quality of life (IVID), index of housing (IVIV), index of urbanization (IURBA), density of population (IPND), share of nonagricultural population (PNA), and health and medical variables (DEFCM, NAP, IMED). The three sets of variables just discussed, those with high loadings on poverty, those with high loadings on being well-off, and those with approximately equal effects on being well-off can be broadly associated with rural factors, urban factors, and housing (quality of home and family possessions) plus service amenities, respectively.

The second principal component is designed to extract residual variability in the original data after the effects of the first principal component have been removed. We see that for the residual poverty, the eigenvector of the second principal component indicates lower values of loadings on infant survival (XMORINF), share of nonagricultural population (PNA), availability of doctors (IMED, IODO, IPAR), nutrition (XDESN), percentage of irrigated area (IAPTA), XGINI, NFUT, market surplus (MARKET), and so forth, than the first principal component. The highest loading is assigned by this component to off-farm income (OFFS), meaning that in the residual poverty group, off-farm income from nonfarm jobs is a major factor in reducing poverty. High positive loading is also assigned to medical institutions (INST, IENF), IURBA, and TC. A high negative loading on the percentage of farms receiving technical aid (FARMS) is puzzling.

High values for the third principal component, which is designed to extract maximum remaining variability in the original data after the first two components have explained as much variability as possible, are XGINI, IPTS, FWT, medical variables (IMED, IODO, IENF, and IPAR), XMORINF, and similar variables, indicating that for the poor of that stratum, health variables are more critical. It has high negative loadings on TC, PNA, DEFCM, NAP, LE, TAXES, XOLD, urbanization, and similar health and urbanization variables. Scanning various loadings, one gets the impression that this component is urban poverty oriented.

The spatial expression of these structures is presented in the loadings for each district, given in table 7.12 for the first, second, and third principal components. Since components were computed for fifty-nine of the sixty-six districts of the Republic, the remaining seven districts appear without component scores in these tables and maps.

Recalling that original variables were structured so that their low values implied high incidence of poverty, high negative component scores represent poverty and high positive components indicate the opposite state, that is, economic development. According to this criterion, Santa Fé, Olá, Las Minas, Cañazas, and Donoso districts (the five of them accounting for

Table 7.12   Principal Components Analysis: Districts Listed in Order of Their Ranking as Determined by the First Principal Component

District	PRIN1	PRIN2	PRIN3	FWT	PFFS	IPTS
Chiriquí Grande	—	—	—	89.78	41.23	4.00
San Blas	—	—	—	—	—	22.40
San Lorenzo	—	—	—	81.74	35.13	11.70
Tolé	—	—	—	92.63	31.57	7.70
Pedasí	—	—	—	62.89	26.66	34.20
Balboa	—	—	—	99.39	75.50	23.20
Chiman	—	—	—	100.00	75.17	0.00
Santa Fé	−1.55	0.77	0.47	97.49	52.20	11.70
Ola	−1.47	0.41	0.65	94.41	53.57	7.40
Las Minas	−0.43	0.23	0.31	78.37	44.13	8.10
Cañazas	−1.40	0.63	0.75	94.17	46.22	16.20
Donoso	−1.38	0.52	−0.39	97.77	60.84	0.00
Las Palmas	−1.33	0.61	−0.03	90.67	48.00	3.20
San Francisco	−1.32	0.08	0.29	87.49	38.03	11.70
Calobre	−1.28	0.46	0.08	95.37	56.37	11.70
La Mesa	−1.16	−0.14	0.31	85.84	50.72	14.10
Chagres	−1.11	0.96	0.79	92.48	71.63	19.70
Los Pozos	−1.10	−0.16	−0.21	89.25	39.07	6.40
Río de Jesus	−1.06	−0.20	0.03	68.47	44.44	15.40
La Pintada	−0.92	0.50	0.46	93.88	71.70	17.10
Montijo	−0.86	0.13	0.19	88.05	39.60	19.40
Pinogana	−0.78	0.00	1.29	95.50	85.62	34.80
Renacimiento	−0.74	−0.64	−0.59	95.63	56.31	4.20
Santa Isabel	−0.70	−0.55	1.14	94.97	50.50	22.40
Soná	−0.62	0.50	0.36	81.52	68.19	20.70
Ocú	−0.60	−1.50	−0.24	59.23	42.55	17.00
Capira	−0.56	0.82	−0.53	84.51	63.81	12.40
Chepigana	−0.46	1.20	1.07	98.18	88.67	37.50
Tonosí	−0.44	−1.80	−0.41	91.26	21.81	18.40
Boquerón	−0.39	−0.13	−0.94	88.76	57.21	3.70
Macaracas	0.27	−0.71	0.15	83.31	25.52	23.60
Atalaya	−0.24	−0.20	−0.11	72.34	59.11	23.90
Antón	−0.13	0.31	−0.18	84.65	52.88	22.60
Portobelo	−0.11	1.86	−1.58	79.71	46.95	17.30

2.86 percent of the Republic's population), situated in and to the the south of the central highlands, are the least favorably endowed, reflecting relatively low levels of services, inaccessible terrain, distance decay, low-quality land, low income, often a significant percentage of indigenous population, and so on. At the top of the most favorably endowed are the growth centers, Chitré, Panamá, David, and Colón, and major market towns, such as Aguadulce, La Chorrere, Las Tablas, Arraijan, Los Santos, Changuinola, Bard, and Boquete. Penonome and Soná fall in the middle.

Table 7.12 Continued.

District	PRIN1	PRIN2	PRIN3	FWT	PFFS	IPTS
Remedios	−0.10	−0.65	−1.27	84.57	29.09	10.40
Penonomé	−0.07	0.15	0.60	91.47	54.81	33.30
San Carlos	−0.06	−0.70	−0.03	71.08	60.47	24.60
Pocrí	−0.01	−2.39	0.72	59.50	31.06	38.30
San Félix	−0.01	−0.18	0.79	88.21	17.19	43.70
Gualaca	0.02	0.17	−1.22	88.12	48.15	11.70
Pesé	0.05	−1.11	−0.82	71.64	32.61	15.60
Bocas del Toro	0.06	0.32	0.53	80.00	60.00	32.50
Dolega	0.16	0.34	−0.84	90.58	67.84	14.70
Chame	0.23	0.15	−0.75	85.52	74.87	15.00
Natá	0.34	−0.74	−1.25	78.23	71.42	8.00
Bugaba	0.41	−0.82	−1.11	83.31	41.91	24.10
Alanje	0.41	−1.91	−1.72	75.25	40.65	10.80
Guararé	0.44	−2.33	−1.05	66.98	22.81	15.00
Chepo	0.45	0.58	2.04	85.35	59.03	63.30
Santa María	0.57	−0.85	−0.89	72.59	55.73	17.70
Parita	0.58	−0.94	0.39	60.45	47.87	36.90
Boquete	0.68	−0.54	−1.09	69.87	62.12	21.80
Barú	0.74	−0.24	−0.15	92.31	41.40	33.00
Changuinola	0.98	1.65	1.32	76.55	77.28	54.00
Los Santos	0.99	−1.71	1.39	75.69	32.01	64.40
San Miguelito	1.02	2.20	−2.91	75.36	50.00	2.70
Santiago	1.03	0.33	0.83	79.26	59.32	52.40
Arraiján	1.06	0.73	−2.02	66.83	40.58	15.90
Colón	1.07	1.54	0.33	80.47	68.27	10.20
Las Tablas	1.10	−0.75	1.84	77.27	26.46	17.50
La Chorrera	1.18	0.83	−0.59	71.59	59.69	62.40
Aguadulce	1.85	−0.56	1.14	73.84	61.86	22.90
David	1.97	−0.19	1.62	80.33	41.96	16.80
Panamá	2.28	−0.33	1.42	79.88	50.69	4.80
Chitré	2.46	−0.33	1.42	65.91	50.69	7.50

Note: Only the first three of the total of thirty-seven variable coefficients are reported in this table.

The second principal component emphasizes certain indirect measures of poverty, reflecting the level of public health services, availability of medical services, nutrition, sufficiency of housing, and similar variables. According to this component, the districts in middle-income provinces, in general well linked with growth centers, are less favorably endowed with the indicators that affect the residual variability after the first component has explained the maximum possible. It explains, for instance, why Tonosí, Pocrí, and Guararé are not as favorably endowed as the nearby market

Table 7.13   Regression of per Capita Income on the First Six Principal Components

Variable	Parameter Estimate	t for HO Parameter = 0
Intercept	1,024.22	18.96
PRIN1	485.58	8.91
PRIN2	−2.75	−0.05
PRIN3	−39.09	−0.71
PRIN5	49.67	0.91
PRIN6	20.17	0.37
Root means square error	414.856	
Mean of dependent variable	1,024.22	
Coefficient of variance	40.5046	
R^2	0.6043	
Adj. R^2	0.5670	
Number of observations	58	

Note: Dependent variable is per capita income.

towns of Las Tablas and Los Santos, or why Alanje is not as favorably endowed as David, even though they have good links with the growth centers, and at the same time why they are more favorably endowed than other districts in the interior. It appears that the first component tends to account for interprovince poverty and the second component for interdistrict poverty.

A final refinement of the levels of poverty comes out in the third principal component, which seems to emphasize urban poverty. High levels of urban poverty are associated with the big working-class districts of San Miguelito, Arraijan, Alanje, Portobelo, and Remedios. Highly endowed districts in this component are Chepo, Las Tablas, David, Chitré, and Los Santos. In this analysis, urban poverty indicators appear to take third place, after the first place for rural poverty indicators and the second place for satellite districts' poverty indicators, indirectly reflecting health-medical-nutrition-housing nexus indicators.

As a broad conclusion, the first component accounts largely for poverty in rural areas, where the highest incidence prevails. The second principal component seems to pick up the poverty of satellite districts well linked to growth centers, perhaps because young people's moving to growth centers causes backwash effects on these areas. The third component explains urban poverty. That seems to be the spatial order of poverty suggested by the analysis of this section.

Faced with the problem of multicollinearity and the fact that few individual indicators of poverty used here explain significant fractions of the variability of income, we ran a regression of income on the first six principal components, which is given in table 7.13. The fit is good—the adjusted R^2 is 0.57. In this regression, however, it is not easy to identify individual determinants of poverty or even to interpret the coefficients meaningfully, because the explanatory variables (principal components) are composite values of original variables. What we have broadly learned from the principal components analysis of the preceding section provides some clues to interpreting the regression results, namely, that the first principal component, which is closely associated with rural causes of poverty, has the highest explanatory power. The second and third principal components are dominated by negative loadings. Hence they acquire negative coefficients. The positive and negative values of coefficients of the successive components appear to yield a cyclical curve, so that the coefficients of the fifth and sixth components are positive. None of the coefficients other than that of the first component, however, are significantly different from zero. Consequently, in this overall national regression rural poverty variables throw other variables out. Antipoverty programs for rural areas thus are likely to have a significantly larger impact on poverty than programs directed to other areas.

EIGHT

Poverty in Indian Areas

Any outsider who visits Indian areas is struck by their poverty. But just how poor they are has seldom been subjected to a scientific analysis. The present household survey is the first one of its nature to be carried out in the Indian territory. Accordingly, a separate chapter is devoted to Indian poverty.

The Guaymi Indians are the largest and the poorest among the Indian tribes of Panama. They form about 60 percent of all Indians. Overall, Indians constitute approximately 4.8 percent of the total population. The Guaymi Indian households covered in the National Socioeconomic Survey, 1983, make up about 1.2 percent of the Guaymi population. For these and other statistics, see table 8.1. About 60 percent of Indians profess Catholicism (see UNICEF 1979). In 1850 the Guaymis occupied all the central mountains where they live today as well as large parts of the uplands and plains of Coclé, Veraguas, and Chiriquí.

Over the decades, these Indians have been pushed by the land-hungry mestizos to the mountains, where land has low productivity and is currently subject to rapid erosion. They seem to suspect that they may gradually lose even what land they still occupy. Therefore their most pressing current demand is for the demarcation of a *comarca* (reservation area). Because of this preoccupation, it is possible that their acceptance of the policy recommendations following from the analysis done here may not be as positive as one might hope.

The 1.2 percent socioeconomic survey of Guaymi Indians done for this study used the same questionnaire as for non-Indians. The definition of income is the same, but some of the entries are zero. Given the smallness of the sample (105 households), the standard errors of any subdivision of it, for example, decile incomes, as well as blown-up estimates for the entire Indian community are expected to be rather large. The results should therefore be interpreted with caution.

INCOME

Surprisingly, only 57 percent of the income of Guaymi Indians originates in the agricultural sector; 43 percent is reported to be nonagricultural income, even though 92 percent of the heads of households declare agriculture as their main economic activity. The result seems to suggest that even those whose main occupation is agriculture need nonagricultural income to make ends meet. Another possible reason is that the wage rate of those Indians who are employed in the National Guard or in the non-Indian areas is many times larger than the average earnings in the Guaymi territory. Mean per capita annual income is $302, which should be compared with the national (non-Indian) mean of $1,766, the national critical poverty line of $392, the mean per capita annual income of the non-Indian critically poor of $189, and the mean provincial per capita annual income of the critically poor of $307, $195, and $160, respectively, in the non-Indian areas of the three Indian provinces of Bocas del Toro, Chiriquí, and Veraguas. Interestingly, Indians contribute $8 per head per annum to social security and $3 per head per annum to taxes. This sum of $8 per head comes from 8.7 percent of the Indians who have the social security card (*carnet*), indicating that the remaining 91.3 percent of Indians who do not have the carnet do not hold regular jobs. The UNICEF survey (1979) revealed that 72.8 percent of Guaymis did not have *cedula*, which means they cannot vote. Their nonagricultural property income is zero, as are transfers from government. These aboriginals live by the sweat of their brows. Over 28 percent of agricultural income is self-consumed, and about a quarter of nonagricultural income is in kind.

Per capita annual income varies from $2 in the bottom decile to $151 in the sixth decile to $2,160 in the tenth decile (see table 8.2). Note that the tenth decile's per capita income is 22 percent higher than the mean national income (and 7.15 times higher than the mean income of the Guaymis). Possibly these are families made up of couples with two children (since the mean family size of decile 10 is four), both teaching school and probably also having some income from village land. The bottom 40 percent of population has only 2.6 percent of total income. The top 10 percent has 41.5 percent of total income. The Gini coefficient is 0.6754, compared with the non-Indian Gini coefficient of 0.554 in the Republic and 0.5149 in areas of difficult access. The result is rather surprising. Why, in a society where land is communally owned and that has few modern assets and little human capital, is income so unequally distributed? A clue may lie in the indigenous society's emerging contacts with the outside economy. Those who get jobs and nonpoor wages outside Indian territories—because of their personal traits, schooling, luck, presence of relatives in employment centers, or other reasons—usually take a big leap forward in relation to their compatriots in an otherwise more egalitarian society in the native land. These Indian employees, however, cannot break away from their culture and family ties, so they remain part of their extended families, remit money, return home when on leave and bring household goods, and are usually considered still members of the family. In the first phase of economic

Table 8.1 Indian Population by Province, 1983

Province	Total population (1)	Total Indian Population		Column 2 as % of Column 1 (4)	Total Indian Households		Indian Population Included in Survey		
		Number (2)	% (3)		Number (5)	% (6)	Households (7)	Population (8)	Column 7 as % of Indian Population (9)
Guaymí Indians	511,702	54,285	58.3	10.61	8,093	7.22	105	690	1.27
Bocas del Toro	52,416	17,468	18.8	33.32	2,391	20.05	30	193	1.10
Chiriquí	286,418	30,862	33.2	10.78	4,705	7.62	64	435	1.41
Veraguas	172,868	5,955	6.4	3.44	997	2.60	11	62	1.04
Cunas									
San Blas (Colón)	149,420	27,588	29.6	18.46	3,386	9.73	—	—	—
Chocoes									
Darién	22,023	8,924	9.9	40.52	1,440	31.37	—	—	—
Mixed with non-Indians (mainly Cunas)									
Panama	902,824	2,294	2.5	0.25	332	0.16	—	—	—
Total in country	1,933,998	93,901	100.0	4.81	13,252	3.06	—	—	—

Source: Census of Population, 1980, vol. 1, for the first six columns; National Socioeconomic Survey, 1983, for columns 7, 8, and 9.

development in almost all countries, education has a high rate of return. Therefore those educated couples who get jobs as teachers or in the National Guard invariably tend to earn much higher incomes than their relatives and brothers in the Guaymi territory.

The census-type income of the critically poor is less than half their comprehensive income, whereas for nonpoor Indians it is over two-thirds. Although these magnitudes are low relative to those for the non-Indian population, they reveal that despite their remote areas and subsistence agriculture, Indians are nevertheless integrated into the monetized sector of the Panamanian economy.

THE INCIDENCE AND INTENSITY OF INDIAN POVERTY

Approximately 73.3 percent of Indian households and 77.8 percent of the Indian population fall below the critical poverty line of $375.70 for the three Guaymi Indian provinces of Bocas del Toro, Chiriquí, and Veraguas (see col. 6 of table 8.2). Their poverty gap is $12.6 million (table 8.2). The excess of income above the critical poverty line that the nonpoor 22 percent of Guaymi Indians have is $8.06, about $4.5 million less than the poverty gap (table 8.2, column 9). For example, were the income of Indians equally distributed among Indian families, they would be 20 percent below the national critical poverty line. The critical poverty gap among Guaymi Indians, who form about 2.75 percent of Panama's population, is about 0.30 percent of GDP. The national income of Guaymis is approximately $17 million, or 0.50 percent of the national income of the Republic.

DEMOGRAPHIC CHARACTERISTICS

The mean household size is 6.57. In the entire sample of 105 households, there are only two persons (women) sixty years old or older. Evidently the life expectancy of Indians is very low in relation to that of non-Indians, so there may not be much incentive for self-employed Indians to contribute to the social security system for old-age pensions.

There are perceptible humps in the middle deciles in respect to almost all groups of the population, indicating a proportionately larger number of families in these deciles. For instance, deciles 5 through 7 have nearly one female spouse per household, whereas households in all other deciles have fewer spouses (the top decile has on the average one-half spouse per household) and have about two children eighteen years old or older per household, while others have fewer (the top decile has fewer than one). The family size of the sixth decile is 8.7 and that of the top decile is 4.0, and so on. The three reference deciles are below the critical poverty line, but among Indians they form the middle class. It appears that the middle

Table 8.2 Adjusted Family, per Capita, and Mean Annual Incomes by Decile, Indian Areas, 1983

Household Decile	Survey				Adjusted Mean Incomes			Income of Blown-Up Population	
	Annual Family Income (1)	Number of Families (2)	Number of Relatives (3)	Adult-Equivalent Persons[a] (4)	Family Income (5)	Per Capita Income (6)	Adult-Equivalent Income (7)	Poverty Gap[b] ($ million) (8)	Nonpoverty Surplus ($ million) (9)
Total	208,328	105	690	577	1,984	302	361	12.600	8.058
1	144	10	70	59	14	2	3	2.175	—
2	1,036	10	84	68	104	12	15	2.541	—
3	1,303	10	59	43	130	22	30	2.029	—
4	2,939	10	63	54	294	47	54	1.722	—
5	5,038	11	60	49	458	84	103	1.455	—
6	14,511	11	96	78	1,319	151	186	1.792	—
7	15,644	11	70	57	1,422	223	275	0.886	—
8	30,889	11	75	68	2,808	412	454	0.175	0.186
9	50,414	11	73	65	4,583	691	776	—	1.922
10	86,410	10	40	36	8,641	2,160	2,400	—	5.950

[a] For calculating adult-equivalent income, the following weights were used: adults = 1.0, ages 0–4 = 0.42, ages 5–14 = 0.63.
[b] Critical poverty line for Bocas del Toro, Chiriquí, and Veraguas = $376.70. The estimates reported in the text were done from individual observations and may not agree exactly with those in the last columns of this table.

decile's larger family size is due to relatively better nutrition and the upper decile's smaller family size reflects the effect of income. This result is consistent with the fertility behavior of Indians estimated in chapter 7.

EDUCATIONAL CHARACTERISTICS

The illiteracy rate among all heads of households is 53 percent; among those over thirty-five (oldish group), 64 percent; and among those thirty-five or under (younger group), 47 percent. About 17 percent of the younger age group and 4 percent of the oldish group have some years of secondary school. None have reached the university or vocational education levels. Illiteracy is almost uniformly spread across all deciles. Secondary education, on the other hand, is clearly associated with the top deciles. Anyone who acquires some years of secondary education tends to get out of critical poverty.

In general, Indian children have middle-level grades spread almost uniformly across all deciles. Over 36 percent in the twelve-and-under group and 50 percent in the above-twelve group have repeated grades.' According to the UNICEF survey (1979), 81 percent started going to school at ages six to nine, 15 percent at ages ten to fourteen, and 3 percent at age fifteen and higher. District-level data (not reported in tabular form here) indicate that in none of the age-groups in the districts of the Indian territory does enrollment exceed 75 percent. In Chiriquí Grande the enrollment rate barely exceeds 50 percent during the peak age of eight through ten years. After that age the dropout rate begins to rise. The highest enrollment occurs at age ten in most districts. On both sides of that age the enrollment curve forms an inverted parabola (see table 7.6). Approximately a quarter of the children who do not attend school report reasons that reflect a lack of motivation or unpreparedness for school as the main cause; another quarter stay away from sheer poverty (e.g., lack of school uniform), and (interestingly) no more than a tenth say that school is too far away. Thus a major schooling problem in the Guaymi territory is a lack of motivation and of early school enrollment. The case for preschool education for Indian children—who lack informal educational environment altogether—is thus much stronger than for other children.

HEALTH CHARACTERISTICS

Although one does not see starving children in Panama, the estimates of the Ministry of Health put child retardation (defined by underweight and subnormal height) due to malnutrition at about a quarter of the total. According to this source, this includes 64.6 percent of the Cuna children in San Blas; 70.8 percent of the Guaymi children in Chiriquí Grande (Bocas

Table 8.3 Expenditure Patterns per Month of Guaymi Indians, National Socioeconomic Survey, 1983

Monthly Expenses	Expenditure ($) by Decile						
	Total	1	2	3	4	5–9	10
1 Family income	165.0	1.2	8.7	10.8	24.3	26.0	720.0
2 Home food	32.9	2.5	8.0	15.2	39.6	41.4	52.3
3 Restaurant food	4.0	0.0	0.0	0.0	2.5	0.4	37.0
4 School transport	0.3	0.0	0.0	0.0	0.0	0.3	2.0
5 Public transport	0.1	0.0	0.0	0.0	0.0	0.2	0.0
6 Own transport	0.0	0.0	0.0	0.0	0.0	0.0	0.0
7 Gas	0.1	0.0	0.0	0.0	0.0	0.1	0.0
8 Electricity	0.2	0.0	0.0	0.0	0.0	0.2	0.5
9 Water	0.1	0.0	0.0	0.0	0.1	0.1	0.2
10 Monthly school fee	0.3	0.0	0.0	0.0	0.0	0.2	2.0
11 Lottery	0.3	0.0	0.0	0.0	0.0	0.1	3.0
12 Clothes	4.0	0.0	0.0	0.0	0.0	6.7	5.0
13 Expenses of students living outside home	2.6	0.0	0.0	0.0	0.0	3.4	8.5
14 Other expenses	2.9	0.0	2.3	2.3	2.0	3.1	7.0
15 Graduation expenses	1.1	0.0	0.3	0.4	0.6	0.9	2.3
16 Cooks	1.5	1.0	0.6	0.1	3.7	1.9	0.0
17 Durable goods credits	0.3	0.0	0.0	0.0	0.0	0.0	3.0
18 Graduation expenses in cash	0.0	0.0	0.0	0.0	0.0	0.0	
19 Total expenses	50.6	3.5	11.2	18.0	48.5	59.5	122.8
20 Savings	0.0	0.0	0.0	0.0	0.0	0.0	0.0
21 Addition 19 + 20	50.6	4.5	11.2	18.0	48.5	59.5	122.8
22 Total food expenses	36.9	2.5	8.0	15.2	42.1	41.9	89.3
23 Total education expenses	5.8	1.0	0.9	0.5	4.3	7.2	14.8
24 Mortgage	0.0	0.0	0.0	0.0	0.0	0.0	0.0
25 Rent	0.0	0.0	0.0	0.0	0.0	0.0	0.0
26 Rent imputed to owner-occupied home	10.4	0.1	0.9	1.1	2.5	13.2	32.5
27 Total expenses	61.0	3.6	12.1	19.1	51.0	72.7	155.3
28 Households	105.0	10.0	10.0	10.0	10.0	55.0	10.0

del Toro), 55 percent in Tolé (Chiriquí), and 54.7 percent in Santa Fé (Veraguas); and 43.9 percent of Chocoe Indians in Pinogana (Darién). Diseases caused by undernourishment are rampant in Indian areas. Thus, according to the UNICEF study (1979), among the Guaymi children 19.4 percent suffer from tuberculosis, 25.4 percent from tosferina whooping cough, 30.4 percent from measles, 61.7 percent from grippe, 40.3 percent from skin diseases, and 59.3 percent from worms. Child mortality and stillbirth rates are 28 percent and 6 percent, respectively. Accordingly, the preschool program discussed in the preceding section will have a higher productivity if accompanied by dietary education and nutritional improvement as well as health training and medical facilities. Already the government of Panama has taken effective measures to that end. Thus it is estimated that 55 percent of official schools provide some free food to children and 35 percent of private schools provide free food to 8.6 percent of their pupils. Theoretically, almost anybody who needs medical assistance receives it. However, about 9 percent of households report inability to obtain medical assistance because the health post is too far away. Such assistance is distributed almost uniformly across all deciles. Indians have very few amenities at home: there is no television and no electricity; very few homes have sanitary services; a high percentage of the population depends on river water for drinking; and so on.

EXPENDITURE PATTERNS

Expenditure patterns of Guaymi Indians are classified in table 8.3. In interpreting this table, note that, unlike the measurement of comprehensive income, expenditures are presented without any adjustments except that, to complete the balance sheet, the rental value of owner-occupied homes (100 percent in the Guaymi territory) is treated as a component of consumption expenditure.

The obvious wide gap between the estimated income per family ($165 per month) and reported consumption expenditure per family ($61 per month) arises because income is comprehensive and includes self-consumption and in-kind receipts, while consumption expenditure is limited to monetary expenditure as reported by interviewees. For instance, the 30 percent self-consumption of food in Indian areas was added to income but was not aggregated with food expenditure. Moreover, blown-up incomes were adjusted to match the corresponding category in the national accounts, the adjustment factor being the same as calculated for non-Indian incomes. No such adjustment was done for expenditures. In this respect, note also that all persons are in general prone to forget parts of their consumption, especially self-consumption. This is true of the rich, who may consciously or unconsciously fail to report in-kind consumption of such services as company cars. It is also true of the poor, who may neglect to report what they consume outside their homes directly from crops and fruit trees in the fields. However, while such components are susceptible to being understated on both sides of the balance sheet of the rich, in the case of the rural poor, especially the agricultural poor, under certain conditions they are apt to be accounted for in income and neglected in consumption. The amount of programming that was done in generating correct incomes was not duplicated for expenditures of Indians.

Subject to the stated qualifications, we see that, on the average, 60 percent of the monetary expenditure of Indians goes to buy food. When self-consumption of food is added, the average food share goes up to 77 percent.

The mean food share of the entire Indian population, however, is somewhat misleading, inasmuch as 100 percent of the monetary expenditure of the bottom 90 percent of the population is for food. For all practical purposes, the only nonfood monetary expenditure is incurred by the top decile, which accounts for 41.5 percent of the total income. Compare this with the non-Indians' mean food share of 41 percent, the mean of the bottom two deciles of 56 percent, and that of the top decile of 26 percent. Expenditure of Indians on electricity is only 0.1 percent of monetary expenditure.

A Comparison with Other Poor Groups

The averages of a few pertinent variables for Guaymi farms and three other farm groups (two poor, one nonpoor) of Panama are given in table 8.4. We see that the Guaymis and the Mestizos and Latinos in areas of difficult access have per capita incomes that do not rise above the critical poverty line. At the same time, agricultural income per farm in non-Indian areas of difficult access is 2.98 times as high, and the mean size of farms is 3.7 times as large as in Indian areas. Crop farmers, as distinguished from livestock farmers, in the Republic do not fare better than Indians in terms of output per farm. The average crop-farm sizes of the two groups are almost the same (see table 8.4). Crop agricultural technology in general in Panama is rather underdeveloped.

Indians do not report any concessional credit or technical assistance, whereas crop farmers in general and non-Indians in areas of difficult access report sizable amounts of these services. Indians use no chemical fertilizer; non-Indian mountain farmers use a bit ($1.53 per farm per year); crop farmers of the Republic spend $2.48 annually on fertilizer, while nonpoor farm owners spend $232 per year. Likewise, the education levels of Indians are lower, though not very much lower, than those of their counterparts in other areas.

Table 8.4 Average Values of Certain Pertinent Variables by Chosen Groups of Farms

| | | Average Annual Value | | | |
| | | Republic | | | |
Variable	Definition	Livestock or (Nonpoor) Farms	Crop Farms	Guaymi Area	Non-Indian Areas of Difficult Access
L1	Per capita income ($)	1,327	—	302	386
L85	Agricultural output per farm ($)	1,707	529	586	1,347
L88	Machinery, rental cost ($)	209	3.56	3.02	10.00
L90	Land (hectares)	82	4.59	5.6	20.97
L92	Seeds, cost ($)	39	1.51	1.05	1.35
L93	Other inputs, cost ($)	98	1.57	1.10	3.95
L40	Education of head (years)	4.9	3.86	2.46	2.81
—	Livestock per family (head)	3.07	0.15	0.51	1.22
—	Pigs per family (number)	0.95	0.17	0.71	1.18
L81/L85	Share of crop value in total value (ratio)	0.050	0.982	0.658	0.687
L94	Those receiving technical assistance (%)	0.102	0.027	0.0	0.033
L98	Those receiving concessional credit (%)	0.527	0.276	0.0	0.541
—	Commercialization (ratio)	0.45	0.401	0.27	0.45
L89	Cost of fertilizer per farm ($)	232	2.48	0.0	1.53
L86*L87	Labor (man-years)	0.95	0.87	0.95	1.22

Source: National Socioeconomic Survey, 1983.

SUMMARY AND CONCLUSIONS

Highland peoples from Andean mountains to Ethiopian dunes to the Himalayas are very poor. Their problems are more or less common: explosion of population, desertification of land, difficult access, and backward agriculture. The mountain natives of Panama suffer from similar problems but seem to have one distinction. Whereas the Nepalese and the Himachal Pradeshis of the Himalayas and the inhabitants of the Ethiopian mountains are on the average not much poorer than the population in the surrounding plains, the Guaymi Indians seem to be critically poor amid relatively well-off people whose country has been classified by the World Bank as an upper-middle-income developing country.

The per capita annual income of Guaymi Indians is $302, which is $73 below the poverty line. About 78 percent of Guaymis are critically poor.

Their poverty gap is $12.6 million, or 0.36 percent of national income. Forming 2.75 percent of the Republic's population, Guaymi Indians have only 0.05 percent of national income. About 17 percent of heads of households who are thirty-five and younger and only four percent of those over thirty-five have completed some years of secondary education. Guaymi children start going to school on the average two to three years late. For this reason and others, over 36 percent in the twelve-and-under age group and over 50 percent in the above-twelve age group repeat grades. In none of the primary-school age groups in Indian districts does the enrollment rate exceed 75 percent. In several Indian districts the enrollment rates are much lower. Approximately a quarter of the school-age children who do not attend school report reasons that reflect unpreparedness or a lack of motivation. The case for preschool education for Indian children is thus much stronger and more urgent than for other children.

The rate of return to schooling among Indians is higher than the average in the Republic. Potentially it is even higher, as modern technology from the advanced segments of the country trickles down to the Indian territory. Indians are becoming increasingly conscious of the value of education. The differences in educational achievement among Indians seem largely due to difference in the availability of schools.

Among the most productive types of investment in Guaymi agriculture are those that introduce agricultural techniques and practices that are yield-increasing and labor-using, such as the seed-fertilizer technology of the green revolution. Such techniques are not readily available; they have to be developed. That requires biotechnological research, which Panama lacks. One of the major policy recommendations of this study is for agricultural research of the type indicated (see chap. 13). Superior agricultural techniques, improved seeds, and new crops cannot, however, be introduced in a vacuum. Especially in these areas, several other types of investments and services are also required. These include road linkages with market towns, availability of credit, extension services, machinery for land clearance, reforestation to prevent soil erosion, and so on. Indian agriculture thus needs massive investment.

Setting Priorities

Investment resources are, however, not unlimited. Priorities have to be set. Among all these investments, preschool education (see more on it in chap. 7) and productivity-increasing agricultural research seem to promise superior and surer results with spreading effects. Therefore these two investments deserve priority. Agricultural productivity merits priority because in rural poor communities in areas of difficult access, self-sufficiency in food comes first. Preschool education warrants priority because without it a very small proportion of Indian students can finish high school. Educated boys can get out and migrate to industrial-commercial centers. Those who stay behind should be able to produce enough to feed their families well and have some surplus to raise animals and poultry and produce milk. It is true that access roads are very important, but not only are they too costly to be undertaken to any effective degree in the present state of Panama's debt and other financial problems, but their trickle-down effect on the development of Indian agriculture is not likely to be as rapid as the direct effect of a green revolution. Extension services are also essential, but the horse must be put before the cart: new agricultural practices and inputs must be developed first. Credit is necessary, too, but even private banks may be attracted to do business with Indians if they find that Indians will raise a surplus to sell. Reforestation and the comarca? Yes. The comarca is the number one demand of Indians, and it will provide the security of land and a productive factor in which Indians can invest without fear of being deprived by more powerful, more affluent sections of the population. The Latinos have pushed them so far back from the plains to the hills over the past century—indeed even during the past quarter-century—that they are afraid they might lose whatever is left. Although that is primarily a political and legal matter, it has no conflict with the priorities in allocating economic resources. Likewise, deforestation is a national loss, and reforestation cannot be postponed without serious damage to the national ecology, but particularly the Guaymi economy. For a winnable war on permanent poverty, productivity-increasing agricultural research (including the prevention of soil erosion) and preschool education deserve top priority.

NINE

Unemployment and Poverty

In industrial countries, unemployment and poverty have been found to be highly correlated. In the United States, for instance, while the overall mean rate of unemployment during 1986 was approximately 7 percent, that among black youths was about 40 percent. A majority of black youths had a low level of schooling and either belonged to poor families and so were doomed to stay in poverty if unemployed at that age, or became poor owing to lack of employment even if they did not come from a poverty background. A similar correlation has generally been assumed to exist in developing countries. Accordingly, in both developed and developing countries, concern with poverty often ends complacently in efforts aimed at reducing unemployment, often by creating public-service jobs with or without job training. The question addressed here is not whether reducing unemployment is more or less important than alleviating poverty. Rather, the question is whether a general employment policy per se can make a significant dent in poverty. Little research has been done in LDCs to verify such a relationship, see Morley (1984).

The characterization of the poor and unemployment in Chapter 7 yielded the preliminary result that unemployment in Panama is scarcely a problem of the poor. Rather, it is predominantly a problem of the nonpoor. This chapter pursues that analysis further. The possible relation between poverty and unemployment is analyzed from a number of aspects.

I will explore answers to several questions bearing directly or indirectly on the relationship, if any, between poverty and unemployment, including the following: Does unemployment perceptibly cause poverty? Alternatively, does the removal of unemployment significantly mitigate poverty? Does the incidence of unemployment fall more heavily on the poor or the nonpoor? More precisely, what fraction of jobs created by general employment policy go to the permanently poor relative to their proportions? What is the employment multiplier or the trickle-down effect for the poor? Are the unemployed now mostly poor even if they did not come from poor families initially? Is there any correlation between unemployment and underemployment? Is the intensity of unemployment (as measured by the number of persons unemployed in a household) higher in poor families than in nonpoor families? Are the unemployed in poor families, as against nonpoor families, largely *primary* workers (heads of households) or mostly *secondary* workers (those who are ordinarily dependent on the head of household, such as spouses and adult children)? What is the relative rate of unemployed secondary workers in families of different strata when the family's primary worker is also unemployed? Do unemployed secondary workers come predominantly from nonpoor or poor backgrounds? Is the rate of unemployment different in sectors and industries that generally employ poor workers? To what extent does unemployment in nonpoor sectors affect employment in poor sectors?

In industrial countries, answers to these questions tend to establish that poverty and unemployment are highly correlated. Ironic though it may sound, the present research suggests that in Panama—and in LDCs in general, for that matter—there is little correlation between the two economic maladies. The result has important implications for antipoverty policies.

Is There a Qualitative Relationship between Poverty and Unemployment/Underemployment?

Let me start with an overview of the incidence of underemployment and unemployment by income classes and a few other dimensions. The next section will verify whether there is any association between unemployed primary workers and unemployed secondary workers. Then I will go on to an econometric analysis of unemployment among primary and secondary workers.

The Incidence of Unemployment and Underemployment

In 1982 the rate of open unemployment was 8.4 percent (it rose to 9.7 percent in 1983); the discouraged-worker rate was about 2 percent; visible underemployment was about 3 percent in rural areas and approximately 1 percent in urban areas; and disguised underemployment ran as high as 23 percent in the rural sector and 4 percent in the urban sector (see table 9.1). Here let us concentrate on two major categories of unemployment— open unemployment or simply unemployment, and disguised underemployment or simply underemployment.

A pattern of the two rates by deciles (of population by family income at the time of the survey) is sketched in figure 9.1. The results suggest that unemployment prevails largely in the middle deciles, while underemployment declines consistently and sharply from low to high deciles.

With a view to getting some idea about the economic positions of primary workers before they became unemployed, we cross-tabulated them by industries and occupations in which they are employed or were employed before losing their jobs.

Table 9.1 Underemployment by Industry, 1982

State of Employment	Agriculture (1)	Mining and Quarry (2)	Manufacturing (3)	Electricity (4)	Construction (5)	Commerce (6)	Transport (7)	Finance and Insurance (8)	Personal Services (9)	Community Services (10)	Total (11)
1. Inactives											
a. Row %	6.26	0.00	16.88	0.00	4.72	16.00	0.49	2.74	34.87	18.04	0.91
b. Column %	0.21	0.00	1.49	0.00	0.59	1.03	0.07	0.55	3.24	0.84	
2. Fully employed											
a. Row %	17.11	0.05	12.20	1.94	8.66	15.99	7.90	5.92	5.19	25.05	67.68
b. Column %	42.02	35.40	80.48	97.66	80.46	76.89	86.25	89.37	35.93	89.48	
3. Disguisedly underemployed											
a. Row %	62.56	0.10	3.19	0.05	2.43	6.50	1.74	0.44	20.13	2.86	21.84
b. Column %	49.59	25.34	6.80	0.81	7.30	10.08	6.13	2.17	45.00	3.20	
4. Openly underemployed											
a. Row %	40.86	0.00	9.79	0.00	5.42	11.29	5.08	2.20	16.71	8.65	4.49
b. Column %	6.66	0.00	4.28	0.00	3.34	3.60	3.59	2.24	7.69	2.05	
5. Underemployed in primary job											
a. Row %	63.07	0.00	0.00	0.00	4.00	4.84	4.00	2.14	3.72	18.23	0.19
b. Column %	0.42	0.00	0.00	0.00	0.10	0.06	0.22	0.09	0.07	0.18	
6. Unemployed											
a. Row %	6.12	0.72	14.55	0.42	12.21	23.97	4.73	5.13	16.11	16.04	4.90
b. Column %	1.09	39.26	6.95	1.53	8.21	8.34	8.74	5.61	8.08	4.15	
Total											
Number	159,554	517	59,441	7,782	42,175	81,546	35,881	25,057	56,576	109,760	578,193
%	27.55	0.09	10.26	1.84	7.28	14.08	6.19	4.48	9.77	18.05	100.00

Source: Panamá, Controller General, *Household Survey, 1982.*

Note: Open underemployment is measured by the shortfall of the number of hours from forty per week as a percentage of forty hours, annualized. Disguised underemployment is defined by the proportion of the shortfall of work income from the respective provinces' mean minimum wage of those workers, whether employees or self-employed, who work at least forty hours per week. Maids were omitted from this subsample. The minimum wage rates used are given below in U.S. dollars per month: Panamá 140, Colón 140, Chiriguí 124, Herrera 115, Veraguas 115, Bocas del Toro 119, Darién 106,

Unemployment and Underemployment by Industry and Occupation

The two phenomena are practically segmented by industry and occupation. Disguised underemployment is closely associated with low-productivity and so low-paid industries, namely, agriculture and personal services (table 9.1, row 3). On the other hand unemployment is concentrated in high-productivity and so high-paid industries such as construction, mining, and commerce (table 9.1, row 6).

This result, however, tells us only half the truth: the unemployed were evidently not poor when they had jobs. They may be poor now. A test of possible correlation between unemployment and underemployment might throw some light on this issue.

Is There a Correlation between Unemployment and Underemployment?

Table 9.2 presents the correlation triangle between pairs of various types and components of unemployment and underemployment. The results indicate that no correlation exists between unemployment and disguised underemployment. Disguised underemployment and open underemployment, on the other hand, are correlated, particularly in rural areas. Open underemployment shows no correlation with disguised underemployment of women or adolescents. There is thus some suggestion that unemployment and open underemployment or partial employment are sister phenomena. Unemployed and disguisedly underemployed workers are unrelated, noncompeting groups.

The absence of any correlation between the stated two groups persists even when income is held constant, as we see from the following regressions:

$$\text{Republic: } X_1 = 13{,}187 + 4.0X_6 - 22.0Y; R^2 = 0.25$$
$$(0.3) \qquad (-1.18)$$
$$\text{Urban: } \quad X_1 = 11{,}310 + 3.86X_6 - 39.5Y; R^2 = 0.46,$$
$$(0.25) \qquad (-2.15)$$

where Y is worker's income (mean decile income in these regressions), X_1 is underemployment, X_6 is unemployment, and the numbers in parentheses are t values. Almost all components of un/underemployment are negatively correlated with per capita family income (Y).

To summarize, the results of this section suggest that the target groups suffering from the two maladies are different. The causes are likely to be different, both between families and between rural and urban sectors, and therefore the policies aimed at remedying these maladies are also likely to be different. Accordingly, highly desirable though reducing unemployment

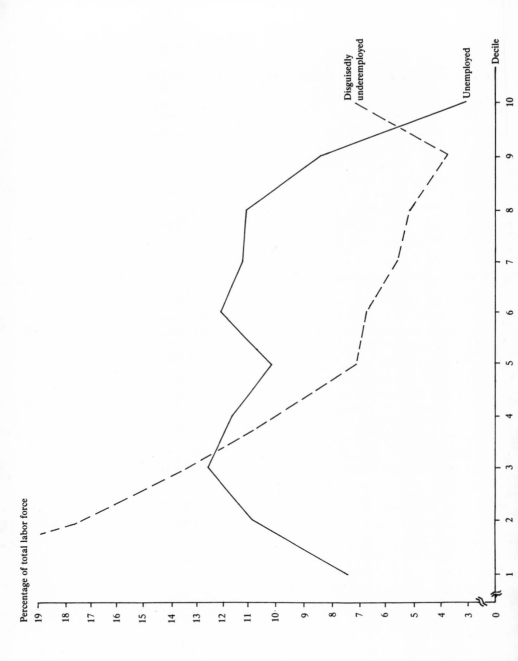

Percentage of total labor force

Disguisedly underemployed

Unemployed

Decile

Table 9.2   Zero-Order Correlation Triangle, 1984

	X_3	X_4	X_5	X_6	X_7	X_8	X_9	Y	Mean
X_2	0.91	0.61	0.69	0.77	0.71	−0.32	0.38	−0.71	2,631
X_3		0.73	0.81	0.67	0.80	−0.27	0.45	−0.66	1,349
						(0.45)		(0.04)	
X_4			0.97	0.23	0.97	−0.13	0.81	−0.47	12,707
				(0.53)		(0.70)		(0.16)	
X_5				0.27	0.99	−0.31	0.68	−0.62	6,010
				(0.44)		(3.9)		(0.05)	
X_6					0.32	−0.15	0.20	−0.44	140
					(0.37)	(0.68)	(0.58)	(0.20)	
X_7						−0.35	0.68	−0.67	11,412
						(0.32)		(0.03)	
X_8							0.40	0.88	3,926
X_9								0.04	2,514
Y								(0.92)	91

Note: Simple correlations between decile means. The number of observations is ten. Standard errors are given in parentheses. The correlations that are reported without standard errors are statistically different from zero. The variables are defined below:

X_1 = Total households with underemployed workers
X_2 = Open underemployment: households
X_3 = Open underemployment: heads of households
X_4 = Disguised underemployment: households
X_5 = Disguised underemployment: heads of households
X_6 = Long-run unemployment: employees
X_7 = Disguised underemployment: men
X_8 = Disguised underemployment: women
X_9 = Disguised underemployment: adolescents
Y = Per capita income (decile mean) in 1982 dollars.

is, an antipoverty policy has to be addressed to underemployment much more than unemployment.

So far we have seen mostly aggregate results for all ages. The classification of the unemployed by age and education should throw more light on the relationship under investigation.

Unemployment or Underemployment by Age

Of working-age persons, the 18 percent who are below twenty years old account for 25 percent of the nation's unemployment (read row percentages in table 9.3), even though the unemployment rate within the entire group (including those who are in college, etc., and are not seeking jobs) is only 6 percent. The single chunk of 36 percent of the nation's unemployment is made up by the young twenty- to twenty-four-year-old entrants, forming

Table 9.3 Underemployment by Age, 1982

State of Employment	≤19	20-24	25-29	30-34	35-39	40-44	45-49	50-54	55-59	60-64	≥65	Total Including Inactives	Total Excluding Inactives
1. Inactives												46.29	
a. Row %	28.48	11.80	7.65	6.45	5.82	5.01	5.18	4.98	5.46	5.79	13.42		
b. Column %	72.71	38.92	30.64	28.96	29.44	31.34	36.07	40.23	52.69	64.00	76.73		
2. Fully employed												35.65	(66.31)
a. Row %	4.59	13.56	16.26	15.56	13.67	10.69	8.64	6.82	4.54	2.60	3.07		
b. Column %	9.03	34.44	50.14	53.76	53.20	51.54	46.81	42.37	33.72	22.10	13.53		
3. Disguisedly underemployed												11.15	(20.74)
a. Row %	17.64	15.92	10.25	9.75	9.55	8.31	7.39	6.81	4.48	3.92	5.97		
b. Column %	10.85	12.64	9.08	10.54	11.62	12.52	12.51	13.24	10.42	10.42	6.23		
4. Openly underemployed												2.31	(4.30)
a. Row %	10.33	14.56	11.39	13.29	13.83	8.94	8.95	6.00	4.21	4.82	3.67		
b. Column %	1.32	2.40	2.27	3.09	3.35	2.79	3.14	2.41	2.02	2.65	1.05		
5. Underemployed in primary job												0.09	(0.17)
a. Row %	0.00	2.42	11.72	16.84	12.65	13.86	10.70	11.26	16.00	2.42	2.14		
b. Column %	0.00	0.02	0.10	0.15	0.13	0.18	0.15	0.18	0.31	0.05	0.02		
6. Unemployed												4.51	(8.4)
a. Row %	24.50	36.03	17.86	7.99	4.60	2.68	1.02	1.29	0.89	0.72	0.79		
b. Column %	6.09	11.59	6.96	3.49	2.26	1.63	1.33	1.56	0.84	0.78	0.44		
Total													
Number	206,798	131,889	117,651	104,480	84,367	75,072	65,415	54,722	47,803	47,803	92,317	1,140,618	
%	18.13	14.03	11.56	10.81	9.16	7.46	6.78	5.74	4.80	4.19	8.09	100.00	(100.00)

Source: Tabulated from Panamá, Controller General, *Household Survey, 1982.*

12 percent of the work force. The young workers of Panama up to age twenty-nine, who together form 44 percent of the work force, account for 78.4 percent of the nation's unemployment.

About 33 percent of the unemployed males and 19 percent of the unemployed females are heads of households. The age group thirty to fifty-nine has an unemployment rate of only 2 percent. Thus this large group of experienced workers, made up almost entirely of heads of households, is fortunate to escape the unemployment disaster.

The results seem to support the life cycle phenomenon identified earlier. Given practically no unemployment in the age group thirty to fifty-nine (table 9.3 and fig. 9.2), when the overall unemployment is verging on a two-digit rate, even if the below-thirty unemployed workers were poor because of unemployment, a large proportion of them are unlikely to remain permanently poor. Nevertheless, even temporary poverty is bad. The next problem therefore is to verify who among the unemployed is poor. I will proceed to that inquiry in several steps.

Unemployment or Underemployment and Education

Table 9.4 and figure 9.3 present associations between un/underemployment and education. We see that the highest unemployment prevails not among illiterates or workers with low schooling levels, but among workers with seven to twelve years of schooling in urban areas and four to six years of schooling in rural areas. In contrast, the highest disguised underemployment occurs among workers with less than six years of schooling. In other words, education reduces underemployment but increases unemployment.

One is tempted to conclude that through schooling many escape the proverbial frying pan (underemployment) to fall into the fire (unemployment) and therefore that education is not a desirable solution to poverty. That, however, is a trivial conclusion. Education of the poor will at worst redistribute poverty more equally and, at best, redistribute wealth more equitably. More educated people also create jobs for one another as they become more productive and enterprising, thereby priming supply to create its own demand. Besides, the reduction in underemployment mitigates permanent poverty, and the possible increase in unemployment probably causes no more than temporary poverty while the economy is in recession. Furthermore, even if education does temporarily create more unemployment, it serves to dramatize the plight of labor, whereas underemployment rarely appears as a dramatic phenomenon. Governments characteristically respond more expeditiously and more effectively to crises than to lingering states. Yet another favorable effect of education, especially college education, discernible from table 9.4 is that it leads to a substantial increase in labor force participation. The rate of inactivity declines from 53 percent

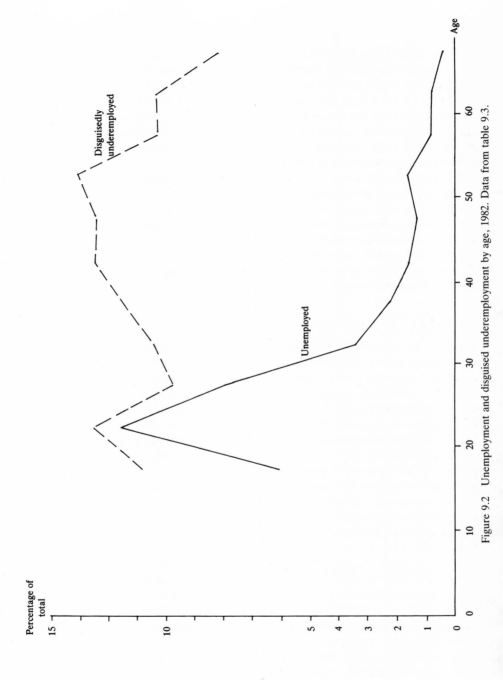

Figure 9.2   Unemployment and disguised underemployment by age, 1982. Data from table 9.3.

for the bottom education class to 16 percent for the top education class (see row 1b of table 9.4). Finally, education raises the earning level and provides the foundation for further learning and even higher earnings.

Several of the results of table 9.4 are well documented. One thing that is newly learned from this study is that in an upper-middle-income developing country such as Panama, to escape the underemployment malady and therefore poverty, one must cross the threshold of minimum schooling. That minimum for Panama is higher than a middle-school education (see row 5 in table 9.4). A desirable level of education to maximize one's chances to get out of underemployment and poverty is from high-school education to two years of college. An even more desirable level of education to escape both underemployment and unemployment is at least four years of college in urban areas, as may be verified from table 9.4, row 6 in particular and row 2 as supplementary information.

Thus, insofar as employment is concerned, terminating school with a primary education does not do one much good. (As we will see in chap. 12, however, primary education of mothers has been found to reduce poverty by lowering the fertility rate.) A policy implication of this result for Panama, therefore, is to make high-school education free and compulsory. This is not an unthinkable goal in this group of countries. Panama's northern neighbor, Costa Rica, has made high-school education free. At least partly because of this policy (combined with other policies, such as the elimination of the military to make education and other social policies financially viable and to eliminate the chances of military coups d'etat), Costa Rica has reaped some enviable results. Thus its society is more egalitarian, democratic, peaceful, and stable (unparalleled in this region), and it has experienced a higher rate of economic growth in the past several decades than any other Central American country.

A conclusion of this section that ought to be underlined is that a disproportionately high incidence of unemployment is found among those with ten to twelve years of schooling. Which income classes these workers are most likely to belong to is the subject of the next section.

Unemployment or Underemployment by Education and Income

A cross-tabulation of the unemployed by education and income deciles (table not shown) reveals that nearly half of the unemployed in the age group twenty to twenty-four have ten to twelve years of schooling. The ratios of the row percentages of this education class to the means of row percentages are greater than unity, by and large, for the upper-half deciles and lower than unity for the lower-half deciles, implying that the incidence of unemployment is higher among the nonpoor than the poor. The incidence tilts toward the middle and lower-middle income groups in lower

Table 9.4 Underemployment by Education, 1982

State of Employment	\[Years of School Completed\] ≤3	4–6	7–9	10–12	13–15	16–17	≥18	Total[a]
1. Inactives								
a. Row %	22.32	32.01	21.01	19.26	3.79	0.95	0.66	46.29
b. Column %	53.46	44.52	51.53	44.66	39.28	20.02	16.17	
2. Fully employed								
a. Row %	11.25	30.88	18.20	24.59	6.62	4.37	4.09	35.65 (66.31)
b. Column %	20.75	33.08	34.38	43.91	52.86	70.91	77.10	
3. Disguisedly underemployed								
a. Row %	36.04	47.40	10.71	4.90	0.36	0.39	0.20	11.15 (20.74)
b. Column %	20.73	15.88	6.32	2.73	0.91	1.98	1.18	
4. Openly underemployed								
a. Row %	29.37	43.59	11.76	10.53	1.08	2.10	1.57	2.31 (4.30)
b. Column %	3.51	3.02	1.44	1.22	0.56	2.21	1.91	
5. Underemployed in primary job								
a. Row %	22.95	50.51	3.72	2.42	0.00	0.00	20.37	0.09 (0.17)
b. Column %	0.11	0.14	0.02	0.01	0.00	0.00	1.01	
6. Unemployed								
a. Row %	5.91	24.77	26.42	33.08	66.33	2.38	1.10	4.51 (8.4)
b. Column %	1.38	3.36	5.31	7.47	6.40	4.88	2.63	
Total								
Number	220,411	379,624	215,266	227,758	50,000	25,064	21,595	100 (100.0)
%	19.32	33.28	18.87	19.97	4.46	2.20	1.89	

Source: Tabulated from Panamá, Controller General, *Household Survey, 1982.*

[a]The numbers in parentheses in the last column are percentages of each category among economically active persons.

education classes, toward lower education classes in the nineteen-and-under age group (in relation to the twenty to twenty-four age group), and toward higher education and higher income classes in higher age groups. As one moves from the diagonal cells to the northeast and southwest cells, the values become smaller and smaller, so that the cells near the northeast and the southwest corners end up with very low to zero values. The higher values lie along the diagonal, which is thick in the middle. There is thus some support for the hypothesis that most of the unemployed come from nonpoor, most probably middle, classes. It is also interesting that even college-educated persons are not immune to being unemployed, especially in rural areas.

To summarize the results of the preceding three sections, insofar as education and age are concerned, broadly speaking, high disguised underemployment prevails among those across all ages who have no more than primary education in rural areas and among those of all ages with middle-school education in urban areas. Unemployment occurs among those below thirty years of age, especially those between twenty and twenty-four, with middle-school education in rural areas and high-school to two-year-college education in urban areas. The result underscores the earlier conclusion that, important though it is to reduce unemployment, its removal is not likely to make a significant dent in critical poverty. A long-term antipoverty program requires measures that enable the rural poor to acquire a high-school education and the urban poor to get vocational training. In the short run, particularly during recessions, unemployment may tend to increase. That will, however, reflect only transitory growing pains. When the economic situation of the Latin American countries improves so that Panama's entrepôt trade and offshore banking industry recover and Panama gets out of the recession, unemployment may no longer take priority. But the problem of poverty will remain. The remedy for poverty suggested by this section may be summed up as follows: high-school education for the urban poor, agricultural development for the rural poor.

So far I have concentrated on the characteristics of individual workers. The focus of our analysis, however, is the family, which is the appropriate unit for a study of poverty. Accordingly, let me move on to analyze the characteristics of the unemployed by family status.

ARE THE UNEMPLOYED PRIMARY WORKERS OR SECONDARY WORKERS?

A key question in determining the relation between poverty and unemployment is, are the unemployed primary workers (heads of households) or secondary workers (all other workers)? Although unemployment is bad enough for either category of workers, the unemployment of the primary

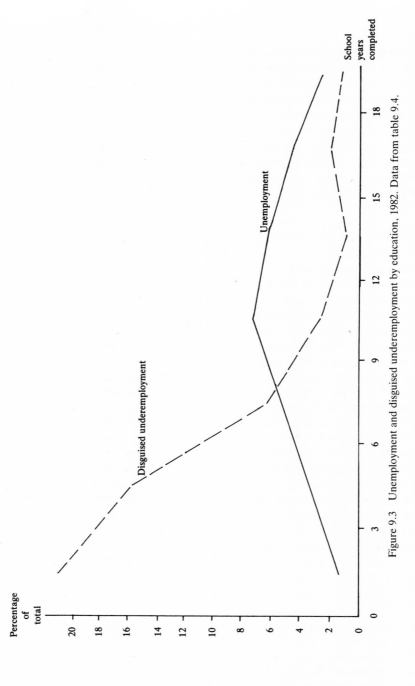

Figure 9.3 Unemployment and disguised underemployment by education, 1982. Data from table 9.4.

180

breadwinner of a family must in general be a greater disaster for the family than that of a secondary worker. In other words, the higher (lower) the incidence of unemployment among secondary (primary) workers, the weaker (stronger), in general, is likely to be the relation between unemployment and poverty.

At the macro level, 33 percent of unemployed men and 19 percent of unemployed women are heads of households. In this section I carry out a disaggregate analysis by characterizing primary and secondary workers by employment status, family income, area of residence, age, education, family size, and similar traits.

Characteristics of Unemployed Secondary Workers by Income of the Primary Worker

The rate of unemployment of nineteen-year-olds, in the first through fourth (poor) deciles, based on the income of the head of household, is 2.55 per household reporting one or more nineteen-year-old unemployed workers (table 9.5). In the fifth through ninth (nonpoor) deciles, the corresponding percentage is 3.25 per household reporting unemployment of nineteen-year-olds.

Above that age the percentage of workers reporting unemployment declines sharply in all deciles, to one person per household in the age group twenty to twenty-four, approximately one out of ten in the age group twenty-five to thirty-nine, and approximately one in twenty in the age group forty to sixty-five. It is reduced to fewer than one in fifty among retirees over sixty-five.

The unemployment rate among secondary workers is higher in urban than rural areas (nothing new); higher among those below twenty-five than among older groups (also well documented); higher among those with secondary education than among others (not widely know); and higher among the lower-middle to middle deciles than among the upper deciles (one of the important facts bared by this study). The last two facts need further analysis for more precise results.

Characteristics of Unemployed Secondary Workers by Education of the Primary Worker

Table 9.6 presents the education of the primary worker in relation to that of the unemployed and underemployed members of the household. Unemployment is three times as high in urban areas as in rural areas among the members of households with illiterate heads; twice as high in urban areas as in rural areas for members of households whose heads have less than primary education; but less than half as high in urban areas as in rural

Table 9.5 Unemployment among Primary and Secondary Workers by Income of Head of Household, National Socioeconomic Survey, 1983

Decile of Head of Household	Area	Age	Education^a	Family Size	Number Unemployed	Number of Households with Un/Underemployed Members	Number Un/underemployed as % of Total
					All Members of Family, Including Head		
1-4					45,359	428,261	10.59
5-9					22,292	169,895	13.12
10					21,708	215,116	10.09
1-4		19			1,359	43,250	3.14
		20-24			1,812	400	453.00
		25-39			7,463	7,493	99.60
		40-64			8,086	67,779	11.93
		65			4,529	79,862	5.67
			<P		402	21,751	1.85
			P		5,085	65,912	7.71
			S		11,543	61,601	18.74
			Un		3,035	6,664	57.55
			N		940	1,690	55.62
				1	889	34,028	2.61
				2	944	11,021	8.57
				3-5	1,143	12,654	9.03
				6-8	9,566	73,062	13.09
				9	7,208	52,622	13.44
5-9					3,431	19,536	17.56
		20-24			2,174	404	538.12
		25-39			8,704	10,228	85.10
		40-64			7,390	82,046	9.01
		65			2,942	94,501	3.11
			<P		498	27,937	1.78

	P	1,458	39,033	3.74
	S	9,753	98,097	9.94
	Un	6,972	44,609	15.63
	N	3,044	22,996	13.24
5–9	1	481	10,381	4.63
	2	433	18,795	2.30
	3–5	1,541	31,624	4.87
	6–8	9,810	116,229	8.44
	9+	6,448	41,261	15.63
		3,476	7,207	48.23
19		149	120	124.17
20–24		476	936	50.85
25–39		483	16,939	2.85
40–64		251	20,524	1.22
65+	<P	0	4,731	—
	P	269	3,112	8.64
	S	488	10,720	4.55
	M	363	11,184	3.25
	N	239	17,508	1.37
10		0	726	—
	1	171	8,013	2.13
	2	243	9,642	2.52
	3–5	626	22,753	2.75
	6–8	319	2,637	12.10
	9+	0	205	—
1–4	1	11,245	46,461	24.20
	2	11,047	123,434	8.95
5–9	1	16,366	153,006	10.70
	2	5,342	62,110	8.60
10	1	1,217	37,853	3.22
	2	142	5,397	2.63

[a]The symbols <P, P, S, M, Un, and N stand for preprimary, primary, secondary, more than secondary, and university education, and nil. The codes in column 2 distinguish urban (1) and rural (2) areas.

Table 9.6 Unemployment among Primary and Secondary Workers according to Education of Head of Household, National Socioeconomic Survey, 1983

Education of Head	Area	Education Levels of Un/Underemployeds	Number of Unemployeds	Number of Underemployeds[a]	Number of Households	Rate of Unemployment as % of Total	Rate of Underemployment as % of Total[a]
	U		28,828	5,393	237,320	12.15	2.27
	R		16,531	35,417	190,941	8.66	18.55
<P	U		6,083	1,564	31,638	19.23	4.94
<P	R		6,843	17,899	76,499	8.95	23.40
P	U		14,756	2,169	106,106	13.91	2.04
P	R		6,642	6,877	64,232	10.34	10.71
S	U		4,432	870	54,324	8.16	1.60
S	R		513	229	8,133	6.31	2.82
Un	U		2,201	190	39,071	5.63	0.49
Un	R		267	0	3,123	8.55	0.00
N	U		1,356	600	6,181	21.94	9.71
N	R		2,266	10,412	38,954	5.82	26.73
	1	<P	1,790	800	31,558	5.67	2.54
	1	P	2,679	416	80	6.83	1.31
	1	S	1,304	80	0	2.00	0.25
	1	Un	310	215	0	0.80	0.60
	1	N	0	53	0	0.00	0.18
	2	<P	3,329	13,516	76,499	4.29	17.66
	2	P	2,472	3,618	0	2.63	4.73
	2	S	876	275	0	0.86	0.36
	2	Un	106	0	0	0.11	—
	2	N	60	490	0	0.08	0.64

P	1	<P	492	113	0	0.58	0.15
	1	P	8,350	1,791	106,106	6.37	1.69
	1	S	4,271	212	0	1.81	0.20
	1	Un	1,589	53	0	0.77	0.05
	1	N	54	0	0	0.05	—
	2	<P	292	181	0	0.24	0.17
	2	P	5,191	6,544	64,232	7.29	10.19
	2	S	1,052	73	0	1.12	0.11
	2	Un	107	0	0	0.12	—
	2	N	0	79	0	0.00	0.12
s	1	<P	0	29	0	0.00	0.05
	1	P	1,378	412	54,324	1.30	0.64
	1	S	2,460	400	0	3.57	0.74
	1	Un	594	0	0	0.95	—
	1	N	0	29	0	0.00	0.05
	2	<P	0	0	0	0.00	—
	2	P	169	31	8,133	0.31	0.06
	2	S	300	162	0	3.07	1.99
	2	Un	44	0	0	0.00	—
	2	N	0	36	0	0.00	0.44

Table 9.6 Continued.

Education of Head	Area	Education Levels of Un/Underemployeds	Number of Unemployeds	Number of Underemployeds[a]	Number of Households	Rate of Unemployment as % of Total	Rate of Underemployment as % of Total[a]
Un	1	<P	0	30	0	0.00	0.37
	1	P	292	0	0	3.59	—
	1	S	666	0	0	3.28	0.41
	1	Un	1,243	160	39,071	2.06	—
	1	N	0	0	0	0.00	—
	2	<P	0	0	0	0.00	—
	2	P	0	0	0	0.00	—
	2	S	37	0	0	0.09	—
	2	Un	230	0	3,123	7.36	—
	2	N	0	0	0	0.00	—
N	1	<P	596	30	0	—	—
	1	P	406	252	0	—	—
	1	S	167	0	0	—	—
	1	Un	0	0	0	—	—
	1	N	187	318	6,181	—	—
	2	<P	313	1,216	0	—	—
	2	P	847	1,978	0	—	—
	2	S	37	232	0	—	—
	2	Un	0	0	0	—	—
	2	N	1,069	6,986	38,954	—	—

Note: The symbols stand for the following: U, urban, R, rural; <P, P, S, Un, and N, preprimary, primary, secondary, and university education, and nil. The numbers in column 2 stand for urban (1) and rural (2) areas.

[a] The underemployment of this table records simply the proportion of persons underemployed to any degree. The measure has not been converted to equivalent employment.

areas for members of households with university-educated heads. Since jobs requiring higher education are mostly in urban centers, the factors that favor the city graduates include information, contacts, quality of education, and probably segmentation of superior and inferior markets. (The segmented labor markets hypothesis will be tested in chap. 10.)

The incidence of unemployment (as distinguished from the absolute number of the unemployed) tends to converge on secondary- and primary-educated heads of households and secondary- and university-educated secondary workers, irrespective of whether the heads have higher or lower levels of education than the secondary workers.

The unemployment and education relationships between primary and secondary workers have become a bit clearer; namely, the greatest unemployment tends to fall on those with middle educational levels who are unlikely to be from poor families. Even if they are, the unemployed secondary workers are not necessarily poor as long as the heads are employed.

Unemployment within subgroups is relatively high in the urban informal sector, in large families, among those below age twenty-five, and among those with primary and secondary education. Although large families and the informal sector, on the average, may reflect low per capita incomes relative to their opposite compatriots, that is not necessarily the case, for we do not yet know the relative proportions of unemployed heads of household to unemployed secondary workers in the two sectors. That brings us, finally, to the tables in which these characteristics are cross-tabulated.

Characteristics of Unemployed and Underemployed Secondary Workers in the Households of Unemployed or Underemployed Primary Workers

Of the 428,261 heads of households in Panama, with a total of 45,359 unemployed persons, 14,802 (41 percent of the unemployed of 3.37 percent of the total heads) are openly unemployed and 24,247 (5.72 percent of the heads) are disguisedly underemployed (tables 9.1 and 9.5). The 14,802 unemployed heads have in their families 2,146 (16,948 − 14,802) unemployed and 1,345 disguisedly underemployed members. The 24,247 disguisedly underemployed heads are accompanied by 2,005 unemployed and 1,739 disguisedly underemployed members. Thus up to 7,235 (2,146 + 1,345 + 2,005 + 1,739) heads (forming 1.68 percent of the national heads) face the double calamity of being themselves unemployed or underemployed and having at least one other member of their family in either of the two states. Of these, the 3,491 (0.81 percent) unemployed heads with one or more unemployed or underemployed members must be in a precarious economic plight. We do not know, however, whether the 3,491 unemployed are permanently or temporarily so. All that can be said statistically is that of the 9.3 percent unemployed during the year 1983, at least 0.81 percent are likely to be critically poor because not only the head breadwinner but at least one other member is unemployed. Further research is needed to pinpoint families whose primary worker has been unemployed for several months or years. If there are such families, they deserve to be given priority in any program of employment generation or poverty relief. In any case, it can be said that at least about 10 percent of the unemployed are in poverty.

The statistics by household size suggest that in the urban sector, unemployment among the secondary members of the households of disguisedly underemployed heads exists only in households with six to eight members. It appears that among the poor only large households can afford to have any unemployed members. In the rural sector, unemployment is uniformly spread across all sizes of households (as is underemployment). Unemployment among the secondary members of households with unemployed heads occurs almost uniformly across all household sizes in both urban and rural areas, except that in very large urban households of nine members or more it is about twice as high as in other sizes, both urban and rural.

The results thus do not reject the hypothesis that the members of households headed by underemployed persons (invariably poor) cannot afford to be unemployed, except in large homes that can afford to keep an unemployed member searching for a job while sharing subsistence with the family.

From this foray into various associations of primary workers with secondary workers, we may derive the following broad conclusions: unemployment is higher among secondary workers than among primary workers; underemployment is by and large uniformly spread between heads and nonheads as well as among heads in all deciles; underemployed heads scarcely seem able to afford to be unemployed or have members of their families unemployed; the incidence of unemployment is high among primary- to secondary-educated heads of households and among high-school-educated secondary workers in middle to lower-middle deciles.

An Econometric Test of the Relation between Unemployment and Poverty

The analysis of the preceding two sections has failed to discover perceptible associations between unemployment and poverty. In this section I make a finer test of possible interrelation between unemployment and poverty and, by implication, between the traditional employment-creating policy and poverty. This is done indirectly by searching for functional relation, if any, between the unemployment/employment of the primary worker and the unemployment/employment of the secondary worker within the same family. For this purpose we did a multinomial analysis of the probability that secondary workers will be unemployed/employed when the head of household is unemployed/employed. The following four logistic regressions, which are reported in detail in tables 9.7 through 9.10, were run:

1. The probability that secondary workers will be unemployed when the head of household is unemployed—dependent variable USWUH or simply *UU*—where an observation (a family) takes the value of unity for *UU* and zero otherwise (table 9.7).
2. The probability that secondary workers will be unemployed in the household of an employed head—dependent variable USWEH or simply *UE* (table 9.8).
3. The probability that secondary workers will be employed when the head is not—dependent variable ESEUH or simply *EU* (table 9.9).
4. The probability that secondary workers will be employed when the head is employed—dependent variable ESWEH or simply *EE* (table 9.10).

The Variable *UU*

Other things being equal, the probability of falling into category *UU*—secondary workers' being unemployed when the head of household is unemployed—is unaffected by age and family income. The education variable throws out all other variables, including per capita family income. Every school year of education of the primary worker above the mean education reduces the probability of *UU* by 10.5 percent. The education of unemployed secondary workers has a positive sign (tends to increase the probability of *UU*) but is not significantly different from zero. The results suggest that it is the secondary workers in the households of educated primary workers who are, or tend to report being, unemployed when the primary worker is unemployed, irrespective of their education. Alternatively stated, the secondary workers in the household of an unemployed head with little education probably do low-productivity jobs and fail to report themselves as unemployed. The results thus suggest that unemployment tends to prevail among nonpoor families.

Note also that the mean education level of unemployed heads is approximately 6.28 years and that of employment-seeking secondary workers is significantly higher, 7.43 years. Higher education levels than these probably mean the completion of high school and even some years of university. At those levels the probability of a son's being unemployed when his father is unemployed increases. Very few university-educated heads, however,

Table 9.7 Logistic Function for the Subsample UU, 1983
(Dependent Variable: USWUH)

Variable	Beta	Standard Error	Chi-Square	Mean
Intercept	−6.1072	0.5090	143.96	0.0031
Y	−0.0006	—	—	1,407.7820
ESW	0.0035	0.0523	0.00	7.4337
EH	−0.1047	0.0545	3.69	6.2812
DA	1.8731	0.4427	17.91	0.4945
DS	0.8788	0.3685	5.65	0.2652
DAG1	0.4383	0.5918	0.55	0.0610
DAG2	0.1902	0.4244	0.20	0.2471
DAG4	−0.4606	0.5970	0.60	0.2471
DAG5	0.1762	0.8031	0.05	0.0599

$R = 0.210$
10,811 observations
10,777 USWUH = 0
   34 USWUH = 1

Fraction of concordant pairs of predicted probabilities and responses: 0.25
Rank correlation between predicted probability and response: 0.21

Note: Variables are defined below:

USWUH: Unemployed secondary worker, unemployed head of household
USWEH: Unemployed secondary worker, employed head of household
ESWUH: Employed secondary worker, unemployed head of household
ESWEH: Employed secondary worker, employed head of household
    Y: Per capita family income
  ESW: Education level of secondary worker
   EH: Education level of head of household
   DA: 1 for the agricultural sector, 0 otherwise
   DS: 1 for informal sector, 0 otherwise
 DAG1: 1 for age 19, 0 otherwise
 DAG2: 1 for age group 20–24, 0 otherwise
 DAG4: 1 for age group 40–59, 0 otherwise
 DAG5: 1 for age group ≥60

The sample sizes in the regressions of tables 9.7–9.10 are smaller than those appearing in table 9.6 because the SAS program picks up only those observations of the dependent variables that also have observations on the independent variables, whereas no such condition was imposed in the earlier tables.

Table 9.8 Logistic Function for Subsample UE, 1983
(Dependent Variable: USWEH)

Variable	Beta	Standard Error	Chi-Square	Mean
Intercept	−4.38353	0.1541	809.37	0.0450
Y	−0.0004	—	—	1,407.7820
ESW	0.0850	0.0147	33.38	7.4337
EH	−0.0086	0.0139	0.39	6.2812
DA	0.6451	0.1170	30.41	0.4945
DS	1.5230	0.1059	206.87	0.2652
DAG1	0.5782	0.1608	12.93	0.0610
DAG2	0.5285	0.1120	22.25	0.2471
DAG4	−0.6807	0.2075	10.76	0.2471
DAG5	−1.5290	0.5912	6.69	0.0599

$R = 0.388$
10,811 observations
10,324 USWEH = 0
  487 USWEH = 1

Fraction of concordant pairs of predicted probabilities and responses: 0.78
Rank correlation between predicted probability and response: 0.61

Note: For variable definitions, see note to table 9.7.

Table 9.9 Logistic Function for Subsample EU, 1983
(Dependent Variable: ESWUH)

Variable	Beta	Standard Error	Chi-Square	Mean
Intercept	−3.2365	0.1525	450.35	0.0250
Y	−0.0004	—	—	1,407.7820
ESW	−0.0099	0.0201	0.24	7.4337
EH	0.0543	0.0187	8.46	6.2812
DA	−0.1357	0.1540	0.78	0.4945
DS	−0.9359	0.1728	9.62	0.2652
DAG1	−0.2934	0.3108	0.89	0.0610
DAG2	0.0060	0.1635	0.00	0.2471
DAG4	−0.0282	0.1614	0.03	0.2471
DAG5	−0.6992	0.3583	3.81	0.0599

$R = 0.114$
10,811 observations
10,541 ESWUH = 0
  270 ESWUH = 1

Fraction of concordant pairs of predicted probabilities and responses: 0
Rank correlation between predicted probability and response: 0

Note: For variable definitions, see note to table 9.7.

Table 9.10   Logistic Function for Subsample EE, 1983
(Dependent Variable: ESWEH)

Variable	Beta	Standard Error	Chi-Square	Mean
Intercept	3.0781	0.1086	833.69	0.9268
Y	0.0004	—	—	1,407.7820
ESW	−0.0487	0.0120	17.66	7.4337
EH	−0.0070	0.0111	0.40	6.2812
DA	−0.4370	0.0913	22.91	0.4945
DS	−0.8993	0.0809	123.68	0.2652
DAG1	−0.3423	0.1381	6.14	0.0610
DAG2	−0.3592	0.0904	15.78	0.2471
DAG4	0.2497	0.1226	4.15	0.2471
DAG5	0.8520	0.2836	9.02	0.0599

$R = 0.268$
10,811 observations
   791 ESWEH = 0
10.020 ESWEH = 1

Note: For variable definitions, see note to table 9.7.

are unemployed. Almost all unemployed persons who have university education are secondary workers.

The Variable *UE*

Almost all variables of the regression tend to influence the unemployment of secondary workers in households with employed heads (table 9.8). The signs of the education variables are the same as in the *UU* regression, but the significance levels are reversed: the probability that secondary workers will be unemployed in households with employed heads increases by 8.5 percent for every additional year of schooling. The probability tends to increase if one is over twenty-five.

The Variable *EU*

The probability that secondary workers will be employed in households with unemployed heads declines with the schooling of the secondary worker and rises with the schooling of the head. This is consistent with the result of the *UE* sample in reverse: other things being equal, the higher the education of the secondary worker and—since higher education goes with higher earning capacity in general—the further away one is from potential poverty, the higher the probability of one's being unemployed.

The Variable *EE*

The probability that secondary workers will be employed in the household of an employed primary worker is reduced with the education of the secondary worker and is unaffected by the education of the primary worker. The probability of a secondary worker's falling into the *EE* category is reduced by about one-third if one is in age group nineteen to twenty-four (with age group twenty-five to thirty-nine as the base).

Conclusion

The results of the estimates of the unemployment and employment relationships of the primary and secondary workers within a household by logistic regressions support the results based on the analysis of cross-tabulations. Schooling plays an important role in the probability of a secondary worker's being employed or unemployed in relation to the head's being unemployed or employed. A higher level of schooling of the unemployed head tends to reduce the probability that the family's secondary workers will be unemployed (the schooling of the secondary worker in this case is unimportant). In the alternative situation, the schooling of secondary workers tends to increase the probability that secondary workers will be unemployed when the primary worker is employed (the schooling of the primary worker in this case is irrelevant). Thus there is some evidence of a trade-off (during periods of high unemployment) in seeking/having employment between the secondary workers and the head: when the head is unemployed the secondary workers have a lower probability of remaining unemployed the higher the schooling of the head (probably seeking jobs more seriously and finding them, or taking whatever job comes up even if it amounts to becoming underemployed by doing low-productivity work). When the head is employed, secondary workers have a probability of being unemployed or otherwise declaring themselves unemployed the higher their level of schooling.

In short, the results of the logistic regression analysis support earlier findings that unemployment is not a major problem of the poor. Rather, it is a major problem among the nonpoor. Unemployment and poverty are thus areas in which applying to LDCs policies derived from research in developed countries would be a mistake. For instance, in the United States the incidence of unemployment is much higher among blacks under age twenty-five (in general from poor households) than among whites under twenty-five (in general nonpoor). The reverse has been suggested (in this research) to be the case in Panama: the incidence is higher among nonpoor young workers than among poor young workers. The stage of economic development and the type of the economic structure are among the factors that explain these differences.

CONCLUSIONS

No matter from which angle we look at the relationship, the hypothesis that unemployment is largely (though not exclusively) a problem of the nonpoor is not rejected. The poor cannot afford to be unemployed. Consequently, highly important though a reduction in unemployment is, it is unlikely to make a significant dent in poverty in developing countries. Therefore it is not difficult to understand the frustration of the LDC policymakers who pin their hopes on general employment-expansion projects to mitigate poverty. In this study the micro approach of creating capacities among (augmenting the human and nonhuman assets at the disposal of) the poor and raising their productivity emerges as more effective than the macro approach of creating jobs in general (as distinguished from selective jobs for poor target groups).

PART FOUR
Behavioral Analysis

TEN

Family Structure, Earnings Functions, Intergenerational Transfers, and Poverty

This chapter, along with the succeeding three, is devoted in part to an empirical verification of the theory developed in chapter 2. It also clarifies certain theoretical issues concerning marriage and poverty. It presents earnings functions, poverty incidence functions, intergenerational transfer functions, and estimates of several other behavioral relations relating to family structure.

The nucleus of income earners of a household or family is formed by the head of household and the spouse. The joint income of husband and wife is more basic a measure for the welfare of a household than the earnings of individual spouses. In chapters 7–9 we diagnosed the degree of unemployment and underemployment among various classes of households. Further search for the causes of unemployment/underemployment and poverty leads us to dig into the work and child-service behavior and related characteristics of husband and wife—the subject matter of this chapter. Jointness of family formation and earnings is also explored.

The family has long been recognized as playing a vital role in determining both personal economic success and the intergenerational transmission of inequality. The debate goes back at least to Plato, who suggested that the nature of inequality would be radically altered if children were removed from their natural parents at birth. Over the years, many important economists have stressed the importance of a person's origin and family circumstances in determining economic success. For instance, Alfred Marshall pointed to the influence of parents on educational and occupational choices and on other human capital investments of their offspring, focusing specifically on the family's ability to finance such investments in their progeny. John Stuart Mill pointed to the connection between family environment and subsequent economic fortunes. These ideas have been reinforced by

The research for this chapter was done by Sherwin Rosen, University of Chicago. The chapter is based largely on Rosen's report on the topic to the Critical Poverty Project of Panama (Rosen 1985). For this book, however, I expanded and reorganized Rosen's study somewhat. Responsibility for errors and weaknesses that might have crept in during the reorganization falls on me.

modern research on the distribution of income and of poverty and its determinants in the past two decades. This research enterprise has been supported by the increasing availability of data on the indicators of personal economic success and by parallel and extensive developments in the theory of human capital and the economic theory of the family. However, most of this research has been applied only to a few countries, owing to limitations of data. The excellent and extensive survey information made available by the National Socioeconomic Survey, 1983, allows some of these ideas to be examined for the first time in Panama's economy.

LIFE CYCLE ISSUES ONCE AGAIN

Two versions of the life cycle theory of poverty were reviewed in chapter 1. Some empirical evidence for this theory was found in chapter 7. In this connection I should mention that there are many dimensions to the concept of poverty and economic well-being, to be sure, but this study, like most others done from the perspective of economics, concentrates on personal income and its determinants—in a word, on command over market resources—as the primary index of interest. This index has the virtue of plausible objectivity and is generally thought to be strongly correlated with other measures of welfare.

The modern theory of personal economic well-being has evolved over the years toward a distinct life cycle orientation, in which income-earning prospects over a lifetime and personal wealth are the central concepts of analysis. A person's ability to produce income and thus support the consumption standard that goes along with it is fundamentally determined by the quantity and quality of resources controlled, and command over resources systematically changes over one's life span. When employed in the market sector, these resources combine with their prices to determine wealth; when employed in the nonmarket sector, they are valued implicitly by productive efficiency and the opportunity cost of time. This study concentrates largely on market values and earning power in the market sector, because those data are more readily available. However, note that a significant share of Panama's population resides and is employed in rural areas where market transactions are less frequent and self-production is more important. This nontrivial segment of the population is treated elsewhere.

The overwhelming fraction of the population, however, is employed in the market sector, both in urban areas and on those farms where cash crops account for a large share of the income. Panama is largely a market economy whose origins rest firmly on its long-standing position as a world trading center. From outward appearances it seems to be a relatively fluid society compared with most, accommodating a very diverse population through a relatively liberal immigration policy. There is a significant migration within the country as well, largely from rural to urban areas and characteristic of a developing economy. Many people described Panamanian society to me as a melting pot, and the phrase seems apt. In fact, a striking finding of the empirical work reported below is that the sources and structure of earnings in this society strongly resemble those of more developed countries where the data are available to perform the calculations.

Life cycle theory makes a distinction between human resources, or human capital, and nonhuman resources and capital. Human capital is the stock of skills and productive knowledge people embody in their roles as economic agents. Part of these skills are inherited through the genetic transmission of talents and other valuable traits. But in at least equal measure they are acquired and learned at considerable cost and personal sacrifice. Personal learning and skill-developing activities are fruitfully viewed as investments, and to make the best use of its human resources a society must be structured so that its human capital investments are directed toward their most highly valued social uses. If a significant share of human resources is acquired through investment, then earnings capacity systematically changes over the life cycle. It is smallest at the age of entry into the labor market and grows through work experience and on-the-job training as the person ages.

However, earnings prospects at the time of entry into the labor force are themselves determined by economic choices and opportunities. Of these, two main activities may be distinguished. One is formal education, where both cognitive and associative skills are acquired. In Panama formal education is financed and provided by both the state and the church, and of course many of the older immigrants were educated abroad. The other is investment in children, especially young children in the home. These interact in important ways in the direct production of skill and earning capacity. There is also an indirect linkage between the family environment and resources and the personal development of marketable skills, insofar as limitations on family wealth imply constraints on investment in human capital. Therefore some persistence in the intergenerational transmission of inequality is inherent in all societies, owing both to genetic inheritance and also to the inheritance of home environments, family resources, and direct bequests of nonhuman wealth. This remains true even in the presence of public subsidies and direct public provision of education and other human capital investments, because direct out-of-pocket expenses are only part of total investment expense: opportunities forgone are at least as important. Perhaps the ultimate test of inequity and inequality in a society is a measure of the "memory" in the system—that is, how long an advantage or disadvantage in one generation, whatever its source, gets carried over to the next and subsequent generations. The less persistence and memory in the system, the greater the social and economic mobility built into it.

The connection between the family and inequality gains increasing importance because of enormous secular changes in the composition of families and in the role of women in the economy. Panama shows little exception to the general trend of increasing labor force participation and market activities among women. The changing role of women, from serving in the traditional household as the primary provider of nonmarket goods and raising children, to being equal partner in providing market goods, has two opposing effects on inequality. Less household and nonmarket production decreases the household's economic welfare because valuable production has been displaced, even though such values are seldom counted in official statistics of income and output. This point gets magnified when there is frequent household dissolution and significant marital instability. The other side of the coin is that market goods substitute for nonmarket production, and greater access to market goods and the monetary wealth it entails may help overcome financial barriers to human capital and other investments in productive capacity.

THE THEORY OF MARRIAGE

The contemporary *theory of household production* underlines the division of labor between husband and wife in producing market goods (or earning market wages) and in providing household services, including family leisure and children. Wives bear children. The postwar *theory of family formation* suggests that couples having a particular set of traits, such as higher education levels, have been observed to plan, space, and rear children somewhat differently than couples with another set of traits. Accordingly, the maximization of family production may cause the market-observed inequalities of income to understate the families' real income and welfare.

Marriage not only brings together two brains and two sets of personal traits, it also buttresses the *environments* husband and wife come from, including family connections and personal contacts. For instance, some research studies have revealed that the mother-in-law has a greater influence on a person's occupational attainment than does the mother, reflecting the role of "contacts." Thus the analysis of poverty will not be complete without studying the behavior and characteristics of households formed by married couples. A pertinent question being posed is, Does marriage lessen or exacerbate the incidence of poverty? If it is found that there are factors inherent in marriage that increase poverty or income inequality, then the next questions is, Are such factors amenable to correction through feasible policies? Before we delve into these questions, a formal statement of the theory of family structure is in order.

A marriage "market" itself alters the distribution of economic welfare among families if marriage involves "assortive mating." The idea is based on the fact that marriage (or more generally, long-term arrangements without the formalities of marriage) involves a relationship of exchange in which partners are selected and sorted to each other. The basis for exchange will differ among alternative partners: some partners are inherently more desirable than others and offer more favorable exchange relationships. In the end, partners are sorted, roughly, to maximize the gains from marriage, and to the extent that there are interactions among partner types in determining the productivity of the match, assortive mating on productivity grounds is to be expected. If the interaction in match quality is positive, individuals with more favorable prospects will tend to be matched in equilibrium. This means that people with less favorable prospects can find only less favorable partners. Hence a positive, multiplicative effect of personal characteristics of partners results in greater overall inequality than if these effects were not present.

These ideas can be formalized in a relatively simple and highly stylized fashion as follows: Let z be an index of the output of a marriage, and let x and y denote univariate indexes of the "quality" of potential marriage partners (x for men, y for women). To represent the diversity of people in the marriage market, the supply of men of quality x is written as $\phi(x)$ and the supply of women of quality y is written $\theta(y)$. Thus ϕ and θ are density functions. The output of the marriage is related to x and y according to production function $x = f(x,y)$. f_x and f_y are positive, reflecting positive marginal products of personal characteristics in producing marital output. A more general formulation would also distinguish among several types of outputs—for example, between household production and market production—but these more complex models will not be considered here, because they just detract from the main point to be made.

A marriage or assignment function matches an x to a y (or vice versa). Thus, in equilibrium we have $x = X(y)$ or equivalently $y = Y(x)$, where $Y(x)$ is the inverse function of $X(y)$. These functions indicate which type of woman is found with which type of man in the marital equilibrium. The derivatives of these functions (assuming they are defined) tell us about assortive mating. For example, if $dx/dy = X'(y) > 0$, then the better-quality men are mated to the better quality women and there is positive assortment. If $X'(y) < 0$, then men and women are mated inverse to their qualities and there is negative assortment. Finally, if $X'(y) = 0$, there is no tendency for systematic correlation between characteristics of partners in the population overall, and mating is "random." A central proposition in the economic problem of assignment states that $dx/dy \gtreqless 0$ as $f_{xy} \gtreqless 0$. The cross-derivative f_{xy} indicates how the marginal product of x changes as y increases. So if the marginal productivity of a high-quality woman increases when she marries a higher-quality man, then it is efficient for x and y to be positively associated. And if the marginal product of one decreases the quality of the other, then efficiency is promoted by negative assortment.

To see how the marriage market produces this result and to display the trading and sharing arrangements in marriage most clearly, define $R(x)$ and $S(y)$ as the return to men and women of type x and y respectively from a marriage. These functions show how the output of the marriage is divided between partners. Thus we have, by definition, $R(x) + S(y) = f(x, y) = z$. Imagine (conceptually) that these return functions are determined by a bidding process (proposals) for marriage partners. $S(y)$ is therefore the highest bid that a woman of type y receives from any man, and similarly $R(x)$ is the best offer that a man of type x receives from any woman. For example, all men may inherently prefer a particular woman as a partner, but men of different characteristics can offer different terms. The one that offers the best terms is selected by that woman as her partner in equilibrium.

Adopting the assumption that men propose to women, the return to a man is the total output of the marriage z minus the share going to the woman he marries. Thus a man of type x would choose a partner so as to maximize $z - S(y) = f(x, y) - S(y)$. The first-order condition for optimal choice of y given x is just $f_y'\,(x, y) = S'(y)$, which states that the marginal product of the spouse's contribution to the marriage is equal to her "marginal cost," calculated as the incremental amount the man must pay for a slightly superior wife. Since $R(x)$ is, in equilibrium, the difference between z and S, we must have in addition that $R(x) = \max_y\,[f(x, y) - S(y)]$. It follows that $R'(x) = f_x(x, y)$ in equilibrium, so the marginal product of the man equals his marginal cost (from the woman's point of view) as well.

The second-order condition for the optimal choice of y given x is $f_{yy} - S''(y) < 0$. This is necessary for the marginal condition above to describe a maximum. Since $f_y = S'$ describes the equilibrium choice, comparative statics indicates how x and y vary in equilibrium. Differentiating with respect to x yields $f_{xy} + f_{yy}(dy/dx) = S''(dy/dx)$. Gathering terms, we have $dy/dx = Y'(x) = -f_{xy}/(f_{yy} - S'')$. The denominator of this expression is negative, from the second-order condition, so the sign of dy/dx is the same as the sign of f_{xy}. Therefore there is positive, zero, or negative assortive mating as f_{xy} is positive, zero, or negative.

Now suppose f_{xy} is in fact positive. Then the distribution of z in the population of all marriages is given by $f(x, Y(x))\phi(x)$, where $Y(x)$ is the equilibrium assignment function. The positive interaction and the fact that $Y'(x)$ is positive make the distribution of z more skewed and more unequal than the distributions of traits of either x or y in the male and female subpopulations.

All available evidence suggests positive assortive mating in most societies, and Panama is no exception. The National Socioeconomic Survey, 1983, the basis of this report, was not designed to investigate this issue in detail. However, one statistic is particularly revealing. Considering intact families and irrespective of whether the head of the household is male or female, the correlation between the education of the household head and the education of the spouse is strongly positive. It is +0.6 in this sample. We also know from many studies (outside Panama) that education is strongly positively correlated with measures of ability and with occupational and social status. I will show below that it is also an important correlate of earnings. When these facts are combined with the estimated correlation of 0.6, the inference that males with better prospects marry or live with females with better prospects is difficult to deny.

Several important possibilities follow from this. First, we might expect on the grounds of genetic inheritance and early family background that the children of advantage parents would themselves have an advantage over others in their cohort. That is, the probable rate of return on investments in measured human capital such as education would be larger, and more of them would be undertaken. Second, even in the absence of any natural advantage, the greater ability to finance these investments would produce higher income and wealth prospects for these individuals and would also place them at an advantage in the marriage market.

POVERTY AND EARNINGS FUNCTIONS

The following aspects of human behavior in the context of family composition involve choices, at one stage of one's life or another, that affect one's earnings, and so poverty, and that are thus endogenous to the earnings model: marriage, schooling of children, family size, female labor force participation, marital stability, and earnings and poverty. Carefully specified, the equations for these traits can be arranged recursively. As such, they can be estimated one at a time by least-squares methods, the procedure followed in this chapter.

An overview of the relation between family structure and the incidence of poverty in Panama is presented in table 10.1. The first column is a multivariate logit function showing the functional determinants of the probability that a family is classified as poor. Poverty is defined as falling into the bottom fifth of the per capita distribution of family income. Let p be the probability that one is poor as defined in this way. Then the numbers in the first column of table 10.1 can be interpreted as β coefficients in the following regression:

$$\log p/(1 - p) = \beta X,$$

Table 10.1   Poverty Incidence

Regressors	Poverty Probability (Logit)[a]	Log Food Expenditure[b]	Log Total Expenditure[b]
Characteristics of household head			
Age	−0.078	0.019	0.034
	(0.016)	(0.004)	(0.004)
Age^2 × 1,000	0.599	−0.194	−0.280
	(0.158)	(0.037)	(0.042)
Education	−0.219	0.037	0.048
	(0.015)	(0.003)	(0.003)
Male	−0.817	0.044	0.099
	(0.130)	(0.027)	(0.031)
Spouse present	0.386	0.153	0.138
	(0.111)	(0.024)	(0.028)
Father's education	−0.033	−0.002	−0.005
	(0.021)	(0.003)	(0.004)
Mother's education	−0.015	−0.013	0.016
	(0.022)	(0.004)	(0.004)
Self-employed	1.107	−0.100	−0.200
	(0.086)	(0.010)	(0.022)
Urban	−1.184	0.289	0.365
	(0.109)	(0.021)	(0.024)
Family characteristics			
Children 0–5	0.411	0.023	−0.001
	(0.040)	(0.009)	(0.010)
Children 6–14	0.364	0.059	0.040
	(0.029)	(0.007)	(0.007)
Persons 15–65	−0.066	0.182	0.179
	(0.031)	(0.006)	(0.007)
Persons 65+	0.039	0.157	0.165
	(0.111)	(0.025)	(0.028)
Nonfamily members	—	0.338	0.331
		(0.038)	(0.043)
Province dummies (8)	Yes	Yes	Yes
	(0.257)	(0.050)	(0.057)
Coclé	−0.182	0.121	0.131
	(0.132)	(0.033)	(0.038)
Colón	−1.043	0.229	−0.031
	(0.231)	(0.046)	(0.052)
Chiriquí	−0.992	0.313	0.433
	(0.128)	(0.031)	(0.035)
Intercept	2.779	5.536	6.120
	(0.392)	(0.086)	(0.098)
R^2	—	0.406	0.383

Note: Standard errors in parentheses.

[a] Logit probability function: probability of falling in the lowest 20 percent of the income distribution.

[b] Linear regressions: dependent variable indicated.

where X is a vector of explanatory variables (listed on the left of the table) and β is a vector of regression coefficients. The number attached to each independent variable in the table is the β coefficient that goes along with it. The statistical standard error of that coefficient is shown in parentheses below the point estimate. Thus a positive coefficient indicates that the variable in question is more likely to lead to poverty and a negative coefficient indicates that the variable is less likely to lead to poverty. The independent variables in the table are broken down into three major groupings.

The first group of variables refers to personal characteristics of the household head. The age of the head has been entered as a quadratic and shows a nonmonotonic pattern. The incidence of poverty decreases strongly with age, but the rate of decline becomes milder as the household head ages. At approximately sixty-five years of age the pattern reverses, and the incidence of poverty actually increases with age beyond that point. This finding is impressive support of life cycle theory and shows that measured poverty has a strong life cycle component. This of course reflects the evolution and employment of personal skills and earning capacity over a lifetime. Measured poverty is highest among the young and the old, because their measured incomes are low. For the young this represents only one point on an income stream that is, on average, rising. The average person will have a significantly larger income in middle age than at younger ages, near the time of entry into the labor market. On the other hand, many of the old have retired, and their current measured income is low. It is noteworthy that the concept of income used here is unusually inclusive, allowing for nonearned income (returns on nonhuman capital) and imputations for owner-occupied housing. If these refinements of measurement had not been made, the incidence of poverty among the elderly would be greater than shown here.

The table shows also a powerful effect of education on poverty. Families in which the head has much education are much less likely to be poor (at any age and with any other family characteristics) than families in which the head has little education. As a first pass on an intergenerational linkage, the effect of the education of the head's mother and father are also shown. These also decrease the incidence of poverty. However, the effects are qualitatively small, on the order of one-tenth as large as the direct effect of the head's education. They are also imprecisely estimated and are not statistically significant. At least as measured by poverty incidence, the direct intergenerational effects of education wash out in one generation. However, there remain indirect effects that are examined below.

The table also shows that the self-employed are much more likely to be poor and that people who live in urban places are much less likely to be poor, given similarity in education, age, and other variables. The coefficients on these effects translate into enormous differences between poverty incidence for self-employed workers and for others, and for differences between the urban and rural populations in Panama, on the order of 50 percent or more. Since a large fraction of Panama's population is nonurban, the table strongly suggests that a major problem of measured poverty is in the rural sector and that the nonurban, largely agricultural population accounts for a significant fraction of the poor. Households headed by males also show a much lower incidence of poverty than other households. This is found in other societies as well.

The effect of the presence of a spouse is best discussed in the context of the variables listed under the general heading "family characteristics." All these coefficients together suggest that poverty increases with the number of persons in the household and that the positive coefficient on the spouse present variable is picking up an effect of this nature. The only exception to this is the negative effect of the number of persons aged fifteen to sixty-five, which probably reflects the presence of more earners in the family. The dependence of poverty status on family size is a typical finding in studies of poverty incidence and is almost inherent in a measure of poverty based on per capita family income. It is important to notice that the measure does not impute values for nonmarket production, and specifically for the value of home inputs in the care and upbringing of children. We may surmise that the effects of family size on poverty would be much different if these imputations could be made.

The last part of the logit function presents statistical controls for province of residence, represented by dummy variables. Veraguas province is taken as the basis of comparison and is the poorest province on this account. Bocas del Toro, Colón, Chiriquí, Los Santos, and Panamá are the provinces where the incidence of poverty is lowest *after controlling* for other aspects of families—their size and structure, which are also determinants of poverty status. Coclé comes close to Veraguas in this "pure" incidence measure, whereas Darién and Herrara are in the middle. It is interesting that this interprovince ranking is similar to that obtained when no controls are made for interprovincial differences in family composition.

The last two columns of table 10.1 show least-squares regressions of the determinants of expenditure on food and total expenditure and are meant to serve as somewhat independent and in any case different indicators of poverty. Here, of course, greater expenditure is associated with lesser poverty, and most of the coefficients conform to the results for the poverty logit function. Notice that the positive effect of family size on food and total expenditure is consistent with the interpretation of these variables given above. All in all, the three regressions corroborate each other in depicting the poor.

An empirical investigation of the linkages between family structure, earnings, and human capital investments is contained in the remaining tables. The analysis begins in table 10.2, which shows the determinants of market earnings for males and females. To avoid problems of defining income and making imputations for nonmarket production, these comparisons are limited to nonagricultural workers.

In general, we follow the "human capital function" approach in which earnings are related to age, education, and other variables. Notice that the list of regressors in table 10.2 is relatively sparse: there are no controls for occupation and industrial sector, for example. The focus of the current investigation is on the life cycle aspects of personal investment and employment in some occupation, and industry of employment may change over time and with age. Therefore such effects are properly incorporated in the education and age effects for focusing on the prospects for general human capital investment to yield personal returns. The intensity of employment variable (a proxy for hours worked) and the unemployment variable (at the time of the survey) are meant to serve as statistical controls, to purge the data of differences among respondents in time worked. The earnings concept here refers to total earnings in a ten-month period before the survey, and the time-worked controls make the comparisons roughly in terms of average hourly wage rates.

The first four coefficients are interpreted as reflecting returns to investment in the human capital framework. The dependent variable is the log earnings, and as is well known, the coefficient on years of schooling gives an approximate estimate of rate of return to education. In the pooled regression across both sexes, this return is 7 percent. The regressions for each sex show this is broken down into a return of 6 percent for males and almost 8 percent for females. These estimates are very similar to those found in other countries—for example, the United States and England. It is remarkable that the labor market structure in Panama rewards investment in schooling in a manner very similar to that in other countries. The training variable is a dummy variable indicating whether a person went through a vocational training program on the current job. Its substantial coefficient, on the order of 15 percent, is consistent with a large rate of return to such investment, though there are obvious problems of interpretation owing to selection. It is also interesting that the rate of return to schooling is larger for females than for males (the rate of return to training is slightly smaller for females, but the differences are not statistically significant). This *difference* in returns to schooling between the sexes is somewhat different than is found in other countries. It is consistent with some evidence presented below that labor force participation of females in Panama is strongly conditioned on schooling.

Table 10.2   Determinants of Earnings, by Sex

Regressors	All	Males	Females
Characteristics of household head			
Education	0.069	0.060	0.078
	(0.003)	(0.004)	(0.005)
Training	0.163	0.160	0.145
	(0.024)	(0.030)	(0.035)
Age	0.060	0.066	0.028
	(0.006)	(0.007)	(0.010)
Age^2 × 1,000	−0.570	−0.638	−0.226
	(0.069)	(0.083)	(0.116)
Spouse present	0.130	0.154	−0.076
	(0.037)	(0.043)	(0.076)
Urban	0.063	0.081	0.024
	(0.026)	(0.032)	(0.045)
Male	0.291	—	—
	(0.039)		
Family characteristics			
Father's education	0.014	0.016	0.013
	(0.003)	(0.004)	(0.005)
Mother's education	0.015	0.016	0.011
	(0.004)	(0.005)	(0.006)
Children 0–5	−0.003	0.005	−0.037
	(0.012)	(0.015)	(0.022)
Children 6–14	−0.016	−0.012	−0.028
	(0.009)	(0.011)	(0.014)
Work intensity	—	0.475	0.943
		(0.032)	(0.070)
Unemployment	−0.089	−0.211	0.010
	(0.045)	(0.100)	(0.075)
Province dummies (8)	Yes	Yes	Yes
Bocas del Toro	0.359	0.355	0.306
	(0.070)	(0.084)	(0.122)
Intercept	5.537	5.226	5.404
	(0.134)	(0.163)	(0.212)
R^2	0.421	0.429	0.513

Note: Standard errors in parentheses.

The effects of the quadratic in age show the typical pattern of a concave age-earnings profile over the life cycle. Earnings rise with age, but the rate of increase slows as a person gains more labor market experience. At older ages (beyond age fifty-four for males), earnings begin to fall with age in this cross-sectional data, reflecting both the obsolescence and depreciation of personal skills and gradual withdrawals from the labor market. There are marked differences between males and females in these age-earnings effects. The age-earnings profile is much flatter for women than for men. This too is a characteristic finding for data from other countries, and is generally thought to reflect differential incentives for on-the-job training and investments between the sexes due to (traditionally) less intensive labor force attachments by women.

The presence of a spouse has a major effect on the earnings of men but a statistically insignificant effect on the earnings of women. This too is a characteristic finding from the data of other countries. The substantial effect for men is consistent with the exchange relationship implicit in marriage and the possibilities for division of labor between household members. Married men are able to specialize to a greater extent in market production than unmarried men. There are lesser possibilities for this kind of specialization among women. The coefficient for men is, however, subject to an alternative interpretation. Men with a spouse present may be better prospects in the marriage market than men who remain unmarried. For example, they may be healthier and have more (unmeasured) ability. To the extent that this is true, the effect of a spouse on male earnings reflects left-out variables rather than investment effects. This same point could also be made for the education effects. However, detailed econometric investigation of ability bias in rate-of-return calculations shows that ability effects have only small consequences for the education effects, and there is no reason to believe the situation is any different in Panama.

The coefficient on the male dummy in the pooled regression gives a summary indication of the overall difference in earnings between the average male and the average female after standardizing for the differences in education, age, and other characteristics. The average male in the nonagricultural labor market in Panama earns approximately 30 percent more than the average female, holding characteristics and time worked constant. Although the income concept and some of the other explanatory variables are somewhat different in this sample than those used for similar calculations in other countries, this overall estimate of the average standardized difference is in the range found in the United States. This too corroborates the conclusion above that the underlying institutional structure of earnings determination in Panama is very similar to what is found in more developed countries. Of course the level of earnings is smaller in Panama than in the United States or England, but the sources and structure of the determinants of earnings and the returns to human capital investment are very similar.

The next group of variables shows the effect of family characteristics on earnings. The presence of children in the home would be expected to reduce the earnings of women more than for men, and this expectation is borne out in the estimates. The presence and number of children in the home have no statistical effect on the earnings of men but tend to reduce the earnings of women. However, even for women these effects are relatively small and are not precisely estimated. That the point estimate is larger (in absolute value) for young children than for older ones in the case of women is also consistent with the division of labor in a marriage and the human capital investment viewpoint. However, this difference is imprecisely estimated. The effect of the number of children under age five on earnings is negative, but the confidence interval is fairly wide. This finding is consistent with another one reported below, that the presence of young children does not have as marked an effect on the labor force activities of women in Panama as it does in other countries that have been studied.

Finally, the table shows some direct intergenerational effects on personal earnings of the household head's parents' education. These effects are of course much smaller than those of own education on earnings, but they are positive and most often sharply estimated. There are several possible interpretations for this result, which deserves more elaborate investigation (on much more detailed data, not available here). The most straightforward possibility is that these variables serve as statistical controls for school quality and home inputs. The education effect reported above is based on a simple count of school years completed. It makes no allowance for the type or quality of school attended. One would expect not only that more educated parents would choose more schooling for their children (see below), but also that they would choose higher-quality schooling. Another possibility is that parents' education is a proxy for "labor market connections" and related factors that enable their adult children to gain access to better jobs. For example, it may proxy such things as entry to a family business or into the business of a friend or associate. Unfortunately, all these possibilities cannot be distinguished with the data currently available. Whatever their source, there is clearly a direct connection between family background and personal earnings of adults.

The statistical control effects of urban residence, work intensity, unemployment at the time of the survey, and the province dummy variables all go in the expected direction. Notice that the point estimate ranking of provinces on these indexes is slightly different from that in table 10.3, but most of these differences would not be statistically significant.

THE MARRIAGE FUNCTION AND A JOINT DETERMINATION OF MARRIAGE AND EARNINGS

One of the purposes of this chapter is to discern what influence, if any, marriage has on poverty. A natural way to do this is to compare and analyze the earnings differences between married and never-married persons. Dividing the data between married and never-married individuals, however, creates a selection bias. To remove the selection bias, I follow the Heckman procedure (Heckman 1987). To do that, we estimate a logit marriage function whose results are employed to generate a selection-correction variable, which is used as an independent variable in the earnings function of the entire sample.

The regressions of table 10.3 report a linear probability estimate of being married as well as joint estimates of marriage and earnings. The variable Z corrects the selection bias due to marriage. A few of the coefficients of table 10.3 by themselves are somewhat perplexing, since their signs are reversed, and significantly so. The estimates cast some doubt on the effectiveness of the selection-correction procedure used here. Nevertheless, I use these estimates to decompose the differences of earnings of married males and never-married males. Thus the product of the corresponding coefficients of the selection-corrected earnings function of never-married males and the mean values of the characteristics of married males, that is, the calculations of the incomes of married males by assigning them the earnings function of never-married males, results in a reduction of the income of marrieds by $ln4.82. The corresponding difference—the product of the mean characteristics of never-married males and the earnings function of stable-married males minus the selection-corrected estimates of the earnings of never-married males—comes to $-$ $ln8.39.[1] That is, were males with stable marriages constrained to work in the market conditions (according to the earnings function) of never marrieds, they would earn $ln4.82 less than they do. Contrariwise, had never-married males the opportunity to work in the market conditions (according to the earnings function) of marrieds, they would earn $ln8.39 more than they are estimated to earn in their own group. Using the mean of the two alternative estimates, we may conclude that the earnings capacity of married males is found to be $ln6.604 higher than that of the never married. Several interpretations could be put on these results: (1) They suggest some kind of market segmentation or discrimination against the unmarried. (2) Married males are in general self-selected and are endowed with certain unmeasured abilities/motivations that let them earn more. (3) The male responsibility that comes in the wake of marriage goads men to work harder and earn higher incomes. Note, however, that this is only the earnings side. We have not estimated earnings net of increased liabilities (expenses) resulting

---

1. Denoting married males by subscript m and never-married males by subscript u, mean characteristics by x, and the vectors of the earnings functions of married males and never-married males by b and b', respectively, the estimates of earnings differences in natural logs of dollars discussed in the text were made as follows:

$$\overline{X}_m b_m - \overline{X}_m b'_u = 8.63 - 3.81 = 4.82$$

$$\overline{X}_u b'_u - \overline{X}_u b_m = -0.098 - 8.29 = -8.39.$$

Table 10.3 Probability of Being Married and Selection Bias-Corrected Linear Earnings Functions, 1983

Independent Variable	Linear Probability of Being Married (p)		Linear Earnings Functions (Dependent Variable: L2C)								
			Married: Not Corrected for Selection Bias		Selection-Bias Corrected						
					Combined		Married		Unmarried		
	Coeff.	t	Coeff.	t	Coeff.	t	Coeff.	t	Coeff.	t	
Constant	0.50	11.72	4.22	16.97	8.53	9.9	9.19	24.6	-3.3	3.4	
L14 Number of rooms in house	—	—	0.04	2.84	0.06	4.4	0.06	4.8	0.1	3.3	
L18 Home without sanitary service	—	—	0.32	2.74	0.14	1.3	0.12	1.2	-0.2	-0.8	
L38 School years of head's father	-0.00	-0.1	0.01	1.52	0.01	1.6	0.01	1.9	0.0	0.8	
L39 School years of head's mother	0.00	1.61	0.01	1.68	-0.01	-1.3	-0.01	-1.5	-0.04	-1.9	
L40 School years of household head	0.01	10.10	-0.04	-4.14	-0.14	-9.9	-0.15	-9.9	-0.10	-3.1	
L41 School years of head's spouse	—	—	0.07	11.20	0.05	8.5	0.05	8.6	—	—	
L26 Age of household head	0.01	6.92	0.07	6.60	-0.05	-4.1	-0.04	-3.0	-0.12	-4.8	
L26SQ Age of household head^2	-0.00	-7.81	-0.00	-4.72	0.00	5.4	0.00	3.9	0.00	4.9	

Variable										
L121320 Rental of home	0.00	8.55	0.11	7.15	−0.03	−1.8	−0.02	−1.5	−0.01	−0.3
L56B*56D Intensity of employment* employment dummy	—	—	−0.00	−1.94	0.00	−2.2	0.00	−2.3	0.00	9.0
L50 Occupational status of head	0.00	2.35	—	—	—	—	—	—	—	—
L50*49 Occupational status of head*that_of head's father	—	—	0.00	2.12	0.00	1.7	0.00	2.0	0.00	0.7
L40*56B Head's education*job intensity	—	—	0.12	17.85	0.00	9.9	0.00	9.9	0.00	2.9
L40*50 Head's education*occupational status	—	—	0.00	0.01	−0.00	−6.1	−0.00	−5.8	0.00	−1.8
CHDEP Child dependency ratio	—	—	−0.03	−2.19	0.01	0.4	0.00	0.1	0.13	3.8
D.URBAN Dummy for urban household	0.00	1.69	—	—	—	—	—	—	—	—
L1 Comprehensive per capita family income	−0.00	−12.58	—	—	—	—	—	—	—	—
Z Selection-bias corrected term[a]	—	—	—	—	13.2	9.9	13.1	9.9	13.1	9.9
Adjusted R^2	0.06		0.54		0.61		0.62		0.78	
Number of observations	6,841		1,929		1,883		1,596		28	

Note: [a]To save space, the coefficient value 0.00 is stated where there are more than three zeroes before a nonzero digit after the decimal. Likewise, very large *t* values are squeezed to a space-manageable value of 9.9. The variable Z stands for the correction of selection bias due to marriage. It is entered as $1 - p$ in the "married" subsample and as p in the "never married" subsample, where p is the probability of being married. Asterisk in stub means "interacted with."

213

Table 10.4 Earnings Functions: Male Married Employee, over Twenty-five, Nonagricultural

Independent Variable[a]	Log Earnings Functions: Dependent Variable L2C, Urban Employment Income, or L2A, Overall Family Income							
	LL2C		LL2C		LL2A		LL2A	
	Coeff.	t	Coeff.	t	Coeff.	t	Coeff.	t
Intercept	4.216	16.97	3.571	14.33	4.546	18.37	4.000	15.98
L14 Number of rooms in house	0.042	2.84	0.049	3.44	0.030	2.08	0.036	2.56
L18 Home without sanitary service	0.322	2.74	0.307	2.69	0.149	1.32	0.142	1.24
L38 School years of head's father	0.009	1.52	0.011	1.90	0.016	2.64	0.018	2.98
L39 School years of head's mother	0.012	1.68	0.009	1.27	0.005	0.75	0.003	0.38
L40 School years of household head	-0.040	-4.14	-0.060	-6.29	-0.115	-12.00	-0.132	-13.80
L41 School years of head's spouse	0.066	11.20	0.065	11.38	0.037	6.38	0.037	6.39
L26 Age of household head	0.071	6.60	0.089	8.41	0.073	6.81	0.088	8.30
L26SQ Age of household head[2]	-0.001	-4.72	-0.001	-6.96	0.001	-5.91	-0.001	-7.76
L121320 Rental of home	0.109	7.15	0.111	7.51	0.077	5.11	0.079	5.35
L56B*56D Intensity of employment*employment dummy	-0.001	-1.94	-0.002	-2.16	-0.002	-2.36	-0.002	-2.54
L50*49 Occupational status of head*that of head's father	0.000[b]	2.12	0.000[b]	2.29	0.000[b]	3.65	0.000[b]	3.81
L40*56B Head's education*job intensity	0.126	17.85	0.140	20.06	0.215	30.54	0.227	32.29
L40*50 Head's education*occupational status	0.000	0.01	0.000[b]	0.35	-0.000[b]	-0.78	-0.000[b]	-0.51
CHDEP Child dependency ratio	-0.027	-2.19	-0.037	-3.10	-0.022	-1.80	-0.030	-2.55
K/O Capital/output ratio	—	—	0.006	10.57	—	—	0.005	8.90
Adjusted R^2	0.539		0.564		0.572		0.589	
Dependent variable mean	8.40		8.40		8.06		8.06	
Number of observations	1,929		1,929		1,929		1,929	

Source: Data from National Socioeconomic Survey, 1983; cf. chapter 2, eq. 23.

[a] The symbol L before the numeric variable stands for linear, that is, the absolute value, and LL for log-linear, the natural logarithm, of the variable concerned. The symbol K/O (capital/output ratio in the industry where the head of household works) is a proxy for the demand side of skills, as explained in chapter 2. Asterisk in stub means "interacted with."

[b] For the significance of 0.00 values, see the note to table 10.3.

from marriage and children. The supply side alone cannot tell us whether marriage reduces or exacerbates poverty. Econometric verification of this problem is infested with multiple selection biases and is beyond the scope of this chapter.

A Supply-and-Demand Model of Earnings, Family Background, and Poverty

Next we fit a simultaneous-equations model of the supply of skills and the demand for skills, the empirical relation for which was derived in chapter 2, eq. 23. Recall that the demand side is surrogated by capital/output ratio, K/O. Along with the demand side, we also test a few family background and inheritance variables, for instance, family's wealth and the quality of environment (as proxied by alternative indexes of the value and quality of home), occupational status, education of parents (and spouse, where relevant), and child dependency that might influence the levels of earnings during certain periods of one's life. Another specification variation that we test in this section is the introduction of several interaction terms for the earner's schooling, occupation, and employment.

Table 10.4 reports four regressions for a sample of urban males, two with and two without the demand-for-skill variable, one of each pair for log earnings of the male head of household (LL2A) and the other for log family income of the male head (LL2C). At first let us look at some of the results of the family background variables with and without the demand variable.

It may be seen that the coefficients of all the education variables—head's father's education, head's mother's education, head's spouse's education, and the household head's own education—are significantly different from zero. The only exception is the coefficient of father's education, which is significant at the 10 percent level and not, unlike other education coefficients, at the 1 percent level. Spouse's education is next only to the head's own education in importance. Each year of the spouse's education enables or induces the male head to earn $243 (or 3.5 percent) more income annually. Parents' education presumably stands for family background.

An interesting and important result of this table is that while all education variables retain their significance in the presence of family background variables and the demand variable, the conventional family background variables, too, come out highly significant. In support of one's home being an index of one's *family background* (in addition to father's education as discussed in the preceding section), we noted that in Panama, perhaps more than elsewhere, it is believed that the rich as a class are easy to identify not as much by their incomes (which are not publicly known) as by their residential areas (which are conspicuous). The same applies to the poor, whose areas are also not hidden. The quality of residential areas—as represented by the quality of home, measured in turn by its rental value (Ll2 + L13 + L20, or simply L121320), a variable that resolves the problem of whether the home is rented, bought on mortgage, or fully owned—is used as a proxy for family's *social and neighborhood environment*. A separate variable, number of rooms per home normalized by the number of persons in the family (L14), is used to stand for *home environment*. Both variables are highly significant. The sanitation variable (L18) did not survive in the presence of other indexes of home quality.

Thus, whether family background is surrogated by parents' education or parents' wealth, the results of this chapter suggest that it is a significant factor in one's earnings. We will also see in the succeeding chapter that family background and home environment are very important determinants of children's educational achievement. As a matter of fact, research has revealed that the real effect of family background on earnings works indirectly through education rather than directly. It is not an easy matter to provide a conducive home environment and competitive family background to the children of the poor. If they have to be extricated from their parents' poverty, special compensatory measures will be needed. One such measure is a universal system of preschool education, as was spelled out in chapter 7.

We may further see that the effect of the head's own education on his earnings becomes more significant when it interacts with the intensity of employment (L40*56B) and renders the coefficient of the noninteracted measure of education either insignificant or negative. The coefficient of education interacted with occupation is positive but not significantly so. Although seemingly trivial, the results underscore the embodied nature of investment in man: one must work to derive income from human capital, which not only is perishable when not harnessed to productive work, but also probably requires complementary consumption expenditure when involuntarily unemployed or when voluntarily used as leisure (as a consumption good). Note that in this table the overall effect of education must be calculated from the three coefficients of education (L40), using regression 2:

$$\text{Ln}y = -0.06(\text{L40}) + 0.14(\text{L40*56B}) + 0.0004029(\text{L40*L50}).$$

For example, the earnings of a fully employed (when L56*B = 1) college graduate (when L40 = 16) working in a median occupation (sixth-ranked L50) are probably 128 percent higher than those of a fully employed illiterate worker in the bottom occupation and 32 percent higher than those of a fully employed high-school graduate in an identical (median) occupation. The earnings of a fully employed high-school graduate, in turn, are probably 96 percent higher than those of a fully employed worker with no schooling.

Introducing the variable for the demand for skills improves the fit of the equation, as expected. The coefficient is highly significant. Recalling that K/O is defined as an index of two-digit industries with the overall (mean) K/O ratio = 100, and assuming that the value of the mean capital/output ratio in the urban sector of Panama is 4, the estimated coefficients of K/O of 0.006 (for the head's log earnings) and 0.005 (for family log income) mean that an increase of one point in capital/output ratio of an industry, say from 4 to 5, increases the earnings of the head of household by 6 percent and the income of the family by 5 percent. These coefficients should, however, be used with caution, since the data on capital are known to be subject to wide measurement errors.

A more important outcome of the supply-and-demand model to view is what happens to various supply coefficients in the presence of the demand variable. We see that the absolute values, along with the significance levels, of the coefficients of the following variables go up:

Positive Coefficients	Negative Coefficients
L14: Number of rooms in home	CHDEP: Child dependency ratio
L40*56B: Schooling interacted with intensity of employment	L40: Schooling of head
L38: Schooling of head's father	
L26: Experience of head	L26SQ: Experience squared

The sole coefficient whose absolute value falls is L39: schooling of the male head's mother. The composite effect of schooling on the earnings of fully employed college graduates compared with those without schooling declines from 137 percent to 128 percent and on the overall family income of the head of household from 160 percent to 152 percent. The difference becomes smaller and smaller as the schooling level falls. But the results are not statistically significant—the t value for the net difference between the corresponding sets of coefficients is approximately 1.47. The tendency for the earnings effect of schooling to go down when the effect of demand has been removed (when the demand variable is included in the regression) suggests that demands and supplies of skills are positively correlated. However, since even the probable face-value bias of the mainstream human capital (the supply-only) model is neither substantial nor statistically significant, there is not a great deal of evidence against the validity of the results of that model.

An interesting result of the supply-and-demand model is the estimated negative covariance between K/O and age and between K/O and the economic-status variables (such as those proxied by the value of home and father's schooling). Finally, the positive (negative) covariance between the education of the earner's mother (father) and the demand variable confirms the earlier results of a positive (negative) causal effect of mother's (father's) education on children's education.

In short, while the use of the supply-and-demand model for earnings function is not irrelevant and there is perceptible, though weak, evidence that it might improve the quality of estimates, the gain may not always be worth the cost of additional research. Accordingly, in the remaining estimates of earnings functions, we will largely ignore the demand-for skill-variable.

THE INTERGENERATIONAL PERSISTENCE OF EDUCATIONAL STATUS

Some direct intergenerational linkages between the education of parents and that of their adult children are shown in the regressions in table 10.5. As the general discussion above makes clear, parents' education would be expected to have powerful effects on human capital investments in children through preferences and inheritances and through the greater wealth and relaxation of capital market constraints that are indirectly demonstrated by the powerful effect of education on earnings shown in tables 10.2–4. These expectations are strongly confirmed in table 10.5. Parents' schooling has very strong positive effects on their adult children's educational attainments. It is interesting that the education of either parent has about the same effect for males, but the mother's education has a much larger effect for females than does the education of the father.

The effects of parents' occupation are much less sharply estimated. Adults whose fathers held professional and managerial positions (itself undoubtedly correlated with father's education) tend to attain higher levels of education. However, those whose fathers held other white-collar jobs tend, if anything, to have lower educational attainment, though these effects are not statistically significant. On the other hand, the point estimates are positive for those adults whose fathers were agricultural workers and other laborers. Although most of these effects are not statistically significant, they are for female heads. This finding needs more investigation in the context of Panamanian social structure. I conjecture that it reflects a selection effect, that women who planned to migrate from the rural to the urban sector found it in their interests to attain more education. This still leaves open the question why these incentives appeared to be smaller for men in the same circumstances. However, it is shown below that education is a very powerful determinant of labor force participation for women.

Table 10.5 Educational Attainment of Adults

Independent Variables	Male		Female	
	All	Heads	All	Heads
Father's education	0.310	0.304	0.171	0.137
	(0.018)	(0.018)	(0.019)	(0.041)
Mother's education	0.283	0.289	0.346	0.424
	(0.021)	(0.021)	(0.021)	(0.046)
Father's occupation				
Professional/manager	0.658	0.676	0.540	0.414
	(0.174)	(0.175)	(0.174)	(0.351)
Office/sales	−0.337	0.424	−0.553	−0.2887
	(0.663)	(0.670)	(0.664)	(1.721)
Agriculture/labor	0.779	0.789	0.870	3.211
	(0.556)	(0.549)	(0.532)	(1.184)
Urban	2.654	2.686	2.554	1.828
	(0.111)	(0.112)	(0.113)	(0.235)
Age	−0.066	−0.067	−0.065	−0.079
	(0.003)	(0.003)	(0.003)	(0.006)
Province				
Bocas del Toro	−1.190*	−1.293*	−1.182*	0.394
Coclé	0.303	0.311	0.236	0.309
Colón	0.154*	0.678*	0.734*	1.019
Chiriquí	0.522*	0.427*	0.787*	0.864*
Darién	−0.671*	0.670*	−0.706*	0.667
Herrera	−0.211	−0.240	0.281	0.158
Los Santos	0.612*	0.585*	1.053*	0.739
Panamá	0.819*	0.784*	0.879*	1.221*
Intercept	5.754	5.819	5.613	6.637
	(0.187)	(0.187)	(0.190)	(0.466)
R^2	0.575	0.585	0.489	0.506

Note: Standard errors in parentheses. The asterisk indicates significance at the 5 percent level where standard error is not shown.

The table also shows very large differences between the educational attainments of urban and rural dwellers, on the order of 2 to 2.5 years. This, of course, is characteristic of all economies and of less developed economies in particular. The province dummy control effects are, by and large, consistent with this finding. Provinces where there is greater representation of urban population tend to display greater schooling attainment of their population, though the effect is not perfect (Chiriquí, for example, is an outlier).

The negative effect of age is best interpreted as a simple cohort effect. There has been secular growth in educational attainment in Panama, as throughout the world. Therefore older people in this sample are less likely

Table 10.6   Educational Attainment of Children

Regressors	School Completion		Eldest Child's Schooling (Regression 3)
	Regression 1	Regression 2	
Characteristics of household head			
Age	−0.004	−0.001	0.201
	(0.0011)	(0.003)	(0.056)
Age^2 × 1,000	—	0.003	−0.002
		(0.035)	(0.0005)
Education	0.015	0.015	0.381
	(0.002)	(0.002)	(0.131)
Training	—	0.007	0.601
		(0.014)	(0.280)
Male	−0.062	−0.057	−0.520
	(0.023)	(0.023)	(0.305)
Spouse present	0.074	0.060	1.053
	(0.022)	(0.022)	(0.285)
Mother's schooling	0.004	0.003	0.054
	(0.0018)	(0.002)	(0.046)
Father's schooling	—	0.001	−0.051
		(0.002)	(0.039)
Family characteristics			
Children 0–5	−0.014	—	—
	(0.005)		
Children 6–14	−0.015	—	—
	(0.004)		
Urban	0.058	0.065	2.303
	(0.013)	(0.013)	(0.222)
Province dummies	Yes	Yes	Yes
Bocas del Toro		0.002	−0.329
		(0.032)	(0.810)
Coclé	0.058	0.064	−0.255
	(0.013)	(0.020)	(0.335)
Colón	0.099	0.106	0.529
	(0.026)	(0.029)	(0.515)
Chiriquí	0.071	1.023	
		(0.019)	(0.315)
Darién	−0.078	−0.075	−1.192
	(0.027)	(0.029)	(0.688)
Herrera	—	0.008	−0.064
		(0.020)	(0.355)
Intercept	0.634	0.598	0.857
R^2	0.168	0.172	0.402

Note: Standard errors in parentheses.

to have attained as much education as younger people. Another factor in this estimated effect, which cannot be studied with the data available, relates to the positive influence of urbanization. As the economy has become urbanized (also a long-term trend), it is more likely that the younger adults were born and raised in urban areas where school achievement levels are higher, whereas older adults were more likely to have been born and raised in the rural sector.

Table 10.6 brings us forward another generation in the connection between family background and education. Two types of regressions are shown. One is the schooling attainment of the eldest child remaining in the household, measured in years and comparable to the regressions in table 10.5. The other uses the mean index of school completion by school-age children as the dependent variable. This index is a weighted average over all children in the household of the ratio of actual school attainment relative to potential school attainment for that age. Hence it is naturally age adjusted and is especially useful for our purposes, whereas the schooling completed by the eldest child is not age adjusted. Note that these indexes refer to children remaining in the household, not to those who might have already left. However, the results in table 10.5 address that question as well as data available in the survey permit. In other words table 10.5 refers to adult children and table 10.6 to nonadult children.

The results for the school-completion index show a negative effect of age of household head on the school completion of children when age is entered in linear form and no significant effect when it is entered in quadratic form. Since the effect, if any, is numerically small, it seems pointless to dwell at length on this variable. The positive effect of age on the schooling of the eldest child undoubtedly occurs because older parents are likely to have older children and school attainment is correlated with age.

The most powerful and sharply estimated effects in this table are the positive effects of the head's education on the educational attainment of children. The *t*-statistics for these coefficients are very large, in the 7–10 range. The number in the third column is in many ways comparable to those in table 10.5 and shows about the same effect. The specifications are somewhat different in the two tables, owing to some data limitations, and so cannot be directly compared. But the coefficient of 0.381 on the schooling completed by the eldest child is very close to the estimated effects of father's and mother's education on the educational attainment of adult children. It would be interesting to know how the linkages between family background and educational attainment have changed in Panama over the years. One of the main reasons for public education is to help relax financial constraints on the educational choices of young people, and one would expect this to dull the effect of family background and environment on education over time. This topic is clearly worth much more intensive study and would help determine how access to human capital investments by young people has changed over time in Panama.

It is surprising that there are minimal effects of training of the head on school completion of children. Evidently there is imperfect substitution between general education and vocational training in this respect. However, the case is not entirely clear because training shows a significant positive effect on school years completed by the eldest child. Another unexpected result is that male-headed households on average exhibit less school completion of children, ceteris paribus, in this sample. This is difficult to explain on either economic grounds or other grounds. Notice, however, that there is a very strong positive effect on children's educational attainment if a spouse is present in the household. This is consistent with the value of spouses in household production and in encouraging more schooling by children.

Table 10.6 allows a third generation linkage to be examined for school choices. Grandmothers' education appears to have a positive effect on the school completion of their grandchildren. Although positive, the numerical effect is small. Furthermore, when both grandmothers' and grandfathers' education are included, the effects are not statistically significant. Apparently most of the connection between generations in educational choices is confined to one generation. The effect of urban residence is comparable in size to that found in table 10.5.

Table 10.6 also shows a powerful and negative effect of the number of children on their educational attainment. In the economic theory of the household, a distinction is made between the quantity and quality of children. Quality in this context refers to human capital investment. This quantity/quality substitution is clearly indicated here: households with many children do not invest in the education of each child to nearly the same extent as households with fewer children do, other things equal. This is a direct consequence of wealth constraints on human capital investments: there are fewer resources to go around per child in the larger families. To the extent that large families have many "unwanted" children, perhaps some social policy is implied. But it would be rash to jump to that conclusion on the basis of these data, because large families may be and probably are mostly planned and desired by parents. In fact there is a presumption that the income effects tend to work to produce negative income elasticities for quantity and positive income elasticities for quality in rational family planning. Then the basic problem is not family size per se, but rather the inequality of parental resources.

FAMILY COMPOSITION AND POVERTY

The issue of family composition is addressed in the regressions in table 10.7. The first two regressions describe the partial correlates of total number of persons in the family (in the household). We see predictable effects of age of the household head, first rising with age and then falling. Again, powerful effects are found for the schooling of the father or mother (head) of the household. These are strongly negative. More educated parents have far fewer children than less educated parents. We have already seen from table 10.6 that educated parents invest more in the education of their children and that parents with fewer children invest more in each one. Hence having been born to a highly educated parent gives a person a clear advantage in probable economic success on both counts.

Of course there are more children in households where the spouse is present and fewer children in urban households than in rural households. Interestingly, there is no relationship between family size and training of the head, total family income (the effect is mildly negative but not statistically significant), and the head's parents' schooling. It is well known that the effects of income are difficult to detect in this kind of regression. The measure used here refers to income (from all sources) over a two-year period, whereas it is "permanent income" that is the relevant concept for this problem. Permanent income is often better proxied by education, training, and age than by current income.

Table 10.8 investigates the determinants of labor force activities of women with spouses present. There is a great tradition in applied economics of studying this problem, whose theoretical foundations rest securely in the theory of time allocation and labor supply. The estimates in the table represent something of a "reduced form" relative to that literature, because the wage rate is not entered as an independent variable. The conceptual issues of using wage data in this context are clear enough. For a participation equation it is necessary to impute a wage to those women who do not work, since direct data are not available on nonworkers' wage rates. The imputation must be extrapolated from available information on women who do work. However, there is a selection bias inherent in any such extrapolation because of the economic selection rule for working: one works if the value of time in the market is greater than the value of time in the household. Certainly women who work must value their market time more than their household time for those hours, and oppositely for women who do not work. However, it does not follow that the wage prospects of women who do not work equal the wages observed among those who do work. It may be that wage prospects of nonworking women are higher or lower than those of working women, depending on the variance and correlation in the population of all women between the value of market time

Table 10.7 Family Composition

Regressors	Number of Children Aged 0–14		Total Persons in Family	
	Regression 1	Regression 2	Regression 3	Regression 4
Family characteristics				
Age of head	0.045	0.077	0.179	0.242
	(0.008)	(0.012)	(0.010)	(0.015)
$Age^2 \times 1,000$	−0.773	−1.181	−1.896	−2.556
	(0.066)	(0.115)	(0.101)	(0.149)
Head's schooling	−0.053	—	−0.051	—
	(0.007)		(0.009)	
Father's schooling	—	−0.032	—	−0.028
		(0.010)		(0.012)
Mother's schooling	—	−0.031	—	−0.062
		(0.009)		(0.012)
Training	0.004	—	−0.004	—
	(0.059)		(0.079)	
Male heaad	−0.707	—	−0.953	—
	(0.067)		(0.088)	
Spouse present	1.329	—	2.436	—
	(0.056)		(0.075)	
Self-employed	—	0.091	—	0.111
		(0.063)		(0.081)
Income $\times$ 10,000	—	−0.041	—	0.036
		(0.059)		(0.076)
Head's father's schooling	−0.000	−0.001	−0.014	−0.005
	(0.008)	(0.010)	(0.011)	(0.014)
Head's mother's schooling	−0.0129	−0.008	−0.035	−0.030
	(0.010)	(0.012)	(0.013)	(0.016)
Urban	−0.216	−0.348	−0.039	−0.072
	(0.053)	(0.072)	(0.071)	(0.093)
Province dummies (8)	Yes	Yes	Yes	Yes
Bocas del Toro	−0.606	−0.362	−0.789	−0.470
	(0.123)	(0.192)	(0.165)	(0.247)
Coclé	0.022	0.022	0.021	0.021
	(0.083)	(0.108)	(0.111)	(0.139)
Colón	−0.234	−0.188	−0.364	−0.253
	(0.113)	(0.148)	(0.152)	(0.191)
Chiriquí	−0.070	0.032	0.013	0.082
	(0.077)	(0.105)	(0.104)	(0.136)
Intercept	1.872	2.101	0.499	0.850
R^2	0.213	0.181	0.246	0.152

Note: Dependent variables are given in column headings. Standard errors in parentheses.

and the value of home time. Limitations of time and resources preclude treating those issues here. A similar problem arises in an hours-worked equation, where it is necessary to impute a marginal wage rate instead of an average wage rate. The hours-worked data available in this sample are not sufficiently refined to warrant extensive extrapolations of that nature. Hence the wage elasticity of women's labor supply remains to be investigated in Panama.

MARKET PARTICIPATION AND POVERTY

The reduced-form nature of the results in table 10.8 can be explained as follows. Consider a labor-supply equation in which the index of labor supply is functionally related to the wage and other variables in the household, such as the number of children (a proxy for the productivity of household production), spouse's income, and other things. As we have seen, the determinants of wages (see table 10.2 and the surrounding discussion) are found in such things as age and education. This can be represented as an earnings function, in which the wage appears on the left-hand side. The reduced form substitutes the wage equation, the determinants of wages, into the labor-supply equation in place of the wage. This of course presents an identification problem, because a variable might have an effect in two distinct ways. For example, consider education. We know from table 10.2 that education has a powerful effect on wage prospects. However, the theory of the household also suggests that education would have a positive effect on productivity in the home. The effect of education in the reduced-form labor-supply equation therefore captures the influence of both forces, and the separate effects cannot be ascertained.

The regression in table 10.8 uses a dummy variable for participation or nonparticipation (specifically, an answer to whether the person is economically active) in the first two columns. Another form uses an index of work intensity in which the economic activity variable is an important component. This variable is defined in the General Appendix and will not be discussed here, because it is clear that the results are practically identical in the two forms. Evidently work intensity and the participation variable are highly correlated in this sample.

The most striking result in the table is the powerful positive effect of education in promoting market participation. More educated women with spouses present are much more likely to work than less educated women with spouses present. Evidently education increases the market prospects of women.

Women whose spouses are self-employed tend to work less than other women. We saw in table 10.1 that self-employment is likely to be associated with low family income and a greater probability of poverty. One would

Table 10.8 Nonagricultural Market Participation of Women with Spouse Present

Regressors	Participation[a]		Work Intensity[b]	
	Regression 1	Regression 2	Regression 3	Regression 4
Characteristics of household heads				
Age	0.026	0.024	0.026	0.025
	(0.008)	(0.008)	(0.008)	(0.008)
Age^2 × 1,000	−0.270	−0.250	−0.270	−0.256
	(0.089)	(0.091)	(0.089)	(0.090)
Education	0.050	0.044	0.050	0.044
	(0.0027)	(0.003)	(0.0026)	(0.0029)
Urban	—	0.085	—	0.077
		(0.026)		(0.025)
Spouse characteristics				
Spouse's income	−0.028	−0.075	−0.022	−0.073
(× 1,000)	(0.023)	(0.024)	(0.022)	(0.024)
Spouse self-employed	—	−0.060	—	−0.059
		(0.026)		(0.026)
Spouse's age	−0.0040	−0.0035	−0.0042	−0.0034
	(0.0016)	(0.0016)	(0.0016)	(0.0016)
Family composition				
Children 0–5	−0.024	−0.020	−0.023	−0.018
	(0.012)	(0.012)	(0.012)	(0.012)
Children 6–14	0.0078	0.0073	0.0095	0.0095
	(0.0095)	(0.0096)	(0.0094)	(0.0094)
Persons 15–65	—	−0.015	—	−0.017
		(0.009)		(0.008)
Persons 65 +	0.022	0.0065	0.041	0.024
	(0.041)	(0.041)	(0.040)	(0.040)
Child schooling index	—	−0.047	—	—
		(0.030)		
Family characteristics				
Transfer income	—	−0.262	—	−0.284
(× 10,000)		(0.099)		(0.098)
Poverty income	—	0.177	—	0.182
(× 10,000)		(0.044)		(0.044)
House size	—	0.0163	—	0.019
		(0.008)		(0.008)
Intercept	−0.497	−0.441	−0.489	−0.480
Province dummies[c]	Yes	Yes	Yes	Yes
R^2	0.283	0.308	0.290	0.315

Note: Standard errors in parentheses.

[a] Linear probability model, dependent variable = 1 if woman is economically active, dependent, variable = 0 if inactive.

[b] Linear regression: dependent variable is employment intensity index in nonagriculture.

[c] Not significant: spouse's occupation, education, and economic activity.

expect the women whose spouses are self-employed to work more frequently for this reason, but that is not the case. Evidently these women find that their home productivity is larger than their wage prospects and that it is not in their interest to work. Since this is a subpopulation whose incidence of poverty is very large, more detailed investigation of these issues is warranted.

The most striking departure of these data from the results in other countries is the trivial effect of the presence of children on the labor force activities of women with spouses present. In most other data known to me, the single most powerful explanatory variable of married women's labor force participation is children in the home. Small children do indeed discourage market work among women in Panama, but the size of the effect is relatively small (and just marginally significant). If anything, older children tend to encourage market work somewhat (but this effect is definitely not significant). The amount of children's schooling also has a very small negative effect, but it is not statistically significant. The differences between women in Panama and in other countries (especially the United States) on this account remains to be explained. There is always the possibility that the result found here is peculiar to this sample. Additional work on other samples is warranted. One potential and interesting source of these differences is the corresponding difference in the production of child care services between Panama and the more developed countries.

Finally, the results for income and household characteristics have obvious interpretations as proxies for something else. Women are less likely to work the more not working increases their nonmarket productivity. This interpretation is reinforced by the finding above that the market rate of return to education of women is substantial, indeed higher than for men.

The effects of age show that older women are less likely to work than younger women. The peak in the estimated participation rate occurs about age forty-eight. Notice that the size of the family and the presence of children are controlled for this regression. I conjecture that this reflects largely a cohort effect and also a retirement effect. We know that in other societies participation of women has a distinct cohort basis and also that women who never worked when younger are less likely to work at older ages. We also see that women who live in urban areas are much more likely to report themselves as working than women in rural areas. This is a standard result and is due to greater opportunities for working in the market sector in urban areas and also to larger productivity of household time in rural areas.

The theory of labor supply makes explicit the connection between a woman's market activities and her spouse's wealth and earnings. Given the wage prospects of the woman, an increase in spouse's income should reduce the woman's labor supply, owing to an income effect. Here the wage is not held constant, and we expect some correlation on assortive mating grounds between the husband's income and the woman's labor market prospects. Nonetheless, the effect of the spouse's income on the woman's labor supply is negative in these data, so the income effect dominates. Notice, however, that the regression coefficient is small. Given the age of the woman, the table also shows that market participation is less likely the older the spouse. This presumably reflects unmeasured components of family resources, similar to an income effect. It also may reflect greater home productivity of women with significantly older spouses if transfer income is received. Since the bulk of transfer income in Panama comes from social security payments, this variable proxies a retirement effect. Women in families where property income is large are more likely to work. Property income allows substitution of purchased inputs for direct home production. It also might be correlated with wage prospects. Its effect is substantially different from that of spouse's earnings, however, and the differences cannot be easily reconciled.

Table 10.9 shows similar regression results for female-headed households where no spouse is present. The fit and general quality of results for women in the agricultural sector are very poor. There are basically no systematic independent variables that predict labor market activities of these women. However, the results for women in the nonagricultural sector are qualitatively similar to those for women with spouses present. Here market participation declines more sharply with age than in table 10.8. The effect of education is extremely powerful, but not quite so large as for married women. The results for the effects of children are even less apparent than for married women with spouses present. On the other hand, the effects of property and transfer income are somewhat larger. These kinds of results are to be expected for women who are the sole wage earners in a family.

MARITAL SEPARATION AND POVERTY

The final table represents a tentative and preliminary attempt to find the correlates of marital separation among women in Panama. It is clear that this attempt is largely unsuccessful. There are few significant differences in the propensity toward marital and related separations based on personal characteristics and family characteristics. The dependent variable takes on the value of 1.0 for intact families and a value of 0 for families where no male spouse is present. It is clear that the nature of most of these variables, such as age, education, and the like (other possibilities were entered but did not exhibit explanatory power), are too crude to be of value in understanding marital instability. The substantial result in table 10.10 is that children constitute a stabilizing force in marital arrangements in Panama,

Table 10.9 Market Participation, Female Heads of Households, Spouse Not Present

Regressors	Nonagriculture		Agriculture	
	Participation	Intensity	Participation	Intensity
Characteristics of household head				
Age	0.037	0.039	0.021	−0.015
	(0.018)	(0.017)	(0.015)	(0.058)
Age² × 1,000	−0.483	−0.553	−0.194	0.184
	(0.212)	(0.201)	(0.158)	(0.627)
Education	0.039	0.045	0.017	0.0047
	(0.0056)	(0.005)	(0.009)	(0.029)
Urban	0.266	0.214	0.018	—
	(0.051)	(0.048)	(0.055)	
Family composition				
Children 0–5	−0.025	−0.025	0.011	−0.051
	(0.028)	(0.027)	(0.025)	(0.101)
Children 6–14	0.023	0.0004	0.010	0.067
	(0.020)	(0.019)	(0.020)	(0.079)
Persons 65 +	0.044	0.021	0.071	−0.174
	(0.096)	(0.091)	(0.102)	(0.403)
Child schooling index	0.128	n.s.	n.s.	n.s.
	(0.078)			
Income				
Property income	0.269	0.307	n.s.	n.s.
(× 10,000)	(0.158)	(0.151)		
Transfer income	−0.492	−0.487	n.s.	n.s.
(× 10,000)	(0.088)	(0.084)		
House size	n.s.	0.032	−0.031	n.s.
		(0.018)	(0.019)	
Intercept	−0.616	−0.712	−0.343	0.897
Province dummies (8)	Yes	Yes	Yes	Yes
R^2	0.325	0.402	0.134	0.056

Note: n.s. = not significant. Standard errors in parentheses.

as throughout the world. However, there remains the chicken-and-egg question. The presence of children might prevent a marital separation, but inherently more stable marriages are also likely to result in more children. The causal connections here remain to be investigated.

SUMMARY AND POLICY IMPLICATIONS

The earnings functions indicate that the incidence of poverty decreases strongly with age, but the rate of decline becomes milder as the household head ages. At about sixty-five years of age the pattern reverses, and the

Table 10.10   Marital Separation, Females; Linear Probability

Regressors	Nonagriculture	Agriculture
Age	−0.007	0.000
	(0.007)	(0.004)
Age^2 × 1,000	0.061	−0.046
	(0.083)	(0.049)
Education	0.001	−0.005
	(0.002)	(0.002)
Urban	−0.009	0.016
	(0.023)	(0.018)
Children 0–5	0.023	0.004
	(0.012)	(0.007)
Children 6–14	0.026	0.015
	(0.009)	(0.006)
Province dummies (8)	Yes	Yes
R^2	0.032	0.036

Note: Standard errors in parentheses.

incidence of poverty increases with age beyond that point. In other words, measured poverty has a strong life cycle component.

Education has a powerful effect on poverty incidence. Parents' education as well as their family wealth depicts strong intergenerational linkages, but the direct (as distinguished from indirect) intergenerational effects of education are relatively weak and wash out in one generation.

The presence of a spouse has a major effect on the earnings of men but a statistically insignificant effect on the earnings of women, a finding that is characteristic of the data for other countries. The substantial effect for men is consistent with the exchange relationship implicit in marriage and the possibilities for division of labor between household members. Married men are able to specialize in market production to a greater extent than unmarried men. There are lesser possibilities for this kind of specialization among women. It is, however, possible to put alternative interpretations on this result.

The earnings capacity of married males is found to be higher than that of never-married men. Among possible interpretations of this result are some kind of market segmentation or discrimination against the unmarried; self-selection of married males, inasmuch as they may be endowed with certain unmeasured abilities or motivations that help them earn more; and the responsibility that comes in the wake of marriage that goads one to work harder and earn a higher income. We have, however, not estimated earnings net of increased liabilities (expenses) resulting from marriage and children.

A test of the supply-and-demand model of earnings suggests that the demand-for-skill variable has a significant coefficient. However, while the use of the supply-and-demand model for earnings function is not irrelevant and there is perceptible, though weak, evidence that it might improve the quality of estimates, the gain may not always be worth the cost of additional research.

The most striking result of the econometric analysis of this chapter is the powerful and positive effect of education in promoting market participation. More educated women with spouses present are much more likely to work than less educated with spouses present. This effect seems to dominate the opposite (negative) effect of spouses' income on women's labor force participation. Evidently education increases the market prospects of women more than it increases their nonmarket productivity.

The results for income and household characteristics have obvious interpretations as proxies for something else. Women are less likely to work if they receive transfer income. Since the bulk of transfer income in Panama comes from social security payments, this variable proxies a retirement effect. Women in families where property income is large are more likely to work. Property income allows substitution of purchased inputs for direct home production. It also might be correlated with wage prospects. Its effect is substantially different from that of spouse's earnings, however, and the differences cannot be easily reconciled.

The regression results for female-headed households where no spouse is present give poor results for rural areas. There are basically no systematic independent variables that predict the labor market activities of these women. However, the results for women in the nonagricultural sector are qualitatively similar to those for women with spouses present. Here the age pattern of market participation declines more sharply with age than that for women with spouses present. The effect of education is extremely powerful, but not quite as large as for married women. The results for the effects of children are less apparent. On the other hand, the effects of property and transfer income are somewhat larger. These kinds of results are to be expected for women who are the sole wage earners in a family.

A major result of this study, one that was rather surprising, is the marked similarity of results for Panama compared with countries such as Canada, England, and the United States. In all cases there are substantial returns to education. There are also marked intergenerational linkages in educational choices through family institutions. Taking education as the single best proxy for human capital investment, there is a clear connection between the human capital investments of parents and their children. Parents with more human capital have higher-quality children and fewer children. Women with more human capital are more likely to be employed in the market sector than women who have less. The major difference between the results for Panama and those for other countries lies in the minor effect of the presence of children on women's work, and perhaps in the somewhat higher rate of return to education for women in Panama. It is clear that education has a special role for women in Panama and that it is a crucial determinant of their economic success. That the Panamanian economy rewards education among women so highly may be a part of a longer-term transition in which women are becoming fully integrated into the market-place and market opportunities for women with more education are at present much larger than for women with less.

The general similarity of these results to those found for several of the more developed economies in the nonagricultural sector is consistent with the view that there is considerable social and economic mobility in the nonagricultural sector in Panama. The more deep-seated problems of poverty in Panama lie in the rural areas and in the agricultural sector. In that sector, however, similar investment in human capital is beneficial mainly in enabling migrants to get nonpoor urban jobs. In the present state of Panama's agriculture, there is little evidence that education is a good investment. Chapter 13 addresses my final analysis for the agricultural sector.

The main policy implication of this chapter is the need to provide jobs or some kind of cottage-industry work to the illiterate women of today and high-school education to their children.

ELEVEN

Earnings Behavior of Indians

Inside the Guaymi Indian territory, practically the only source of income is subsistence agriculture. Some Indians, however, have managed to get employment outside their territory as well as in the National Guard and the local school system. In view of this, we study two types of earnings behavior among Indians: earnings functions, comparable to those for Panamanians in general (chap. 10), and agricultural production functions, parallel to those for non-Indian territories (chap. 13).

EARNINGS FUNCTIONS FOR INDIANS

Earnings functions for indians in their territory are presented in tables 11.1 (logistic regression) and 11.2 (ordinary least squares with selection-correction variable). We see that education comes out with a significant coefficient in all three regressions of table 11.2: the first without selection correction, the second with linearly specified selection correction, and the third with nonlinearly specified selection correction. The fit is very good: the adjusted R^2 for the three regressions is 0.75, 0.77, and 0.80. The coefficient of education is 0.117 in the standard regression and 0.169 in the selection-correction regression when the schooling variable is not interacted with the predicted value of the correction term. The difference of 0.052 ($0.169 - 0.117$) is due to the truncation or selection bias in the standard regression. The result may be interpreted to suggest that the situation in the Guaymi Indian territory is such that education cannot realize its potential within its boundaries. The rate of return from investment in schooling would be 6 percent higher if the Guaymi areas enjoyed the same level of technology as the rest of the country. Given the mean per capita income of $473 of the subsample picked up by the computer in table 11.2, the direct and indirect actual value of the mean value-marginal product of a year of schooling of an average person is $80 per year (a 17 percent increase in income), and the potential value-marginal product is $160 (a 34 percent increase in income). Clearly this is a case of market segmentation between Indian territories and the rest of the country.

A somewhat puzzling result is that the experience profile has the wrong signs. Unlike the usual inverted-parabolic income curve with respect to experience or age (which for Indians is practically the same as age), the incomes of the Guaymi Indians seem to increase according to a normal

Table 11.1   Earnings Functions: Logistic Regression, Probability of Being Indigent, Guaymi Indian Areas, 1983

Independent Variable		Beta Coefficient	Standard Error	Chi-Square
Code	Definition			
Intercept		−8.961	14.45	0.38
L44AA	1 if head of household has had technical training, 0 otherwise	−10.092	—	—
L26AA	Experience in years, defined as age minus 6 + years of schooling	0.484	—	—
L26AA2	Experience squared	−0.006	—	—
L400	Years of schooling of head of household	−0.619	0.63	0.96
D1	1 if household is in Bocas del Toro, 0 otherwise (Chiriquí serves as the base province)	−1.608	2.60	0.38
D9	1 if household is in Veraguas, 0 otherwise	12.261	—	—

−2 log likelihood for model containing intercept only = 35.59
Model chi square = 26.36 with six degrees of freedom

Note: Dependent variable: 1 if household is indigent, 0 otherwise. The indigency cutoff line for Indians is assumed to be the same as for non-Indian Panamanians.

parabola. The experience coefficients are, however, not estimated with conventionally acceptable levels of precision. One interpretation that can be put on the face value of this result is that in Indian areas, where for all practical purposes brute labor is the only factor of production, human dexterity probably wanes with age after its peak at prime youth and that there is little productive experience available in this traditional, purely agrarian society.

The coefficients of province dummies are not significantly different from zero, suggesting that all Guaymi territories have a more or less similar economic structure and Guaymi Indians are more or less homogeneous people. That is not surprising, since Indian areas in all the three provinces are mountainous and contiguous.

AN ALTERNATE (POLYNOMIAL) FUNCTIONAL FORM FOR CORRECTING THE SELECTION BIAS

Conventionally, the variable estimated for possible selection bias in tests of dual labor markets and other segmentation hypotheses is entered linearly as a regressor in the relevant regressions. As in the case of the probability function for dual labor markets, however, there is no necessarily simple functional relationship between earnings and the explanatory variables, including the estimated selection-bias-correction variable. With a view to gauging possible improvement in the results from alternative functional forms, I made some experiments on the sample of Indians. For this purpose, the selection-correction variable was generated, following Heckman (1987), by a logistic regression of households below the indigency line on the relevant explanatory variables for a sample of Guaymi Indians (see table 11.2). The number of observations of this sample is not large, since several were eliminated because there were no nonzero values for the specified variables for the already small sample of Indians, but there still are seven to eighteen degrees of freedom not used up in different regressions. The Indian sample was used for an additional reason—namely, because there is more reason to believe that the traditional economy and the household resources of the Indian territory are more homogeneous than those of the dynamic modern economy of the Republic. Accordingly, the division of the Indian sample (where land, practically the only nonhuman resource, is by and large communally owned) into indigent and nonindigent subsamples is likely to be an artificial one, except for the human factor, insofar as individuals may be poor or nonpoor owing to differences in physical strength or dexterity, mental capacity, age, or handicaps. In other words, we expect the division of the Indian sample to have a truncation bias.

The results are presented in table 11.2; there we see that the statistically significant coefficient of education goes up by 450 percent and its significance goes up by 18 percent. At the same time the coefficient of education's interaction with the selectivity-correction variable acquires the negative sign with a value of -0.35—a net increase of about 6 percent in the rate of return to schooling. The coefficients of experience and their significance levels also go up perceptibly, but these changes may be misleading inasmuch as the coefficients of their interaction terms with $Z1$ have the opposite signs. Two of the coefficients of the cubic profile of the selectivity-correction variable ($Z1$) are significantly different from zero, as are some of those of the interacted variables. Note that because of the interaction terms and the cubic profile of the functional form of table 10.10, the composite (net) effect of an independent variable depends not only on its own linear, quadratic, or cubic transformation (as the case may be), but also on the levels of other interacted variables.

The important result to be noted here is that indigents have an earnings function that is probably different from that of nonindigents among Indians. Some analysts might be tempted to interpret this result as a support for an ad hoc approach—that is, for the inapplicability of any economic theory to the analysis of poverty. Contrary to that, this result is indeed a support for the validity of poverty theory—the results for the poor and the nonpoor

Table 11.2 Earnings Functions for Indians: National Socioeconomic Survey of Guaymi Indians, 1983

	Type of Regression					
	Standard OLS		Corrected for Selection Bias			
Variable	Coefficient	*t*-Value	Coefficient	*t*-Value	Coefficient	*t*-value
Constant	7.50	4.52	5.81	2.91	8.33	2.64
L44AA	0.20	0.30	0.10	0.12	0.19	0.15
L26AA	−0.036	−0.54	−0.00006	−0.001	−0.32	−1.43
L26AA2	0.0013	1.23	0.001	0.88	0.015	2.00
L400	0.117	1.81	0.169	1.99	0.526	2.13
DPI	−2.53	−4.32	—	—	3.63	1.04
DI	0.118	0.27	0.583	1.10	1.237	1.49
D9	−0.782	−0.53	−1.532	−2.19	2739.3	0.44
Z1	—	—	16.5	1.49	20.19	1.37
Z2	—	—	−51.85	−1.75	−110.1	−2.92
Z3	—	—	37.33	1.94	79.37	2.94
DPI*Z1	—	—	−2.72	−2.92	−7.27	−1.67
D1*Z1	—	—	—	—	−1.89	−1.42
D9*Z1	—	—	—	—	−2741.5	−0.45
L26AA*Z1	—	—	—	—	0.75	1.43
L26AA2*Z1	—	—	—	—	−0.019	−1.96
L400*Z1	—	—	—	—	−0.349	−0.72
Adjusted R^2	0.75	—	0.77	—	0.80	—
Dependent variable mean	6.159	—	6.159	—	6.159	—
Number of Observations	26		26		26	

Note: The variables are defined below:
Dependent variable = Family income in dollars in natural logarithms
L44AA: 1 if head of household has had technical training, 0 otherwise
L26AA: Experience in years, defined as age minus 6 + years of schooling
L26AA2:   Experience squared
L400:   Years of schooling of head of household
DPI: Dummy for indigency, defined as lower quarter of households
D1:   1 if household is in Bocas del Toro, 0 otherwise (Chiriquí province serves as the base)
D9:   1 if household is in Veraquas, 0 otherwise
Z1:   Predicted probability of a household's being indigent, as estimated from the logistic function this variable serves to correct the selection bias.
Z2:   Z1 squared
Z3:   Z1 cubed
D1*Z1:   D1 − multiplied by Z1, that is, Z1 interacted with D1; the other variables postmultiplied by Z1 are similarly interacted.

Table 11.3 Agricultural Production Functions, Guaymi Indian Areas, National Socioeconomic Survey, 1983

	Variable	Parameter Estimate	t-Value
Intercept		5.010	2.941
LL86L87	Man-years, family and hired	0.986	2.092
LL88	Rental cost of machinery	0.312	1.780
LL90	Land in hectares actually used	0.175	1.258
LL92	Cost of seeds	0.285	0.537
LL93	All other inputs	−0.137	−0.614
L81A/L85	Ratio of crop to gross agricultural output	−0.968	−1.025
L26	Age of head of household	0.028	0.421
L98	Dummy: can get credit easily = 1	−0.357	−0.831
L26SQ	Age Squared	−0.001	−0.332
L40	School years of head of household	0.134	1.136
L44		−0.413	−0.383
LL90B	Percentage of land held with title	−0.059	−0.375
MINVCA	Beginning-year inventory livestock	0.108	0.880
MINVPI	Beginning-year inventory pigs	−0.256	−1.555
COMER	Commercialization of agricultural output	−0.274	−0.601
L25A	Sex of head of household	0.196	0.157
L41	School years of spouse	−0.043	−0.363
L56D	Head fully employed = 1	2.568	3.234
Adjusted R^2		0.4176	
Number of observations		40	
Dependent variable mean (logarithm)		6.39385	
Coefficient of variation		12.23	

Note: Prefix L means linear; LL means log linear. Dependent variable is LL85, total gross agricultural income.

samples are derived from the application of the same theory, the theory developed in this study (chap. 2).

AGRICULTURAL PRODUCTION FUNCTION

An agricultural production function is reported in table 11.3. We see that labor tends to explain almost all output. Only two coefficients are significantly different from zero, and both are related to labor—aggregate man-years and the dummy for full employment. The coefficient of farm machinery can also be stretched to an acceptable significance level—with t value of 1.78 and nineteen degrees of freedom, it is significantly different from zero at the 10 percent level. The coefficients of land and the schooling

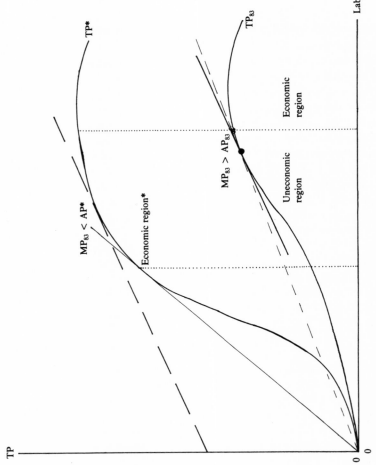

Figure 11.1   Present $MP_{83} > AP_{83}$ and potential $MP_{83} < AP^*$. (TP = total product, AP = average product, MP = marginal product of labor, V = value, Q = quantity, P = price, and an asterisk indicates potential value.) $VAP_{83} = AP_{83}*P_{83} = \$598 = VMP_{83}$, where subscript 83 means the year 1983.

238

of the head of household are not measured with precision, though they acquire the right signs.

Scale economies as measured by the sum of the coefficient of labor and capital are surprisingly high, 1.298. They rise to 1.473 if the coefficient of land (not measured with precision) is also added. From this result it appears that Indians face some serious input constraints. Their farms are too small to exploit realizable scale economies. The constraint apparently comes from machinery and new inputs, for if land were the constraint, families would tend to pool their communally owned land to cultivate cooperatively or in some other form by which scale economies can be reaped. Moreover, the contribution of land is not statistically significant. The share of labor in total output comes to 76 percent.

The value-marginal product (VMP) of labor in the Guaymi agriculture is a shade higher than the value of its average product ($598), though not significantly so. The Guaymis' economy is thus characterized by a very low level of technology. Its fixed factor is nature and a little man-made capital. The value-marginal product of machinery (not measured very precisely) is indicated to be exorbitantly high at its face value: $62.00 per dollar rental cost of machinery per year. Its average input cost, however, is only $3.02 per year. Evidently machinery carries with it embodied technical change whose effect is a substantial upward shift in the production function, as illustrated in figure 11.1. The value-marginal product of machinery probably also picks up the effects of most of the left-out modern inputs. In the present context, however, it is not the estimated high VMP of machinery that needs to be taken special note of. First, machinery picks up the effects of improved technology, and second, its coefficient is not measured with precision. Rather it is improving the low state of the art, the chuzo technology, that yields high returns. Recall from chapter 3 that the yield of rice in mechanized farms is about three times as high as on the chuzo farms. Even more important than mechanization is the productivity growth from potential seed/fertilizer technology, in which Panama lags behind but that can probably be developed. I will return to this topic in chapter 13.

In the present state of technology the proportion of labor to land is actually too low. The Guaymi agricultural production, indeed, seems to be taking place in the uneconomic region or, at best, at the boundary of the economic and uneconomic regions, as illustrated in figure 11.1. There exists the paradoxical scarcity of labor (for manual agriculture) in a labor-abundant territory. Labor is all the Guaymis have. Therefore any investment that will increase the productivity of the abundant factor (labor) will naturally have a high payoff. The total output curve lies so close to the horizontal axis (is so low in fig. 11.1) that in the present state the averages seem to be as enlightening about the Guaymi economy as marginal values.

In summary, the production function results indicate that Indian agriculture is woefully underdeveloped. Unlike the traditional dual economy in most rural economies of the world, however, Indian agriculture is characterized by approximately as high a marginal product of labor as its average product.

The ratio of output shares of labor and capital is 3:1. The output elasticity of labor is nearly 1. Consequently children still remain the most productive capital of the Guaymis even without schooling. At the present low level of agricultural technology, there is little educated labor can do that unskilled labor cannot. The observed high return to labor seems mainly in nonagricultural vocations—teaching, service in the National Guard, off-farm jobs outside the Indian areas, and the like.

CONCLUSIONS

The findings from the Indian sample are consistent with theoretical expectations that the productivities of schooling and experience will be positively related to levels of technology. In the primitive society of Indians, neither variable yields returns anywhere approaching those prevailing in non-Indian areas.

Complementary evidence for the same result comes from the fitted polynomian functional form, in which education's interaction with other relevant variables indicates significant changes from education's independent effect.

Indian agriculture, the mainstay of the Guaymis, is very primitive. It is carried on largely by variable factors, essentially labor, such that marginal and average products of labor are almost equal.

The earnings, production, and poverty functions that explain the behavior of modern Panamanians do the same for the tribal Indians, but their resources are so meager they can hardly make ends meet, much less invest in themselves or their children. Public investment in their education, health, infrastructure, and agriculture is going to have a high payoff. The kind of public investment from which they will benefit most is the topic of chapter 13.

T W E L V E

Fertility and Poverty

Numerous studies have documented certain broad relationships between poverty, fertility, infant mortality, and child malnutrition. In comparisons of societies at different times and of different income groups within a particular society, we find that the degree of poverty is positively correlated with measures of fertility, infant mortality, and malnutrition. Indeed, all four indexes are positively related: high levels of poverty, fertility, infant mortality, and malnutrition in children go together. Evidence from Panama shows that these indexes are positively correlated in Panamanian society as well.[1]

That an association between these four important indexes of well-being exists, however, does not tell us whether one particular condition "causes" another. Nor does it tell us how policy actions might be designed to change one or more of these indexes. Demographic studies have been useful for clarifying some of the fertility relationships and have been especially valuable in enabling more careful measurement of fertility behavior. Public health and nutrition studies have also been useful in providing better measurement of mortality and malnutrition and showing their association with poverty. A number of important studies of this type have already been completed in Panama.[2]

Economists have also been concerned with the relationship discussed above. A large number of studies based on an economic perspective of family behavior have now been undertaken in other countries and have demonstrated that the "structure" of the economic model can bring new insight and understanding of the causalities involved in the correlations discussed above. The implications of the economic model have been supported by most data sets, and where this is the case economists can offer additional policy implications beyond those afforded by other approaches.

Panama has experienced (and is currently experiencing) rapid demographic change. Available data show that indexes of fertility have declined at a rate roughly equal to that exhibited by Taiwan in the 1950s and 1960s and by Colombia in the 1960s and 1970s. Crude birthrates (average number

This chapter was written by Robert Evenson of Yale University. It is almost a verbatim reproduction of the report on fertility and poverty prepared for the Critical Poverty Project of Panama by Robert Evenson, Yale University (Evenson 1985).

1. See De La Cruz (1983).
2. See Bermudez (1980) and Panama, Ministry of Health (1983).

of live births per 1,000 population per year) have fallen from about thirty-seven as recently as 1970 to about twenty-five at the end of 1983. Available data also show that infant mortality rates have declined, and that they began to decline earlier than did birthrates. Surveys further show a rise in the use of contraception, particularly sterilization, coinciding with the decline in fertility.[3]

Available data from at least three special demographic surveys—the 1973–76 Contraceptive Use Survey (CUS), the 1976 World Fertility Survey (WFS), and the 1979 Contraceptive Prevalence Survey (CPS)—have already been analyzed from a demographic perspective. Additionally, a recent study of Nutritional Functional Classification based on the 1980 National Nutrition Survey (NNS) has classified the relation between malnutrition indicators and poverty-related groups.

The task of this chapter is not to duplicate this prior work in Panama or to attempt to reinterpret it. It is rather to complement it by bringing an economic perspective to bear on the available data. This perspective will enable a somewhat more integrative interpretation of the relationship between poverty, fertility, and child health. The chapter is organized as follows: the first section will sketch out the basic economic model, and the second will report econometric tests of the basic model, and parametric estimates based on three data sets: the 1973–76 CUS, the 1976 WFS, and the 1980 NNS. The third section explores possible relationships between infant mortality, family size, and breast-feeding and work activities of mothers in Panama. The final section discusses the policy implications of the findings.

THE ECONOMIC MODEL

The economic model of the household has been applied to demographic behavior for some time now.[4] It has shown that economic variables such as employment opportunities and human capital skills, as well as income and wealth, do affect demographic behavior. The model has the following basic relationships:

$$U = u(N, H, M, L, Z) \tag{1}$$

Equation (1) is a household utility function showing that aggregate household utility (or satisfaction or well-being) is related positively to the number of children (N) and the health of these children (H); negatively

3. These trends are documented in the publication of the Departamento de Población, Division de Planificación Social of the Ministero de Planificación y Política Económica, Panama (Panama, MIPPE 1984).
4. See Evenson and Rosenzweig (1977) and Rosenzweig, Schultz, and Wolpin (1980) for examples of models of this type.

to infant mortality (M); positively to leisure (L); and positively to other consumption goods (Z):

$$N = N(X_n, T_n, K, S, C)$$
$$H = H(X_h, T_h, B, K, S)$$
$$M = M(X_m, T_m, B, K, S) \tag{2}$$
$$Z = Z(X_z, T_z, K, S).$$

The equations in (2) are technical relationships of a "production" type showing that the "household" goods N, H, M, and Z are produced from market goods (X_n, X_h, X_m, X_z) such as foods, medicine, and clothing; time inputs (T_n, T_h, T_m, T_z); capital stock (K), including community capital investments in sanitation programs and so on; and from basic skills (S) of the manager of these producing activities (usually the mother). In the case of the child services relationship, contraceptive effect (C) also enters the relationship. Breastfeeding (B_f) affects health and mortality.

$$L + \sum_i T_i + T_w = T \ (T_i \text{ includes breast-feeding time})$$
$$Y + WT_w = \sum_i P_i X_i. \tag{3}$$

The equations in (3) represent time and budget constraints. Leisure (L), plus time spent in household production, plus time spent working, must add to a constant for all family workers. Similarly, money income from labor (WT_w) and nonlabor sources (Y) must not exceed spending on market goods.

The economic model presumes that families maximize utility (1) subject to the technical constraints implied by (2) and the physical and financial constraints implied by (3). This does not mean every household will be equally efficient, because skills vary greatly between households, as do endowments of household capital (K) and other forms of income-yielding capital (such as land). Essentially, this model says that households act in their own best interest as they see it. They face different economic and social conditions (e.g., wages, prices, and community capital may vary from community to community). Thus poverty is consistent with maximizing behavior. Poverty is determined by limited endowments of capital, by limited skill acquisition, by low wages and high prices, and by limited public investment in health and other services. The direct manifestations of poverty are observed in N, H, M, L, and Z.

Econometric analysis based on this model takes two forms, and these are complementary in nature. The first and major type of analysis is to estimate reduced-form or "jointly determined" equation systems. The optimizing activity of the household implies that each variable that the household can vary in order to maximize eq. (1) is related to those constraints, prices, and inherited characteristics that it cannot vary. In econometric language, this states that the full set of endogenous variables is jointly determined by the full set of exogenous variables. The resulting system then is:

$$Z_i = Z_i(P_n, P_h, P_m, P_z, P_c, W, K, K^*, S),$$
(4)

where $Z_i = N, H, M, Z, T_n, T_h, T_m, T_w, L$, and C.

Equation set (4) looks like a "reduced form" of a simultaneous equation system, but it really is not. In this system there is no causality per se between the endogenous variables. This may appear puzzling to demographers, who generally regard infant mortality as causing changes in fertility, and to others who may regard contraceptive effort as causing changes in fertility.

Actually, there is a causality between endogenous variables embedded in equation set (2), and we would like to actually estimate (2) because it is of considerable interest. We can, however, indirectly make inferences about (2) from (4). For example, if more highly skilled home managers are better able to use contraceptive technology, C will be significant in system (4). Nonetheless, we will attempt to measure the mortality (M) and health (H) equations of system (2) directly in this study.

The mortality equation is of particular interest because it does have a possible response in it. Families actually engage in remedial behavior regarding child health. This remedial behavior may reflect a response to information about particular unanticipated characteristics of the environment as well as to anticipated effects.

This indicates that system (2) should be written as:

$$N = N(M, X_n, T_n, K, S, C)$$

$$H = H(M, X_n, T_h, K, B_f, S, T)$$

$$M = M(N, X_m, T_m, K^*, B_f, S)$$
(2')

$$Z = Z(X_z, T_z, K, S).$$

Now we are faced with a type of simultaneous equation problem. A recent paper by Rosenzweig and Schultz (1983) suggests a way to deal with this problem. We will proceed in a similar fashion by first estimating the equations as specified in (4) for N, T_n, X_n, X_m and then estimating the H and M equations in (2'), replacing actual N, T_m, X_n, X_m, B_f with predicted values from (4). This will provide us with estimates of the biological relationships implied by (2'). Then we will proceed to compute the residuals from the (2') equations using actual rather than predicted values of N, T_m, and so on. Finally, we will regress N, B_f and other endogenous variables on these residuals to estimate the true type (4) relationship.

The relevance of this work for poverty issues can be seen in two ways in the empirical work. First, we will engage in some testing to see whether these relationships differ for the poor and the nonpoor. Second, since many of the variables are policy variables, and since these may be differentially related to poverty (e.g., health centers and social security programs may not be readily available to the poor) they will have poverty-related implications.

ECONOMETRIC ESTIMATES

The basic household maximization problem set forth in the previous section provides us with a reasonable guide for econometric work. It also provides us with some a priori basis for expecting certain effects. This section will report estimates for equation system (4) from three different data sets for Panama. In the next section we will turn to an estimation of equation system (2') in an attempt to clarify the relation between mortality and fertility. In equation system (4) we will treat infant mortality as exogenous and not under the control of the family.

Table 12.1 provides a summary of the estimates of the impacts of the most important exogenous variables in system (4) on the family from three data sets for Panama. Appendix 12A describes the three sample surveys used here, the 1976 WFS, the 1973–76 CUS, and the 1980 NNS. Standard error, R^2, F-statistics, and related statistical information are provided in the appendix tables of regressions. Table 12.1 reports estimated coefficients and indicates the significance for them of the value of t-statistics. Both OLS and Logistic estimation techniques are used.

The estimates for certain control type variables, defined in the General Appendix, are not reported in table 12.1. For instance, all equations include age-class dummy variables for the mothers to control for different stages in the family life cycle. In addition, the proportion of sons born to the family and one or two other variables were included. These variables have little policy interest, so they are not reported in table 12.1 and will not be discussed here. Note that most of these equations also include a mortality rate variable (number of child deaths per child ever born). More will be said about this in the second stage of this analysis.

The economic model of the previous section does not yield many unambiguous predictions of the signs to be expected in table 12.1. Nonetheless, with reasonable assumptions regarding complementarity and substitutability and the size of income effects, we can sign many of these effects. Furthermore, we have results from a substantial number of studies based on other data sets that we can compare with these results. In discussing table 12.1, I will proceed by discussing the effects of each group of inde-

Independent Variables	Number of Pregnancies			Months Breast-fed (76 WFS)	Abortions	
	76 WFS	73–76 CUS	80 NNS		76 WFS	73–76 CU
Parent's schooling						
Mother's completion of primary school	−0.403**	−0.784**	−0.769**	0.682**	0.012	−0.076**
Mother's completion of secondary school	−0.808**	−1.213**	−1.239**	−1.262**	−0.080**	−0.078**
Mother's completion of university	−0.919**	−1.787**	−1.616**	−1.500**	−0.082**	−0.026
Father's years of schooling	−0.070**			−0.087**	0.0058**	
Father's years of schooling × mother's years of schooling	0.000			−0.000	−0.00058**	
Mother's completion of primary school × POOR	−0.417**		0.170	−0.076	−0.011	
Mother's prior work experience						
Professional	−1.252**			−1.325	0.017	
Skilled	−0.839**			−0.983	0.007	
Sales related	−0.545			−0.739	−0.004	
Unskilled work	−0.239**			−0.267*	0.005	
Income and wages						
Income class poor	0.177	0.679**	1.492**	0.242	−0.005	0.018
Income class medium		0.413**	−1.095**			0.030
Income class high		0.362	0.259			0.055
Mother's wage			−0.010		0.006	−0.013
Father's wage			−0.036**		−0.012	−0.016
Child's wage			0.039**		0.001	0.026*
Location						
Metropolitan rural	1.308			0.167	−0.032*	
POOR × rural	0.213			0.233	0.023**	
Other rural	1.087**			0.218	−0.041	
Other urban	0.847**		0.003	0.799	−0.077*	
Moved rural urban	0.433*			0.317	−0.015	
Town-urban	0.338			0.311	0.019	
Public services						
Health services	−0.0669*					
Social security	−0.0079**					
Health × POOR	−0.0051					
Social security × POOR	0.0110**					

| | Contraception Use (76 WFS) | | | | Malnutrition (80 NNS) | |
	Sterilization	Pill or IUD	Last Closed Interval	Last Open Interval	Acute	Chronic
rents' schooling						
Mother's completion of primary school	0.153	0.447**	0.370**	0.258*	0.313	0.702**
Mother's completion of secondary school	0.246	0.888**	0.792**	0.662**	−0.543*	−1.263**
Mother's completion of university	0.137	0.866**	1.092**	1.013**	−0.347**	−2.543**
Father's years of schooling	0.038	0.034*	0.012	0.035*		
ther's years of schooling × mother's years of schooling	−0.005**	−0.001	−0.000	0.001		
other's completion of primary school × POOR	0.162	0.199	0.247	0.178	−0.827*	0.271
other's prior work experience						
Professional	0.110	0.127	−0.018	−0.283		
Skilled	−0.285*	0.418**	0.256*	−0.051		
Sales related	0.056	0.447**	0.344**	0.072		
Unskilled work	0.046	0.166*	0.117	0.069		
come and wages						
Income class poor	−0.115	0.174	−0.471**	−0.247*	0.714	0.537*
Income class medium					0.415*	0.167
Income class high					0.300	−0.394*
Mother's wage					0.006	−0.013
Father's wage					−0.012	−0.016
Child wage					−0.001	0.026*
cation						
Metropolitan rural	0.264	0.037	0.049	0.183		
POOR × rural	0.513**	−0.203	0.247	−0.136		
Other rural	0.140	−0.347	0.313	0.271		
Other urban	0.063	−0.574	−0.536	0.181	0.015*	−0.002
Moved rural urban	−0.69	0.029	−0.195	0.212		
Town-urban	0.000	0.215	0.094	0.013		
blic services						
Health services					−0.001	−0.000
Social security					−0.016**	−0.009**
Health × POOR					0.001	−0.007
Social security × OOR					0.001	0.014**

*ignificant at the 10 percent level.
Significant at the 1 percent level.

247

pendent (exogenous) variables. As can be noted, the data sets differ in the availability of measures for independent variables. Nonetheless, most relevant variables are available in one form or another for all three data sets. In this discussion we will attempt to compare the estimates with the a priori expectations based on economic logic.

None of the estimates in table 12.1 with statistical significance are actually in conflict with a priori economic reasoning. Furthermore, most of the cases where we have a strong a priori basis for expecting a particular sign are statistically significant. Thus we have a high degree of confirmation of the economic model.

Let us turn to discussion of the results by groups of independent variables.

Parents' Schooling

This cluster of variables illustrates quite well the claim of high consistency of results with a priori reasoning. We recognize, of course, that economists are not the only researchers treating this variable as an important determinant of fertility. The interpretation they place on the variable may differ somewhat from that placed on it by demographers. The economic argument is that schooling is an index of skills in home production activities including contraception. These skills enable more effective contraception, particularly of the conventional type, and this translates into fewer pregnancies. They also allow more efficient home and food management, and this should translate into lower incidence of malnutrition. We would expect more educated mothers to have fewer pregnancies and to use more of the conventional contraceptive methods, but not necessarily to use more sterilization and induced abortions as fertility-control measures. Furthermore, we would expect consistency by level of schooling; higher levels of schooling should have larger effects.

These expectations are strongly borne out in all three data sets. The three schooling dummy variables measure effects relative to the left-out class—mothers with less than primary schooling. Mothers with primary schooling have from 0.4 to 0.77 fewer births, holding all other factors constant, than mothers without primary schooling. Furthermore, they use more of the conventional contraceptives (pills and IUDs) and used more contraceptives in the last closed interval (even though these contraceptives failed to prevent the closing of the interval with a birth) and in the current open interval since the last birth. They also have shorter breast-feeding periods. Finally, they have a lower incidence of chronically malnourished children. These findings are strengthened not only by the consistency of effect on different dimensions of family behavior but also by the fact that higher levels of schooling produce larger effects.

We would generally expect fathers' schooling to be less important than mothers' schooling but to generally have the same effects. The interaction term is designed to see whether one parent's schooling complements the other's (positive sign) or is a type of substitute (negative sign). The results suggest substitution—but are not very significant.

That schooling does not significantly affect sterilization is consistent with the view that it enables women to practice conventional contraception more efficiently. I should note, however, that we did not have a particularly good fit on the sterilization equation. The argument could be applied to the fact that breast-feeding is negatively affected by schooling. Breast-feeding is a form of contraception. However, it is also possible that some taste factors associated with education may be involved. Significant effects for work before marriage emerge in the breast-feeding equation. We may be picking up some association between breast-feeding and current work in the schooling variables. It is important to note in connection with breast-feeding that schooling, although reducing breast-feeding, also quite clearly reduces the incidence of malnutrition.

The interaction of primary schooling with a poverty dummy (POOR) is one of several designed to determine whether a difference in schooling impact exists between the poor and nonpoor. We are interested in knowing whether the primary schooling effect holds for the poor as well as the nonpoor in our data. Our data do show two differential effects, both indicating that the schooling effect is more important for the poor than the nonpoor. In the first 76WFS equation primary schooling has a -0.403 effect on pregnancies for the nonpoor and a $-0.403 - 0.417 = -0.820$ effect for the poor. Further primary schooling has a significant negative effect on incidence of acute malnutrition for the poor—but not for the nonpoor.

Mother's Prior Work Experience

We are treating work before marriage as an inherited and thus exogenous variable in the WFS data set. This may be somewhat questionable, but since it has some policy relevance, this adds to the argument for the treatment given here. We would expect early career orientation to constitute the acquisition of specialized skills not held by mothers without prior work experience. This skill will then affect behavior after marriage, including of course work after marriage (which is treated as an endogenous variable below; also see the General Appendix). The direction of the effects of these skills should be similar to that associated with schooling.

The expectation is generally borne out. Prior work experience (the left-out class is mothers without prior work experience) reduces fertility and increases the use of conventional contraception. It has little impact on abortions and sterilizations, and it does reduce breast-feeding. As with schooling, this effect on breast-feeding may be at least partially channeled through current work.

Income and Wages

The income data in the data sets are not ideal. It was possible to define a POOR class for all three data sets, however, and a medium and high income class for the 73–76 CUS and the 80 NNS. In all cases the leftout class is the higher-income class. For the 76 WFS the POOR dummy is picking up effects relative to the nonpoor. For the other two data sets it is relative to the very high income class. (The definition of the POOR class for the 76 WFS was based on occupational and schooling data; see the General Appendix).

Part of our motivation for including this variable is to discover distinctive poverty effects. To some extent these variables are picking up effects that other variables have missed. Note that several POOR interactions are included in the specifications as well as the direct dummy variables.

The poverty variable appears to have a clear positive impact on fertility. Where we have included an interaction with schooling, it appears that the schooling effect is strengthened by poverty. Poverty also eliminates the effect of social security on fertility (see below). Poverty conditions also appear to reduce contraceptive use.

Poverty has the separate effect of increasing the incidence of malnutrition. Poverty appears, however, to enhance the negative schooling impact on malnutrition and to eliminate the negative effect of social security.

The wage results for the 80 NNS survey are the only case where strong a priori expectations are not met by the estimates. We expect that high child wages will induce higher fertility because as the value of children's work goes up the real costs associated with children go down. This will tend to have two effects on malnutrition. On the one hand, larger family size is likely to increase malnutrition. On the other, child health will be valued more because wages are higher. The expectations of a positive effect on fertility are borne out. It appears that the negative effect of fertility on child malnutrition may dominate. High child wages are associated with higher malnutrition.

We also expect that rises in the value of women's time will induce women to work more, to have fewer children, and to have better nutrition (see Evenson and Rosenzweig 1977). This is not borne out by the data. Economic reasoning also suggests that father's wage levels should affect fertility positively, or at least not negatively, provided other income data are properly measured. That father's wage effects are negative, though not entirely implausible, suggests measurement problems. (This effect should be positive if it is primarily an income effect. Since fathers do not engage in much child care, a rise in their wages should not raise the cost of raising children unless it induces a rise in the value of the mother's time.)

Location

Location dummy variables suggest that rural locations do have higher fertility than urban locations, especially the Panama City metropolitan area (the left-out reference group in the WFS). It also appears that a move before marriage to an urban location affects fertility negatively. It may be considered a bit of a puzzle that rural locations are not associated with significantly lower contraception use in the 1976 WFS. This result suggests either that the greater number of pregnancies in the rural areas is genuinely desired or that contraception is less efficient in the rural and nonmetropolitan areas than in the metropolitan areas.

Many studies have shown that work opportunities for children are higher in rural areas. Since we have not captured this in other variables, we are probably picking it up with the rural dummy variables. The argument for different contraceptive efficiency is more difficult to make. It is supported to some extent by the high likelihood of sterilization in rural areas, since sterilization may be a response to contraceptive inefficiency. Interestingly, the only significant rural-poverty interaction effect is in the sterilization equation. The rural poor undergo more sterilizations. This appears, however, to be more the result of government policy to push for sterilization in particular regions than a response to perceived contraceptive inefficiency.

Public Services

Of the three data sets, only the 1980 NNS provided locations by district for the households samples. For this sample it was possible to assign two public service variables at the district level to each household. The first was an index of health services, an average of doctors, dentists, nurses, and hospitals per capita. The second was an index of social security coverage. Each variable was interacted with the POOR income class dummy variable, in an attempt to differentiate between general effects of these public sector variables and effects specifically on the poor.

The results are instructive. Both health services and social security have a fertility-reducing effect. Social security coverage also reduces malnutrition. However, for the poor the story is different. The data indicate that the poor do not benefit to any appreciable extent from social security. They do appear to benefit from the health services, in terms of reduced fertility. (Note that the effect on the poor is the sum of the variable effect and the interaction effect.)

This finding is perhaps not surprising if one looks at the coverage of the social security system. It does have important policy implications. Policymakers in Panama should be aware that incomplete coverage of important programs has discriminatory effects on the population. We have not been able to address the issue of fertility and poverty among Indian families because they are not included in the data bases. The findings with respect to public services in this study, however, suggest that the lack of access to health services, social security, and schooling by the Indian population is severely discriminatory in its effect.

MORTALITY, FAMILY SIZE, BREAST-FEEDING, AND MOTHER'S WORK

Regression system (4) is a reduced-form system that does not allow us to examine structural relationships directly. We are particularly interested in the structural relationship between infant mortality and family size as depicted in equation set (2′). (We are also interested in a similar health relationship but do not have adequate data to estimate it.) Specifically, if we could estimate the mortality function in (2′) we could then sort out the replacement response from the real production effect in the correlation between pregnancies and mortality. We could also determine the breast-feeding response to infant deaths. In approaching this problem we shall use of model put forth by Rosenzweig and Schultz.[5]

We begin by specifying an error structure in mortality on health relationship with two components:

$$M = M(N, X_m, T_m, K^*, e_1, e_2). \tag{5}$$

In this specification e_1 is a stochastic term that does not reveal itself until after a child is born. It is not under the control of the family and constitutes a "surprise" to them. The family behavior regarding mortality can then be modeled as having a planned component and a "response to surprise" component.

We cannot estimate (5) directly by OLS because the endogenous variables in (5) n, X_m, T_m have both planned and response components, and the response components will be correlated with the error terms. The procedure employed to avoid this problem entails the following steps:

1. We first estimate behavioral equations from system (4) predicting the endogenous inputs in (5).

---

5. Rosenzweig and Schultz (1983) apply this to infant mortality in the United States.

2. We then estimate (5) replacing the actual endogenous variables with predicted values. This is a consistent 2SLS procedure for estimating the parameters in (5). Actually, for consistency we do this in an iterated manner by treating mortality as exogenous in the first-round estimate of predicted fertility. In a second round we use predicted mortality for (5) in the predicted fertility equation and then estimate a new mortality equation.

3. We then form the residual $M - \hat{\hat{M}}$ where $\hat{\hat{M}}$ is predicted mortality using the consistent 2SLS parameter estimates and the actual endogenous variables. These residuals now are estimations of $e_1 + e_2$; that is, they contain the responses to surprise of the endogenous variables.

4. We can now regress each endogenous variable on $M - \hat{\hat{M}}$ in order to obtain an estimate of the response to surprise effect.

The General Appendix reports the results of the first step. Equations predicting pregnancies (PRFERT), breast-feeding (PRBFEED), rural-urban migration (PRRURUB), professional work by mother (PRPROF), and skilled work by mother (PRUNSK) are reported. The first two equations are summarized in table 12.1. Work experience before marriage is used as the major set of identifying variables.

Table 12.2 reports the 2SLS mortality function estimates. A simple linear equation is used. The results are remarkable in terms of the strong statistical association between family size, breast-feeding, work, schooling, and poverty. We find that an increase in family size increases infant mortality, while an increase in the duration of breast-feeding reduces mortality. Parents' schooling reduces infant mortality, as does work in professional and skilled occupations. We also find that mortality is higher in rural areas and among the poor.

These estimates have obvious policy implications. Before discussing them, however, we will proceed to steps 3 and 4 to determine how much of the actual behavior in endogenous variables can be considered a response to surprise regarding mortality. Table 12.3 reports the regressions of actual fertility and breast feeding on the $M - \hat{M}$ residuals.

The coefficients in the system (4) regressions are also reported. These estimates indicate that only 28 percent of the apparent response of pregnancies to infant deaths is in fact a true replacement response. They also indicate that the true response to mortality in breast-feeding actually exceeds the apparent response. Both family size and breast-feeding have real effects on mortality, of course.

Table 12.2   Mortality Function Estimates

Variable	Parameter Estimate	Standard Error	t for HO Parameter $= 0$	Prob. t
Intercept	0.533	0.023	23.259	0.000
PRFERT	0.156	0.002	67.627	0.000
PRBFEED	−0.244	0.004	−66.445	0.000
RURALURB	0.023	0.009	2.399	0.019
PPROF	−0.007	0.003	−2.550	0.010
PSKILL	−0.015	0.003	−5.935	0.000
PSALES	0.017	0.003	6.275	0.000
PUNSKILL	0.003	0.002	1.221	0.222
METRUR	0.001	0.006	0.214	0.030
OTHURB	0.014	0.005	2.993	0.002
OTHRUR	0.202	0.006	34.482	0.000
HOSED	−0.010	0.001	−12.593	0.000
EDIMT	−0.000	0.000	−0.924	0.355
PRIMCOMP	0.123	0.013	−9.402	0.000
SECCOMP	−0.188	0.026	−7.094	0.000
COLLEGE	0.185	0.028	−6.616	0.000
PODRI	0.091	0.004	23.126	0.000

Source	d.f.	Sum of Squares	Mean Square	F-Value	PROS F
Model	16	34.174	2.136	399.725	0.000
error	3,186	17.024	0.005		
C total	3,202	51.199			
Root MSE		0.074	R^2	0.667	
		0.051		0.666	
		142.710			

Table 12.3   Regressions of Pregnancies and Breast-Feeding on M $-$ $\hat{\text{M}}$

Variable	Intercept	Coefficient	F-Value	Coefficient in System (4) Regression
Pregnancies	4.004 (0.049)	0.5116 (0.070)	53.22	1.837
Months breast-fed	4.266 (0.039)	−0.3742 (0.055)	4,533.85	−1.407

Note: Standard errors in parentheses.

POLICY IMPLICATIONS

The adage that the "rich get richer and the poor have children" suggests a general belief that some families choose to be poor and to have large families. The economic model postulated in this chapter, and supported by the empirical data, argues otherwise. Families appear to maximize utility as best they can. They do not choose to be poor. If they are poor, it is because of factors they do not control. Some of the confusion inherent in the adage betrays a lack of understanding regarding the value of children to their families. Parents value children, and in certain economic circumstances children are "bargains" relative to other goods—when their earning opportunities are good, when expectations regarding schooling are modest, and when the cost of avoiding their births is high.

Children were bargains in most socioeconomic groups in Panama twenty years ago. They are no longer the bargains they were. Contraception is now low cost for most of Panamanian society. The provision of health services and social security has changed the economics of contraception in profound ways. So has the extension of schooling opportunities. Our data show that the poor have not shared fully in the gains produced by the social security system, but appear to show that they have benefited as much as the nonpoor from the provision of schooling.

The conditions that produce high levels of fertility at the "micro" household level can, of course, have "macro" effects. In fact, the economic argument for an active family planning program is not that individual households are acting irrationally, but rather that their actions have "externalities." That is, high fertility leads to a high rate of growth of the supply of labor to labor markets or family enterprises. Expanding the supply of labor relative to a fixed (or at least a slow-growing) resource and capital base will lower the marginal product of labor and hence real labor income. Individual households do not take this effect into account when they make their contraception decisions. (It is, of course, true that high rates of technical change can cause real incomes to rise even in countries with rapid population growth; e.g., Brazil in the 1970s. Nonetheless, rapid population growth will reduce the rate of growth in real incomes.)

It is not easy, however, to estimate the size and importance of this externality or to determine the relative burden it places on the poor and nonpoor. Relatively simple partial equilibrium analysis, as well as more sophisticated general equilibrium analysis, shows that income from labor services will fall relative to income from other sources when the labor supply is growing rapidly. Since the poor earn all or most of their income from labor (this is true even for the self-employed), there is a clear presumption that *the externality burden of high fertility falls most heavily on the poor*. The burden is further accentuated when the agricultural and rural sector of the economy is "short-changed" in terms of public services. When governments fail to invest in the development of technology suited to the geoclimatic regions of the country and in related extension, schooling, roads, and markets, food prices will rise relative to those of other consumer goods. This is because high fertility leads to a high rate of growth in demand, and, even though the labor force grows as rapidly, other factors of production do not. Since the poor spend a higher proportion of their income on food than the nonpoor, they clearly are further disadvantaged.

A brief review of Panama's policy toward agriculture suggests inadequate investment in technology and technology-related infrastructure. (One should not confuse mechanization with technology. Substituting machines for human and animal labor is not a change in technology but merely a movement along the isoquant. Real technical change enables the same production with fewer inputs—an inward shift of the isoquant.) In part because of this inadequate investment and the consequent slow growth to stagnation in production, a series of price-raising distortions have been introduced. These distortions have almost certainly harmed the poor and worsened their relative position in society.

Our findings regarding the relation between pregnancies and infant mortality provide an even stronger justification for intervention to reduce the number of births in Panama. Policymakers cannot presume that the relation between pregnancies and infant mortality is simply a replacement response to unexpected deaths. Much of that relationship unhappily is a "real" effect whereby additional births in many families increase the probability of infant deaths. Averting births in these circumstances not only causes a rise in real incomes for Panama's poor, it lowers child mortality. Although our data do not permit a full exploration of the point, it appears reasonable that it would also reduce malnutrition.

This study does suggest some directions for policy action in the areas of family planning, health, and nutrition that would improve the health and welfare of Panama's poor. The most obvious and most difficult goal is to achieve some improvement in the incomes of the poor. Our estimates show that this would reduce pregnancies, increase contraception, and reduce malnutrition and mortality. It is probably reasonable to conclude that raising the real income of the poor is the most important policy action to be taken to improve their welfare. This conclusion is, however, not novel. And since our interest is in the full range of policies that not only could directly affect the poor but could also have the indirect effect of reducing poverty itself, it is important that we identify other policy instruments.

Our study does identify several such instruments. Parents' schooling is identified as a very important factor with strong welfare-improving effects. It reduces pregnancies, infant mortality, and malnutrition. It improves the efficiency of contraception. Poor mothers benefit even more than the nonpoor from schooling. Clearly, providing universal primary schooling to all segments of society, *especially the poor,* should be a major goal in Panama. Education is important enough that compensatory programs for young schooling dropouts are justified, as are specialized young-adult education programs stressing nutrition and health.

A second area for intervention is employment opportunities for young women. Women who have work experience before marriage, particularly in the skilled occupations, do better in later life in terms of contraception, pregnancies, and child health, education held constant, even though they breast-feed less. Labor market policies to eliminate sex discrimination, to provide specialized training to young women, and to encourage women to enter the labor market and delay marriage will have welfare-improving effects. If targeted to the poor, they could have dramatic effects.

Data on locations show that rural settings are conducive to significantly higher numbers of pregnancies than urban locations, but not necessarily to significantly lower levels of contraceptive use. This is in part because farm families have stronger incentives for large families than do urban families because of employment opportunities. Unfortunately, this translates into higher infant mortality and probably malnutrition as well. A recent study of malnutrition based on the 1980 NNS identified fifteen "functional groups" for Panama and showed that the incidence of malnutrition was higher in small-farm agricultural households.

This indicates that rural areas, particularly some of the functional groups in rural areas, deserve to be target groups for nutritional, educational, employment, and other programs. Actually the subclass of the poor within these groups should be the critical target group. It also suggests that Panama should not have a policy of blocking or deferring migration from rural to urban areas or from agricultural to nonagricultural occupations. The fact is that many of the poor will improve their lot only through such migration.

Finally, the two public service variables, provision of health service and provision of social security, have been shown to have important effects. Health services appear to reduce pregnancies for both poor and nonpoor. Some of this effect for the poor may be through sterilization programs targeted to the rural poor. These programs do not appear to have affected malnutrition, however. Panama's social security system reduces pregnancies and appears to improve child health. Unfortunately, it has little or no beneficial impact on Panama's poor—presumably because they are not covered. Clearly this finding calls for an assessment of ways to extend this important system to everyone in the Panamanian society. For a proposal to this end, see chapter 14.

This conclusion applies a fortiori to Panama's Indian population, whose health and fertility situation is even worse (see chap. 11). This group has not had equal access to the programs that have had such a profound impact on Panamanian society.

Panama has indeed been undergoing change in its patterns of fertility, mortality, and child health, and the direction of change is clearly positive. Furthermore, much—perhaps most—of the change is attributable to government policies over the past two decades. Programs of schooling, health services, employment change, and social security have drastically improved the welfare of the population. That fact should not be lost in the discussion dealing with future policies to achieve further change.

Appendix 12A
Fertility Data Sources

THE 1976 WORLD FERTILITY SURVEY (WFS)

The World Fertility Survey for Panama is part of an international study covering a number of countries. It was not designed by economists for the type of analysis undertaken here. Hence it has certain limitations, the most serious being the lack of wage and income data. It is also weak on public program variables, and the data set available to us does not have district identifiers. This lack of district data reflects the interests of the statisticians working on this study (and for that matter other surveys as well). They are primarily concerned with computing means and other statistics for groups of households sufficiently large to be representative. They are not concerned with the researcher whose objective is simply to use "observations" in a statistical model. The absence of district identifiers prevents us from assigning public-sector variables to our observations.

OLS regression estimates were done for cases where the dependent variable is continuous, and logistic regression estimates were used where the dependent variable was of a zero/one type. The following notes on variable definitions are relevant; they also indicate the exogenous variables included in the regressions though not reported in the text. Regression tables are not reported here to save space.

AGE 2–AGE 6 are dummy variables for mother's age.

AGE 2 = 1 for age 20–24, 0 for other age groups

AGE 3 = 1 for age 25–29, 0 for other age groups

AGE 4 = 1 for age 30–34, 0 for other age groups

AGE 5 = 1 for age 35–39, 0 for other age groups

AGE 6 = 1 for age 40–44, 0 for other age groups

The "left-out" reference group comprises women aged between forty-five and forty nine. No women younger than twenty are included in the regressions.

METRUR = 1 if the household is a rural household in the Panama metropolitan area

OTHURB = 1 if the household is an urban household outside the metropolitan area

OTHRUR = 1 if the household is a rural household outside the metropolitan area

HUSED = Years of schooling of husband

EDINT = HUSED × years of schooling of mother

PRIMCOMP = 1 if mother completed primary school

SECCOMP = 1 if mother completed secondary school

COLLEGE = 1 if mother has schooling beyond secondary school

(The "left-out" reference group is mother with less than primary school.)

PODRI = 1 if both parents have primary schooling or less and do not work or work in agricultural, household, or unskilled occupations

RURALURB = 1 if mother migrated from rural to urban location

TOWNURB = 1 if mother migrated from town to urban location

PPROF = 1 if mother worked in a professional occupation before marriage

PSKILL = 1 if mother worked in a skilled occupation before marriage

PSALES = 1 if mother worked in a clerical, sales, or farm occupation before marriage

PUNSKILL = 1 if mother worked in an agricultural, household, or unskilled occupation before marriage

(The reference group is mothers who did not work before marriage.)

POORRUR = POOR × (METRUR + OTHRUR)

PROPSON = Sons born/total children born = ½ if no children

V203 = Spontaneous abortions

PRFERT = Rate of fertility (children born per 1,000 adult women ages 15–45)

PRBFEED = Proportion of breast-feeding mothers

OCCHNGE = 1 if the mother upgraded her occupation after marriage

MORT = Child death/children ever born, = 0 if no children

THE 1973–76 CONTRACEPTIVE USE SURVEY (CUS)

The 1973–76 CUS was conducted in 1976 and contains some recall data. It is a selected sample of family planning program participants. We have not attempted any selectivity corrections, since we do not have data on nonparticipants. The evidence from this study plays only a minor role in the analysis of the chapter. It is essentially serving as corroborative evidence.

The OLS results of pregnancies and induced abortions were reported in table 12.1. The regressions of the use of contraceptives were not discussed in the text because of the possibility of selection bias. On the whole, they corroborate the contraceptive use results based on the 1976 WFS.

The independent variables are similar to those in the 1976 WFS. PRIM, SEC, and UNIV are schooling dummies (the reference group is women not completing primary schooling). AGE 2–AGE 5 are age-class dummies. (The reference group is women older than forty.)

INC 1–INC 5 are income class dummy variables (the reference group is the highest income group 6). PUBEMP, CANAL, and WORKING are occupation classes for fathers, public employment, canal-sector employment, and other employment. (The reference group is the unemployed.) MORT is the ratio of child deaths to children ever born.

THE 1980 NATIONAL NUTRITIONAL SURVEY (NNS)

The 1980 NNS is potentially a very rich data set. For the purposes of this study only a limited set of the data was made available. It was significant, however, for an analysis of pregnancies and child health status. This data set includes a district identification variable, thus letting us assign public-sector variables to individual observations. This data set also includes income measures. The income data from this source, however, are not considered trustworthy.

Several papers based on this study (by Parillon et al.) have concentrated on the definition of "functional groups" where these groups differ substantially in terms of the risk of acute or chronic malnutrition. It is a question of some interest, therefore, whether the economic model underlying this chapter is competing with or complementary to the functional group model. It is possible, for example, that when "functional group" distinctions are made little or no added explanation can be obtained from the economic model and vice versa.

THIRTEEN

Agriculture and Rural Poverty

The preceding three chapters analyzed the earnings and related socioeconomic behavior of men and women mainly in the nonagricultural sector. Some explorations cut across sectors, for example, poverty as affected by marriage, fertility, nutrition, and schooling. In this final chapter on behavioral analysis, the focus shifts from the urban employee as the main productive micro unit for understanding poverty to the rural family farm as the basic economic unit.

PRODUCTION FUNCTIONS AND EARNINGS FUNCTIONS DISTINGUISHED

The theoretical basis for analyzing poverty in the rural or agricultural sector is the same as for the urban sector, but the environment and the nature of the economy, as well as the availability of certain variables, are somewhat different. Recall that the theoretical model of this study is anchored on the usual optimizing behavior, with constraints consisting of inherited fortunes (subdivided into inherited human capital and inherited nonhuman wealth); acquired earnings capacity (also subdivided into human and nonhuman capital); environment (consisting of the immediate society's or neighborhood's level of human and nonhuman resources as well as family background); luck of various sorts; supply factors (e.g., easy access to schools); and market conditions (macro forces, market segmentation, etc.). The empirical correlates of these theoretical variables were identified and classified into five sets: environment and family background; personal characteristics (such as age, education, and experience); innate or inherited traits (such as ability, opportunity, and mobility); supply variables (such as access to quality schools); and market conditions.

In the context of agricultural income behavior these categories have to be redefined to some extent, because in Panama agriculture and rural economy are more or less synonymous terms and have both population and spatial dimensions. In contrast, nonagricultural occupations are largely found in urban areas, and for them the spatial dimension is insignificant. Thus environment in agriculture includes all those factors connected with

This chapter was written by Anthony Tang, Vanderbilt University and the Chinese University of Hong Kong with minor collaboration by the author. It is based largely on his report on rural poverty to the Critical Poverty Project of Panama (Tang 1985). I assume responsibility for any errors or weaknesses.

neighborhood, society, family status, and the state of technology, which are equally relevant for the urban sector. Besides, it includes physical environment, such as linkages with growth centers and market towns, terrain, quality of land, and the degree to which an area suffers from the vagaries of weather as well as "distance decay." Accordingly, while for all practical purposes transportation and road connections are irrelevant for individualized earnings functions in the nonagricultural sector, they are critical variables for agricultural development and rural family incomes. Thus the density of roads, physical properties of terrain, linkages to market towns and growth centers, degree of monetization, marketed surplus, and similar physical environment variables belong in agricultural functions.

Another basic difference between agricultural and nonagricultural functions is that for a vast majority of workers in the latter sector, income means the earnings from one's labor and embodied human capital. Even if that were not the case, estimating individualized production functions would be impracticable, because the production data on nonhuman productive assets of individual families, though not completely irrelevant, are unavailable. This is an advantage for income analysis in agriculture in that the data for both human capital and physical assets of farm firms are in general part and parcel of the farm family surveys. Accordingly, earnings functions for agriculture become essentially production functions of individual households. To derive the shadow wage or value-marginal product of labor of the rate of return to one's human capital, it is possible to hold the effects of most other inputs of production constant, which is not practicable for the employee groups that dominate the urban sector. Income from all owned resources—the relevant concept of income for poverty analysis—can in principle be estimated jointly as well as separately from the production function in the agricultural sector.

Agricultural production functions therefore form the main econometric work in this chapter. The primary objective of using fitted production functions for poverty analysis is to determine output elasticities and value-marginal products of individual resources. These parameters are crucial for resource allocation in general and for discerning which factors of production will most benefit the poor. The results throw light not only on the direction the allocation of resources should take for efficiency and equity objectives in the present state of the art, but also on which kind of technological improvements should be sought—for instance, through research and development—to attain the same objectives less painfully.

Types of Farms Analyzed

The main variables and other symbols used in this chapter and others are defined in the General Appendix. A farm household is defined as one whose head gives farming as his or her principal occupation. Income is net of business expenses and comprehensive of all sources and types (monetary and in kind, via imputation of owner-occupied dwellings and home-consumed farm output). Agricultural output is made up of sales, home consumption, and changes in livestock inventories during the year. Value added is gross output net of certain production expenses of the family farm. (Corporate farms, cooperatives, and other non-family-operated farms are excluded from the sample used in this chapter.) We also exclude backyard farming in the form of a fruit tree or a couple of chickens or tomato plants, as well as larger farms whose land is nominally held rather than farmed. Farms with land yielding less than $10 per hectare per year are also excluded. These households form a separate subsample denoted as rural nonfarm, for which a production function is irrelevant. For these farms we fit broadly defined family earnings functions of the type analyzed in chapters 10 and 11.

RURAL FARM FAMILIES POOR AND NONPOOR COMPARED

Table 13.1 tells the statistical story of the poor and the nonpoor families in the rural farm sector in the 1970s. Since the table is nearly self-explanatory, only the highlights will be touched on. First, we turn to *family characteristics* and the similarities: The poor rural farm families do not have low incomes because of the age of the household head (41.3 years), the head's sex (98.8 percent male), a small family work force (2.6 working age persona vs. 2.5 for the nonpoor), or ill health in the family. It should be noted here that age, work-force size, and health conditions are significant determinants of production and income, as will be seen in the later sections on regression analysis. Table 13.1 shows that the poor and the nonpoor do not differ in these regards. This is an argument for joint use of regressions and of cross-tabulations of family and production characteristics on the poor and nonpoor farm households.

Not surprisingly, there are far more differences than similarities in family and production characteristics between the poor and the nonpoor rural farm families. The poor farm families have fewer household heads with technical training (1.4 percent against 5.7 percent for the nonpoor); their heads have less formal schooling (3 years vs. 3.7); and the heads' spouses are less well educated (3.1 years vs. 4.2). There are also intergenerational links at work, as may be seen from the following. Poverty household heads tend to have less well educated fathers (1.0 years vs. 1.3) and mothers (0.8 years vs. 1.1), and they invest less in their children, as is clear from the schooling of the adult children (oldest adult child's education of 5.2 years vs. 7.2 for the nonpoor).

Turning to the production characteristics of the families, we see that the poor and the nonpoor have about the same family work-force size— 1.13 and 1.04, respectively. Here the similarity ends. Poor farm families

Table 13.1 Characteristics of Poverty and Nonpoverty Farm and Nonfarm Households Compared, Census of Agriculture, 1970

Characteristics	Variable	PF	NPF
		Farm Households	
Family characteristics			
Similar characteristics			
Age of household head (years)	L26	41.3	44.0
Sex of head (% male)	L25A	98.8	98.8
Number of persons of working age (16–65)	L28	2.6	2.5
Needed and secured medical care (%)	L46	63.3	63.2
Different characteristics			
Head received technical training (%)	L44	1.4	5.7
Education of head (years)	L40	3.0	3.7
Education of head's spouse	L41	3.1	4.2
Education of head's father	L38	1.0	1.3
Education of head's mother	L39	0.8	1.1
Education of oldest child >18	L42	5.2	7.2
Income and production attributes			
Similar attribute			
Number of family workers	L86	1.13	1.04
Different attributes			
Gross value of agricultural output ($)	L85	463	3,290
Value added by agriculture ($)	VA	303	2,433
Net family comprehensive income ($)	L1	804	4,340
Wages paid to hired workers ($)	L87	44	261
Rent value of farm capital ($)	L88	52	202
Land in farms (ha)	L90	23	48
Farms receiving technical assistance (%)	L94	1.6	6.9
Farms with credit access (%)	L98	22.0	44.0
Land held without title (%)	L90B	66.0	62.0
Land irrigated (%)	L96	0.7	1.5
Value of crop sold ($)	L81A	272	1,792

Value of cattle sold ($)	L82	41	781
Value of pigs sold ($)	L83	11	56
Value of poultry and dairy sold ($)	L84	42	544
Fertilizer and pesticides ($)	L89	26	228
Farm output from crops (%)	L81A/L85	69.0	58.0
Current input use ($)	INPTS	59.0	376
Output marketed (%)	COMER	28.0	54.0
Number of cattle (head)	MINVCA	2.9	13.9
Number of pigs	MINVPI	1.3	2.2
Value of livestock purchased ($)	VPUCP	5.4	18.8

District location factors (1970–75)

Similar factors

Growth dynamics: population growth (%)	TAC	1.7	1.7
Life expectancy (years)		50.0	51.0
1970 PF incidence		21.0	21.0

Different factors:

Marketing: farms doing marketing on foot (%) (1970 date)		73.0	14.0

		Nonfarm Households	
Similar characteristics			
Age of household head (years)	L26	52.6	50.1
Number of persons of working age (16–65)	L28	2.6	2.5
Needed and secured medical care (%)	L46	70.9	77.9
Different characteristics			
Head received technical training (%)	L44	3.1	17.7
Education of head (years)	L40	3.0	5.1
Education of head's spouse	L41	3.5	5.8
Education of head's father	L38	0.9	1.9
Education of head's mother	L39	1.0	1.8
Education of oldest child >18	L42	5.0	8.0
Family size	L31	5.3	4.3
Number of 6–18-year-olds in school	L33	1.4	1.1
Net family comprehensive income ($)	L1	366	1,896

Table 13.2 Mean Values of Variables in Livestock and Crop Farms, National Socioeconomic Survey, 1983

	Agricultural Variable	Livestock Farms		Crop Farms	
		Mean	Standard Deviation	Mean	Standard Deviation
LL85	Output	7.44	1.42	6.27	1.27
LL86+L87	Lab	−0.05	0.98	−0.14	0.86
LL88	Rental of **K** (Capital)	2.08	2.57	1.27	1.89
LL90	Land used	2.89	2.14	1.52	1.42
LL92	Seed cost	0.49	1.43	0.41	1.16
LL93	Other inputs	2.53	2.61	0.45	1.32
L81/L85	Crop/agricultural value	0.05	0.06	0.98	0.04
L94	Received technical assistance	0.10	0.30	0.02	0.16
DSC	Dummy sharecrop	0.02	0.14	0.01	0.08
L26	Age of head (years)	42.48	10.51	42.05	10.55
LL96	Proportion irrigated	−2.28	0.21	−2.28	0.22
L98	Can get subsidized credit	0.53	0.50	0.28	0.45
L40	Schooling of head	4.91	3.53	3.86	2.46
L44	Technical training of head	0.12	0.32	0.05	0.22
LL90B	Titled-land ratio	−1.05	1.12	−0.77	1.07
DM	Metropolitan dummy	0.07	0.25	0.08	0.28
LMIPUCA	Purchased cattle	3.07	2.73	0.15	0.66
LMIPUPI	Purchased pigs	0.95	1.83	0.17	0.76
LE	Life expectancy	62.03	22.70	40.76	23.39
COMER	Index of commercialization	0.44	0.38	0.40	0.41
L25A	Sex of head of household	0.93	0.26	0.95	0.22
L41	Schooling of spouse	5.50	3.79	3.81	3.06
L38	Schooling of head's father	1.46	2.39	1.43	2.22
L58	Schooling of head's father	0.18	0.38	0.21	0.41
LL89	Disguised unemployment of head	1.32	2.29	0.91	1.86
L588687	Disguised unemployment of family	0.16	0.51	0.22	0.57
Number of observations		353		674	

Note: The means of this table are expressed in the same units as used for the corresponding variables in table 13.3. In particular, the values of output, have gross output, value added, and total net income from all sources of $463, $303, and $804, respectively, as compared with $3,290, $2,433, and $4,340 for the nonpoor. The latter have not only an eightfold gross and net farm output, but also a larger capacity to earn nonfarm income. They have more and better resources at their disposal, as table 13.1 amply demonstrates. Thus they have twice the land, four times the capital, nine times the fertilizer and pesticides, and six times the current inputs taken as a group. They are more livestock oriented, more commercial, more irrigated, and better situated in terms of access to markets, credit, technical assistance, and, more marginally, to land title. With respect to locational factors of the districts in which the farms are situated, there appears to be no advantage in favor of either category of farms. These locational variables are, however, generally significant as explanatory variables in the later regressions on the production and earnings functions.

Rural Farm Families: Livestock Farms versus Crop Farms

To see whether livestock production functions are different from crop production functions, we studied the following two subsamples separately: farms that earn 80 percent or more of their income from cattle (and other livestock) and farms that earn 80 percent or more of their incomes from crop production. The mean values of output and various inputs and related variables of the two types of farms are given in table 13.2.

We see that the mean income ($1,706, or ln $7.44) of livestock farms is 3.22 times as high as the mean income of crop farms (ln $6.27 or $529). The negative ln values mean an absolute value of less than unity. Thus, man-years per family in both types of farms are fewer than one. Livestock farms use twice as much machinery, 4 times as much land, 8 times as many "other inputs," and 1.5 times as much fertilizer as crop farms. The ratio of sales to output and the proportion of male household heads in total are practically the same in both cases, approximately 44 percent and 94 percent, respectively. The livestock farms have an average of 21 head of cattle and 2.6 pigs per farm. Crop farms have a little over 1 pig and 1 cow per farm. In the subsample picked up, the crop value/total output ratio is 0.98 as against 0.05 in animal farms. Education of the head of household for crop farms is 3.86 school years compared with 4.91 for livestock farms. It is interesting to note a regression result in anticipation; the coefficient of school years for crop farms is highly significant, whereas it is not significantly different from zero for livestock farms.

Rural Nonfarm Families: Poor and Nonpoor Compared

As with the families in the rural farm sector, the poor and nonpoor in the rural nonfarm sector share several common characteristics in age of the household head (52.6 and 50.1, respectively—both are about ten years older than the rural farm heads), size of family work force (2.6 and 2.5), and state of health (71 to 78 percent of families needed and secured health care in the preceding year). Low family income does not seem to be the outcome of youth or old age, unusual family structure, or health problems. The income difference ($366 vs. $1,896) is proportionally as large as in the case of rural farm families (a ratio of 1:5 in both cases), but the rural nonfarm family incomes in absolute terms are a little less than half the incomes of the rural farm families for both the poor and nonpoor subcategories.

The same intergenerational income transmission mechanism is observed through schooling effects, serving to perpetuate (not so rigidly, of course, as to disallow mobility) income differences between the poor and the nonpoor. The poor, in present-generation terms, have larger families (5.3 vs. 4.3) and less training and schooling for their household heads and the heads' spouses.

AGRICULTURAL PRODUCTION FUNCTIONS (APF)

Three sets of variables are introduced to explain or account for output variability among farms. The first set consists of what are usually called conventional agricultural inputs—labor, land, and capital (machinery, implements, livestock)—and of various kinds of current inputs. The former set of inputs forms the basis for considerations of scale economies. Using shorthand vector notations (X for the vector of conventional inputs, Y for the vector of household characteristics, and Z for the vector of locational district characteristics) the APF regression as computed here is of the following form (where Q is gross value of agricultural output):

$$Q = AX^{\alpha}e^{(\beta Y + \gamma Z)}; \text{ or in natural log,}$$
$$\ln Q = \ln A + \alpha \ln X + \beta Y + \gamma Z. \tag{1}$$

Conventional Inputs

The parameter estimates of the overall production function (regression 1, table 13.3) yield a sum of coefficients of 1.005, implying constant returns to scale. (This estimate of 1.005 is suggestive since α in eq. (1) is affected by disaggregation of the inputs.) That is to say, if a farmer doubles all his conventional inputs, he doubles his output (Q). In this regression, the parameters of the conventional inputs are the output elasticities of these inputs. Family labor's elasticity is estimated at 0.07, which says that for every 1 percent increase in family labor (L86) a 0.07 percent rise in output follows. However, this coefficient is not statistically significant. Hired labor

(L87) is paid a wage at $4.50 per day plus 11 percent social security tax (if the minimum rural wage is observed), hence the farmer must use it at a time (peak season) and in a manner where marginal productivity justifies hiring. Our regression result is reassuring with a highly significant parameter estimate (positive). Farm capital (L88—machinery, implements), land (L90), livestock inventories (cattle and pigs as a form of capital) and livestock purchase (in supplement of the initial inventories), and current inputs (used up in the production period such as seeds, fertilizers, pesticides, feed) all contributed to production in an expected manner. Livestock (particularly cattle) variables seem to carry unusually large output elasticities compared with those of traditionally important inputs such as labor and land.

A few words of explanation about livestock are in order. Livestock production is important in Panama. The survey data show that 40 percent of gross value of agricultural output in 1983 was from livestock. Unlike crop production, where contribution to its output comes from many inputs, livestock farming in Panama is based primarily on breeding and fattening cattle on ranch land. It is not surprising that livestock inventories and (pasture) land should have the largest output elasticities, which also reflect income shares to these inputs. The sum of their elasticities is 0.72 out of a total of 1.005 for all the conventional inputs.

Household and Farm Characteristics

Among the *farm characteristics,* irrigation (L96), credit access (L98), and degree of commercialization (COMER) have strong positive influences on production. There are useful policy suggestions here, centering on the importance of infrastructural investment and marketing improvement. On the other hand, sharecropping (of little importance in Panama), technical assistance or extension, and use of land without title do not carry significant parameter estimates, although a more rigorous test of the contributions of such variables will come from the value-added function (VAF). The specialization index (measuring the relative importance of crop production to livestock production (L81AL85), which is expected to shed some light on the location of Panamanian comparative advantage in agriculture, did not show any significance. However, this question too is best answered by the VAF regression. In anticipation, we note that the latter regression supports a clear inference that Panama's comparative agricultural advantage is in livestock production. Comparing the results for cattle versus pigs in the APF regression, we can further infer that cattle production is the central point of advantage. (More detail on this in the VAF section.)

Two *household characteristics* variables contributed to agricultural production: education (mean 3.8 years) and age (mean 42.5 years) of the

Table 13.3 Regressions of Microproduction Functions, National Socioeconomic Survey, 1983

Variable	All — Regression 1 Coefficient	All — Regression 1 t	All — Regression 2 Coefficient	All — Regression 2 t	≥80% Livestock — Regression 3 Coefficient	≥80% Livestock — Regression 3 t	≥80% Crop — Regression 4 Coefficient	≥80% Crop — Regression 4 t
Intercept	4.777	11.01	5.116	8.99	4.949	4.13	6.523	4.66
L25A	0.132	0.35	0.164	0.44	0.118	0.14	0.641	1.01
L26	0.008	2.77	0.010	0.86	0.002	0.07	0.015	0.82
L26SQ	—		0.000	0.30	0.000	0.17	−0.000	−0.11
L38	0.020	1.51	0.025	1.85	0.020	0.83	0.028	1.29
L40	0.023	1.90	0.022	1.86	0.012	0.54	0.050	2.01
L41	0.003	0.24	0.004	0.34	0.010	−0.51	0.000	−0.02
L44	−0.050	−0.45	0.072	−0.63	−0.128	−0.69	−0.008	−0.04
L46	−0.029	−0.49	—		—		—	
L58	0.140	2.11	0.053	0.52	0.061	0.32	0.165	0.36
L588687	—		0.061	0.74	−0.020	−0.16	0.137	1.27
LL86	0.076	1.46	—		—		—	
LL87	0.053	3.99	—		—		—	
LL86+L87	—		0.088	2.63	0.126	2.13	0.044	0.78
LL88	0.052	3.24	0.056	3.35	0.001	0.03	0.109	3.54
LL89	0.062	3.61	0.079	4.59	0.030	1.37	0.095	3.07
LL90	0.118	6.08	0.127	7.02	0.133	4.01	0.173	5.38
L90B	0.042	0.71	0.021	0.83	0.024	0.47	0.048	1.14
LL92	0.034	1.37	0.048	1.97	0.023	0.55	0.057	1.34
LL93	—		0.011	0.64	0.002	0.08	0.034	0.94
LL94	0.099	0.78	0.091	0.70	0.070	0.38	0.022	0.08

Variable	(1) coef.	(1) t	(2) coef.	(2) t	(3) coef.	(3) t	(4) coef.	(4) t
LL96	0.606	2.22	0.170	1.64	-0.005	-0.02	0.348	2.03
L98	0.182	2.62	0.217	2.56	0.244	2.00	0.245	2.42
L81AL85	0.013	0.15	0.023	0.26	1.264	1.37	-1.835	-1.75
TAC	0.003	0.18	—	—	—	—	—	—
DM	-0.034	-0.31	0.076	0.76	0.654	3.28	0.044	-0.29
LE	0.004	1.49	0.000	0.68	0.002	0.82	-0.003	-1.37
PF	-0.011	-2.98	—	—	—	—	—	—
COMER	0.931	12.49	0.974	13.03	1.017	6.81	0.116	7.99
DSC	0.194	0.88	0.200	0.90	0.145	0.41	—	—
LMINVCA	0.238	8.04	—	—	—	—	—	—
LMINVPI	0.178	4.29	—	—	—	—	—	—
LVPUCA	0.140	8.68	—	—	—	—	—	—
LVPUPI	0.053	2.41	—	—	—	—	—	—
LSTOCK	—	—	0.254	12.91	0.318	11.57	0.051	0.73
LPIGS	—	—	0.088	4.33	0.066	2.29	0.135	2.47
R^2	0.6381		0.6322		0.7052		0.5192	
Number of observations	996		996		237		465	

Note: All variables are defined in the General Appendix. In addition, the variables used in the tables of this chapter are defined either in the body of table 13.2 or below:

L46:	Dummy: secured medical assistance at health post = 1, 0 otherwise
TAC:	Population growth rate
PF:	Poverty farms
DSC:	Dummy: Sharecropping = 1, 0 otherwise
LMINVCA:	Beginning-year inventory of cattle
LMINVPI:	Beginning-year inventory of pigs
LSTOCK:	L (MINVCA + MINVPI) = total livestock
LPIGS:	L (MINVPI + MPUPI) = total pigs

271

household head. Here again, these variables (L40 and L26), and others such as education of the head's spouse and father (with insignificant parameter estimates), are expected to show up more clearly in the VAF. Few household heads receive technical training (L44—about 2 percent), and the variable is not significant in the regression. Only 5.5 percent of the household heads were female; the sex variable (L25A) is not significant. The percentage of heads employed who answered "they can do more work"—meant to be a measure of disguised unemployment—averaged 20 percent for the sample. This variable, interestingly enough, turns out to have a positive effect on agricultural production. In looking ahead, we note that its effect is persistently (and in most cases significantly) positive in the value-added function and the two income-earnings functions. It appears that the variable reflects not so much underemployment as the energy and motivation of the respondents. A person with a strong work ethic not only does his work well but may wish for more work even when he is "fully employed." This quality may well be what was showing through the regression results. Individual farms operate under the influences of each locality's characteristics, which condition the farmers' capacity to operate their farms efficiently. However, the farm-specific commercialization and specialization indexes are likely to capture the impact of the locational factors on the individual farmers—displacing the district variables of road density and the remote farming dummy. However, the metropolitan location dummy variable (DM) is retained to test the effect on farm productivity of part-time farming concentrated near large cities. For 1983 DM shows essentially no effect on farming efficiency, perhaps suggesting two countervailing forces at work: more efficient markets serving agriculture in such locations, with a positive effect on production, and part-time farming with its negative productivity implications. It is, however, highly significant in the livestock production function (see below). The growth dynamics variable (represented by district population growth rates) is supposed to reflect labor and other market improvements in high growth areas, enabling farms to make family labor adjustments and other changes to narrow the gap in labor returns between agriculture and nonagriculture. This variable (TAC) is not significant in the APF (see ahead for firmer results in VAF), although it carries the predicted sign. District health conditions as measured by life expectancy (LE) has the predicted positive effect, significant at the 6 percent level. The incidence of poverty farms (PF) is supposed to reflect the unfavorable effect of concentrations of poverty farms on the workings of the output, input, and credit markets in a district and on the psychology and sociology of the community. The time lag, we hope, will bring out possible intergenerational effects of poverty. The PF variable produced the predicted negative effect on 1983 farm productivity; the negative coefficient is highly significant statistically.

Livestock Production Functions

Regression 2 differs from regression 1 in the following respects: it treats all labor (family and hired), cattle (preexisting and purchased), and pigs (preexisting and purchased) as single variables. It interacts the variable "willingness to work more even when fully occupied" with both family and hired labor (L588687), assuming, for instance, that if family labor is underemployed hired labor would be also. Finally, it allows the usual parabolic shape for the age-experience variable by introducing age squared along with its linear measure. Interestingly, the R^2's are identical; the combined labor coefficient is significant and higher than either one separately but lower than the sum of the two components in regression 1; the magnitudes (and significance levels) of the animal-input variables go up but are lower than the sum of the coefficients of components—suggesting (though weakly) that subdividing almost (but perhaps not quite) identical factors of production tends to overestimate scale economies. Neither the age squared nor the L58 interaction is significant. Other coefficients undergo little change.

The livestock regression (3) has a superior fit. Here the output elasticity or the share of labor (0.126) is statistically significant, higher than that in the crop production function (reg. 4) and approximately equal to the sum of the two labor components of regression 1. The coefficient of land is highly significant and matches in magnitude those in other regressions, signifying that land, as expected, is a productive factor as pasture for animals. Interestingly, the coefficient of machinery is zero, even though animal farms use twice as much as crop farms. Presumably such machinery is used in fixed proportions to animals—for example, number of milking machines per one hundred cows, with the probability that its effect will be picked up by LIMIPUCA. Cost of seeds tends to acquire more significance in regression 4, as expected.

Students of economics have often wondered why the two-product transformation curves are drawn concave to the origin in textbooks and why specializing in one product reduces the marginal rate of substitution. In regressions 3 and 4 we find an empirical verification. The livestock-production regression with mean crop share (L81AL85) of 0.050 has a positive coefficient of 1.26 ($t = 1.37$). The crop-output regression with mean L81AL85 of 0.982, on the other hand, has a negative coefficient of -1.84 ($t = -1.75$). Thus the two types of farms have reached such high proportions of monoproduct specialization that diversification seems economical.

The availability of credit (L98) has identical positive and significant coefficients in both regressions. Credit is productive and important for all production in modern times. This is an area where the poor suffer. Naturally, those poor who do not have title to land lack the collateral to borrow money.

The metropolitan dummy is highly significant for livestock but not significant at all for crops. Recall that it was not significant in regression 1 either. The Schultz hypothesis that agriculture tends to be more progressive near industrial-urban centers where factor-product markets are more efficient seems to apply to livestock farms but not to crop farms in Panama. The possible explanation for this dichotomy discussed above in connection with regression 1 seems to be strengthened—namely, that most so-called crop farms in the metropolitan area are part-time vocations and therefore less productive than crop farms in the rest of the country, while most livestock farms of this area are full-time farms. The recent trend toward vegetarianism might change this situation.

A final contrast is to be noted with respect to fertilizer. Its coefficient (elasticity) is 0.095 ($t = 3.1$) in crop farms, and not significantly different from zero in livestock farms, yet livestock farms use more fertilizer ($3.80 per hectare) than crop farms ($2.50 per hectare). This is an instance of constraints and capacities: The campesinos cannot expand the use of fertilizer, probably owing to shortage of credit, high price, local unavailability, or lack of knowledge of fertilizer.

VALUE-ADDED REGRESSION RESULTS

Production Characteristics

One of the interpretations of VAF is that it allows ordinary regressions (OLS) to capture the total effect (direct and indirect) of variables such as education on production through the parameter estimates. The argument, in fact, applies to all the exogenous variables that influence the productivity of the endogenous variables. The list includes such conventional inputs as family labor and land. If more land is used output goes up, other things being equal—the direct effect. But more land may also induce farmers to use more fertilizers in order to remain in a profit-maximizing position— the indirect output effect of land. Family labor (L86) has a more-or-less significant total effect on value added or net agricultural production. (Value added is gross output net of all current inputs, service value of farm per capita, and value of livestock purchased. It was about 67 percent of gross output value in 1983, so defined.) Its total effect differs little (0.10 from VAF) from its direct effect (0.08 from APF). This small difference in output elasticity is consistent with family labor's low coefficient, seen earlier in the APF section; it means little or no upward shift in the marginal product curve of the endogenous inputs when family labor input is increased and hence little indirect effect.

Another interpretation of VAF regressions is derived from the management or entrepreneurial bias, because the entrepreneurial input cannot be measured. Those of the included variables that are closely correlated with the left-out variables will tend to pick up the effect of the latter. Differential entrepreneurial input depends upon the producer's differential ingenuity, risk mindedness, gut reactions, drive, determination, ability, knowledge, availability of cooperant resources, and so on. One single variable that has been found to be more systematically correlated with most of these unmeasurable traits for modal or majority of producers (excepting special cases) is education (see, e.g., Welch 1970). Accordingly, while in production functions variables are and should be, in principle, complementary (in the sense that an increase in the quantity of one raises the marginal product of another), such that some of the effects of the purchased or hired inputs that are left out may be picked up by several of the included variables, education is likely to assume a major part of them. The difference between the coefficient of education in APF and VAF would reflect the entrepreneurial effect of education. To the extent that some effects are picked up by other variables, such as land, the entrepreneurial contribution of eduction would be understood to appear through land.

Note that here the variables are deliberately left out even though data on their measures are available. This is desirable because we assume that the entrepreneur—the head of the farm family in this case—decides how much, for example, fertilizer and new techniques he or she would use: they are endogenously determined. Note also that the same effect can appear in production functions when out-of-pocket costs of inputs are left out. It is logical, however, to subtract the cost of these inputs from both sides of the equation, which means the relevant dependent variable is value added, not Q.

The explanatory power of land increased greatly in the VAF regression, with output elasticity rising from 0.12 to 0.26; its high marginal product as compared with family labor is clear from the large indirect production effect under profit-maximizing behavior (see table 13.4). This result in turn supports the significant inference of optimizing behavior on the part of Panamanian farmers. On the other hand, if the indirect effect is nil or weak, we have the inference of low MP (as is drawn above in the case of family labor), or else a lack of optimizing behavior or, more plausibly, presence of constraints operating on the decision maker, or both. Of course, it could also be due to mere statistical effect or measurement errors.

In contrast to the weak and insignificant results as estimated from the APF, here farms receiving technical assistance acquire a significant coefficient. This effort has been rather limited in Panama—see Evenson (1985a) on Agricultural Research. In the National Socioeconomic Survey, 1983, an average of only 5 percent of farms are reached by extension. Farms

Table 13.4   Agricultural Value-Added Function, 1983

Variable		Parameter Estimate	t for HO Parameter
Intercept		4.656	8.911
LL86	Family labor	0.098	1.528
LL90	Land actually used	0.260	13.241
L81AL85	Crop/agricultural value	−0.585	−6.389
L94	Received technical assistance	0.648	4.116
DSC	Sharecropping dummy	0.214	0.729
COMER	Index of commercialization	0.925	10.246
L25A	Sex of head	0.270	0.602
L96	Proportion irrigated	1.041	3.080
L98	Can get subsidized credit	0.288	3.904
L26	Age of head	0.012	3.665
L40	Schooling of head	0.030	1.950
L44	Technical training of head	−0.042	−0.302
L46	Secured medical assistance	−0.140	−1.942
L90B	Titled-land ratio	0.064	0.896
TAC	Population rate	0.035	1.671
DM	Metropolitan dummy	−0.151	−1.127
LE	Life expectancy	0.005	1.485
PF	Poverty farms	−0.013	−3.041
L41	Schooling of head's spouse	0.029	2.120
L38	Schooling of head's father	0.038	2.267
L58	Disguised unemployment	0.105	1.302
Adjusted R^2		0.4547	
Number of observations		964	

specializing in livestock production benefited more in net output (see table 13.2). Only 2.7 percent of those specializing in crops received technical assistance. Their parameter estimates are 0.071 and 0.022, respectively, in the production functions for livestock and crops. In the VAF, the coefficient of technical assistance rises to 0.65. Compared with regression 1, the coefficient of L81/L85 falls from 0.013 to −0.585. The combined results of regressions 1–4 of table 13.3 on specialization support the inference that Panama's comparative advantage lies in livestock production (i.e., cattle, given its overwhelming importance and its low domestic/international price ratio compared with the greater-than-one ratios for virtually all other animal and plant products), but that it has been overexploited. This inference is all the more forceful since the empirical result comes about despite the significant domestic price distortions against the relative price of beef. Alternatively, an abundant supply of beef has pushed its price relatively low. The modernization dummy (L75CD) on fertilizer use (not introduced in the APF because of the presence of fertilizer as a current input) is highly significant with a dummy coefficient of 0.26, as expected for modern inputs, other things being equal.

The commercialization index (COMER) is consistently the most important determinant of net or gross output. Its coefficient varies between 0.92 and 1.01 in all the regressions. Since it is a dummy coefficient, its magnitude is to be measured from the general intercept term, 4.66 in regression 4. Further stressing the roll of markets, farms with access to the organized credit market (L98) tend to enjoy a 1.2 percent higher income for mere access to credit. Another source of income gain is irrigation (L96). Irrigation as a source of income is virtually untapped. The National Socioeconomic Survey (SES) shows that only about 1 percent of the land in farms was irrigated in 1983. Given Panama's substantial annual yield variability and the strong value-added response from the regressions, it is probable that irrigation is a rewarding form of investment. A full analysis is beyond the scope of this study. Its returns are given fuller expression if seed varieties and fertilization are improved. With Panama's average yield of rice—a crop that has received the government's special attention in its agricultural import-substituting program—amounting to only about one-third the East Asian standards and the traditional chuzo farms' yield in turn about one-third that of the mechanized farms, the potential for yield-raising modernization seems high.

Turning to land tenure aspects, neither sharecropping (DSC) nor the issue of land held without title (90B) seem to affect value added, negatively or otherwise. Sharecropping (or tenancy in general) is of little significance in Panama. According to the SES, only 1.3 percent of the farms reported having paid rent in kind in 1983. The survey farms reported 63 percent of land as without title. It is likely that the problem's negative effect on production may have been caused by the credit-access variable, which is in fact inversely correlated with percentage of land without title. The negative correlation (though relatively weak given that one of the variables is a dummy) supports the common contention in Panama that it is difficult to obtain credit without titled land as security. At any rate, the regression result on L90B supports the inference that, apart from the likely blocking of credit access, lack of title does not seem to have more direct consequences such as discouraging land improvement. Certain other indirect consequences are difficult to capture through regression analysis at the micro farm level. One such possible consequence is the impediment to leasing untitled land. Panama's land reform statute, as we understand it, holds out the possibility that a landholder may lose untitled land if occupancy passes to a tenant or may otherwise find himself unable to collect rent or get the land back for lack of the legal leverage that comes with fee-simple ownership. The country's exceedingly low tenancy rate may be a result of those uncertainties attached to half or more of all the farmland. Impediment to leasing in turn tends to perpetuate the country's badly skewed farm size distribution (Gini = 0.78 in 1970 and about unchanged in 1980). Extensive public land, freely available by pushing even deeper inland onto higher elevations, also continues to encourage slash-and-burn agriculture. Overall, there is probably a strong case for government action in this area, particularly when the remedy is linked with other action programs to develop agriculture.

Household Characteristics

Schooling of the household head (L40), the head's spouse (L41), and the head's father (L38) has significant positive net production effect of about the same magnitude in all three cases, a three to four percent increase per one year of increase in schooling. Schooling of the head's mother (L39) has no significant effect. The mean schooling for L40, L41, L38, and L39 is respectively 3.8, 4.1, 1.3, and 1.2 years, in table 13.4. It is 4.9 years for L40, 5.5 years for L41, and 1.4 years for L38 in the livestock subsample. Note the intergenerational increase in schooling and the intergenerational income transmission through education (though not in the mother's case). Note also the spouse's schooling effect on net farm output. The effects under the VAF are substantially greater than under the APF in the case of the head's spouse and father, suggesting their role in farm record keeping and management, whose effect is captured by the VAF, as opposed to doing actual work in the fields, of which there was little, according to the APF regression. The latter seems to be the main task of the head or the farmer, whose schooling parameter estimate turns out to be virtually unchanged between the two regressions.

Age of the head has a positive impact on value added. The variable (L26) probably may affect production in a nonlinear fashion. A squared term, however, was without success. Sex of the head (L25A) appears to be irrelevant in a farming context, as is technical training by the head (L44). The apparent measure of disguised unemployment, as in the APF, has a positive production effect, suggesting that the variable is reflecting the work ethic instead, as argued in the APF section. A recent health problem in the household detracts from farm activity and production, suggesting the presence of some transitory income despite the survey's design and our attempt to suppress it through definitions of certain variables, especially the output variable, by including, for example, livestock inventory change and by using the larger of the annual outputs for 1982 and 1983.

District Locational Variables

As in the APF regression dynamic, rapidly growing local economies (measured by the population-growth proxy, TAC) seem to promote performance of local farms, presumably by expanding market opportunities for output and inputs. District life expectancy (LE), as a proxy for the physical well-being, strength, and productivity of local farm persons, contributes to net agricultural production. Metropolitan location (DM = 1) seems to lower farming performance (though the negative coefficient is not quite significant) owing to the preeminence of part-time farming, which apparently overwhelmed the positive influences of metropolitan markets. Concentration of poverty farms (as defined in our earlier report on 1970 census farms), as in the APF regression, seems to so condition the economic-sociological-psychological environment of the district as to reduce the efficiency of the local farms. The coefficient of PF is negative and significant.

VALUE-MARGINAL PRODUCTS AND RATES OF RETURN

Value-marginal products (VMPs) for the mean values of inputs are given in table 13.5, (based on reg. 1 of table 13.3 and VAF of table 13.4) and table 13.6 (based on regs. 3 and 4). It should be mentioned that mean VMPs are rather approximate indicators for resource allocation. In figure 13.1, for example, the means of inputs labor and capital may lie at A for all farms, at B for capital-intensive (mechanized) farms, and at C for labor-intensive (e.g., chuzo) farms. The duality of B and C may exist side by side for various reasons, such as market segmentation, inaccessibility to credit by C farms, high-quantity discounts and low overhead and startup costs per unit of cooperant factors, such as land, for hiring machinery by B farms, and so on. Mean marginal products calculated at A may not be applicable to either typical farm. At point A, for instance, measured VMP of capital may be much higher than it really is to B farms that actually use capital. We present some estimates for farms of type B, for instance, the VMP of fertilizer to fertilizer-using farms. For the most part, however, mean marginal products are reported, based on the predicted output at the mean values of inputs, assuming means are close to modal value of inputs.

We see from table 13.5 that value-marginal product (VMP) of land amounts to $9.02 on poverty farms (or PF, as represented by their geometric mean farm) and $11.80 on the more productive nonpoverty farms (NPF). Note that, as explained in some detail in the notes to table 13.5, the use of geometric mean farms narrows considerably the differences that exist between PFs and NPFs when arithmetic means are employed to rep-

Table 13.5 Mean Value-Marginal Products, Poverty Farms and Nonpoverty Farms (Dollars per Year per Unit of Respective Input and Rates of Return)

Factor or Input	Poverty Farms (PF) (GVAO = $443) (VA = $400)	Nonpoverty Farms (NPF) (GVAO = $990) (VA = $725)	Unit
Land	$9.02 (1.48)	$11.80 (1.94)	Per hectare
Labor	$35.35 (24.41)	$84.70 (58.49)	Per man-year
Capital	$7.89 (2.43)	$6.53 (2.01)	Per dollar of rental value of machines and implements
Current inputs	$4.72 (1.31)	$3.18 (0.88)	Per dollar of outlay
Irrigation	$2.68 (1.21)	$6.00 (2.70)	Per one-point change in percentage of land irrigated
Irrigation	$11.72[a] (5.29)	$12.52[a] (5.64)	Per hectare of irrigated land
Livestock (cattle)	$72.22 (8.96)	$82.10 (10.22)	Per head of inventory
Livestock (cattle)	28.9%[b] (3.6)	32.8%[b] (4.1)	Rate of gross return (on cost per head)
Education of household head[c]	$12.00 (6.15)	$21.75 (11.15)	Per year of schooling
Education of household head[c]	4.8%[d] (2.5)	8.7%[d] (4.4)	Rate of return
Age in experience of household head[c]	$5.16 (1.41)	$9.35 (2.6)	Per year of experience

Note: Standard errors in parentheses. All calculations are for the geometric mean farms, poor and nonpoor. Geometric mean (GM) farms are synthetic farms (for each of the two groups of farms, poverty and nonpoverty) with GM inputs and GM farm-household characteristics. These GMs of the explanatory variables are substituted in the APF regression (table 13.3) to generate the estimated gross value of agricultural output (GVAO) of the GM farms. The latter estimates are $443 for the GM poverty farm and $990 for the GM nonpoverty farm, compared with $225 and $910, respectively, for the GM of GVAO calculated from the data. The GMs for GVAO are, in turn, to be compared with the arithmetic means of GVAO for the PF and NPF groups, $463 and $3,290. In interpreting the comparative VMPs and rate of returns between PF and NPF, it is important to remember the special meaning of the GMs and how much closer they are to one another than if conventional averages are used. See illustration in figure 13.1.

[a]Irrigation coverage is minimal in Panama. The survey data show that only 0.7 percent of the land of the GMPF and 1.53 percent of the GMNPF was irrigated. The GM sizes were, respectively, 22.9 and 47.9 hectares; hence a one percentage point increase in relative irrigated area translates into 0.229 and 0.479 hectares, respectively, for the PF and NPF. The latter figures are divided into the estimates of the preceding line ($2.68 and $6.00) to obtain VMP per hectare as shown.

[b]Calculated on the basis of cost of $250 per head of cattle inventory, as is consistent with the average price adopted by the Census Bureau of Panama.

[c]Estimated parameters are from the VAF in table 13.4 to capture both the direct and indirect effects to these variables on production. The GM farms are based on the GMs of the explanatory variables in the VAF; their values added are the regression estimates from the substituted GMs in the explanatory variables.

[d]Based on a 1983 social cost of $250 per year of elementary school per pupil. The returns to schooling of the spouse are virtually identical.

Table 13.6 Mean Value-Marginal Products, Livestock and Crop Farms, 1983 (Dollars per Year or Rate of Return)

	Factor or Input	Livestock Farms		Crop Farms		Unit
L86L87	Labor	$179.2	(2.07)	$18.98	(0.76)	Per worker per year
L88	Capital	$0.12	(0.21)	$11.47	(3.40)	Per dollar rental per year
L90	Land	$9.9	(3.81)	$14.17	(4.89)	Per hectare per year
L96	Irrigation	—	(—)	$31.00	(2.00)	Per irrigated hectare per year
L90B	Land with title	$93.3	(0.43)[a]	$38.88	(1.09)[a]	Per percentage-point increase per year
L90B		$2.19	(0.43)	$1.82	(1.09)	Per hectare of titled land per year
Cattle		$20.0	(9.47)	$16.41	(0.67)	Per head of cattle per year
Cattle		$8.0[b]	(9.47)	$6.56[b]	(0.67)	Percent rate of return on cattle per year
Pigs		$34.6	(2.34)	$42.65	(2.28)	Per pig per year
L40	Education of head	$16.7	(0.52)	$18.80	(2.01)	Per school year per year
L40		6.7[b]	(0.52)	7.5[b]	(2.01)	Percent rate of return per school year
COMER	Index of commercialization	$13.3	(6.25)	$1.88	(7.16)	Per percentage-point change per farm of mean size (18 hectares for livestock and 4.6 hectares for crop farms) per year
L81/L85	Crop ratio	$144.0	(1.36)	−$0.75	(−1.69)	Per percentage-point change per year per farm of sizes stated above

Note: The numbers in parentheses are *t*-values.

[a] The ratios of land held with title are 0.349 for livestock farms and 0.463 for crop farms. (Surprisingly, the ratio is higher for crop farms.)

[b] Given the mean farm size of 17.99 hectares and 4.6 hectares and the number of farms in the sample of 237 livestock farms and 465 crop farms, a one-percentage-point increase in L90B comes to 42.7 hectares and 1.82 hectares, respectively. When these numbers are divided into the respective VMPs per percentage-point increase of 93.3 and 38.88, they yield the stated rates of return. Similar calculations were used to obtain the relevant values for COMER and specialization (L81/L85).

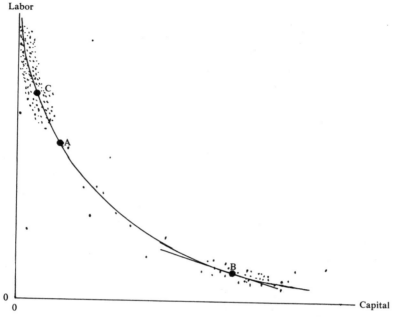

Figure 13.1   Significance of mean VMPs, an illustration. For a discussion of how constraints on farms in the neighborhood of C prevent them from moving to the neighborhood of B, see the discussion in the text.

resent them. Also, the outputs of our GM farms are estimated from the APF and VAF regressions by substituting the GMs of the explanatory variables into the equations. These further narrow the PF/NPF differences compared with the differences of the GMs of the output data (GVAO and VA). In short, it is well to remember in interpreting the estimates that follow on VMP and rates of returns that the differences between the PF and NPF would be grossly overstated compared with those reported in table 13.5 had ordinary averages been used to represent the "typical" PF and NPF. A suggestive magnitude of the understatement is found in the first note to table 13.5. The implied rates of return are probably not implausible when calculated from the relatively low farmland values in Panama. The VMP of (family) labor is a low $35.35 per man-year in the PF sector, reflecting considerable disguised unemployment (not caught by the SES questionnaire). Underemployment appears to be substantial even in the NPF sector, with an estimated VMP of just under $85. Capital appears to be seriously underutilized, especially on PFs, its VMP being several times its service flow price. Use of current inputs is also suboptimal, especially on PFs, suggesting in part the influence of capital rationing under uncertainty in production and price (not completely removed by price support). The latter risk-averting behavior also helps explain the disequilibrium in use of hired labor. Livestock inventory, as a separate form of farm capital, yields good returns in Panama. Cattle VMP of $72 to $82 on PFs and NPFs translates into 29 to 33 percent rates of returns. Note that GVAO is calculated on a perpetual inventory basis and net of livestock purchase. However, VMP is otherwise a gross output concept.

Turning to the variables that modify the productivity of the conventional inputs above, irrigation (little used in Panama) essentially doubles the VMP of the land. Irrigating a hectare of land (at the Panamanian level of water application) adds $12 to $13 to the unit yield on PFs and NPs. Note that these estimates are subject to sizable standard errors. Given the relative abundance of land (albeit poorly distributed), the sizable current and capital costs of irrigation, and the country's adaptation to "dryland" farming (as in Panama's North American–style dry rice farming in contrast to wet, flooded-field rice farming in Asia), the returns are probably too low to justify widespread use of irrigation, unless new technologies and new marketing opportunities should alter the basic terms of reference.

So much for the production characteristics of the farm. Of the household characteristics, education and age (or experience) of the farm operator both matter. As calculated from the VAF regression in table 13.3, whose estimated parameter captures both the direct and the indirect effects of education on production, an additional year of schooling for the farm operator (household head) raised annual farm income by $12 on PFs and $21.75 on NPFs. Translated into perpetual annual income flows and based on a 1983 schooling cost to Panama of $250 per pupil per year, these estimated income gains support rates of returns of 4.8 percent per year for the PFs and 8.7 percent for the NPFs. These are not exciting returns. They suggest relative stagnation in the state of the art and in forces operating on the demand side. A tilt toward production policies is suggested not so much for the sake of balance per se as to capture the high returns promised by a policy to exploit the disequilibrium promises. It is to be noted for emphasis that the problem is all the more serious as it bears on the PFs. The PFs have less schooling that the NPFs (2.96 vs. 3.67 years). To pull themselves up, they will need more schooling, but additional schooling brings them lower rates of returns than it does the larger, higher-income farms. Such is the vicious circle of poverty.

Age or experience differs little between the PFs and NPFs (41.29 vs. 43.99). Its effect on value added is positive but small, $5.16 and $9.35 per year of additional experience for the two types of farms.

The VMPs calculated for livestock and crop farms support most of the results discussed above for the overall function. Some of the differences between livestock and crop farms are enlightening. The VMP of labor

($179 per man-year) in livestock farms is much closer to the market wage than is the case for other farms. The range of VMPs of cattle goes from $20 (table 13.6) to $82 (table 13.5). The cattle economy seems to be over-expanded in relation to the pig economy in both types of farms. The rate of return from fertilizer is amazingly high, 1,400 percent. Evidently the use of fertilizer represents much more than chemicals. Presumably, superior technology and entrepreneurial input are embodied in the use of fertilizer.

The rates of return from schooling in agriculture are respectable, 7–8 percent, but not spectacular, once again reflecting the traditional state of Panamanian agriculture in which not much use can be made of education. In the current state of technology, schooling is remunerative mainly for those seeking nonagricultural employment.

The rate of return on machinery is a whopping 1,147 percent on crop farms, suggesting either supply or financial constraints, or some other type, on the use of machinery. In livestock farms the rate is competitive (12 percent), suggesting fewer physical or financial constraints and more efficient allocation and markets.

We have seen that in the prevailing state of the art in Panama VMPs of land and labor on poor farms are a pittance. The two conventional factors of production under reference, land and labor, are at best all that the poor in general possess. Small farmers own some land, though not much. They seem to have plenty of underused family labor. Others have only their labor and no land or capital. Also overexpanded is the cattle population in Panama.

The two modern inputs whose VMPs are given above, machinery and fertilizer, have surprisingly high rates of return. For all farms the rates of return are approximately 7 percent in perpetuity for education, 700 percent for machinery, and even more for fertilizer. In the present state of the art and with their present distribution, endowments—not only raw labor and land—have miserably low value-marginal products, and the rate of return to education is also modest.

In short, the main remedy for reducing rural poverty lies in increasing the productivity of land and labor as well as in promoting and creating the conditions for the use of fertilizer, high-yield seeds, and machinery (in an otherwise chuzo economy). The productivity of land and labor can possibly be increased by developing land-intensive innovations, and that of labor might be raised by schooling, training, and extension services. Neither augmenting small farmers' land nor increasing the number of hands in the family seems to hold much hope for ameliorating their economic plight unless the level of technology is raised.

The earnings capacity of poor farmers is more vividly brought out in table 13.7, which gives mean quantities of fixed factors owned and oper-

Table 13.7 Mean Quantities of Factors Owned (F), Mean VMPs Produced, and Mean Incomes Realized (Y) per Farm, Poor and Nonpoor Farms, 1983

Sample and Variable	Land	Labor	Capital	Education	Cattle	Pigs	Observed VAP	Comprehensive Y
Sample of table 13.5 and Regression 1 (996 Observations)								
1. *Poor*								
F	23.0	1.3	5.2	3.0	2.9	1.3	—	—
VMP	9.02	35.35	7.9	4.8	72.0	42.6	—	—
Y	207.0	46.0	41.0	14.0	209.0	55.0	303.0	804.0
2. *Nonpoor*								
F	48.0	1.25	20.2	3.7	13.9	2.2	—	—
VMP	11.8	84.7	6.5	21.8	82.0	34.6	—	—
Y	566.0	106.0	131.0	80.0	1,140.0	76.0	2,433.0	4,340.0
Sample of Regression 2 (996 Observations)								
3. *Poor*								
F	30.0	1.18	3.3	3.03	4.1	1.4	—	—
VMP	2.88	51.0	1.16	15.0	42.4	43.3	—	—
Y	86.0	60.0	3.8	46.0	174.0	59.0	303.0	804.0
4. *Nonpoor*								
F	56.4	1.22	37.2	4.0	22.3	2.7	—	—
VMP	11.1	353.0	0.4	109.0	10.0	59.0	—	—
Y	623.0	431.0	144.0	434.0	223.0	159.0	2,423.0[a]	4,340.0[a]

Sample of Regression 3: Livestock Farms (237 Observations)

5.	F	18.0	0.95	8.0	4.9	21.6	2.6	—
	VMP	9.9	179.2	0.12	16.7	20.0	34.6	—
	Y	178.0	170.0	96.0	82.0	432.0	90.0	1,143.0

Sample of Regression 4: Crop Farms (465 Observations)

6.	F	4.6	0.9	3.6	3.9	1.2	1.2	—
	VMP	14.2	19.0	11.5	18.8	16.4	42.7	—
	Y	65.0	17.0	41.0	73.0	19.0	51.0	354.0[b]

Simple Mean of 1, 3, and 6: Poor Farms[c]

F	21.0	1.1	13.0	3.3	2.7	1.3	—
VMP	9.0	35.0	10.0	26.0	43.0	43.0	—
Y	119.0	41.0	40.0	44.0	134.0	55.0	320.0

Simple Mean of 2, 4, and 5: Nonpoor Farms[c]

F	41.0	1.41	21.8	4.2	19.3	2.5	—
VMP	10.9	206.0	2.3	49.0	39.0	43.0	—
Y	456.0	236.0	124.0	199.0	600.0	108.0	2,433.0

4,340.0

[a]From table 13.1.
[b]From table 13.2.
[c]Because of simple means, the product of F and VMP may not equal Y. Since the numbers are subject to large standard errors, sophisticated calculations were not done. The products of F (number of units of the respective factor) and VMP in the individual panels, however, are correctly calculated to obtain Y (income).

287

ated, the VMPs of the respective factors, and incomes attributable to these factors for poor farms, crop farms (also relatively poor), and livestock farms. We see that the human and nonhuman factors of which poor farms have relatively more command (labor and land) have low shadow prices (value-marginal products) in relation to market prices (not reported). They are from one-quarter to one-sixth lower for poor farms than for rich farms. The factors of which the poor have little relative to the nonpoor, specifically capital, enjoy high shadow prices, and substantially higher for poor farms (if they possess them) than for nonpoor farms. Factor shares are identical for both classes of farms (a property of the Cobb-Douglas production function). Almost all inputs, owned or purchased, except labor, are significantly higher per hectare in nonpoor farms. Finally, the levels of technical assistance received, availability of credit, and irrigation facilities are much higher on nonpoor farms than on poor farms.

Which assets of small farmers may be augmented to raise them sufficiently above the poverty line? In the present state of technology, evidently none except mechanization hold any prospects, but mechanization is beyond their capacity. Land has very low VMP. Even education will not do them much good in their chuzo agriculture. If they migrate to urban areas with schooling less than high school, in all probability they will end in urban poverty. There seems little hope for small farmers to get out of poverty without a technology that increases the marginal productivity of land and man, or without at least high-school education so they can get nonpoor jobs in nonagricultural occupations.

Thus, the reasons for the frustration of Panamanian policymakers in not being able to reduce the poverty of campesinos despite agrarian reform, asentamientos, subsidized credit, support prices, and other incentives are a bit clearer. Policies that are not addressed to increasing the productivity of rural man and land have little chance of reducing rural poverty.

RURAL NONFARM FAMILY (RNFF) EARNINGS FUNCTION

Turning to the RNFF earnings function (whose results appear in table 13.8), first note that no farm inputs are present. This affords a basis for using a strictly linear function with interaction terms where relevant on a priori grounds. The linear function in this case produces a superior fit. Its coefficients stand for marginal effects that are equal to average effects and are directly translated into dollars and cents. The dependent variable used here is family (instead of individual or household) income, since a large number of families have some farm income that is not attributable to any one member of the family. Not surprisingly, the size of the family work force (L28) is a significant determinant of total family earnings. Such a finding, though hardly startling, is reassuring, since it confirms internal

Table 13.8   Rural Nonfarm Family Earnings Function

	Variable	Parameter Estimate	t for HO Parameter-0
Intercept		−7,143.64	−1.821
L28	Persons aged 15–65	769.65	2.819
L25A	Sex of household head	38.51	0.011
L26	Age of head (years)	105.78	3.342
L40	Schooling of head (years)	315.24	2.664
L41	Schooling of head's spouse (years)	642.16	5.903
L38	Schooling of head's father (years)	299.23	2.249
L34	Has refrigerator = 1, otherwise 0	257.26	0.711
L46	Secured medical assistance = 1	−415.50	−0.659
AE	Principal employment in agriculture	−2,293.57	−3.346
AESQ	AE squared	9.11	0.004
L58	Disguised unemployment of head	−37.86	−0.055
TAC	Population growth rate	338.13	1.413
DM	Metropolitan dummy	−748.39	−0.666
HEALTH	Life expectancy	10.44	0.706
Adjusted R^2		0.4969	
Number of observations		275	

consistency of the SES data. Its coefficient says that, other things being equal, an additional member in the family work force adds $770 to the family's annual income in the rural nonfarm sector of Panama. Given the mean RNFF income of $3,510 (and the mean family work force of 2.6 persons sixteen to sixty-five years of age), the incremental earning means a 22 percent increase to the average family, the rest of income being attributable to other factors. Age of the head of household, which in the rural nonfarm setting might be a proxy for experience matters, adds $106 to annual family income for each year of gain in age, that is, experience.

Schooling adds much more per year (of additional education): $315 for the head of household (L40), $299 for the head's father (L38), and, interestingly, $642 for the head's spouse (wife in most cases; L41). The result supports the findings of chapter 7 and other chapters to the effect that while education may not have a high payoff in farming at the present level of agricultural technology, it is essential for jobs in the nonagricultural or urban modern sector. Rural-urban migration of persons with at most primary education is in general unlikely to get migrants out of poverty; high-school education may.

Although education of the head's mother has no apparent effect, the *direct* intergenerational transmission of income is there through the father. The contribution of the mother's education to the next generation has been found in many studies to be *indirect* by exerting a positive influence on the children's schooling and outlook. These indirect intergenerational relationships are the subject of chapters 10 and 11 above. As with the rural farm families, occupation has a great deal to do with the incomes of the rural nonfarm families. Having one's principal occupation in agriculture (65 percent of all RNFF, compared with 85 percent for RFF) reduces income to $2,294 from a mean RNFF income of $3,510. As has been confirmed elsewhere in the book, the burden of poverty in Panama is primarily agricultural.

POLICY IMPLICATIONS

At the outset, we remind readers that the larger context in which agricultural policy issues are to be viewed is concerned with antipoverty programs that are growth promoting, or at least not growth inhibiting. It is thus a frame of reference requiring consideration of long-term effects. In deriving the following list of policy implications, we draw on the insights afforded by the regression results on the workings of the possible policy instrument variables, including the price variable studied in chapter 3 and elsewhere.

Value of Assets

Which assets will ameliorate the economic conditions of the poor the most? Augmenting poor farmers' ownership of the traditional asset, land, with its VMP ranging from $3 to only $14 per hectare per year, will not harm them. But it will solve not their poverty problem. At the prevailing level of technology, were land alone used to reduce the poverty of rural farm families, the 47 percent critically poor of farm families would each need 73 hectares of additional land to rise above the critical poverty line.[1] There is not enough land available to fulfill this order, since the mean size of landholdings of nonpoor farm families is at most 56 hectares.

Accordingly, some other resource must be found. Family labor has an even lower VMP relative to market wage and is, indeed, disguisedly underemployed to a high degree. At present, education has a very modest rate of return in agriculture. Mechanization and modern inputs, proxied by fertilizer, have high VMPs. Their use by poor farmers, however, is constrained by several factors: there probably isn't enough machinery in

---

1. The predicted level of the present income of the average critically poor farm family, as in table 13.7, is $354 (using the higher estimate among all subsamples), its mean landholdings are 21 hectares, and the mean VMP of land in poor and nonpoor farms is at most $14.20. The critical poverty line for a family of 4.5 members is $1,692 (= $376*4.5). For this family to rise above the critical poverty line by owning more land, it needs 73 hectares (= {[$1,692 − $354]/$14.20} − 21).

Panama for all farms; the scale of most poor farms is too small to use machinery economically. Despite the high expected rate of return from mechanization and fertilizer, the incomes of a large majority of campesinos are so small and the ratio of titled land to total land they possess is so small that few private banks are willing to advance them the requisite credit. Finally, the extension service for whatever technology goes with fertilizer and mechanization is woefully lacking. Despite all these constraints, however, the slack can be taken up if scattered campesinos can combine to increase the scale of their farms and pool their resources, however meager, to provide security to creditors and organization to hire the services of managers and other technical personnel. For this purpose, a type of farm association profitably exploited in East Asian countries is worth considering (see below).

The solution to rural poverty thus lies not in mechanization but in developing the right type of technology for the small farmer—not confined to movement along the isoquant, but rather in continual inward shifts of the isoquant. Once again the experience of the green revolution of the South and Southeast Asian countries deserves serious attention. Productivity-increasing agricultural research is probably the most profitable known investment in current times that serves a dual purpose: it is pro-poor, and it is growth promoting.

Technology of the green revolution type is the objective, and it involves the usual investment risk. Research might not bear fruit or might take a long time (say, up to a decade) to show results. These imponderables have to be accepted without giving up the effort. One should also remember, moreover, that the development of seed and fertilizer technology has to be accompanied by complementary programs. Education becomes an extremely important complementary factor, for which programs have to start now, because the gestation period for an educated labor force is even longer than that for a possible green revolution. Ownership of land will then be a potent factor not only in reducing poverty but also in making the present poor well-off, for the average productivity and the VMP of land will rise significantly, as they have in other countries that have experienced the green revolution. This technology is complementary to land and is labor intensive. For instance, as may be seen from panel A of table 13.9, 30 percent of family farms cultivate less than 3 hectares of land. Currently over a quarter of farms with 3 hectares of land derive farm incomes that are below the critical poverty line.

When the green revolution comes, an institution that effectively meets the credit needs of poor farmers is essential. Equally important are nonfarm employment opportunities, such as the creation of agroindustrial small businesses. The key programs that need to be planned now are the education program and productivity-increasing agricultural research. Panama

Table 13.9 Cross-Tabulations of Farm Size and Farm Income Class, National
Socioeconomic Survey, 1983

Annual Farm Income Classes ($)	Number of Farms by Size Classes (Ha)						
	Total	0.1–0.4	0.5–2.9	3.0–9.9	10.0–49.9	50.0–499.9	≥500
	A. All Farms						
Total	1,436	31	394	307	463	213	28
<200	208	10	104	44	50	—	—
200–699	522	15	185	99	187	36	—
700–1,199	226	3	59	65	65	32	2
1,200–2,099	153	2	24	29	57	36	5
2,100–4,799	177	1	17	46	59	48	6
4,800–9,599	71	—	3	13	24	28	3
9,600–17,999	46	—	1	8	14	18	5
≥18,000	33	—	1	3	7	15	7
	B. Backyard Farms and Farms Held for Speculation[a]						
Total	499	57	140	90	103	52	7
<200	434	57	140	90	103	42	2
200–699	15	0	0	0	0	10	5

[a]Backyard farms are defined as farms that have income of $10 or less per hectare. This is the
unexpanded sample of farms in the National Socioeconomic Survey, 1983.

has already invested generously in schools. Rural children, however, need
a headstart. For that a preschool program is highly productive and desirable. Action programs for both investments—preschool education for rural
children and biotechnical research—have been elaborated elsewhere in this
book.

Price-Control Reform

The number of commodities whose prices the Panamanian Price Regulation
Office fixes or controls is estimated to run to five digits. Evidently the role
of relative prices in signaling where scarce resources should be directed to
reduce relative scarcities tends to be stifled. As we saw in chapter 3 and
elsewhere, agricultural prices, for both the producer and the consumer,
are too high in Panama relative to border prices. The IMA (Instituto
Mechanaria de Agricultura) supports a number of agricultural prices and
fixes retail prices for an equally large number of imported and home-
produced food products. This price control system has helped maintain
Panama's high-cost agriculture. A reform of the agricultural price control
system is therefore in order. Since agricultural prices have been the subject

matter of a thorough inquiry by the Minnesota University group of economists, we shall not duplicate it here but shall simply add that a change in price policy is in order even from the poverty point of view.

For Panama, whose present frame of reference is more akin to that of the developed countries with its high support and consumer prices, it makes little sense to invest scarce administrative and fiscal resources in price controls. The utility of such an undertaking diminishes as economic development proceeds apace. It is a difficult and costly undertaking if the full theoretical benefits are to be realized. It is far more sensible to invest in a comprehensive development program for agriculture while gradually phasing out the present antipoor and basically inept price intervention scheme.

Mechanization versus Increased Productivity

There is a need to divert the present trend in Panamanian agriculture from mechanization to productivity-increasing practices and techniques. In the present, rather stagnant state of food agriculture, poor farmers' supply response to price incentives appears to be weak in Panama. Technical conditions on the production side and input supply conditions need to be improved for more elastic responses to take place.

Investment in education and health, though it promotes welfare and enhances nonagricultural employment, has thus far produced low returns in Panama's agriculture. This, together with the finding of relatively low productivity of the conventional inputs, suggests an imbalance in the country's rural development package, overemphasizing the "social welfare" aspects at the expense of production-related investments, as in agricultural research, development, and technical extension and in infrastructure and institutions bearing on production and marketing. The importance of improving market access for the Panamanian producers (especially the small ones) regarding both output and inputs cannot be overemphasized.

Land Reform

There is need for a complete cadastral survey and program of granting titles to land. Size distribution of the operating units is a serious problem in Panama. The disparity between the poverty and nonpoverty farms is sharp. The problem is, fortunately, more amenable to solution in Panama owing to the unique prevalence of land held without title. About half of the farmland may thus be considered public domain pending final titling. "Land reform" in this context should begin with a complete cadastral survey to delineate all land by ownership, by untitled holdings, and by leasing status and to establish land use and land quality classification according to soil types and other relevant characteristics. The survey can be conducted expeditiously with modern aerial photographic technology. Part or all of the cost may be recovered by a title fee to be borne by the recipients of the titles under a formal program to redistribute land in public domain.

Expansion of Land Tax

Land tax exists in Panama in name only. It can be made a vehicle of revenue gathering as well, can damp speculative holding of land, and can promote land's productive use. An idea of speculative landholding can be had from the data of table 13.9. Of the 449 farms that earn $10 or less per hectare, 7 (or 1.6 percent) have 5,000 or more hectares of land, and 52 (or 11.6 percent) fall in farm size 50.0 to 499.9 hectares. A land tax will reduce the rate of return in the form of capital gains. It will make speculative holding of land less attractive and push land toward productive use.

The geography and topography of the country are not conducive to low-cost infrastructural development. Providing the costly infrastructure—an essential ingredient in any substantive comprehensive rural development in Panama, given its present deplorable status—is almost certain to exceed the resource capacity of the government. Part of this burden should fall on the farmers who benefit from it. A land tax properly structured with the help of the cadastral survey, so as to provide incentive for economical land use, suggests itself. Title fees, to incorporate a modest land evaluation, such as two times the normal annual yield of the land in the area, would also be desirable to help finance this and other development needs of agriculture. Payment of the fee may be in installments. Proper structuring of the lump sum levy and the land tax is never easy. An expedient way would be to require each landowner to assess his or her own holding under the legal provision that the government has the right to purchase it at the self-assessed value when gross undervaluation is suspected.

Farmers' Associations

Collective farms (asentamientos) are one type of farm organization Panama has experimented with. Scattered campesinos, too, can benefit from scale economies by pooling their resources and availing themselves of modern methods of business organization. A somewhat modified system of cooperative farms has been profitably exploited in Taiwan and other East Asian countries. This type of farmers' association (FA)—probably most developed in Taiwan—is an appealing form of organization that a government can readily promote as an economical and effective way to provide numerous private services to the farms and households in villages as well as to handle public functions entrusted to it by the government. The operating

FAs are local units organized under a standard charter. They are subject to some oversight and coordination by the provincial FAs, in which the operating FAs have representation and that hold annual or semiannual meetings attended by local elected representatives. At the apex there is the national FA, with responsibility for national oversight and coordination. Operating FAs are the heart of the multitier system. They are true cooperatives with voluntary membership restricted to bona fide farmers (with nonvoting associate membership for local nonfarmers interested in agriculture) who elect their own officers and directors. The directors in turn hire a trained manager to operate the FA day to day. A full-service operating FA offers such services as banking, storing, processing, marketing, buying, renting, and so on. Panama's current close friendship with Taiwan may be taken advantage of to obtain technical and financial aid from that country, which has successfully exploited this form of farm producers' association.

Increased Crop Yields

There is need for an agricultural technology for poor farmers. Productivity-increasing agricultural research must aim at enhancing agricultural growth and reducing rural poverty as well as urban poverty.[2] We saw in chapter 3 that, except for a modest increase in rice output, the production of other staples, such as corn and beans, has stagnated since the 1960s. During the same period, per capita apparent consumption of all three food staples declined significantly. The yield of staple food commodities is estimated to be very low. For instance, in the middle of the 1970s, the yield of rice in Panama was estimated to be less than a third of the yield in major rice-producing countries.

Owing to the development of the seed-fertilizer technology known as the green revolution in the Punjab of India, the yield of wheat doubled during the four-year period 1965–69 and has since been increasing at a high rate. The yield of rice has experienced similar increases. Food prices in Panama are estimated to be from 150 percent to 500 percent higher than border prices.

Thus, not only has the level of food prices in Panama been high, but the rate of increase too has been higher than elsewhere. During the 1970s, the price index of food rose roughly by a quarter more than the price index of nonfood commodities. Worse still, the prices of poorman's food increased by one-third more than the prices of the food of the nonpoor.

2. An evaluation of Panama's agricultural research was made by Robert Evenson. The proposal for expanding Panama's agricultural research as an antipoverty policy follows from the results of his research and evaluation (Evenson 1984).

In the years 1980 and 1981, the Agricultural Research Institute (Instituto de Investigación Agropecuaria de Panamá [IDIAP]) spent a little over $3 million (or about 0.1 percent of GNP) annually on current account and about half of it on capital account for agricultural research. This includes $6 million in aid from the USAID (to be used over a period of five years) to strengthen the technical capacity and physical facilities of the institute. Less than $100,000, or 6 percent of the total, was allocated to research on agriculture. The rest went to institutional development (75 percent), livestock research (14 percent), and the production (as distinguished from development) of seeds (5 percent) (Panama, IDIAP 1981, 11).

Given Panama's rather weak performance in increasing the yield of its staple crops during the past fifteen years, when several developing countries have experienced green revolutions, the top priority for research should perhaps go to the development of high-yield varieties of seeds, especially for unirrigated areas. Funds appear to be spent mainly on extension research (which is usually expected to yield quick though unspectacular results). Relatively low priority seems to be given to developing innovations in agricultural practices and high-yield varieties of seeds (whose payoff is usually high but is uncertain and generally has a long gestation period). In this area there is need to reconsider priorities. Imported technology is highly biased against farm labor and small farms. A major payoff should be expected from research in high-yield varieties of rice. This research thus has a high potential, both for the amelioration of poverty and for national economic growth.

An important conclusion of the brief survey of Panama's food sector is that in investment in agricultural productivity Panama lags far behind its peers. Even though, in the face of the possible "spill-in" nature of agricultural research in Central America, it is not apparent whether relatively large expenditure on a central farm experiment station or other big research center is justified, there is clear need for a central research unit for directing and coordinating scattered on-farm research units. Such a central unit would require a critical mass of agronomists and other scientists (with postgraduate degrees, including some with postdoctoral training at leading universities or agricultural centers of the world). Panama has a highly developed medical and health science system but not a comparable agricultural production science system. This is due in part to the 1970s focus on social services and agricultural institutions to the relative neglect of production technology. A national capacity for developing at least biotechnology should be created, since it cannot be easily imported. It is the kind of technology that tends to benefit the poor, and there is a large scope for improvement in this area.

The limited extent and present organization of domestic agricultural research leave the agricultural sector to be influenced entirely by imported technology, which is highly biased against farm labor and small farms. This study therefore poses the following questions aimed at clarifying policy.

Can an expanded system of agricultural research do better than it has in the past?

Is it moving in the right direction?

How much larger should it be?

Where will the scientists come from?

In search for answers to these questions, we find that much of Panama's research budget is spent on extension research (even though extension services of the Ministry of Agricultural Development [MIDA] are rather meager). This direction is not very productive; it needs to be reoriented toward production research. It is not concentrating on achieving a "critical mass" of scientists in selected fields. The productive research system of Panama is composed of a "portfolio" of research projects, dominated by components designed to produce only managerial technology. This may deliver goods in the short run, but in the long run Panama's portfolio must include a strong biotechnology component. As now organized, Panama's system is basically capable of technology screening and managerial technology development. At the same time, Panama cannot afford to build a large system with first-rate scientists in all the basic sciences. But it clearly has to move toward the plant breeding area, which does not require massive investment in equipment and is quite compatible with the present policy of on-farm research that is currently dominating IDIAP's overall approach to agricultural growth. The quantum of research by IDIAP might have to increase two or three times. The creation of IDIAP with the sole function of research has been a very appropriate institutional development in Panama, but its size needs to be expanded. Any expansion or reorganization of agricultural research must be under the direction of IDIAP. Strong complementarities exist between research and graduate teaching, especially in the agricultural area, where field experiments have both research and teaching value. We think the case is strong for creating a university-based research graduate study center that is part of an integrated research and teaching center. By integration we mean operation under one administration. In the long run Panama should avoid the high cost of getting all its scientists trained abroad.

PART FIVE

Policy Analysis

FOURTEEN

Policy Analysis

This chapter surveys Panama's major socioeconomic policies with a view to assessing their effects on the poor, irrespective of whether their primary objective is to alleviate poverty. Six major categories of policies are included: the social security system of Panama, public enterprises and public utilities, taxes, public services or public expenditures, investment incentive schemes and price policies, and public investment policy. These policies are assembled in this chapter because at least for certain parts the method of analysis is by and large the same. Several other policies are evaluated or derived in other parts of the book. They fall into different contexts and use different methods of analysis—for example, policies on agricultural research, preschool education, employment, child health and family planning, and small business.

GENERAL METHOD OF POLICY ANALYSIS

The general approach to the analysis of almost all the reference policies is derived from theories on taxes and expenditures. The interest in determining the redistributive effects of taxes and expenditures in developing countries arose around the beginning of the 1960s, and Panama was one of the first in this research. Two of the studies done on the public finance of Panama in those years—McLure's 1971 report on the distribution of tax burden in Panama (published 1974) and my own 1972 report on the distribution of the benefits of government expenditure in Panama (Sahota 1977)—remain standard in the field. A number of such studies have been done for other countries since, but the standards of tax and expenditure allocation that we used in the context of Panama have barely been improved, except to the extent that superior data have become available and general equilibrium models have been developed instead of partial equilibrium analyses, as in Pindyck (1973), Sahota (1975), Sahota and Rocca (1985), and others.

The present study goes beyond taxes and expenditures to analyze most of the policies and public institutions that tend to influence distribution and poverty. It is an overall policy analysis rather than a mere budget study.

Precise methods of allocating the antipoverty (or pro-poverty or neutrality) effects of particular policies will be discussed in their respective sections below. The general approach consists of first translating individual policies in terms of taxes or quasi-taxes; expenditures, quasi-expenditures, or tax expenditures; and subsidies and transfers, and then estimating their benefits and burdens by income class. The analysis is carried out in a partial equilibrium context, even though taxes and expenditures clearly have general equilibrium consequences. The main reason for not using the general equilibrium analysis is the lack of data. An additional rationalization is that partial equilibrium analysis is simpler and more easily understood by policymakers. Moreover, in the case of long-term redistribution among income classes, indirect and secondary effects may to a large extent be mutually neutralizing. The study is divided into seven sections:

Intergenerational and intragenerational redistribution effects of the social security system

Antipoverty effects of the price and production policies of autonomous and semiautonomous public enterprises, which will be called parastatals or public enterprises

The distribution of the benefits of government expenditures, including expenditures of parastatals that are directly financed from the central budget—for example, the National Radio, the University of Panama, IFARHU, and others

The distribution of the burden of taxes

The redistributive effects of price policies and investment incentive schemes

The distribution of the benefits of public investment

The final section collects the results of all six policies.

Before we turn to the evaluation of policies, it is important to describe the basic income distribution series that will be used throughout this chapter.

Income Distribution

The most basic series of data for analyzing the incidence of policies is the distribution of comprehensive income. The population census of Panama, like censuses all over the world, collects data only on monetary income. Accordingly, the monetary income of the *Population Census, 1980* was adjusted for nonmonetary income as well as certain categories of national accounts not reported in the household surveys—for example, undistributed and unreported profits. It was supplemented by information from the *Household Survey, 1982.*

The ratios of nonmonetary income to monetary income by income classes derived from the *Income Survey, 1970* were used to adjust the 1980 census incomes to develop comprehensive incomes. This is apparently a rough adjustment, since neither the income distribution nor the self-consumption ratios of different classes may have remained constant. The changes, if any, in income distribution and self-consumption over the decade, however, are not likely to be so appreciable as to render the indicated adjustment futile. The self-consumption component for low-income rural classes, for instance, is so large—over 100 percent of monetary income (see chap. 4)—that neglecting it would give misleading results.

Equally important is the adjustment for undistributed profits, which represent an income (or forced savings) of the same sort for rich stockholders as social security contributions do for wage earners. The dividends reported in the *Income Survey, 1970* for the cities of Panamá and Colón came to only 0.07 percent of personal income, whereas aggregate profits accounted for approximately 6 percent of national income. The reported profits of individual families were therefore adjusted to the level of true profits. A result of this adjustment is that the reported incomes of the top bracket go up by 44 percent, from approximately $21,000 to $37,000 per annum. The resulting distribution appears in table 4.1.

WHO BENEFITS FROM PANAMA'S SOCIAL SECURITY SYSTEM?

Social Security Contributions as Quasi-Taxes

Social security contributions fall in between pure taxation and pure long-term savings or old-age and health insurance. They have the nature of savings in that it is mainly contributors who get major social security benefits such as old-age pensions. Insofar as benefits are paid out of current collections, and insofar as they are only partially funded and are fractionally related to the equity component, contributions conform to taxes. Moreover, the time span between contributions and old-age pensions (the major single component of social security benefits) is so long that the present value of distant benefits at, for instance, age twenty-five of a pension expected at age sixty-five looks rather small. Thus, even if an actuarially fair relationship existed between contributions and pensions, to the average contributor it might appear vague. Accordingly, in this study social security contributions are treated as quasi-taxes and are allocated to various income classes according to wages.

Data

The main data source is a merge file prepared especially for the Critical Poverty Project from several different tapes of the Social Security Administration (Panama, Social Security Department 1984). The entire file consists of a stratified sample of 3,500 active and 1,000 inactive men and women subscribers as of 1983. For this section, however, a subsample of all men and women who retired during the period 1978–83 was chosen.

The file consists of the life cycle earning history of each subject from the introduction of the social security system in 1943 to date. Unfortunately, there are several gaps in the data in the 1940s, 1950s, and early 1960s. Thus the analysis was based primarily on the data for the 1970s and 1980s. For additional description, see the notes to table 14.1.

The second main source of data is the *Household Survey, 1982*. This is the latest routine (almost annual) survey on incomes. It reports monetary incomes by sources, including old-age pensions. It has many more variables than the social security data file, but it reports only benefits, without any information on contributions. Moreover, it is a cross section, whereas the social security data tape reports the life history of the earnings, contributions, and old-age benefits of individual subscribers. The third source used here is the 1980 census of population, from which we derive certain characteristics of retirees.

Benefits

Social security benefits are divided into three components: all nonpension, current-account benefits, such as those for health, maternity, temporary incapacity, work injury, funeral expenses, and other welfare ($130 million in 1980); old-age pensions ($69.46 million in 1980); and benefits from capital expenditure. Even though nearly one-fifth of wages are contributed to the social security system, like other Latin American countries, Panama has no social unemployment insurance, though it has old-age and health insurance.

Welfare and Institutional Benefits

The benefits in this category are available not only to covered workers and their dependents but, under a recent merger of public health and social security health programs, to noncovered persons also. In 1982, 15 percent of those who received public health services were not covered under the social security system. As such, 15 percent of health and welfare benefits under the latter category were allocated based on population and 85 percent based on wages.

Retirement Benefits

In 1982, pensioners formed 2.3 percent of total population and 11.9 percent of social security subscribers. Alternatively stated, there are currently 8.4

workers covered by social security to every retiree. The marginal ratio of covered to retired persons, that is, the ratio of new subscribers to new pensioners, as of the early 1980s, is 7.3, giving a transitory elasticity of retirees with respect to subscribers of 1.15. The covered worker to retiree ratio thus seems to be approaching a plateau of 7.3.

The main preoccupation of social security experts in recent years has been with the solvency of the social security system. This is the main theme in Burkhauser's report (1984). Its income distribution effects have been neglected. This study focuses on the latter, which by implication also throws light on the system's solvency from a different angle. Three aspects of the redistribution of retirement benefits are analyzed: intergenerational redistribution resulting from retirement benefits; intragenerational redistribution of pensions among pensioners; and intragenerational redistribution of pensions among families. Before discussing redistribution, a description of the data base is in order.

Estimates of Equity

The separation of the equity built up by participants of the system through cumulated contributions and transfer components of old-age benefits is the first step for a redistribution analysis. The necessary calculations for actual historical data are done in the first fourteen columns and those based on the prevailing (1983) rates in the last column of table 14.1. Sequential column headings describe the calculation procedure, making the table self-explanatory. To understand the method, the table should be read. Briefly, the first column specifies the standard income classes in the year 1980, which are used throughout this study. The next three columns are data. Column 5 gives the replacement rate, defined as the ratio of first month's retirement benefits to the mean monthly salary during the three years before retirement. The next five columns report the present value in 1980 of the past forty years' contributions to social security and that of retirement benefits for the expected life after mandatory retirement at age sixty. The last four columns present the benefit/contribution and the transfer/equity ratios.

Intergenerational Redistribution Resulting from Retirement Benefits

The computation of intergenerational transfers is described in table 14.1. The benefit/contribution ratios of column 11 and the transfer/equity ratios (which are simply the benefit/contribution ratio minus one) of column 14 measure intergenerational redistribution from the working population to the retired population. When the former ratio is above unity—when the latter ratio is positive—a redistribution from the working population to

Table 14.1 Distribution of Social Security Contributions and Old-Age Pensions, Historical Contribution Rates, 1978–83

					Present Value		
Income Class (1)	Frequency (2)	Median Monthly Wage of Last Three Years up to Retirement during 1978–83 (3)	Median First Month Benefits at Retirement during 1978–83[a] (4)	Columns 4/3 = Replacement rate (5)	Median Monthly Wage Cumulated over Forty-Year Working Life Before Retirement[b] (6)	Median Monthly Contributions Cumulated over Working Life[c] Per Person (7)	Per Class (8)
1. 1–75	32	−42	100	2.38	1,680	151	4,832
2. 76–100	22	87	100	1.15	3,480	315	6,864
3. 101–25	18	111	111	1.00	4,440	398	7,164
4. 126–75	59	154	154	1.00	6,160	553	32,627
5. 176–250	80	205	198	0.97	8,200	736	58,880
6. 251–400	120	308	284	0.92	12,320	1,106	132,720
7. 401–600	60	481	381	0.79	19,240	1,727	103,620
8. 601–800	24	676	619	0.91	27,040	2,427	58,248
9. 801–1,000	16	904	694	0.77	36,160	3,245	51,920
10. 1,001–1,500	12	1,158	883	0.76	46,320	4,157	49,884
11. 1,500+	11	1,811	913	0.50	72,440	6,501	71,511
Total	454	—	—	—	—	—	578,270
Mean	—	—	—	—	—	—	1,274

Note: All values are expressed in 1983 prices.

[a]According to the social security law, a pension cannot exceed the mean of the highest salaries of any three to five years (depending upon the length of service), except that there are minimum (and maximum) limits. The minimum limit was $100 in 1980 and $145 in 1983, which very nearly coincided with the respective years' minimum wage. The maximum limit was $1,000 (and under certain conditions $1,500) in 1983. The tabulation of the data revealed that the median salaries of the first two of the eleven brackets were below the lower limit of retirement benefits and median persons were above the minimum statutory pension. Also the median pensions of the third and fourth brackets exceeded the respective brackets' above-the-minimum-wage median earnings. Owing to lack of any cogent explanation, those discrepancies were considered to be due to errors in data for the low-paid subscribers. Accordingly, the following adjustments were made; the maximum benefits for the first two brackets were reduced to minimum pension, and the maximum benefits for the third and fourth brackets were lowered to the levels of the respective brackets' median earnings.

| Present Value of Retirement Benefits for Expected Retirement Life of 18.3 years[d] | | Columns 10/8 = Benefit/ Contribution Ratio or Intergenerational Redistribution (11) | Intragenerational Redistribution | | Column 11 − Unity = Transfer/ Equity Ratio (14) | Transfer Equity Ratio (1983 Rates) (15) |
Per Person (9)	Per Class (10)		Column 11 − 3.38 = Change as Multiple of Own Equity (12)	Column 11/3.38 = Change Relative to Mean (13)		
1,438	46,016	9.52	6.14	2.82	8.52	3.76
1,438	31,836	4.61	1.23	1.16	3.61	1.00
1,597	28,746	4.01	0.63	1.19	3.01	1.00
2,215	130,685	4.01	0.63	1.19	3.01	1.00
2,848	227,840	3.87	0.49	1.14	2.87	0.93
4,085	490,200	3.69	0.31	1.09	2.69	0.84
5,480	328,800	3.17	−0.21	0.94	2.17	0.58
8,904	213,696	3.67	0.29	1.09	2.67	0.83
9,982	159,712	3.08	−0.30		2.08	0.53
12,701	152,412	3.06	−0.32	0.91	2.06	0.52
13,133	144,463	2.02	−1.36	0.60	1.02	0.01
—	1,945,206	—	—	—	—	—
—	4,304	3.38	0.00	1.00	2.38	0.69

[b]During the thirty years before 1980, per capita real income in Panama rose at an annual rate of 2.6 percent. It was assumed that during the four decades till 1980, real wage rate also increased, on the average, at the same rate. It was further assumed, somewhat herocially, that the real rate of interest, too, was equal to the rate of growth of productivity (or wage) per worker. Under these rather simplifying assumptions, the present value in 1980 of the wage rates in each of the past forty years turns out to be equal to the terminal wage rate.

[c]The rates of social security contributions (employee plus employer shares) for different periods were as follows: 1960–61: 5.0 percent; 1961–62: 9.0 percent; 1963–74: 10.5 percent; 1975–80: 15.5 percent; 1981–83: 18.0 percent.

[d]The expected life at the retirement age of sixty in Panama is 18.3 years. Since we are estimating the equity value of contributions, the relevant rate of increase in benefits is zero. For the calculations of columns 9 and 10, the real rate of discount is assumed to be the same as that for the past forty years.

retirees is implied, because benefits paid by the former to retirees exceed the equity accumulated by retirees. The benefit/contribution ratio is approximately 2 for the highest income bracket, ranges from 3 to 5 among middle classes, and rises to nearly 10 for the poor among retirees. Since there is a minimum to social security pensions, workers earning below minimum wage are apt to have a high incentive to join the system (if they can) and get multifold transfers from the society, unless their subjective discount rate is also extremely high. The system is indeed very generous. For every dollar that the present generation of retirees put into the system it is getting back $3.38 (when conformably compounded and discounted).

Several reasons for the calculated generosity of the system can be identified: (1) it is natural for the first generation of retirees to reap windfall gains, because during almost their entire lives they subscribed to the system at the low rates of 5 to 10 percent, whereas the present subscribers put into the system 18 percent of their wages with practically no ceiling on contributions from wages. (2) During the past fifteen years, the proportion of covered workers to total workers rose rapidly, from 17 percent in 1968 to 55.5 percent in 1982, while the proportion of pensioners in total population increased at a lower rate, from 0.86 percent in 1968 to 2.3 percent in 1982. If actuarial estimates were influenced by these two changes, the system would look more solvent than it really is, and generous benefits would appear feasible. (3) The social security philosophy has changed from its emphasis mainly on health insurance in the early years to that of retiree income maintenance in recent years. Thus long-term subscribers to the system in Panama can retire at almost the highest three- to five-year mean salary, except when it hits the ceiling. (4) The Torrijos government's redistributive policy may in part have an effect. (5) Finally, the crunch came with the onset of the late 1970s recession and rising unemployment, which exposed the inner incompatibility of the pre-1980 structure of social security taxes and benefits.

To see how redistributive the 1983 structure of taxes (at 18 percent of wages) and benefits is, we present parallel calculations in column 15. We see that even the present structure would involve transfer from the young to the old, though the mean transfer component is now only 69 percent of equity as against 238 percent in column 14. The magnitude of transfers in the 1983 structure, from the ordinarily better-off young (progenies) to the less well-off old (parents or grandparents), does not seem to offend the prevailing notion of fairness in taxation and public services. Nonetheless, though younger generations are in general better off than were older generations in their working lives, in Panama retirement beneficiaries, with only 0.2 dependency ratio, are by no test worse off than the working population, with an average dependency ratio of 2.25 (and among the middle-income wage earners over 3). I shall elaborate upon this remark in the next section.

A sensitivity analysis of the results of table 14.1 was done by using the real rates of interest and discount equal to the rate of growth of GNP (5.5) instead of that of per capita income (2.6) of table 14.1. The transfer/equity ratios calculated at this rate of interest indicate that at this high interest rate, the transfer component in the historical structure is still quite significant. According to the 1983 structure, on the other hand, the transfer is reversed; that is, it occurs from the old to the young. The crucial parameter thus is the rate of interest. An internal rate of return of 6.5 percent in the past and one of 5.2 percent for the 1983 rates would reduce transfer component to zero. Two questions are relevant in this context. Would wage laborers be capable of earning real interest rates significantly higher than 2.6 on their savings? Does the Social Security Administration earn a significantly higher real rate of return on social security funds?

Most would agree that the answers to these questions are probably no. From all counts, thus, the common rate of interest and discount, equal on the average to the rate of per capita productivity growth, seems more plausible than any other. Hence there is no strong prima facie evidence against the results obtained in table 14.1.

The data on the retirement behavior of covered workers tend to support this conclusion. Indeed, it is perhaps because the subjective value to beneficiaries of the basic level of pensions looks so high relative to increments of pension associated with the number of years of service that as soon as early retirement was legalized in 1975, a large majority of workers started taking it. By the year 1981, early retirees formed 25 percent of total pensioners with 36 percent of the total value of pensions, as against 35 percent for normal-age retirees with 45 percent of the value of pensions, the rest being survivors and incapacitated pensioners (Panama, Republic of Panama, Caja de Seguro Social, 1982, table 166a). Currently, five out of nine workers are taking early retirement.

Intracohort Redistribution of Old-Age Benefits among Retirees

Retirement benefits are clearly redistributive among retirees. This is evident from columns 12 and 13 of table 14.1. Among the present retirees, those in the high-pension bracket receive only 60 percent of the median, while low-pension retirees get nearly three times the median benefit/equity ratio of 3.38 (column 13). Alternatively stated, low-pension retirees receive 614 percent of their equity more than the median beneficiary, while high-pension retirees receives 136 percent of their equity less than the median retiree, who received 238 percent more than his or her equity (col. 12).

The relative gain or loss among retirees is the same whether we use the 2.6 percent or the 5.5 percent rate of interest.

The distribution of benefits among pensioners is highly egalitarian, as we see from the calculations reported in table 14.2. The Gini coefficient of pensions is 0.21 for the urban areas and 0.14 for rural areas as against those of overall monetary income of 0.46 for urban areas and 0.54 for rural areas. Since the dependency ratio among retirees is only 0.2, those pensioners who reside independent of their children live in a highly egalitarian society of their own.

Distribution between pensioners as a class and the rest of society. The calculated egalitarianism is somewhat misleading, however, when pensioners are viewed as part of the entire society. Pensioners, by and large, belong to the middle class, as is apparent from the last two rows of table 14.2. In 1982 the mean level of pension was approximately twice as high in urban areas and approximately four times as high in rural areas as the adult-equivalent overall monetary income in the respective sectors. Pensioners forming 2.7 percent of the population account for 8 percent of total personal income (see table 14.2, last column). The minimum pension for retirees with a 0.2 dependency ratio is fixed at the same level as minimum wage for younger workers with much higher dependency ratio (about 3). Most retirement beneficiaries probably live by themselves and thus maintain a relatively higher standard of living. Over 7.27 percent of households with heads under sixty have one or more persons in the age group sixty or older living with them, while 5.1 percent of older persons live independent of heads under sixty. The former presumably comprise the rural elderly and others without retirement pensions.

Conclusions of the analysis of this section are that the social security system is highly income-equalizing in the middle ranges of income; that among the lower half of the population it creates a privileged class; and that it does not reach the poor. It can be converted into a highly pro-poor institution, however, by extending its coverage to all citizens irrespective of past contributions. In Panama this can be done by lowering the benefit/ contribution ratio in general and by introducing appropriate conditions and incentives for rural and poor people to subscribe to the system.

Intragenerational Redistribution of Retirement Benefits among Families

So far we have compared social security benefits of retirees against the incomes of others. Not to be ignored is the fact that many retirees have nonpension incomes and, in addition, continue holding jobs (even though that is illegal). In 1982, when the unemployment rate had peaked (8.4 percent), 8 percent of retired men and 9 percent of retired women held more than one job. This percentage is higher among middle-pension retirees than among low- and high-pension retirees. It was naturally higher during the 1960s (when employment was full) than in recent years. The percentage of middle-pension multiple jobholders among total retirees holding multiple jobs was about the same among men but significantly higher among women in the 1960s than in the 1980s. Thus an average pensioner enjoys a relatively higher standard of living than either an average retired or an average working person, perhaps partly because he or she is more resourceful.

Finally, a comparison of the distribution of pensioners with the distribution of currently fully employed workers reveals that even in this case pensioners, particularly those in rural areas, are discernibly better off than the working population. More than half of the old live with heads of households who are under sixty. In any case, retirees have to be allocated to income classes in our overall scheme of classwise benefits and costs of public policies. This is done according to the distribution of pensions by income classes. The results are given in table 14.3.

Benefits from the Capital Budget of the Social Security System

In addition to the operation of health institutions, payment of pensions, and other recurrent expenditures, the Social Security Administration uses part of its funds to invest in government bonds, loans for housing, and similar construction for health, education, and other purposes. The administration advances these loans at concessional rates. According to the latest regulations concerning such loans, resolutions 4-84 and 5-84, dated February 1, 1984, of the Ministry of Planning, lending institutions were directed to charge only 8 percent interest on their loans to agriculture and housing when the market rate of interest (as mentioned in the same resolutions) was 12 percent. Oral interviews with mortgage banks show, however, that 12 percent is a preferential rate. The market rate is a couple of percentage points higher. Accordingly, an interest subsidy of 6 percent was used.

In 1980, social security taxes from all sources amounted to $238.5 million, and income from loans and investments totaled $45.4 million. Current expenditure on health and pensions was $207.4 million. Of the remainder ($76.5 million) of the revenue, $48.2 million was estimated to be invested in government bonds and $28.3 million was lent as mortgages for housing. The distribution of housing mortgages by income classes, as available in the *Estadística de Seguro Social*, was used as the base to allocate the 6 percent implicit subsidy on $28.3 million in mortgages. The results appear in table 14.3. We see that this part of the budget is clearly antipoor.

The treatment of $45.5 million in income from past loans is somewhat tricky. In the Social Security Administration's budget this category appears

Table 14.2 Distribution of Retirement Pensions in *Household Survey, 1982*

| | Deciles of Persons in the Nation as a Whole | | | | | | | | | | |
	1	2	3	4	5	6	7	8	9	10	Total
	Number of Persons in Thousands										
Urban	21	38	57	72	102	105	118	134	146	162	955
Rural	160	143	124	109	79	76	63	47	35	19	855
Total	181	181	181	181	181	181	181	181	181	181	1,810
	Number of Pensioners										
Urban	72	263	1,062	814	2,637	3,141	3,646	6,686	9,860	12,355	40,536
Rural	122	337	533	850	1,126	949	1,450	1,450	1,998	579	9,102
	Total Amount of Overall Monetary Income in Millions of Dollars (monthly)										
Urban	0.05	0.53	0.41	2.58	4.78	6.40	9.45	14.81	22.75	61.02	123.78
Rural	0.42	1.86	2.95	3.81	3.73	4.58	4.95	5.05	5.44	5.97	38.76

Total Amount of Pensions in Thousands of Dollars (monthly)												
Urban	5	52	151	161	395	438	705	1,358	2,557	5,184	11,026	
Rural	5	60	95	136	191	192	257	391	333	244	1,905	
Mean Adult-Equivalent Monthly Income ($)												
Urban	3	17	30	44	57	72	94	123	178	422	148	
Rural	3	16	29	43	57	72	93	124	178	358	48	
Amount of Pension per Pensioner per Month ($)												
Urban	69	196	142	198	150	139	199	203	259	420	272	
Rural	42	179	179	160	170	203	177	196	287	421	209	
Ratio of Pension per Pensioner to Overall Monetary Income per Adult-Equivalent Person												
Urban	23.0	12.0	4.7	4.5	2.6	1.9	2.1	1.7	1.5	1.0	2.1	
Rural	14.0	11.0	6.0	3.7	3.0	2.8	1.9	1.6	1.6	1.2	4.1	

Note: Gini coefficients: overall monetary income—urban 0.46, rural 0.54; pensions—urban 0.21, rural 0.14.

Table 14.3 Distribution of Net Benefits of Social Security System as Percentage of Income, Urban and Rural Sectors, 1980

					Income Classes[a]							
	1	2	3	4	5	6	7	8	9	10	11	Total
Urban												
A. Benefits												
Health and welfare	1.07	9.22	9.34	8.47	7.52	6.62	5.55	5.96	5.89	3.51	1.79	4.73
Pensions	2.69	4.42	3.25	2.80	2.82	2.89	3.40	3.67	3.59	2.13	1.08	2.59
Capital income	0.27	0.16	0.20	0.21	0.20	0.18	0.60	2.36	3.02	3.23	2.30	1.91
Subsidy to housing	0.01	—	—	0.01	0.01	—	0.02	0.09	0.11	0.12	0.09	0.07
Total	4.04	13.80	12.79	11.49	10.55	9.69	9.57	12.06	12.61	8.99	5.26	9.30
B. Taxes	7.06	12.43	13.95	13.53	12.70	11.83	10.26	11.40	11.47	6.85	3.48	8.71
A minus B: net benetifs	2.58	1.37	−1.16	−2.04	−2.15	−2.14	−0.69	0.66	1.14	2.14	1.78	0.59
Rural												
A. Benefits												
Health and welfare	2.97	4.63	4.28	4.02	3.76	3.07	2.67	2.41	2.48	2.08	1.44	3.00
Pensions	2.26	1.01	0.98	1.10	1.16	1.42	1.64	1.74	1.47	1.14	0.78	1.19
Capital income	1.15	0.14	0.14	0.12	0.09	0.07	0.05	0.05	0.03	0.06	0.03	0.08
Subsidy to housing	2.01	—	0.01	—	—	—	—	—	—	—	—	—
Total	3.39	5.78	5.41	5.24	5.01	4.56	4.36	4.20	3.98	3.28	2.25	4.27

B. Taxes	1.34	4.38	4.42	4.82	5.24	4.64	4.39	4.14	4.44	3.81	2.62	4.00
A minus B: net benefits	2.05	1.40	0.99	0.42	−0.23	−0.08	−0.03	0.06	−0.46	−0.53	−0.37	0.27

Republic

A. Benefits

Health and welfare	2.56	5.65	6.07	5.98	5.74	5.26	4.77	3.72	5.29	3.36	1.76	4.26
Pensions	1.61	1.76	1.78	1.85	2.04	2.33	2.92	2.34	3.22	2.02	1.06	2.20
Capital income	1.17	0.14	0.16	0.16	0.15	0.14	0.45	1.34	2.49	2.88	2.11	1.41
Subsidy to housing	0.01	0.01	0.01	0.01	0.01	0.01	0.02	0.05	0.09	0.11	0.08	0.05
Total	4.35	7.56	8.02	8.00	7.94	7.74	8.16	7.45	11.09	8.37	5.01	7.92
B. Taxes	2.17	6.16	7.79	8.65	9.18	9.06	8.66	7.06	10.23	6.51	3.41	7.43
A minus B: net benefits	1.18	1.40	0.23	−0.65	−1.24	−1.32	−0.50	0.45	0.86	1.86	1.60	0.49

[a]Income classes are defined in table 14.1, column 1.

as income along with taxes, but it is not a burden on present subscribers; it is rather a benefit item, an income for present (and future) beneficiaries from investments cumulated over the lifetime of the fund. Several alternative catagories relating to capital are candidates for the measure of benefits from this budgetary component. Should the investment of $76.5 million from current income be allocated to beneficiaries, in which case the accounting burdens and benefits are exactly balanced? However, investment per se is not a measure of benefits. Should only the rate of return from the current-year investment be allocated as benefits? In this case current income will exceed current outgo. Should explicit and implicit benefits on the cumulated stock of housing and bonds be estimated for the purpose? Should capital income be ignored because its cost was borne by subscribers in the past and it is in any case reinvested rather than consumed? Or should the explicit income from cumulated capital be allocated to appropriate beneficiaries? After weighing the conceptual and practical pros and cons of each, the last candidate was chosen, and the sum of $45.4 million was allocated according to the distribution of mortgages for housing. The resulting allocation is reported in table 14.3.

Overall Results

In interpreting table 14.3 one must keep in mind that these results conceal redistribution (discussed in the foregoing sections) within retirees and between retirees and the working population. The table summarizes the effect of that redistribution on average families of different income classes.

The interfamily distribution of net benefits seems to have no relationship with interretiree distribution of net benefits, nor is there any reason to expect a similar pattern. The distribution of net benefits is parabolic. Low-income and upper-income families emerge as net beneficiaries, while middle-income classes are the losers. The main source of net gain by upper-income classes is evidently the exemption of nonlabor income from social security taxes. Net losses of middle classes are probably due to the fact that they are mostly wage earners with little in-kind or profit income and thus are subject to high social security taxes relative to their incomes. Low-income families receive low benefits but come out net gainers because they pay even lower taxes. The differences in the family cultures of low and middle classes in keeping or not keeping their old with them may in part explain the parabolic shape of the curve of net benefits.

Summary, Conclusions, and Policy Implications

The social security system is one of the most remarkable social institutions that the countries of the world have introduced during the past half-century.

It is a built-in stabilizer of economic ups and downs and is therefore conducive to growth; it is redistributive and in general pro-poor, without being a disincentive to work, save, invest, and take risks as, for instance, personal income tax is; it is relatively easy and economical to administer; although in essence a socialist institution, it is entirely acceptable and conformable to free-enterprise economies; and it is a source of investment funds. An additional property desirable from a redistribution point of view that many developed countries of the world—for instance the United States—lack but that Panama's social security system incorporates is the proportionality (i.e., nonregressivity) of the tax with respect to wages, with no upper limit on contributions except in the case of the thirteenth-month contributions, which currently have an upper limit of $400 per month.

On the benefit side, Panama's system is highly equalizing among beneficiaries but unequalizing between inactive beneficiaries and active subscribers, between the agricultural sector and the urban sector, and between the very poor of the nation and the not-so-poor social security beneficiaries. This state of affairs presents a great opportunity to Panama to reduce critical poverty and income inequalities in general, without imposing any additional cost on subscribers and without causing undue hardship to present or future beneficiaries. Currently, among those sixty years old or older, 9.6 percent in rural areas and 42.1 percent in urban areas, or 25.3 percent of all old people, receive social security benefits ranging between $145 and $1,500 per month, with a mean pension of $275 in urban areas and $209 in rural areas. The benefits are from twice (in urban areas) to four times (in rural areas) as high as the adult-equivalent income of the respective sectors.

Given Panama's critical poverty line (for the minimum food basket only) of $36 per person per month for urban areas and $29 for rural areas or $72 per old couple per month for urban areas and $62 for rural areas in 1983, the social security benefits of retirees have to be reduced at most by half (still leaving them with higher than adult-equivalent incomes) to remove old-age critical poverty (as just defined) from Panama in one easy step. In other words, every senior citizen, whether or not he or she has subscribed to the social security system, should get retirement benefits.

In general, any social policy will be resisted by potential losers. The indicated redistribution within the old-age cohort, which has the proverbial one foot in the grave, should, however, be less repugnant than other known policies involving redistribution of equivalent magnitudes. The change may be brought about by simply not raising pensions annually until inflation and real growth reduce the real value of current-level pensions to desirable levels, while at the same time beginning to transfer modest benefits to nonparticipants.

The question of incentives for low-income workers, especially in rural areas, to join the social security system needs to be addressed, so that future senior citizens do not have to feel that they live on the dole from compatriots who were smarter, better endowed, or luckier to get pensionable jobs in the modern sector. A major thrust that is needed in this regard is to bring rural labor into the social security tax net.

A supplementary measure to reduce old-age poverty is to rescind the 1975 law by which retirement age was lowered by five years. Better still, it may be raised by five years over the earlier mandatory retirement age, or by ten years over the present optional retirement age, to sixty-five for men and sixty for women. The current early retirement age (of fifty-five for men and fifty for women), which seems to be so attractive that more than half of workers now take early retirement, has several disadvantages. It is a waste of experienced human resources, because fifty-five years is not an age to stop working. Retirees simply shift from the jobs they are specialized in to jobs for which they are less suited. If this leads to a fall in labor force participation, for which there is some evidence, that is even worse from the point of view of national economic growth. It defeats its purpose of reducing unemployment among the young, because the retirees continue working anyway, and in less efficient jobs. It is an inefficient way of creating jobs for new entrants. It puts a financial strain on the social security system. It exacerbates the inequity of the system between inactive retirees and active subscribers. Finally, it strains the legal system, which prohibits employment of retirees, who nevertheless continue holding multiple jobs. Indeed, the benefits of those who take early retirement are about one-quarter higher than those who retire at the normal age, implying that early retirees fall into higher wage brackets. Cumulated contributions of men to the social security fund during the ten years from age fifty-five through sixty-four are almost even with cumulated increments to future retirement benefits for the remaining expected life.

WHO BENEFITS FROM PANAMA'S PUBLIC ENTERPRISES?

There are over three dozen public enterprises in Panama, accounting for approximately one-eighth of value added in the economy. In combination, they form an important instrument of government policy for regional, sectoral, and overall growth as well as for exports, redistribution, employment, and other social and economic services. In this study we analyze mainly the redistribution and antipoverty effects of the operations of these enterprises, insofar as they are discernible from their balance sheets.

Panama's public enterprises range from those producing purely private goods (e.g., Victoria Sugar Corporation, CALV), to natural monopolies (e.g., the National Institute of Telecommunications, INTEL), to those providing mixed public-and-private goods (such as the University of Panama), and to almost purely local, regional, or sectoral public goods (for example, the services provided by the Institute of Aqueducts and Sewerage, IDAAN). To the extent that these institutions deviate from zero profits, some redistribution may take place. In that case a deficit is equivalent to a subsidy, and a surplus represents a tax on the enterprise, whose direct incidence will in general fall on the consumers of the product but in some cases may be borne, partly or wholly, by factors employed or even by suppliers of raw materials. In this study we measure only direct profits and losses, according to the general theory of tax-subsidy incidence.

Calculating Economic Costs and Benefits

This section is devoted to calculating the economic costs and benefits of the production, commercial, and other activities of public enterprises. This is done by evaluating the true balance of the enterprise's finances by posing a counterfactual situation in which the enterprise is required to run on private business lines, receiving/giving no subsidies, borrowing/lending and buying/selling in competitive markets, and enjoying no differential tax treatment.

Economic surpluses or deficits for individual public enterprises were calculated from balance sheets as follows:

1. Current income minus current expenditure, net of transfers, subsidies, and loans, gives surplus on current account.

2. Net subsidies and transfers to the enterprise concerned from the year it was started or 1973, whichever happened last, to the latest year for which data are available, that is, 1983, were treated as quasi-loans for the purpose in hand. The application of the market rate of interest (of 15 percent), compounded and cumulated to the year 1983, is treated as an economic cost of these resources, that is, it is subtracted from the current surplus of item (1) above. For this purpose, no distinction was made between current-account payment and investment, for in the long run all interest has to come out of the current budget.

3. The subsidy component of concessional loans is similarly compounded and cumulated to the present year and added to current costs. Concessional loans are available to the agricultural and housing sectors. Housing loans are handled by the Ministry of Housing and the Social Security Administration, which are analyzed elsewhere. Among the public enterprises that administer concessional loans to agriculture are the Agricultural Development Bank (BDA) and the National Bank of Panama (BNP). The estimated economic deficits and surpluses are given in table 14.4.

Table 14.4 Economic Surplus or Deficit, Public Enterprises, 1983 (Thousands of Dollars)

Public Enterprise	Current Deficit (−) or Surplus (+) (1)	Net Transfers and Subsidies (2)	(1) + (2) = Economic Deficit (−) or Surplus (+) (3)
Domestic operations			
*1. Banco Hipo. Nacional	− 9,057	+ 6,685	− 2,372
*2. Caja de Ahorros	+ 607	+ 172	+ 779
*3. Air Panama	+ 2,876	− 2,212	+ 574
**4. Ferrocarril de Panamá	− 4,383	− 661	− 5,044
**5. Ferrocarril Nacional Chiriquí	− 466	− 161	− 627
6. Autori Portuar Nacional	+ 6,064	+ 7,283	+ 1,219
7. Aeronautica Civil	+ 4,111	− 16,671	− 12,560
8. IDAAN	+ 9,154	− 6,222	+ 2,932
9. Departmento de Aseo	+ 9,154	− 6,222	+ 2,932
**10. IRHE	+ 51,452	− 34,886	+ 16,566
**11. INTEL	+ 35,603	+ 4,644	+ 40,247
*12. Contadora Panamá	+ 658	− 835	− 177
*13. COFINA	− 2,324	− 1,778	− 4,102
14. CODEMIN[a]	− 78	0	− 78
*15. Cemento Bayano	− 1,232	− 10,536	− 11,768
16. IPAT	− 1,768	− 5,523	− 7,291
*17. CALV	− 15,350	− 16,438	− 31,788
*18. ATLAPA	− 1,629	− 1,097	− 2,726
19. Zona Libre	+ 2,064	+ 1,085	+ 3,149
20. BNP[b]	+ 3,697	+ 3,543	+ 7,240
BNP	− 3,040	0	− 3,040
BNP	+ 3,040	0	+ 3,040
*21. Hipodromo	+ 2,487	+ 52,724	+ 55,211
*22. Loteria	+ 43,932	+ 96,701	+ 140,633
*23. Casionos Nacionales	+ 17,589	+ 26,383	+ 43,972
*24. Bingos Nacionales	+ 329	+ 575	+ 904
25. ENASEM	+ 640	0	+ 640
*26. BDA[c]	− 3,446	− 6,751	− 10,197
BDA	0	− 1,964	− 1,964
27. IMA[d]	− 941	− 7,300	− 8,241
IMA	+ 2,651	0	+ 2,651
*28. ENDEMA	− 720	− 991	− 1,711
*29. ISA	+ 340	− 65	+ 275
30. IDIAP	− 2,204	− 1,585	− 3,789
31. Consejo Nacional Banano	− 127	− 409	− 536
32. Corporación Int. de Bocas	+ 51	− 244	− 193
33. Co. de Int. Bayano	+ 783	− 4,500	− 3,717
*34. Citricos de Chiriquí	+ 57	− 306	− 249
35. IPACOOP	− 1,193	− 299	− 1,492

Table 14.4 Continued.

Public Enterprise	Current Deficit ($-$) or Surplus ($+$) (1)	Net Transfers and Subsidies (2)	(1) + (2) = Economic Deficit ($-$) or Surplus ($+$) (3)
Import tax exemptions of all enterprises (1982)	$-40,640^e$	0^e	$-40,640^{e,f}$
Surplus	$+187,856$	$+199,795$	$+318,813$
Deficit on domestic tax exemptions	$-47,958$	$-121,434$	$-114,881^f$
Deficit, including import tax exemptions	$-88,598$	$-121,434$	$-155,521^f$
Net surplus	$+99,258$	$+78,361$	$+163,292^f$
Net without casinos, lottery, and racecourse	$+35,259$	$-97,447$	$-76,524^f$
Private-goods enterprises producing deficits	$-34,466$	$-75,620$	$-60,600^f$
Private-goods enterprises producing surpluses	$+165,235$	$+187,884$	$+311,300^f$

Note: Entries with one asterisk are categorized broadly as private-goods-producing public enterprises; those with two asterisks are natural monopolies; and others are dominated by public-goods elements, local or national.

ªIn the absence of a clear-cut picture of what the fate of the Cerro Colorado Mining Corporation (CODEMIN) will be in the future, it is currently engaged solely in maintaining its establishment and fixed structure. From a long-term viewpoint, it may be considered a gestation period. If the mine is developed, it may become a socially profitable project. Currently, therefore, it has only costs, including cumulated costs, and no income. In view of this, only the current-year costs (49 percent of which are borne by foreign investors) are treated here. Accumulated deficits according to the procedure used in this table, however, amount to $8.416 million.

ᵇThe BNP levies a surcharge on loans to nonagricultural borrowers, the income from which is used to subsidize agricultural loans at a concessional interest rate of 9 percent (instead of the market rate of 13–15 percent). The total amount of this agricultural loan was $3,040,000 in 1983. It is shown in three lines to underline the fact that its distribution does not cancel out. Its allocation is explained in table 14.5.

ᶜThe BDA is one of the two institutions that gives concessional loans to agriculture. The benefits go directly to agricultural borrowers. These benefits are shown separately in the second line.

ᵈFor IMA, the first line gives the account for the cost and management of support prices and other institutional operations. The second line reports the profits on imported food.

ᵉPast exemptions on import taxes are ignored.

ᶠThese are column totals. Being aggregates of net values, the figures of columns 1 and 2 for the separate items do not necessarily add up to these totals.

321

4. In addition to the implicit or explicit transfers and subsidies on their domestic operations just discussed, public enterprises are granted import tax exemptions similar to those enjoyed by private enterprises under export or other incentive schemes (*incentivados*). The estimated aggregate tax exemption of all public enterprises in 1982 was $40.64 million. These are reported in the last section of table 14.4.

Of the thirty-five enterprises reported in table 14.4, about twenty show economic deficits and fifteen show surpluses. The three major gambling institutions—casinos, lottery, and racecourse—with their combined profits more than cancel out the deficits of other enterprises. The annual flow of cumulated true surpluses of profit-earning enterprises—when past profits transferred to the central government budget are treated as loans to the government and compound interest is calculated on them—as of 1983 was $319 million. The annual flow of the cumulated true deficit of other enterprises was $115 million on domestic concessions, or about 2.6 percent of gross national product. Including import tax exemptions, it came to $156 million. According to this measure, there was a net surplus of $163 million. Excluding the three major gambling institutions, the aggregate balance turns into a net deficit of $77 million. The three private-goods gambling institutions are thus lucrative revenue gatherers, whether taxes or quasi-taxes on these activities are actuated by revenue motives or sumptuary motives.

The Allocation Procedure

Public enterprises producing social or other types of goods that are financed from central budget, for example, the INAC, will be included in the section on public expenditure below. The social security system was analyzed above. The autonomous and semiautonomous public enterprises (other than the social security system) are analyzed here. The deficit of $114.88 million on domestic concessions and $40.64 million on import tax exemptions (of table 14.4) is treated as quasi-subsidy, and the surplus of $318.81 million (table 14.4) is treated as quasi-tax. The allocation of the benefits of these quasi-subsidies and the burden of quasi-taxes is described enterprise by enterprise in table 14.5.

The net balance is somewhat misleading, since it conceals the performance of individual enterprises. We must therefore look at each enterprise separately. From the point of view of whether they should earn economic surpluses or incur economic deficits, public enterprises may be divided into four broad classes.

Natural monopolies and enterprises producing social goods.   According to the theory of optimal pricing, deficits are required, and consequently subsidies from the general budget are justified for natural monopolies (firms with declining average cost curves) such as INTEL, and for enterprises producing social goods, for example, IDIAP.

Public enterprises producing private goods. Efficient pricing for enterprises producing private goods (usually with nondeclining average cost curves, e.g., CALV) will result in profits unless cost curves are horizontal, though from a practical standpoint most governments, at least on paper, require such public enterprises to stand on their own feet.

Merit and demerit goods and revenues—purpose public enterprises. Sumptuary taxes or price margins above marginal cost curves are in order for demerit goods, for example, a tax on horse racing if betting is considered socially undesirable. Naturally, surpluses are called for when the avowed purpose of a private-goods enterprise is revenue collection, for example, national casinos.

Mixed goods.   In actual practice, there are no purely social and no purely private goods. There is a whole range of mixed goods, with some social-good components and some private-good components, which may be and are provided both publicly and privately—for example, education. ATLAPA (public convention center) and ENASEM (public seed company) may fall in this category. Depending upon the proportions of social- and private-good components, public enterprises of this nature may or may not be required to maintain surplus budgets.

A cursory glance at table 14.4 indicates that many public enterprises do not, in general, follow efficient pricing practices. For instance Chiriquí Citrus Company, Bayano Cement Company, Victoria Sugar Corporation, and similar private-goods enterprises should earn profits, but actually they incur deficits. On the other hand, according to the efficiency pricing criteria, natural monopolies, like INTEL (public telephone company), and IRHE (public electricity company), should follow the marginal cost pricing rule and incur deficits, whereas in Panama, as in many other countries, they collect large surpluses. It is also a question mark whether the government gathers more revenue by operating its own casinos and the racecourse than it would if it left these activities to the private sector and levied taxes on them.

A judgment whether on theoretical grounds a public enterprise should produce a surplus or a deficit is perhaps not too hard. To determine how much output and surplus/deficit it should realize is a difficult task that requires estimating sophisticated supply-and-demand equations, which in

Table 14.5   Allocation Criteria for the Surpluses and Deficits of Parastatals, 1983

Public Enterprise	Between Income Classes According to	Between Urban and Rural Sectors according to
1. BHN	Income ($100–600 brackets)	Income
2. Caja de Ahorros	Income ($400+ brackets)	Income
3. Air Panama	Consumption of air transport	All to urban
4. Ferrocarril de Panamá	Income (50%); consumption of train transport (50%)	All to urban
5. Autoridad Portuaria	Income	Income
6. Aeronautica Civil	Consumption of air transport	Income
7. IDAAN	Consumption of water	Income
8. Aseo	Expenditure on trash	All to urban
9. IRHE	Expenditure on electricity	Income
10. INTEL	Expenditure on telephone	Urban 95%, rural, 5%
11. Contadora Panama	Income	All to urban
12. COFINA	Profits (50%) Income (50%)	Income
13. CODEMIN	Weighted mean of 25% to rural according to population; 26% to both sectors according to income; foreign company (49%)	25% to rural, 25% to both sectors according to income
14. Cemento Bayano	Income	Income
15. IPAT	Income	Income
16. Corporación Azucarera la Victoria	Weighted means of urban + rural	Rural (50%), urban (50%) according to income
17. ATLAPA	Profits (50%); income (50%)	All to urban
18. Zona Libre	Total consumption (5%); foreigners (95%)	All to urban
19. BNP	Income Subsidy on agricultural loans according to agricultural sales; tax on nonagricultural according to savings	All subsidy to rural All taxes to urban

Table 14.5 Continued.

Public Enterprise	Between Income Classes According to	Between Urban and Rural Sectors according to
20. Hipodromo	Expenditure on horse racing	All urban
21. Lottery	Expenditure on lottery	Income
22. Casinos	Expenditure on casinos (20%); foreigners (80%)	All to urban
	Expenditure on Bingo	All to urban
24. ENASEM	Agricultural income (50%) Consumption of food (50%)	Urban (50%) Rural (50%)
25. BDA[a]	Agricultural income	All to rural
26. IMA	Profits on imports: food consumption deficit on support prices; agricultural sales	Income All to rural
27. ENDEMA	Agricultural income	All to rural
28. ISA	Agricultural sales	All to rural
29. IDIAP	Agricultural income (50%); consumption of food (50%)	Rural (50%) according to income; both sectors (50%) according to income
30. CONAB	Income	Income
31. Corporación Internacional Bocas del Toro	Income (50%); population (50%)	Income
32. CODEIBA	Population	All to rural
33. Citricos de Chiriquí	Weighted means of urban + rural	50% to rural according to income; 50% to both sectors according to income
34. IPACOOP	Income (first eight brackets)	Income
35. Ferrocarril Nacional de Chiriquí	Consumption of train transport (50%); foreign corporation (50%); ignore	All to rural
36. Import tax exemptions of all enterprises	Mean distribution	Mean distribution

[a]Includes subsidy on agricultural loans.

the present state of data for Panama are beyond the scope of this study. From practical aspects, moreover, governments usually settle on no-profit, no-loss policy for autonomous enterprises. In view of this, we analyze the zero economic profit as the benchmark, and departures from it are assumed to cause either quasi-taxes or quasi-subsidies to the beneficiaries of the enterprise. The criteria of allocating the incidence of quasi-taxes and quasi-subsidies are summarized in table 14.5.

Substantive Results

The incidences of the deficits/surpluses of public enterprises are calculated in table 14.6. We see that when the rich (as defined by the highest income class) are excluded, the overall public enterprise policy is regressive or pro-poor even when lottery is included. The regressivity is by and large monotonic even when the rich are included, if the national lottery is excluded from the measure. The rich generally seem to shun the low-stakes lottery and love high-stakes horse racing. The poor and middle classes thus bear the burden of the quasi-tax on the lottery.

The overall net deficit of public enterprises benefits the rural sector and hurts the urban sector, whether or not the national lottery is included. In the rural sector, it is clearly pro-rich. The benefit to income ratios of the first six income classes (with lottery) are close to zero, whereas they rise to 0.07 for the eighth income class and 0.10 for the top class. The urban areas are the net losers—they consume and produce mainly those products and services of the public sector earning profits that are transferred to the central government budget. Even without the national lottery, the town people are the net losers. The losses are more or less uniform among the poor and middle-income households. The urban rich of the top income class, however, escape with minor losses relative to other urban families. The elasticities of the benefit/income ratios with respect to per capita family income are -0.14 for the Republic, -0.27 for the urban sector, and 0.45 for the rural sector.

On the whole, the policy concerning public enterprises is pro-poor (see table 14.6). Public enterprises augment poor families' incomes by about 2.5 percent. Unfortunately, these families' indulgence in the lottery deprives them of more than they gain from other public enterprises (and from wins in the lottery). No one can blame them for playing, however, for that is the only risk a poor person can afford to take in his or her lifetime in the remote hope of getting out of poverty.

Note that the national lottery embodies a high tax on the poor and the middle class. The tax falls at a progressive rate among the first four income classes, then at a regressive rate. Unless, therefore, the proceeds from the lottery are used at least for the poor so as to cancel out the quasi-tax

Table 14.6 Distribution of Aggregate Surpluses or Quasi-Taxes and Deficits or Quasi-Subsidies of Public Enterprises, 1983

Income Classes	Republic as a Whole					
	Total Deficit (−)	Total Surplus (+)	Net with Lottery ($)	Net with Lottery (%)	Net without Lottery ($)	Net without Lottery (%)
1	− 5,524	+ 6,434	+ 910	+ 0.52	− 4,044	− 2.32
2	− 195	+ 2,586	+ 627	+ 1.37	− 1,311	− 2.86
3	− 3,052	+ 4,738	+ 1,686	+ 2.36	− 1,688	− 2.36
4	− 5,750	+ 10,005	+ 4,255	+ 3.04	− 2,663	− 1.90
5	− 10,194	+ 17,121	+ 6,927	+ 2.56	− 4,639	− 1.71
6	− 18,963	+ 36,914	+ 17,951	+ 3.50	− 4,903	− 0.96
7	− 27,486	+ 50,121	+ 22,635	+ 3.76	− 3,033	− 0.51
8	− 21,812	+ 36,816	+ 15,035	+ 3.47	− 2,092	− 0.48
9	− 14,892	+ 29,704	+ 14,312	+ 4.47	+ 1,397	+ 0.42
10	− 26,947	+ 59,215	+ 32,268	+ 4.19	+ 7,935	+ 1.02
11	− 21,400	+ 29,815	+ 4,415	+ 0.70	− 3,995	− 0.63
Total	− 157,979	+ 279,471	+ 121,492	+ 3.05	− 19,141	− 0.48

Note: Values are in thousands of 1983 dollars.

burden, the poor and the lower-middle classes would be better off were the lottery to operate on a no-profit, no-loss basis. It is, however, a source of investible funds that are used largely for low-income housing.

Policy Implications

The analysis does not end here, for as yet we have not compared the calculated benefits with the opportunity cost of the subsidies given public enterprises to write off their deficits. The opportunity cost or the gains from the use of subsidy funds for alternative uses may be viewed, among other vistas, in terms of either a reduction in overall taxes or an increase in public investment, or at least a reduction in the Republic's budget deficit. Since deficits do not necessarily reflect marginal cost pricing and planned operations and may conceal inefficiency in production and other operations, it would probably be preferable to require all deficit enterprises to balance their budgets. Perhaps one should go a step further and, following MIPPE (Panama, MIPPE 1977), suggest that all public enterprises (other than natural monopolies and industries producing social goods) be run competitively for private profit. The benefits from the investment or distribution of these surpluses would then be the opportunity cost of the benefit distribution of table 14.6.

There are still other alternatives. Public enterprises in Panama account roughly for 12 percent of GDP. Because of the financial drain caused by the deficit budgets of many of the public enterprises producing private goods (roughly about half of the thirty-five enterprises studied here), some experts recommend their reorganization as mixed enterprises of India's type, in which the government holds 51 percent of the shares while 49 percent are sold to the public. In such a system, government retains management control over the enterprise so it cannot be used for antisocial purposes such as monopoly exploitation. Of course, private investors will buy shares only when they are assured of maximization of profits. Private shareholders, with 49 percent weight, will wield enough influence to see that these enterprises are run profitably.

Still others recommend their divestment or privatization. From the viewpoint of workers, that would probably not be the best solution. For one thing, against the supposedly superior efficiency of the private enterprise must be put the cost of dismantling already built-up institutions. For another thing, most of these institutions are supposed to be pro-worker. They were created rather heroically by a courageous leader during a popular military regime, in part to break private monopolies. That most of the private-goods public enterprises are not operating according to optimum pricing rules, that many are a financial drain on general revenue, and that many are likely to remain monopolies in this small country provides a unique opportunity to the government of Panama to use them to ameliorate the condition of poor as distinguished from better-off workers. The remainder of this section discusses what that opportunity is.

Of the thirty-five public enterprises, very broadly twenty supply private goods, including four natural monopolies. Of the four natural monopolies, two (namely Panamá and Chiriquí railroads) are loss projects, while the other two (IRHE and INTEL) make a profit. Eight other enterprises in this category incur losses of $55 million a year, while ten earn profits aggregating to $243 million. Those that earn profits may be considered to be operating according to the private-profit motive, subject to particular constraints imposed by the state. The deficit of $55 million, on the other hand, seems indefensible. Were it possible to eliminate this deficit, the overall yearly surplus of private-goods enterprises would rise to $355 million, or about 8 percent of GDP. This is roughly the income of the lower quartile of the population. It is also about equal to the poverty gap (defined on the basis of twice the critical poverty line).

For this purpose, I propose a modified version of the MIPPE's earlier proposal (Panama, MIPPE 1977) of "creating and distributing new affluence" through public enterprises. The objective of the MIPPE proposal was to privatize public enterprises by making the process attractive to workers. The proposal was that public enterprises should operate on commercial lines, compete with private enterprises, and earn profits. The present proposal is for the purchase of the stock of public enterprises by workers of the nation as a whole.

The new proposal is consistent with the old one insofar as it aims at enabling workers to acquire "new wealth." But it differs in substance, in that the main objective is not privatization per se, since in the prevailing sociopolitical environment that is not feasible. Apart from an intense opposition from workers, the Torrijistas are still strong in the National Guard and the civil government. Privatization may nevertheless ensue as a result of market forces. The means of enabling workers to become fledgling capitalists is to assign them the surpluses of these enterprises in the form of a mutual fund to be operated by a national workers' council, which can be used solely to acquire stock in the name of workers. The stock would be bought on the open market; economic considerations would dictate whether the stock bought was in the private sector or belonged to public enterprises. By implication, the stock of public enterprises too would be subject to purchase by private individuals and enterprises. There is a constraint, however. Some limit must be put on distributing profits. Undistributed profits would go into the Workers' Mutual Fund and be used to subsidize the purchase of stock by the collectivity of workers.

In transferring the claim to the profits of the private-goods public enterprises, the exchequer would lose some of the revenue it receives from parastatals. Although that is inevitable with this policy, a good part of it could be recovered through taxes. For instance, it is quite probable that the government would receive an equivalent amount of tax revenue from the expanded business of privatized casinos run more efficiently than they are now.

WHO BENEFITS FROM GOVERNMENT EXPENDITURE IN PANAMA?

In the reference year 1980, government's current expenditure on goods and services amounted to $471 million, and transfers to public (including debt service) totaled $339 million. Of every dollar of gross domestic product, 33 cents passed through the government budget, of which 25 cents was on current account. The government bought 14.5 percent of the nation's goods and services, against which it rendered public services to the people. For lack of a common yardstick, government output in terms of public services is conventionally assumed to equal input. If money is spent and services are not rendered or are rendered with less than the average efficiency of the nation, real output will be correspondingly less and vice versa, but it is very difficult to measure this discrepancy. Accordingly, the quantity of public services is measured in terms of dollar input. The 1980 value of public services thus came to 14.5 percent of GDP, or $258 per head.

Theory and General Allocation Procedure

Since public services are not priced in the market, their benefits are allocated in accordance with theoretical considerations and empirical observation. Certain standards of allocation have become common in the past decade or so. This study is more or less a replication of the criteria used in my earlier study of Panama (Sahota 1972b).

The theoretical approach that permeates that analysis should be distinguished from an alternative approach used in some studies. The relevant output that public expenditures reflect and that people consume and draw utility from is public services rather than public employment. I consider that the real objective of the true gain from public expenditure consists of public services consumed rather than public jobs landed. This is the approach taken by me (Sahota 1972b, 1975, 1977, 1980, 1985), Musgrave (1975), and others. Some authors—for instance, Thurow (1980, chap. 7)—employ public employment as a measure of benefits. The point needs further discussion.

To understand the true distribution effect of expenditure, one should ordinarily abstract from the Keynesian effects of the generation of net aggregate demand, whether through fiscal or monetary means. Alternatively, it will be more enlightening if the analysis is carried out under alternative conditions of full employment and less than full employment.

In a full-employment situation, quantities of factors may change little. The relative prices of those types of factors and those categories of skills that are employed predominantly by government (such as Ph.D.s) will tend to go up. The relative prices of goods consumed more intensively by the public sector (such as cement and arms) will tend to rise. Under less than full employment, factor quantities employed most likely will rise. Thus price elasticities in the former situation and real multiplier effects in the latter will determine the distribution of gains from public expenditure. For pure budgetary effects (the subject matter of this study) as distinguished from fiscal policy effects, the full-employment situation is more relevant. A simple and realistic assumption in this regard is that, with minor differences, the amount of money spent by the public sector is the amount of money not spent by the private sector. This assumption, in one stroke, reduces the value of "the balanced-budget multiplier" and the net Keynesian multiplier effect to zero. Consequently, we can concentrate on the pure budgetary effect or the differential expenditure effect of the public budget.

It is apparent that allocating benefits of public expenditure to those who get jobs rather than those who consume public services free—for example, allocating education expenditure to schoolteachers instead of pupils—is missing the grain for the chaff. Real gains lie in the consumption of public services. Employment is at best a secondary or indirect effect, which should be considered in terms of relative shifts of demand from those income classes whose resources/products are less intensively employed/consumed in the private sector to those income classes whose resources/goods are more intensively employed/consumed in the public sector, rather than the generation of net effective demand. The losses of those income classes for whose resources/products demand and therefore prices have declined because of tax payments to meet public expenditures and the gains of those income classes for whose resources/products demand and therefore prices have risen, by and large, cancel out, such that the net gain or loss to the economy is zero. Particular groups of households may suffer from differential losses or benefit from differential gains, but the society as a whole experiences no net gain or loss. In this study we abstract from such secondary differential gains and losses of disparate factor intensities of the private and public sector.

Specific Allocation Procedure

The allocation of the current expenditures of various ministries and institutions of central and municipal governments for the year 1980 is briefly described below.

Education

Of all educational expenditure, 25 percent was treated as providing externalities of the social-goods type and was allocated among income classes and across provinces on the basis of population. The remaining 75 percent, available in eight subcategories, was allocated as follows: (1) Expenditure on adult education and literacy was allocated, with minor adjustments, to the two lowest brackets (consisting of about 20 percent of families in 1980; the illiteracy rate in 1980 was 14.2 percent). (2) Expenditure on primary education was allocated equally to all income brackets based on population. The urban/rural division of the province totals was calculated on the urban/rural population basis. (3) Secondary education expenditure was based fifty–fifty on population and income. Between sectors, it was assumed that an average urban family gets twice as much benefit from the provision of secondary education (given higher quality and proximity of schools in urban areas and other similar factors) as an average rural family. (4) The expenditure by the University of Panama was allocated among income classes on the basis of a broad association between income and education levels. As between urban and rural sectors, the expenditure was divided based on the proportion of students in the disciplines mainly related to agriculture. (5) Physical education and (6) special education expenditures were treated in the same way as secondary education. (7) The allocation of the expenditure of the Institute for Development and Utilization of Human Resources (IFARHU) was based on the categories of workers trained according to salary by income bracket. (8) The general administrative and other expenditure was allocated based on the average distribution in terms of income of the first seven categories, except that 25 percent of the overall general administration expenditure was allocated to Panama City, in addition to the city's share of the general allocation.

Public Health

Different expenditure categories of the Ministry of Health were treated on their own merits with regard to their social-goods and locational characteristics. The detailed allocation of public health expenditure was collected from the budget document. In particular, four types of expenditure were distinguished. In the first category were collected expenditures on general administration, research, and part of the expenses of such hospitals as mental, tuberculosis, and children's, which are all in Panama City. It was assumed that even though these hospitals are of the nature of social goods and may benefit the entire nation, the cities where they are actually situated benefit more. Expenditure on these hospitals was divided fifty-fifty between the sector where they are and the general category. The allocation of the other items of this general category was based on the mean of the overall health expenditure.

In the second category, the regional directorate expenditures were allocated to sectors by population. The third category—public health expenditures in rural areas—consists almost entirely of two items, the sanitary engineer's department (whose main function is to build wells, latrines, and aqueducts in rural areas) and veterinary services. The former category of expenditures is available by provinces. The latter is given for the four regions (east, metropolitan, central, and west). These expenditures were allocated to the respective class by agricultural incomes. The fourth category consists of sanitary services, which are available by cities. These were therefore allocated to the urban sector.

The resulting sectoral totals were allocated among different income brackets according to population. The Ministry of Health's expenditure on education was allocated earlier, under education. The results indicate that approximately 93 percent of total health expenditure goes to urban areas, which account for approximately four-fifths of national income.

Public Works

Expenditures on public works are available for a number of categories. The expenditure on highways was allocated by income between the urban and rural sectors. The entire expenditure on streets was assigned to the urban sector. Expenditure on buildings was allocated by location; the bulk of it goes to Panama City.

The remaining expenditures—general administrative, transport services, equipment-maintenance center, inspection and maintenance of public works, director and coordination, docks, and so on—were allocated according to the average pattern of highways, streets, and buildings.

Ministry of Commerce and Industry

The ultimate benefit presumably falls on the consumer of industrial and commercial goods; part of it may stay with factors of production. The expenditure of this ministry was divided between Panama City and the overall country in the ratio of twenty-five to seventy-five. The latter part was allocated according to urban incomes after allocating 10 percent of the total to agriculture. Interbracket allocation was based on income.

The Ministries of Agriculture and Livestock and Labor and Welfare

The expenditure of the Ministry of Agriculture and Livestock was allocated based on 25 percent to urban areas (in the form of agricultural prices lower than in the absence of this expenditure and 75 percent to rural areas according to incomes by size class. The expenditures of the Ministry of Labor and Welfare were allocated based on the urban wage and salary among income brackets and sectors.

All General Government Expenditures

These general expenditures, not already allocated above, were divided into two parts. The first component consists of expenditures that can be spatially located. Included are the current expenditures of the Ministries of Education, Public Work, Health, and Agriculture and Livestock, which can be broadly located geographically. The other category is expenditures that cannot be located geographically. These include such ministries and government organs as the National Assembly, the Presidency, the Controller General's Office, the Ministry of Government and Justice, the Ministry of Finance and Treasury, the Ministry of External Affairs, the Price Regulation Board, the Judiciary, the Public Ministry, and the Election Tribunal. Owing to the differential advantage of the location of these ministries in

Panama City, 25 percent of these general expenditures were allocated to this category. The balance was allocated among sectors (and brackets) according to income.

Municipal Expenditure

Panama has virtually a unitary government. The country is divided into nine provinces (plus one additional political unit of San Blas), but there are no provincial governments. Municipal governments have limited functions/powers. Several of the traditional municipal functions are performed by different departments and autonomous enterprises of the central government. Geographic allocation of municipal expenditures is determined by the location of the municipality concerned. The urban/rural allocation follows the census classification, which is available from published sources. Direct municipal government expenditures are available by four categories, allocated, by and large, on the same basis as the corresponding central government expenditures. About 20 percent of municipal expenditure goes to education.

Empirical Results

The results for the Republic are presented in table 14.7. A few pertinent results for urban and rural sectors are also discussed without reporting detailed sectoral tables. The following conclusions, in particular, are worth noting.

On the basis of relative, as distinguished from absolute, income augmentation, public services are doubtlessly pro-poor between income classes, provinces, and sectors. The degree of progressivity is more or less the same across all provinces. Herrera and Darién get the highest and the metropolitan provinces the lowest relative benefits of public services. The reverse, however, is the picture in terms of absolute per capita amounts, in which Panamá gobbles up nearly six times as much as the least-benefited provinces of Coclé and Colón and twice as much as Darién (see the last column of table 14.7).

The poorest three classes, comprising 28 percent of households, receive public services that augment their private incomes by 31 to 35 percent in urban areas and 27 to 30 percent in rural areas. The poor of Colón benefit more and the rich of Colón benefit less than the corresponding classes in any other province except Darién.

Interclass redistribution is more clearly brought out by the calculations of "differential benefits," given in lines 3–5 (fractional or multiple deviations from the mean) and 6–8 (absolute deviations from the mean). The rich lose approximately 6 percent of their incomes and the poor gain ap-

Table 14.7 Distribution of Incidence of Taxes and Expenditures, 1983 (as Ratio of Family Income)

Sector	Income Classes											Total	Per Capita Expenditure ($)
	1	2	3	4	5	6	7	8	9	10	11		
Republic total (%)	6.61	10.3	11.35	12.66	12.92	13.65	14.86	16.69	18.24	20.69	23.19	16.95	
Taxes													
0 Urban	0.35	0.35	0.31	0.30	0.22	0.19	0.15	0.11	0.12	0.10	0.09	0.15	116
1 Rural	0.28	0.30	0.27	0.25	0.20	0.16	0.14	0.13	0.11	0.12	0.10	0.19	55
2 Republic	0.31	0.33	0.29	0.32	0.22	0.18	0.15	0.12	0.11	0.10	0.10	0.16	89
Public Expenditures													
3 Line 0/0.145[a]	2.43	2.39	2.10	2.04	1.52	1.29	1.06	0.74	0.79	0.69	0.63	1.00	—
4 Line 1/0.190[a]	1.49	1.58	1.42	1.32	1.03	0.84	0.73	0.68	0.56	0.61	0.54	1.00	—
5 Line 2/0.155[a]	2.01	2.13	2.19	2.03	1.42	1.17	0.98	0.77	0.74	0.66	0.59	1.00	—
6 Line 0 minus 0.145[b]	0.21	0.20	0.16	0.15	0.08	0.04	0.01	-0.04	-0.03	-0.05	0.05	0.00	—
7 Line 1 minus 0.190[b]	0.10	0.11	0.08	0.06	0.01	-0.03	-0.05	-0.06	-0.08	-0.08	0.08	0.00	—
8 Line 2 minus 0.155[b]	0.16	0.18	0.14	0.16	0.07	0.03	-0.01	-0.04	-0.04	-0.05	0.06	0.00	—
9 National income/household ($000)		2.27[d]		3.18	4.42	6.67	10.28	14.34	18.45	30.44	58.25	8.78	—
10 Proportion of national income		0.07[d]		0.04	0.07	0.13	0.15	0.11	0.08	0.19	0.15	1.00	—
11 Proportion of households		0.28[d]		0.10	0.14	0.17	0.13	0.07	0.04	0.06	0.02	1.00	—
12 Line 9/8,781[c]		0.26[d]		0.36	0.50	0.76	1.17	1.63	2.10	3.47	6.67	1.00	—

[a]The divisors 0.145, 0.190, and 0.155 are calculated from the mean values of the benefits from the last column. The calculations of lines 3, 4, and 5 signify the benefit ratios relative to mean values.

[b]The subtraction of mean values—0.145, 0.190, and 0.155—from class values of benefits yields differential benefit ratios.

[c]Line 12 gives household income of each class as a ratio of mean income of $8,781 of column 11 of line 9.

[d]Figures are aggregates for columns 1–3.

335

proximately 16 percent in relation to the mean beneficiary. The household with approximately $10,000 income just about breaks even.

The results suggest that the distribution of public services has become more pro-poor since 1970. Comparisons of the present results with earlier ones are not entirely conformable, because at the time of the earlier studies (Sahota 1972b; McLure 1972), the *Income Survey, 1970* was not available. They thus relied by and large on monetary incomes only. Even the monetary incomes of the *Population Census, 1980* and the *Household Survey, 1982* are considered more reliable than those for the 1970 demographic census and the 1971 census of agriculture used as the data base by Sahota and the 1969 household survey used by McLure. I consider the estimates based on comprehensive incomes of table 14.7 more correct. For conformable comparisons, however, the estimates based on monetary incomes were also made. Normalized benefit measures, that is, ratios of individual class benefits to the mean, for the country as whole are sketched in figure 14.1. The results suggest that public services have become considerably more pro-poor during the decade. More of the low-income households of 1980 lie above the normalized line than those of 1970. In the 1970 estimates, the curve for the upper-income classes had turned up; that is, between middle-income and rich classes, public services were pro-rich. Calculations according to comprehensive income yield an almost monotonically declining curve up to the highest income class. In terms of comprehensive income, the poor seem to benefit less and the rich lose less relative to the mean beneficiary in comparison with the results based on monetary income of either year. There are two possible reasons. One is merely the statistical reason; including in-kind income (which affects largely low-income households) and undistributed profits (which raises the upper-end incomes materially) increases the denominator more than the numerator. Second, the weight of social services in the overall budget has increased significantly during the decade, and they have been oriented more toward low-income households.

WHO BEARS THE BURDEN OF TAXES IN PANAMA?

Public income can be divided into two general categories, tax revenues and nontax revenues. Broadly, a public revenue is a *tax* when it has no direct relation to goods and services provided. It is nontax revenue when a direct quid pro quo does exist. The latter category includes prices, charges, rates, rents, and fees. A price charged by government or semi-government agencies may, however, contain some elements of a quasi-tax or quasi-subsidy. Major nontax revenues and quasi-taxes/subsidies were analyzed in the preceding sections, namely, the social security system and

**Ratio of class benefits
to mean benefits**

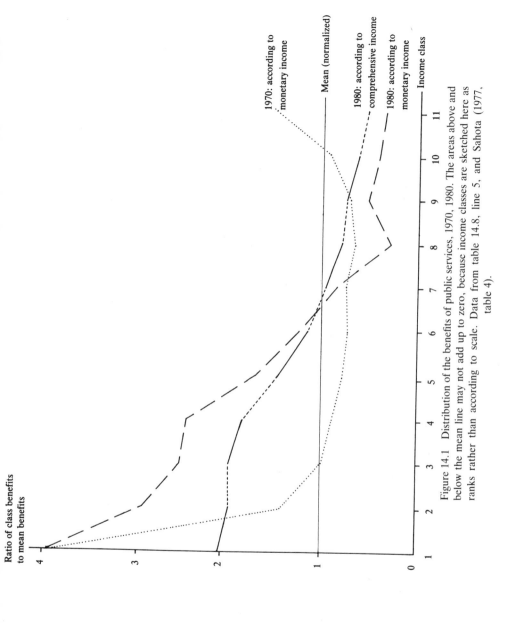

Figure 14.1 Distribution of the benefits of public services, 1970, 1980. The areas above and below the mean line may not add up to zero, because income classes are sketched here as ranks rather than according to scale. Data from table 14.8, line 5, and Sahota (1977, table 4).

public enterprises. Tax revenues are the subject of analysis in the present section.

A few disclaimers concerning this section include an abstraction from what in recent public finance literature have come to be called "tax expenditures," that is, taxes levied and not collected, or collected from some taxpayers but not from others. These will be analyzed in a subsequent section on investment-incentive schemes. Taxes borne by foreigners are ignored in tax burden analysis. Possible implicit costs of "strings attached" to foreign aid to Panama are also ignored. Duplication of revenues and expenditures involved in intergovernmental transfers is eliminated by considering only the impact points of such categories. Several services for which prices or fees are charged but which pass through the government budget and for which no independent accounts are available, even though taxes/charges may be "earmarked," for example, the gasoline tax, are included in the present section. Taxes and expenditures of municipal governments are treated as part of the overall government budget, even though in some Panamanian literature municipal governments are lumped together with public enterprises as the "decentralized public sector."

The Allocation Procedure

The criteria for the allocation of taxes are summarized in table 14.8. The table is self-explanatory, but a few aspects may be elaborated. The data for personal income tax are reported in two parts, tax deductions or withholdings at source (for which no annual returns are required in Panama), and tax payments by nonwage income recipients through annual tax returns. The two sources are classified independently. They have not been integrated into Panamanian tax data, and there is little one can do to correct this divorce between the two series. Accordingly, these were allocated to different income classes independent of each other, as if they were two taxes.

Despite the fact that more high-powered research has been done on its incidence than on that of any other tax, the corporation tax remains highly controversial with regard to the shifting of its incidence. This tax has been the subject of a lively debate between the researchers of the Chicago school, who find that the entire tax is borne by the owners of corporate stock (see, e.g., Cragg, Harberger, and Mieszkowski 1967) and those at Harvard University, whose findings suggest that from one-third to the entire tax is shifted forward to the consumer (see especially Krzyzaniak and Musgrave 1968). With a view to not taking sides between the two great schools, we allocated it fifty-fifty to profit recipients and consumers.

Substantive Results

The results are presented in table 14.7 for the Republic. Those for urban and rural sectors are discussed without reporting separate tables, but the results are sketched in Figure 14.2. We see that Panama's taxes are quite progressive. The ratio of taxes to income goes up from 6.6 percent for the lowest of the eleven income brackets in the country as a whole, from 10.0 percent in urban areas, and from 6 percent in rural areas to a little over 23 percent for the uppermost bracket in almost all sectors. The curves of the distribution of tax burden for the rural sector, urban sector, and overall population are more or less exponential with a quadratic to cubic shape (see fig. 14.2). The elasticities or progressivities of tax ratios with respect to per capita income (using the logarithmic equations), are 0.19, 0.36, and 0.28, respectively, for the urban, rural, and total samples. In the country as a whole, within the relevant, plausible values of the income range, for instance, when per capita income of a class doubles, its tax burden ratio goes up by 28 percent. This may be compared with the corresponding elasticity of 0.23 in McLure's estimates for 1969. The quadratic and cubic equations give relatively more plausible values of the progressivity, but the conclusion is the same, that Panama's tax burden is distributed highly progressively; that is, it is transparently pro-poor.

Among individual taxes, personal income tax and corporation income tax (direct taxes) are the most progressive, as expected. The combined income elasticity of their tax burden ratios is 0.53. The elasticity of the burden of property taxes of all kinds (quasi-direct taxes) is 0.47, almost the same as that of income taxes. The incidence of gasoline tax falls about seven times as heavily on the rich as on the poor. The following, in general, are regressive taxes: sales tax; taxes on beer, soft drinks, liquor, and cigarettes; stamp duty; and municipal taxes. The elasticity of the burden of overall indirect taxes is not different from zero. In fact, in aggregate they have little relation to income.

Somewhat surprisingly, taxes are more progressive in rural areas than in urban areas (see fig. 14.2). A possible reason is a high proportion of tax-free self-consumption among low-income households in rural areas and a high proportion of undistributed profits in overall income among the rich in urban areas. Undistributed profits escape some taxes that distributed profits and other income components are subject to. While the rural rich enjoy low taxes on farmland, the urban rich pay differentially less in income taxes in general.

A comparison with the 1969 estimates by McLure (1972) indicates that taxes have become less progressive, as we see from figure 14.2, where McLure's estimates for his eleven classes are superimposed upon the eleven classes of this study. Even though the distribution of families by income classes and the magnitudes of income ranges may differ, merely ranking

Table 14.8 Allocation Criteria for Taxes, 1983

Tax	Between income Classes according to	Between Urban and Rural Sectors according to
1. Individual income tax[a]	Tax returns according to taxes paid; withholding according to taxes paid (special tabulation)	Same ratios
2. Corporation tax	50% on distribution of overall consumption; 50% on corporate profits of top two brackets according to Pareto distribution	Consumption All to urban
3. Dividend tax	According to corporate profits of top two brackets according to Pareto distribution	All to urban
4. Complementary tax	According to corporate profits of top two brackets according to Pareto distribution	All to urban
5. Colón Free Zone tax	95% to foreigners, 5% on consumption basis (nonfood)	Consumption
6. Tax on transfer of property	Property income (*Household Survey, 1982*, special tabulation)	Income
7. Urban real estate tax, rural land tax	Urban property income (*Household Survey, 1982*, special tabulation) Rental value of land by income classes (*Censo Agropecuario, 1982*, special tabulation)	Urban only Rural only All rural
8. Commercial and other licenses	Same as corporation tax	Same as corporation tax
9. Shipping duties	90% on foreigners, 10% according to income	Income
10. Death duties	Top two income brackets according to square of incomes	Square of incomes
11. Education tax	According to wages	Wages
12. Sales tax	According to nonfood consumption	Nonfood consumption
13. Import taxes	According to consumption	Consumption

14. Export taxes	All on foreigners	Zero
15. Tax on insurance premiums	According to income on upper eight brackets	All urban
16. Excise on gasoline	According to gasoline consumption (75%); according to overall consumption (25%)	According to income
17. Excise on airplane tickets	According to expenditure on air travel	All urban
18. Excise on hotels	One-third on foreigners; two-thirds according to income of upper two brackets	All urban
19. Excise on beer and soft drinks	According to consumption of beverages	Income
20. Excise on liquor and wine	According to consumption of alcoholic beverages	Income
21. Excise on tobacco	According to consumption of cigarettes	Income
22. Excise on oil products	One-third public transportation, one-third private transportation, one-third consumption	Income
23. Excise on perfumes	According to consumption of perfume	Income
24. Racecourse	According to consumption of horse racing	All urban
25. Judicial stamp duties	According to income	Income
26. Other taxes[b]	According to income	Income
27. Income from Canal (royalty + shipping)	All to foreigners	Zero
28. Tax on anonymous corporations	Foreigners (40%), consumption (30%), profits (30%)	All urban
29. Public register	Same as for property tax	According to income
30. Pipeline	97% foreigners, 3% according to income	Income
31. Municipal taxes	According to consumption	All urban

[a]For explanations, see text.
[b]These taxes include private markets, banks, civil register, consular duties, authentication of signature, tax on exemptions, improvement duties, penalties, and tax on deposits.

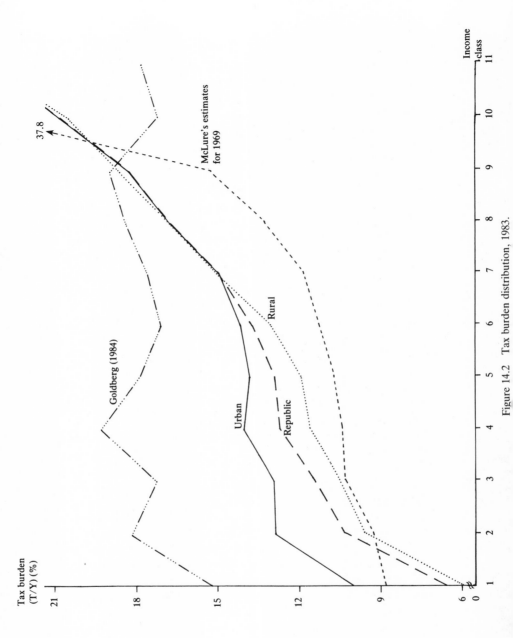

Figure 14.2 Tax burden distribution, 1983.

342

income classes brings out the contrast meaningfully. Caution should be observed in drawing conclusions from this comparison, however, in that the data on income distribution, though by no means completely satisfactory now, were rather weak in the years when McLure wrote his work. Subject to these caveats, the progressivity of Panama's taxes is well documented. Our estimates based on more reliable data indicate that the overall tax structure is less progressive than McLure's estimates suggest.

Recently a study has been finished at the Ministry of Treasury and Finance that suggests the tax burden in Panama is regressive—more precisely, that it is distributed according to an inverted parabola, with relatively lower tax burden on the lower-income and upper-income families and higher tax burden on middle-income families (Goldberg 1984, chap. 3; estimates for 1982). A tax-by-tax comparison reveals the following reasons:

1. The Banco Internacional para Desenvolvimiento (BID) study by Goldberg seems to employ monetary income of the 1980 census; we use the same source with adjustments for nonmonetary income.

2. In the summarized overall table of the BID study, the entire incidence of the corporation tax is allocated to consumers; we follow the standard practice of allocating 50 percent of it to consumers and 50 percent to the recipients of profits.

3. The BID study includes social security contributions as taxes. We treat social security taxes and benefits together and present separate estimates for them. They are not added to taxes.

4. There are no other major differences; any minor differences can be ignored.

If we add social security taxes to our estimates of tax burden distribution, we get a picture that is somewhat similar but not quite the same as that in the BID study. When the social security taxes are subtracted from the BID estimates, the resulting series is almost a straight line, as we see in figure 14.2. If nonmonetary incomes are duly taken account of in the BID study, their curve is very likely to show that Panama's taxes (net of social security contributions) are progressive. Thus, remembering that both estimates are subject to standard errors and that both are based on several (largely identical) assumptions with regard to where the ultimate incidence rests, if nonmonetary incomes are accounted for both estimates would yield, by and large, the same conclusion, that taxes other than social security contributions are progressive and that social security taxes may tend not to be progressive in the upper percentiles.

A comparison of the benefits of expenditures and the burdens of taxes is presented in figure 14.3. In a system of progressive (pro-poor) tax burden and regressive (pro-poor) expenditures, the net benefits would naturally

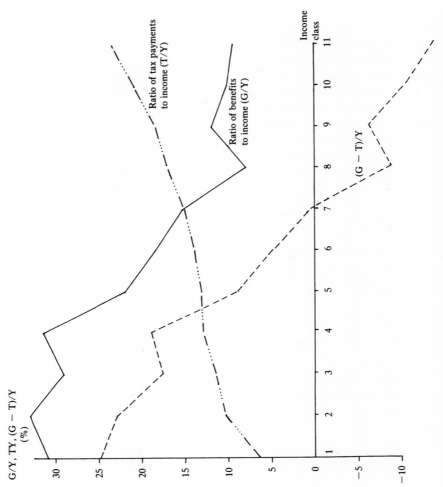

Figure 14.3   Benefits, burdens, and net benefits of taxes and public services, 1983.

344

be pro-poor. What impresses one most is the high degree of pro-poorness of the net budget incidence in Panama. It is significantly higher now than it was fourteen years ago. Not many countries can match the pro-poorness of the Panamanian government's budget. Wealthy families of Panama are the net losers by about 13 percent of their incomes in the government game; the poor are the net gainers, by about 25 percent of their incomes. In the post–World War II era, government sectors have grown rapidly for two main reasons: the belief in the role government plays in rapid national growth, and welfare programs. In general, the rich are opposed to big government, for valid reasons: as a class, though not all families, they are the losers in terms of the net budget incidence, while the high taxes needed for big government are disincentives for them to invest domestically. From the partial viewpoint of reducing poverty, the Panamanian government's budget certainly seems to be playing a positive role. With taxes alone, the Gini index is reduced by two points.

I stated earlier that the aggregate tax burden and aggregate expenditure benefits may not tally exactly, since some of the taxes collected are paid by foreigners and some of the government transfers to households are not benefits in a real sense, for example, interest on public debt (see the discussion above). Accordingly, there may be a discrepancy between the weighted sum of benefits and the weighted sum of burdens, though we do not expect this discrepancy to be significant. Subject to this proviso, the benefit and burden distributions and the resulting net distribution are brought together for an overall view in figure 14.3.

Conclusions

Panama's tax structure is quite progressive. The marginal tax burden ratio increases at a declining rate up to about the fifth income bracket, with a per capita income of about half the mean national income. After that it grows at an increasing rate. In other words, the progression is mild among low-income brackets but becomes strong among upper-income classes. Panama's tax structure thus has desirable pro-poor properties not only because its burden is progressively distributed but also because the degree of change in the progression favors low-income classes. The net budget incidence naturally becomes more steeply pro-poor because Panama's public services too are biased toward the poor. The degree of pro-poorness has increased during the past fifteen years for which comparable estimates are available. Panama's fiscal budget must be counted among the leading welfare budgets of the world. What is now needed, from the viewpoint of poverty, is to maintain the budget. Nevertheless, there are several pockets of public finance where either taxes or expenditures can be made more pro-poor without jeopardizing growth, for example, a land tax with significantly higher revenue than at present.

WHO BENEFITS FROM PANAMA'S INCENTIVE SCHEMES AND PRICE POLICIES?

For a number of years Panama has had extensive programs of export promotion (mainly for the industrial sector), import substitution (largely for agriculture), investment incentives (principally for export industries, industrial location in the interior, and housing), and agricultural price supports. In this section the effects of these policies on poverty are analyzed under four headings: import tax exemptions, export tax concessions, domestic tax exemptions, and agricultural price policy.

The emphasis of incentive schemes has shifted broadly from national growth in the 1950s and 1960s (Law 12 of February 9, 1950, and Law 12 of February 7, 1957) to the export promotion, "rational import substitution," and "geographic dispersal of industry" of the 1970s (Decree 413 of December 30, 1970, and subsequent decrees and laws) and the employment expansion of the late 1970s and early 1980s (e.g., Law 22 of December 1976). The basic incentives have, however, not altered materially. By and large, the firms that sign "contracts with the nation" to produce and sell under the incentive schemes are totally exempt from import duties on all kinds on machinery, equipment, raw materials, and related imports, taxes on profits from exports and other taxes on exports and reexports, and taxes on capital and investment. They are allowed deductions for taxes on domestic inputs, including electricity and telephone and property taxes. Other benefits include loans at subsidized interest or guaranteed by the state; low-priced land in publicly developed industrial parks; research studies at public cost; promotion of small business; and various other fiscal incentives. Nonfiscal promotional measures include protection from foreign competition through quantity restrictions on imports and certain domestic facilities.

Import Tax Exemptions

Basic data on import taxes not collected under these laws are available from published sources. Two independent estimates of aggregate import tax exemptions under various incentive schemes put the value of taxes not collected at 15 percent (PREALC 1980b, table III.18) and 17 percent (Arosemena-Alvarado 1983) of the value added of the respective firms. This is roughly twice the net annual investment of these firms (PREALC 1980b, 50).

Import tax exemptions amount to roughly one-third of the revenue collected from these taxes. The allocation criteria for import tax exemptions are similar to, though not quite the same as, those for domestic taxes. The basic theory underlying this allocation is that cost curves of the industries enjoying import tax exemptions on their inputs and the supply schedules of imported consumer goods shift downward. The differential benefits accruing from these shifts were divided among three participant groups—consumers, workers, and capital owners—according to informed judgment based on the shares of tax-exempt imports between consumer goods and intermediate goods, on the one hand, and factor shares of the industries availing themselves of these benefits (incentivados), on the other hand.

Export Tax Concessions

The country needs exports to service its foreign debt and to buy essential capital as well as intermediate and final consumption goods. As such, no matter who earns profits from expanded exports, the nation as a whole shares in the benefits. Accordingly, 25 percent of export tax exemptions, amounting to $7.3 million in 1982 (Panama, MIPPE 1983b, table 4), was allocated to the entire population according to income. At the same time, the employment of the factors of production in the export-promoted sectors (incentivados) expands at the cost of others (nonincentivados). The remaining 75 percent of tax exemptions therefore are allocated according to factor intensities in different industries. Major incentivados of this scheme are nontraditional industries—clothing, hides, shrimp, cocoa oil, certain agro-based products, and tobacco products—which account for over two-thirds of all the tax concessions under this policy ($5.6 million of a total of $7.3 million). All the noted products belong to two two-digit industries, food and beverages and clothing and footwear. Wage distribution by overall income classes by two-digit industries is available from a special tabulation of the *Household Survey, 1982.* Accordingly, 75 percent of the sum of $7.3 million of the 1982 tax concessions under this scheme was allocated to various income classes according to wage (60 percent) and profit (40 percent) distribution in the two industries.

Domestic Tax Exemptions to the Nonagricultural Sector

Two main types of domestic subsidies to the nonagricultural sector are exemption from property, income, and other taxes to the incentivados of the nonagricultural sector and subsidies and transfers to parastatals. The latter analysis was done above. As discussed earlier, estimates of even fiscal incentives of the former set of subsidies are not easily tractable, not to mention nonfiscal incentives. Estimates for exemptions from property tax to promote construction have been estimated by the Ministry of Finance and Treasury (1984). These come to $11.6 million for urban property tax and $2.1 million for rural property tax for the year 1983. This is probably the major single domestic tax exemption under the incentive schemes. For lack of data, therefore, the rest of domestic tax exemptions under this scheme were ignored. As we analyze the tax concessions of the present section, therefore, this underestimation should be kept in mind.

The allocation of property tax exemptions was done according to the distribution of property income other than that from agricultural land.

Support Prices for Agriculture

The Agricultural Marketing Board (IMA) supports a wide range of agricultural prices, procures the produce to sustain floor prices, and maintains warehouses all over the country. A small margin of its selling price over the respective purchase price in published data represents only a fraction of the cost of its operations. In a normal year, IMA incurs substantial deficits on support prices.

These deficits are largely made up by profits on imported food products, since the border prices are much lower than the internal prices IMA charges for imported and domestically purchased agricultural products. The result is that farm producers receive quasi-subsidies, while consumers of food are subjected to quasi-taxes. A redistribution is thus going on from consumers, especially low-income urban consumers, to farm producers, mainly producers with large sales. The estimated quasi-subsidies and quasi-taxes are separately allocated to different income classes. The allocation criteria were explained and the results analyzed earlier, where the quasi-taxes and quasi-subsidies due to the operations of IMA were treated along with other parastatals. They are reported here insofar as they qualify as domestic subsidies, but they fall into a different class inasmuch as they are not entirely of the nature of investment incentives. Nor are they administered directly as part of the central government budget.

Substantive Results

The results are presented in table 14.9. In this case one must be careful not to interpret these results as net gains. We are analyzing only the production diversion aspects of incentives by abstracting from the production creation aspects of incentives. The gains of incentivados are the losses of nonincentivados. Accordingly, only the differential estimates of the last line of each panel of table 14.9 are relevant.

Among the four categories of incentives analyzed here, the benefit incidence of property tax exemptions is the most and that of the import tax exemptions the least (though still significantly) pro-rich. The weight of import tax exemptions being substantially higher than the rest of subsidies, the former moderates the progressivity of overall incentives. The aggregate benefit distribution has progressivity coefficients of 0.4792, 0.4775, and 1.0636, respectively, for total, urban, and rural samples. The rich enjoy over five times as many benefits relative to their incomes as the poor. While the average benefit ratio is higher in urban areas than in rural areas, the interclass progressivity is higher in rural areas. The rural rich incentivados increase their incomes by 4.3 percent, the urban rich incentivados by 2.3 percent; the rural poor are favorably affected by incentives by about 0.5 percent, and the urban poor by about 0.7 percent. The mean loss to those not affected by incentives is 1.67 percent of their incomes. Differentially, as a result of incentives, the highest bracket augments its income by a little less than 1 percent, while the lowest bracket suffers a loss of over 1 percent.

Conclusions

Considering only the production-diversion aspects and abstracting from the production-creation aspects of incentives, the Panamanian incentive system is significantly pro-rich or antipoor. The superimposition of the production-creation effects, if any, will increase the absolute levels of income but are unlikely to reduce the adverse distributional effects of incentives.

The import-substitution and price policy for agriculture, in particular, has been antipoor. For instance, the IMA makes substantial profits on imported maize (*maiz*) and beans (*rotos*) by buying at low border prices and selling domestically at higher prices. Beans are poorman's food, and maize is the feed of the poorman's animal, the pig. Maize is, however, the major feed for birds and a part of the feed of other livestock also. Pigs can be raised in small units, whereas cattle, both for milk and for meat, are the specialty of large farms. The policy hurts the poor man more because the small buyer (pig raiser) has to buy maize at the high domestic price while the large buyer (cattle producer), under the incentive schemes, can buy it through the IMA at the much lower border price.

Were the import-substitution policy to be replaced by an export-promotion policy for agriculture, the price of beef and milk would rise (since these are practically the only commodities whose prices are lower than border prices), and the prices of maize and beans would fall. As a result, some substitution of pork and poultry products for beef by the nonpoor could be expected. The fall of maize prices and the rise of the price of pork might benefit small farmers. The price of rice, on the other hand, would fall, which would hurt mainly nonpoor farmers, since rice is largely produced on big farms, and would benefit poor consumers.

Table 14.9 Distribution of Differential Benefits under Various Incentive Schemes, 1980

	Income Classes[a]											
	1	2	3	4	5	6	7	8	9	10	11	Total
						Republic						
Import exemption (1980)												
Food, beverages, and tobacco	221	96	171	382	806	1,546	1,843	1,287	1,066	2,890	2,858	13,166
Textiles, clothing, and leather	80	36	62	140	295	569	675	470	389	1,057	1,046	4,819
Wood and furniture	14	5	11	23	49	94	112	78	64	177	173	800
Paper, press, and publishing	63	28	50	113	266	553	771	532	414	1,095	1,099	4,984
Chemicals, oil, rubber, and plastic products	—	—	—	—	11	78	304	447	401	2,229	2,654	6,124
Nonmetallic mineral products	16	7	11	23	45	84	100	72	55	108	65	586
Basic metallics	112	43	73	151	298	570	670	483	371	724	435	3,930
Metallic products, machinery, and equipment	12	4	8	17	32	62	73	52	40	79	47	426
Miscellaneous	69	30	53	119	250	480	574	401	332	900	889	4,097
Subtotal	587	249	439	968	2,052	4,036	5,122	3,822	3,132	9,259	9,266	38,932
Percentage of income	0.4	0.7	0.8	0.9	0.9	1.0	1.1	1.1	1.2	1.5	1.8	1.2
Export exemption (1982)												
Amount ($000)	65	32	60	147	365	714	893	625	552	1,731	2,104	7,288
Percentage of income	0.04	0.07	0.09	0.11	0.14	0.14	0.15	0.15	0.17	0.23	0.34	0.19
Property tax exemptions (1983)												
Amount ($000)	22	18	20	38	198	342	504	1,676	2,429	4,249	1,831	11,327
Percentage of income	0.01	0.04	0.03	0.03	0.07	0.07	0.08	0.39	0.73	0.55	0.29	0.28

Agricultural price policy

Deficits on agricultural price support by IMA[b]											
Profits on food imports by IMA[b]											
304	65	56	23	237	75	1,509	1,746	813	731	305	5,590
Total											
0.45	0.81	0.92	1.04	1.11	1.21	1.33	1.64	2.10	2.28	2.43	1.67
Differential											
−1.22	−0.86	−0.75	−0.63	−0.56	−0.46	−0.34	−0.03	0.43	0.61	0.76	0.00

Rural

12	8	10	18	69	193	355	124	181	290	120	1,380
Total											
Income percentage											
0.01	0.02	0.02	0.02	0.05	0.10	0.22	0.13	0.31	0.34	0.23	0.13
Total											
0.45	0.69	0.80	0.92	1.08	1.14	1.37	1.39	1.59	2.61	4.26	1.36
Differential											
−0.91	−0.67	−0.56	−0.44	−0.28	−0.22	−0.01	−0.03	−0.23	1.25	2.90	0.00

Urban

10	10	10	20	129	149	149	1,552	2,248	3,959	1,711	9,947
Total											
Income percentage											
0.04	0.10	0.04	0.03	0.09	0.05	0.03	0.46	0.82	0.58	0.29	0.34
Total											
0.69	0.97	1.03	1.04	1.23	1.19	1.28	1.70	2.19	2.22	2.25	1.85
Differential											
−0.16	−0.88	−0.82	−0.81	−0.62	−0.66	−0.57	−0.15	0.34	0.37	0.40	0.00

Note: Absolute figures are in thousands of dollars.

[a] Income classes are defined in table 14.1, column 1.

[b] The deficits on price support and profits on food import by IMA are recorded for the sake of completeness of incentive schemes. Since these were included in parastatals in the text above, their distribution is omitted from the total in the last line for the Republic.

Although support prices serve an important role in ensuring stable price (and income) expectations of farmers, they mainly benefit large farmers with a substantial market surplus. A shift of emphasis from price policy to productivity-increasing agricultural research policy is both growth promoting and poverty reducing.

Policy Implications

Domestic subsidies, tax concessions, price supports, and similar policies in Panama have created wide distortions in the economy whose net effect is antipoor. Another set of distortions arises from high and numerous tariff exemptions and export-tax concessions. Both domestic and trade policies need a careful review, first, because they are antipoor and second, because their trade-creating and production-creating effects, as against trade-diverting and production-diverting effects, have not been established. The available statistics indicate a woefully unsatisfactory performance of the incentivados in relation to costs. As a commercial center of the world with free foreign-exchange rate and open borders, Panama ought to be achieving international competitiveness of the degree attained by Hong Kong, Taiwan, Singapore, and similar small commercially oriented, outward-looking countries. It is not so much the existence of the exemptions that needs to be looked into as the high levels and the extensive list of tax exemptions (and therefore price distortion) an incentivado can enjoy.

Most incentive schemes have led to a cheapening of capital. Some other policies have made hiring and firing labor more expensive. Panama's labor code has made firing a worker more costly than hiring one. Insofar as the code pushes domestic investors to adopt laborsaving technology, as has been documented in this study, or discourages potential foreign investors from investing in Panama, a careful look at its rationalization is in order. For it appears that not only the respective share of the welfare cost (as represented by the Harberger triangle) but also a major part of the cost of the "wedge" between the market wage rate and the real cost of an employee to the employer is borne by employees. This is a kind of implicit tax on workers. The law may benefit the nonpoor employed workers, but it hurts those who are immiserized because the supply of jobs is reduced. The reform of this law is likely to be opposed less by workers if presented as a package along with the socialization policy proposed above. As a matter of fact, there will be some built-in convergence of interests in the reform of this law, since workers will sit on both sides of the negotiating table.

Finally, domestic quasi-subsidies, especially those resulting from tax concessions for construction, need to be corrected. The antipoor nature of domestic quasi-subsidies is exacerbated when the pro-rich distribution of concessional mortgage loans by the social security system is added to the tax concessions of this section. It is something of an anomaly to find so many incentives and subsidies for nonpoor and commercial housing when the poor of the nation lack basic services in their shacks and over-crowded abodes.

WHO BENEFITS FROM PANAMA'S PUBLIC INVESTMENT AND PUBLIC DEBT?

Like any other balance sheet, public investment has its two sides—liabilities and assets, or costs and benefits, or outgo and income. Likewise, the government as the borrower receives investible funds. The outgo side consists of debt service or interest on public debt.

Cost of Public Investment

Public debt is in principle incurred for public investment whose benefits are in general made available to the public free of charge. Public debt, internal or external, is in general and justifiably incurred for development purposes, except war debt, in which Panama has been fortunate enough not to have indulged. Ultimately, interest on public debt must come out of tax revenues. Therefore the burden of public debt falls on taxpayers.

On the outgo side, whether debt should be treated as factor capital or as transfer is debatable. The proponents of treating interest payments on public debt as a transfer of the same sort as any other government transfer to families contend that loans to government are made essentially in lieu of taxes, because otherwise lenders would have been subjected to man-datory taxes. They argue that when governments cannot collect enough revenue by taxes, they resort to borrowing and therefore that interest receipts should be treated as transfers (benefits). The opposite argument is that since lenders are free to invest either in private securities and other assets or in government bonds, interest income from public debt is no different from any other factor income. Lenders such as financial investors can switch back and forth from one financial asset to another. The argument is consistent with the Ricardian equivalence theorem according to which today's lending is viewed (by lenders) as a postponement of taxes to be paid tomorrow to service the debt. In this study we follow the latter ap-proach. Interest receipts as transfers are ignored. True benefits of public debt appear, rather, in the form of social returns to investment financed through loans. It is these real benefits whose distribution ought to be studied. The burden of taxes to service the public debt was treated above.

Since there is no special levy to service the debt, the cost is treated to conform to the distribution of the average burden of all taxes.

Benefits of Public Investment

The bulk of public loans during the 1970s were incurred to create or to deficit finance public enterprises, analyzed above. In Panama, current budget deficits are also covered entirely by loans. Accordingly, investment expenditures do not necessarily match loans. The analysis of public enterprises and the budget was done in the preceding section. What remain to be analyzed are the social rates of return from various projects and their allocation to different income groups. For this purpose we follow the partial equilibrium procedure of the preceding sections and estimate mainly the primary benefits of public investment.

A dichotomy one encounters in the analysis of debt-financed public projects is that annual payment of debt service is related to the cumulated stock of debt, whereas the usual investment budget relates to one year's capital formation. It is almost impossible to collect the inventory of the public's capital stock created in the past, not to speak of the cumulated stock of such intangible investment as the cost of research on the present critical poverty project. Returns, too, may be intangible, and public capital invariably has large externalities. Records of publicly created stock, its depreciation, repair, and maintenance, its destruction, and related data simply do not exist. Nevertheless, in the case of the cost of debt service, citizens cannot disclaim the legacy of the past. To cut the story short, since benefits of public capital as represented by annual interest on public debt cannot be estimated, we limit our scope to one year's investment. The reference year for this analysis is 1980.

In Panama no perspective plans of development projects are prepared, like the five-year plans in several developing countries. In this regard, what I observed in 1972 is also true today:

> Planning in Panama is still a collection of projects prepared largely with an eye on concessionary loans from foreign financing agencies. The projects prepared and selected seem to fit into the national priorities. However, the Panamanian plans still seem to lack comprehensiveness and coherence of the dynamic input-output type models where each selected project finds its hole after being fully evaluated in relation to other projects in terms of the national goals and scientifically determined levels of feasible instruments. (Sahota 1972b, 73)

In view of this, it is difficult to estimate the interaction effects and externalities of one project upon another and of all projects on national income. This is an added reason for the partial equilibrium approach in this section.

That is to say, the benefits of each project are estimated independent of other projects.

The Allocation Procedure

In determining the net final incidence of public investment expenditure, both sides (forward incidence on consumers and backward incidence on factors of production) must be taken into account. For example, the effect of agricultural loans accrues largely to farmers. The higher productivity resulting from the use of improved techniques in agriculture facilitated by agricultural credit also benefits the urban consumer through lower food prices. In the case of agricultural price supports, the benefits accrue in proportion to the marketed produce, which means higher returns to big farmers than to subsistence farmers. The reduction in gains to the urban sector, owing to agricultural price supports, will be larger for low-income families, which spend a high proportion of their income on food, than for upper-income families, which spend a much lower percentage. Factor incomes may be further altered in case, for example, agricultural investment financed through subsidized credit induces capital-intensive techniques, thereby worsening labor income in relation to property income. In part these results also depend upon what agricultural input supplies are available and whether loans are tied to one or another type of use. With this reminder, the allocation scheme is summarized in table 14.10, which is self-explanatory. Note, however, that since benefits and costs are measured as percentages of household income, public investments as additions to the stock of economic and social capital must be translated into annual flows of benefits. For this purpose, a stylized rate of return of 10 percent was assumed.

Substantive Results

The calculated allocation of investment benefits is presented in table 14.11. We see that in absolute dollars the rich gain much more than the poor ($385 per household per year for the top class as against $33 per household per year for the bottom class of the Republic). In relative terms, which is a standard criterion used for income distribution, however, public investment is pro-poor in urban areas and pro-rich (pro-latifundistas) in rural areas. For instance, the bottom urban class augments income through public investment by 1.93 percent, the third class by 2.05 percent, the fourth class by 1.97 percent, and the top class by 0.56 percent. The overall distribution for the Republic is pro–middle class rather than pro-poor. A smoothed benefit curve for the Republic would look like an inverted parabola. A poor/poor inequity of public investment lies in the result that

Table 14.10 Allocation Criteria for Public Investment, 1980

	Allocation Criteria	
Project Investment Agency	Between Classes	Between Sectors

Agricultural sector

Project Investment Agency	Between Classes	Between Sectors
I. Hydroelectric projects: MIDA-AID	Same as in current budget	Same as in current budget
1.1. Institutional	50% on income basis, 50% on population basis	Whole country: 50% on income basis, 50% on population basis
1.2. Canal basin	Same as above	Same as above
1.3. Río Caldera basin	Same as above	Same as above
1.4. Río La Villa basin	According to income	100% rural
2. Program of Animal husbandry, MIDA-WB		
3. Aid to investment programs	Same as in current budget	Same as in current budget
II. Agricultural Marketing Board (IMA)	Distribution of support price quasi-subsidies (as in current budget)	Same as in current budget
III. University of Panama (Farm Experiment Stations)	Income and population 50/50	50% rural, 50% nation
IV. National Bank of Panamá	Same as in current budget	All to rural
V. Agricultural Development Bank (BDA)	Same as in current budget	All to rural
IV. Agricultural Research Institute	Same as in III above	Same as in III above

Commerce and industrial sector

Project Investment Agency	Between Classes	Between Sectors
I. Ministry	Income and population 50/50	Income and population 50/50
II. Bayano Cement Public Enterprise	Same as in current budget	Same as in current budget
III. BNP	According to income	According to income
IV. National Financial Corporation	According to income	According to income
V. Colón Free Zone	According to income	According to income

Education sector		
Ministry of Education	Same as in current budget	Same as in current budget
Electricity sector (IRHE)	Same as in current budget (public enterprises)	Same as in current budget
Health sector		
I. Ministry of Health	Same as in current budget	Same as in current budget
II. Social Security	Treated in the section on social security	
III. IDAAN	Same as in current budget	Same as in current budget
IV. Department of Street Cleaning	Same as in current budget	Same as in current budget
Telecommunications sector	Same as in current budget	
Transportation sector		
I. Public works (roads)	Income and population 50/50	Income and population 50/50
II. Port Authority	Same as in current budget	Same as in current budget
III. Civil aeronautics	Same as in current budget	Same as in current budget
Tourism sector	Same as in current budget	Same as in current budget
Housing sector		
I. National Mortgage Bank (RHN)	Same as in current budget	Same as in current budget
II. Savings Bank	Same as in current budget	Same as in current budget
III. Social Security Bank (Caja de Seguro Social)	Included in the section on social security	
Multisectoral projects	Income and population 50/50	Income and population 50/50

357

Table 14.11 Distribution of Benefits of Public Investment, 1980

Institution and Project/Program	Income Class[a]											Total
	1	2	3	4	5	6	7	8	9	10	11	
Total investments ($000)	20,991	7,263	12,184	22,863	37,378	64,891	87,125	52,386	35,438	63,614	33,683	437,822
Flow of benefits												
Percentage of income	1.50	1.96	2.11	2.03	1.71	1.57	1.80	1.50	1.33	1.02	0.66	1.36
Differential (%)	0.14	0.60	0.75	0.67	0.35	0.21	0.44	0.14	−0.03	−0.14	−0.70	0.00
Per household ($)	33.4	41.5	52.1	64.14	75.6	104.6	184.7	215.5	244.6	311.5	384.9	119.7

Source: Cumulated from the data published in Panama, MIPPE, *Annexo: Presupuesto de inversiones publica* (Panama; Republic of Panama, 1980), pp. 11–47, and other unpublished sources.

Note: Absolute figures in thousands of dollars, except "per household."

[a] For the dollar ranges and mean values of income classes, see table 14.1, column 1. The investment by the Social Security Bank has already been included in the analysis of social security benefits above.

while the urban poor are favored relative to the urban rich by overall public investment, the rural poor do not share the benefits proportionately to the rest of the rural population. The Gini coefficient of the distribution of public investment in rural areas is 0.47 as against 0.34 in urban areas, giving a mean Gini coefficient for the Republic of 0.39.

For studying poverty, however, global statistics such as the Gini coefficient are not very helpful. It is more meaningful in this case to look, for example, at the bottom 20 to 50 percent of the population. In terms of relative poverty, the bottom two income classes of rural areas, comprising 38 percent of the rural population, derive negative differential benefits from public investment. The economic position of the rural poor is worsened by 0.64 percent relative to the mean rural household. As regards absolute poverty—the more relevant concept for critical poverty—the rural poor get less, but not much less ($34 per household for the bottom class forming 30 percent of rural households) than the urban poor (with a mean income augmentation of $53 per household for the bottom 35 percent of households). Note that the relevant comparisons between urban and rural sectors are not between the corresponding classes, but between given percentages of ranked households, which are noted in the last line of table 14.12. Line 4 from the bottom brings out these magnitudes even more vividly. Thus, the urban poor receive a higher percentage of 1.93 of their relatively higher household incomes by way of public investment than the rural poor, who receive only 1.42 percent. The mean for the Republic for this class is 1.5, for the top class 0.66 percent.

Policy Implications

How can the rural poor increase their benefits from public investment without impairing the productivity of overall investment? Within the existing economic structure, the rural poor can improve their relative economic position if investment funds are diverted toward the Ministerio de Desenvolvimiento de Agricultura–USAID (MIDA-AID) types of hydroelectric projects, toward agroeconomic research (such as is done under the management of the University of Panama at the farm experiment stations), and toward investment listed under the category of multisectoral projects. The analysis must be viewed in differential terms. That is, investible resources can be diverted toward the indicated type of projects only at the cost of reduced investment in some other projects. Instances of the projects that may be pruned to benefit the rural poor are AI3, aid to investment program; AIV, the programs financed through the National Bank of Panama; BIV, National Finance Corporation; the investment programs of D, IRHE; EIII, IDAAN; F, the telecommunications sector; and I, the housing sector. One of the most productive and highly redistributive rural invest-

Table 14.12 Summary of Distribution of Net Benefits from Six Policies (Republic) and Aggregates (Urban and Rural Sectors), 1980

Net Benefits from Policy	Income Class from 1970 Census of Population											
	1	2	3	4	5	6	7	8	9	10	11	Total
	Republic											
Social security (transfer/equity ratio)[a]	2.05	1.40	0.99	0.42	−0.29	−0.08	−0.03	0.06	−0.46	−0.53	−0.37	0.27
Parastatals with (without) lottery[b]	0.30	0.15	−0.05	−0.26	0.31	0.18	3.29	7.03	5.45	4.66	10.63	2.36
	(2.87)	(4.00)	(4.20)	(4.15)	(4.11)	(4.14)	(7.09)	(10.70)	(9.19)	(8.12)	(12.61)	(5.96)
Public services[c]	28.3	30.1	27.0	25.0	19.5	16.0	13.8	12.8	10.7	11.5	10.3	19.0
Taxes[c]	−6.0	−9.6	−10.5	−11.6	−12.0	−13.0	−15.0	−16.6	−18.5	−20.4	−23.3	−13.6
Incentives (differential)[d]	−0.91	−0.67	−0.56	−0.44	−0.28	−0.22	0.01	−0.03	−0.23	1.25	2.90	0.00
Public investment	1.42	1.97	2.15	2.07	1.85	1.79	2.55	2.89	2.52	2.15	1.77	2.06
Aggregate[e]	25.16	23.55	19.03	15.19	9.19	4.67	4.6	6.15	−0.52	−0.84	1.93	10.09
	Urban											
Aggregate[e]	23.55	18.43	11.1	8.13	11.2	8.12	2.99	−2.57	−5.54	−12.6	−13.06	−7.66
	Rural											
Aggregate[e]	26.44	23.83	17.55	16.51	6.15	0.79	−3.21	−6.25	−8.65	−11.02	−11.68	−2.7

Note: The year of estimates for different policies varies between 1980 (e.g., for public investment) and 1983 (e.g., for public enterprises). However, since benefits and costs are expressed in relation to (as percentages of) income their comparison or aggregation (if aggregation were valid on other grounds, which it is not) is unlikely to cause significant error or bias.

[a] The series of transfer/equity ratios (which are calculated only for participants in social security) is not directly comparable to the distribution series of other benefits and costs (which pertain to all population). It is reproduced here for its own importance.

[b] Like the transfer/equity ratios, the distribution of the net benefits of public enterprises "without lottery" is reported here as an alternative series. For the pros and cons of its inclusion, see under Public Services above.

[c] One may expect that the costs of taxes and the benefits of public expenditures should cancel each other out. This is not necessarily the case, however, since some taxes are borne by foreigners, some nontax revenues finance current expenditure, certain benefits accrue in other policies—for example, the benefits of debt, whose cost is met out of tax revenue, appear in public investment—and so on. For further classification of this point see under Incentive Schemes above.

[d] Recall (see Public Investment above) that we abstract from the production- and trade-creation aspects of incentives and focus only on the production- and trade-diversion aspects of incentives. That is the reason for the inclusion of differential instead of absolute distribution of benefits for this category. Contrast this with the next line for public investment, for which absolute values of production-creation are relevant.

[e] For a number of reasons, an aggregation of the net benefits of the six policies would not be valid. The aggregation may be deceptive because, for instance, annual debt service, which is ordinarily met out of annual tax revenues, is calculated on cumulated past borrowings. On the other hand, for the reasons discussed above, the benefits of public debt are estimated only on one year's investment. Similarly, on the cost side, the burden of the entire quasi-tax revenue (surplus) from the national lottery is subtracted from incomes of one year, whereas the benefits of investment of the same funds are treated to emerge as a fraction of the principal, that is, as a flow (roughly 10 percent of the revenue collected). There are other discrepancies of this sort. Accordingly, aggregation either should be avoided or should be interpreted with great care. For those who would take that care, the aggregation is presented in the last line.

ments in the present state of Panama's agriculture, in my judgment, is agricultural research—that is, the right type of agricultural research. This research may open up more productive investment areas, such as the right agricultural techniques, the right modern agricultural inputs, and so on. The results of chapter 3 and Tang's report (1985) indicate a significant lag in this area. Accordingly, the present state of agricultural/agronomic research of Panama was evaluated and the potential of appropriate agricultural research was explored in a study by Evenson (1985a), whose policy implications were discussed in chapter 13.

A SUMMARY OF THE EFFECTS OF SIX POLICIES ON THE POOR

The results of the six policies analyzed according to the methodology of quasi-tax quasi-subsidy incidence in the foregoing sections are collected in table 14.12 (by functions for the Republic and aggregates for sectors). A few series from them are sketched in figure 14.4. The total line of the table, though the one readers would probably like to look at first and last, is somewhat deceptive, because the aggregation of the benefit over different policies as estimated here is not valid. Before drawing any conclusions from it, therefore, one should read the caveats about such an aggregation in note e to the table. In particular, although the distribution reflected by the aggregate is roughly meaningful, the absolute magnitudes are probably not.

Subject to this warning, we can see (fig. 14.4) that Panama's policies are pro-rural between the two sectors, pro-poor among income classes, and antirich in urban areas both as between the urban rich and the rural rich as well as within the urban sector relative to the position of the rural rich within the rural sector. It is more equalizing in the urban sector than in the rural sector. More meaningful in this respect, however, are individual policy results, to which we turn next.

Social Security

On the contribution side, Panama's social security system is less regressive (almost proportional) than most systems of the world, including that of the United States. On the benefit side, the system is highly equalizing among beneficiaries. The benefit/equity ratio is substantially greater than unity for all participants. It is substantially higher toward the lower end relative to upper classes. The system is, however, inequitable between urban areas (which it favors) and rural areas, between inactive beneficiaries and active subscribers, and between the poor of Panama (whom the system bypasses) and the middle-class beneficiaries. When social security contributors and beneficiaries are assigned to their respective families, the distri-

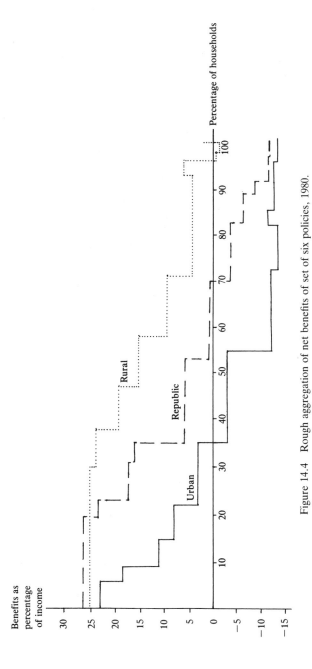

Figure 14.4 Rough aggregation of net benefits of set of six policies, 1980.

bution assumes a parabolic shape—it favors the rich and the poor at the cost of the middle classes.

Based on these results a policy recommendation for the system is that benefits, especially retirement benefits, be extended to all, irrespective of their participation, and that since the system is very generous to pensioners, the rates of present pensions may be cut to half of what they are at present. The covered old-age pensioners will still be the gainers from the social security system. The saving from this reduction will be nearly enough to pay pensions to the one-third of all those rural and other nonparticipant senior citizens who are below the critical poverty line. The problem of incentives and disincentives receives passing attention, but it needs to be looked into more carefully.

Public Enterprises

The overall effect of all the three dozen or so public enterprises analyzed here is mildly pro-poor. Without the national lottery, public enterprises benefit all. The inclusion of the lottery converts benefits into losses to all classes. The benefit curve becomes parabolic, such that the middle classes are the losers relative to families at the two extremes.

When the opportunity cost of deficits/surpluses of public enterprises is introduced, the pro-poor results of the operations of public enterprises change to antipoor. The opportunity cost of deficits of public enterprises may be viewed, among other alternatives, as an equivalent reduction in overall taxes, an equivalent increase of public investment, or an equivalent increase of government's general current expenditure. The interclass redistributive effect of the operations of Panama's public enterprises is significantly less pro-poor than either public investment or overall current public expenditure, while the intersector redistribution is more pro-poor (if the rural sector is considered the poorer of the two sectors).

A policy implication that is suggested by these results and that is consistent with an earlier proposal of the MIPPE is to require public enterprises, other than those that provide "public goods," to at least stand on their own feet. As a matter of fact, there is a strong case for them to operate on commercial lines, compete with private enterprises, and earn profits. A proposal of this study is to turn over private-goods public enterprises to workers. They will generate ownership in the stock of these enterprises equal to economic profits. Individual families would be required to match the additions to their annual shares according to a graduated negative income tax scheme.

Public Services

Public services are impressively pro-poor between income classes, provinces, and sectors. The degree of redistribution is higher between provinces than between classes. The results suggest that the distribution of public services has become more pro-poor since 1970.

There is a good deal of evidence supporting these findings. That is, the pro-poor character of the *inputs* (public services) is consistent with the pro-poor character of the *results* (improved health and longevity, reduction in child mortality, significant rise in literacy, and other benign results).

Further improvements may still be possible here and there without impairing growth, but the progress made so far needs to be consolidated. No major policy change in the allocation of public expenditure is therefore necessary.

Taxes

Panama's tax structure is probably a bit less progressive now than it was when Charles McLure analyzed it for the year 1968, but is still highly progressive. The progression is mild among low-income brackets but becomes strong among upper-income classes. (The second derivative of taxes on income is positive.) Panama's tax structure thus has desirable pro-poor properties not only because its burden is progressively distributed but also because the degree of change in the progression favors low-income classes. Despite the suggestion of a slight decline in the progressivity of the tax structure since 1968, the net budget incidence has become more steeply pro-poor. Evidently this is due to Panama's public services' having become a bit more pro-poor during the same period.

The elasticities of the ratios of the benefits (burden in the case of taxes) to income with respect to per capita family income are given below:

	Public Enterprises	Public Services	Public Investment	Taxes
Republic	−0.14 (−2.9)	−0.46 (−21.4)	−0.26 (−5.0)	0.28 (6.6)
Urban	−0.27 (−1.55)	−0.47 (−15.6)	−0.31 (−10.2)	0.19 (9.7)
Rural	0.45 (7.2)	−0.45 (−10.0)	0.08 (1.3)	0.36 (7.6)

The numbers in parentheses are *t* values. The negative sign of the coefficient of a public expenditure (first three columns) means the respective category is pro-poor. In the case of tax burden, the positive sign is pro-poor.

Thus Panama's fiscal budget has moved significantly toward being a welfare budget. All that is now needed, from the viewpoint of poverty, is to maintain its present structure. Minor adjustments are still in order to improve its pro-poorness without adverse effects on efficiency, but what is needed is to guard against any encroachment upon the pro-poorness that has already been built into Panama's budgetary structure.

Incentive Schemes and Price Policies

In summarizing the results of Panama's incentive and price policies, let me repeat a disclaimer. We have abstracted from the overall growth or production-creating aspects and have concentrated on only the production-diverting aspects of these policies. Thus the gains of the incentivados (including the sharing of gains by the factors of production employed by incentivados and the consumers of their products) are the losses of non-incentivados. The results indicate that the overall investment- and export-incentive schemes as well as price supports and other pricing policies are significantly pro-rich and antipoor. In my judgment the superimposition of the redistributive effects of production-creating and export-promoting policies is unlikely to reduce the adverse redistributional effects of the currently structured incentive policies.

The prevailing maze of subsidies, tax concessions, price supports, and similar policies in Panama has created numerous distortions in the economy that in aggregate turn out to be antipoor. Protection of agricultural staples and high agricultural support prices have imposed upon Panama a high-cost agriculture that is conducive to neither growth nor redistribution. Agricultural prices therefore need to be brought closer to, though not necessarily at par with, world prices, so that inefficient production is weeded out. This is not to say that food production should be left entirely to atomistic, laissez-faire market forces. No country in the world of today, when food embargoes have become tools of international diplomacy, can risk the lifeline of its people by relying mainly on imported food; but we should not forget that several major exporting countries, such as those in the Organization for Economic Cooperation and Development and the United States of America, subsidize their agricultural exports. What is being underscored is that the gap between border prices and internal prices in Panama is rather too wide. Panama needs an agricultural policy that favors comparative advantage and exports instead of the protection of its high-cost agriculture. Its need lies in a policy that promotes biotechnological research aimed at closing the gap in yield between large and small farmers. In this policy, price supports have a definite role. That role must, however, be viewed as the stabilization of agricultural prices, necessary for a viable agriculture, rather than as a means of redistributing income from urban consumers to farm producers.

The policies of tariff walls accompanied by numerous tariff exemptions and export-tax concessions are another major source of distortions. These need a careful review, first, because they are antipoor and, second, because their trade-creating and production-creating effects, as against trade-diverting and production-diverting effects, have not been established. The available statistics indicate a woefully unsatisfactory performance of the incentivados in relation to costs. As a commercial center of the world with free foreign-exchange rate and open borders, Panama ought to be striving for international competitiveness of the degree attained by Hong Kong, Taiwan, Singapore, and similar small commercially oriented, outward-looking countries. It is not so much the existence of the exemptions that needs to be looked into as the high levels and the extensive list of tax exemptions (and therefore price distortion) an incentivado can enjoy.

Finally, domestic quasi-subsidies, especially those resulting from tax concessions for construction, need to be corrected. The antipoor nature of domestic quasi-subsidies is exacerbated when the pro-rich distribution of concessional mortgage loans by the social security system analyzed above is added to the tax concessions of this section. It is somewhat of an anomaly to find so many incentives and subsidies for nonpoor and commercial housing when the poor of the nation are not housed decently at all.

Public Investment

The results of the analysis indicate that public investment is pro-poor in urban areas and pro-rich in rural areas. At the national level mean public investment becomes pro-middle class, at the cost of both the rich and the critically poor. Interestingly, the relative benefit curve is practically the reverse of that for public enterprises. One roughly cancels out the other.

A careful look at individual projects shows that the rural poor can improve their relative economic positions if investment funds are diverted toward the MIDA-AID type of hydroelectric projects, toward agricultural experiment stations, and toward what are classified as multisectoral projects. To increase investment in this type of project, naturally, funds must be reduced for other projects. Some of the projects that might be pruned to release funds for investment that will benefit the rural poor were listed above. One of the most productive and redistributive rural investments in the present state of Panama's agriculture is an appropriate type of agricultural research to seek the right agricultural techniques and new inputs. The analysis indicates a lag in this area that warrants attention.

The critical survey of existing policies in this chapter has not exhausted them all. Several other policies were evaluated in earlier chapters. Here we have examined mainly those policies that were found germane to the methodology of quasi-tax incidence.

If the facts brought to surface by the analysis of the policies and socioeconomic structure of this country, as well as the policy implications following from them that have been spelled out in the relevant chapters, are given due consideration by Panamanian policymakers, the next generation in Panama definitely, and the present generation most probably, will experience much less poverty than that would otherwise prevail.

GENERAL APPENDIX

Definitions of Variables

(All income variables are in thousands of 1983 dollars unless otherwise stated.)

Variable Code	Variable Definition
Income	
1	Per capita comprehensive income (YV), ranking according to this variable
2A	Urban employment income, including in-kind income, head of household
2B	Urban employment income, including in-kind income, spouse
2C	Urban employment income, including in-kind income, total (including other members)
3A	Rural employment income, including in-kind income, head
3B	Rural employment income, including in-kind income, spouse
3C	Rural employment income, including in-kind income, total
4A	Urban own-account income, including self-consumption, head
4B	Urban own-account income, including self-consumption, spouse
4C	Urban own-account income, including self-consumption, total
5	Agricultural own-account income, including self-consumption, family total
6	Urban property income, including imputed property income
7A	Transfer income, total
7AH	Transfer income, head
7AS	Transfer income, spouse
7B	Transfer income, total pensions
7BH	Transfer income, head's pension
7BS	Transfer income, spouse's pension
8	Social security taxes paid by family (including employer's share)
9	Income taxes paid, head
9A	Income taxes paid, all, including head

(All income variables are in thousands of 1983 dollars unless otherwise stated.)

Variable Code	Variable Definition
Home Characteristics	
10	Own house
11	Condemned
12	If own home by mortgage, monthly payment
13	If home rented, monthly rent
14	Number of rooms in house
15	Floor unpaved (dirt floor)
16	Water source inside home
17	Drinking water from river or "other"
18	No sanitary service
19	Has electric light
20	Rental value of fully owned owner-occupied home
121320	L12 + L13 + L20—rent or rental value of home
21	Has television
22	Has refrigerator
23	Has any means of transportation
24	Has automobile
Household Size and Age of Members	
25A	Sex of head of household
25AA	Sex of eldest child ≥ 18
25B	Spouse living in home
26	Age of head of household; 26SQ = age squared
26B	Age of spouse
26C	Age of eldest child ≥ 18
27	Number of persons ≥ 65
28	Number of persons ≥ 15 but < 65
29	Number of children 6–14
30	Number of children 0–5
31	Total persons in family
32	Total persons in household

(All income variables are in thousands of 1983 dollars unless otherwise stated.)

Variable Code	Variable Definition
Education	
33	Number of 6–18-year-olds attending school
34	Number of 6–18-year-olds not attending school
35	Number of school-going persons who repeated grade
36	Mean grade of school-going persons
37	Mean aspiration for children's schooling
38	Number of school years completed by head's father
39	Number of school years completed by head's mother
40	Number of school years completed by head of household
41	Number of school years completed by head's spouse
42	Number of school years completed by eldest child, if > 18
43	Index of school years completed (S) by children 7–18 (of the household concerned)
44	Technical training by head of household (does not include vocational training)
44B	Technical training by spouse
Health	
45	Number of children ≤ 1 year who died last year
46	Secured medical assistance at health post, clinic, or hospital
46B	Needed medical attention but did not secure
47	Reason for not seeking medical assistance
Occupational Characteristics	
48	Job in modern sector, head of household
49	Occupational status of head's father
50	Occupational status of head of household
51	Occupational status of head's spouse
52	Occupational status of eldest child, if > 18
53	Principal economic activity of head of household
54A	Principal economic activity of spouse
54B	Labor force participation rate in family

(All income variables are in thousands of 1983 dollars unless otherwise stated.)

Variable Code	Variable Definition

Employment Characteristics of Head of Household

Variable Code	Variable Definition
55A	Ratio of earnings of second job to earnings of primary job in non-agricultural sector, total for family
55B	Ratio of earnings of second job to earnings of primary job in non-agricultural sector, head of household
55C	Absolute earnings from primary job of head ($)
55D	Absolute earnings from primary job of spouse ($)
55E	Absolute earnings from primary job of eldest child
55T1AA	Absolute earnings from secondary job of family
55T2AA	Absolute earnings from primary job of family
56A	Intensity of employment = ratio of months employed in past six months in nonagricultural sector, family total
56B	Intensity of employment = ratio of months employed in past six months in nonagricultural sector, head of household
56BB	Intensity of employment in nonagricultural sector, spouse
56C	Intensity of employment = ratio of months employed in past six months in nonagricultural sector, all other than head
56D	Whether head employed or unemployed, dummy: 1 for employed, 0 for unemployed
56E	Intensity of employment of other active members of family
57A	Ratio of months worked in year, agricultural sector, family total
57B	Ratio of months worked in year, agricultural sector, head
57BB	Intensity of employment in agricultural sector, spouse
57C	Ratio of months worked in year, agricultural sector, others than head
58	Fully employed but can do more work, or disguised unemployment, head only
59A	Ratio of perceived underemployment in agricultural sector, head only
59B	Ratio of disguised underemployment $(W^{min} - W)/W^{min}$, head only
60A	Own-account business income fixed, family total
60B	Own-account business income fixed, head
61A	Ratio of earnings in off-farm job to that in agricultural job, family total
61B	Ratio of earnings in off-farm job to that in agricultural job, head

(All income variables are in thousands of 1983 dollars unless otherwise stated.)

Variable Code	Variable Definition
Employment Characteristics of Head of Household	
61T11	Absolute amount of off-farm earnings in Q.55, family total
61T22	Absolute amount of agricultural income in Q.54, family total
Consumption Expenditure Patterns	
62	Expenditure on food
63	Expenditure on energy
64	Expenditure on education
65	Expenditure on health
66	Total expenditure
67	Savings reported
L75CD	Modernization dummy: 1 for farms using fertilizer, 0 otherwise
75H1	Farm expenditure on own transportation + fuel
75H2	Farm expenditure on rent and transportation
75I	Farm expenditure on animal feed
75K	Farm expenditure on agricultural insurance
75L	Farm expenditure on veterinarian
75M	Farm expenditure on other
Agricultural Output in 1983 Products	
81A	Gross value of crop output
81B	Marketed surplus in crop production
L81AL85	L81/L85
L81L85	L81*L85 (product of L81 and L85)
82	Value of sales of cattle
83	Value of sales of pigs
84	Value of sales of poultry and dairy products
85	Total gross agricultural output
1983 Inputs	
86	Family labor in man-years
87	Hired labor in man-years
87W	Wage received by agricultural workers

(All income variables are in thousands of 1983 dollars unless otherwise stated.)

Variable Code	Variable Definition
1983 Inputs	
88	Rental cost of machinery and equipment (including transport equipment) and tools
88B	Rental price of machinery
89	Cost of fertilizer and pesticides
90	Land in hectares actually used
90B	Ratio of untitled land to total land
L90B	Percentage of land held with title
91	Rental value of land actually used
91B	Rental price of land
92	Cost of seeds
93	All other inputs
Other Data	
94	Received technical assistance
95	Sharecropper
96	Proportion of irrigated land to total land
97	Received concessional credit this year
98	Can get concessional credit easily
99	Principal problems of community
Variables with Alphabetic Names	
100	PERC = percentile of family
101	AE = economic activity code of head (Q. 35)
102	CO = Occupation code of head (Q. 40)
103	AES = economic activity code of spouse
104	COS = occupation code of spouse
105	AECH = economic activity code of child > 18
106	COCH = occupation code of child > 18
107	AREA = area
108	PROV = province
109	DIST = district

(All income variables are in thousands of 1983 dollars unless otherwise stated.)

Variable Code	Variable Definition
Additional Variables and Symbols	
AE	Principal employment in agriculture; same as variable code 101
AES	Agricultural employment squared
AGE2–AGE5	Age-class dummies (dummy for women older than 40 is used as reference class)
BRINVCA	Beginning inventory of cattle (1982); same as LMINVCA
BRINVPI	Beginning inventory of pigs (1982); same as LMINVPI
CANAL	Occupation class for fathers, Canal sector employment (reference group is the unemployed)
CHDEP	Child dependency ratio
COLLEGE	1 if mother has schooling beyond secondary school, 0 otherwise
COMER	Commercialization: ratio of sales to gross value of output
CUS	Contraceptive Use Survey, 1973–76
DM	Metropolitan dummy: 1 for Panamá and Colón, 0 for other provinces
DSC	Sharecropping dummy: 1 for farms reporting in-kind payment of rent, 0 otherwise
EDINT	HUSED × years of schooling of mother
FA	Farm association
FACTOR	Expansion factor
GVAO	Gross value of agricultural output
H or HH	Head of household
HEALTH	Same as LE
HUSED	Years of schooling of husband
INC1–INC5	Income-class dummies (dummy for the highest income group, number 6, was used as reference class)
L	Before a code, signifies variable; distinguishes code from variable name; e.g., L90 = land
LE	Life expectancy (census data); also abbreviated HEALTH
LL	Before a code, means logarithm of variable; e.g., LL90 = log of land
LMINVCA	Beginning-year inventory of cattle; same as BRINVCA
LMINVPI	Beginning-year inventory of pigs; same as BRINVPI

(All income variables are in thousands of 1983 dollars unless otherwise stated.)

Variable Code	Variable Definition

Additional Variables and Symbols

LPIGS	L(MINVPI + VPUPI) = total pigs
LSTOCK	L(MINVCA + VPUCA) = total cattle
MORT	Child death/child ever born; 0 if no children
NAE	Nonagricultural employment (occupation dummy: 1 if nonagricultural occupation, 0 otherwise)
NNS	National Nutritional Survey, 1980
NPF	Nonpoverty farms
OBS	Number of observations
OCCHNGE	1 if the mother upgraded her occupation after marriage
OLS	Ordinary least-squares method
OTHRUR	1 if the household is a rural household outside the metropolitan areas
OTHURB	1 if the household is an urban household outside the metropolitan areas
PF	Poverty farms, defined as those with overall income below the poverty line
PODRI	1 if both parents have primary schooling or less and do not work or work in agricultural, household, or unskilled occupation, 0 otherwise
POORUR	POOR × (METRUR + OTHRUR)
PPROF	1 if mother worked in a professional occupation before marriage, 0 otherwise
PRBFEED	Proportion of breast-feeding mothers
PRFERT	Rate of fertility, children born per 1,000 adult women age 15–45
PRIM	Primary school
PRIMCOMP	1 if mother completed primary school, 0 otherwise
PROPSON	Sons born/total children born; 1/2 if no children
PSALES	1 if mother worked in a clerical, sales, or farm occupation before marriage, 0 otherwise
PSKILL	1 if mother in a skilled occupation before marriage, 0 otherwise
PUBEMP	Occupation class for fathers, public employment (reference group is the unemployed)
PUNSKILL	1 if mother worked in an agricultural household or unskilled occupation before marriage, 0 otherwise

(All income variables are in thousands of 1983 dollars unless otherwise stated.)

Variable Code	Variable Definition

Additional Variables and Symbols

$\bar{R}^2$	R bar squared, i.e., R^2 adjusted for degrees of freedom used up
RFF	Rural farm family
RNFF	Rural nonfarm family
RURALURB	1 if mother migrated from rural to urban location
SEC	Secondary school
SECCOMP	1 if mother completed secondary school, 0 otherwise
SES	Frequently used to stand for National Socioeconomic Survey, 1983
TAC	Population growth rate; proxy for rapidly growing local economy
TOWNURB	1 if mother migrated from town to urban location
UNIV	University
V203	Spontaneous abortions
VAP	Value of average product
VMP	Value of marginal product
VPUCA	Cattle purchased during the year
VPUPI	Pigs purchased during the year
w^{min}	Minimum wage rate
WFS	World Fertility Survey, London, England (1976)
WORKING	Occupation class for fathers, employment in sectors other than the Canal sector and the public sector (reference group is the unemployed)
Z	Correction of selection bias due to marriage; entered as I–P in the "married" subsample and as P in the "never married" subsample, where p is the probability of being married.
*	When appearing between two numbered variables, stands for multiplication, whose economic meaning is "interaction" between the relevant variables. For instance, L50*49 means the occupational status of the head of household *interacted* with that of the head's father. The following interacted variables appear in several regressions: L56B*56D, L40*56B, L40*50, and others.
Currency	The official currency of the Republic of Panama is called the balboa. It is the same as the United States dollar. Only the United States currency bills circulate. Panama prints no balboas; it only mints coins. United States coins, too, are fully acceptable. All figures expressed in value terms in this study may be read as United States dollar or Panamian balboas; they are identical.

References

Akerlof, George A. 1969. Structural unemployment in a neoclassical framework. *Journal of Political Economy* 77:399–407.

Allen, R. G. D. 1938. *Mathematical analysis for economists.* London: Macmillan.

Altimir, Oscar. 1981. Poverty in Latin America: A review of concepts and data. *Revista de la CEPAL,* April, 65–91.

———. 1982. *The extent of poverty in Latin America.* Staff Working Paper 522. Washington, D.C.: World Bank.

Arosemena-Alvarado, Ricardo. 1980. Distribución del ingreso y crecimiento económico: El caso de Panamá. B.S. diss., Instituto Technológico Autónomo de Mexico.

———. 1983. Incentivos tributarios y desarrollo industrial diagnostico de la evolución reciente. Memorandum to the director of the Ministry of Finance Treasury, August 3.

Bauch, Jerald P., and Elda Maud Rodriguez. 1984. Early childhood education for economic and social growth. Report to the Critical Poverty Project of Panama, MIPPE, mimeographed.

Becker, Gary S. 1964. *Human capital.* New York: Columbia University Press.

———. 1967. Human capital and the personal distribution of income: An analytical approach. Woytinsky Lecture 1, Institute for Public Administration, University of Michigan. (Reprinted in *Human capital,* 2d ed. [New York: Columbia University Press, 1975].)

Becker, Gary S., and Nigel Tomes. 1979. An equilibrium theory of the distribution of income and intergenerational mobility. *Journal of Political Economy,* 87(6): 1153–89.

Bermudez, I. I. C. 1980. Estado nutricional de la población adulta en la Republica de Panamá. Panama, Ministry of Health, mimeographed.

Bienfed, M. 1975. The informal sector and peripheral capitalism: The case of Tanzania. *Human Resources Research* 6(3): 55–70. (Institute of Development Studies Bulletin, University of Sussex.)

Bird, Richard J., and Lue Henry DeWulf. 1973. Taxation and income distribution in Latin America: A critical review of empirical studies. *IMF Staff Papers,* November, 639–82.

Bloom, Benjamin S. 1964. *Stability and change in human characteristics.* New York: John Wiley.

———. 1976. *Human characteristics and school learning.* New York: McGraw-Hill.

Bowles, Samuel, and Herbert Gintis. 1977. The Marxian theory of value and heterogeneous labor: A critique and reformulation. *Cambridge Journal of Economics* 1:173–92.

Burkhauser, Richard. 1984. Technical report on old age poverty: The social security system of Panama. Report to the Critical Poverty Project of the U.N. and Panama, MIPPE, mimeographed.

———. 1986. Social security in Panama: A multiperiod analysis of income distribution. *Journal of Development Economics* 20(1986): 53–64.

Burkhauser, Richard, and Jennifer L. Warlick. 1981. Disentangling the annuity and redistributive aspects of social security. *Review of Income and Wealth* 27(December): 401–21.

Centro de Estudios Torrijista. 1984. *Comandante de los pobres*. Panama: Republic of Panama.

CEPAL (Economic Commission for Latin America). 1980. Quantification, analysis y descripción de la pobreza en Panama (consultant Hugo Lavados). E/CEPAL/PROY. 1/R 40, April.

———. 1981a. Notas sobre las canastas basicas de alimentos en los paises del istmo centroamericano: Características y resultados. CEPAL/MEX/SEM. 416, March 20.

———. 1981b. La pobreza y la satisfacción de necesidades basicas en el istmo centroamericano. CEPAL/MEX/SEM. 4/12, March 31.

———. 1982. Notas sobre la evolución del desarrollo social del istmo centroamericano hasta 1980. E/CEPAL/MEX/1982/L.26/Rev. 1, September 3.

Clausen, A. W. 1985. Poverty in the developing countries, 1985. Address given at the Martin Luther King, Jr., Center, Atlanta, Georgia. World Bank, Washington, D.C., January 11.

Correa, Arora. 1984. Perfil del desempleo. Panama, MIPPE.

Cragg, John G., Arnold C. Harberger, and Peter Mieszkowski. 1967. Empirical evidence on the incidence of the corporation income tax. *Journal of Political Economy* 75(6): 811–21.

De Gordon, Denis T. 1984. La situación nutricional de los niños panamenos de perimer grado primaria en el año de 1982. Panama: Ministry of Health and Ministry of Education.

De La Cruz, Rosa Elena de. 1983. Características demográficas de la familia. Primer seminario de la asociación de Psicólogos de la caja del seguro social, Panama, MIPPE, mimeographed.

De Tray, Dennis N. 1973. Child quality and the demand for children. *Journal of Political Economy* 81(2): S70–95.

Eighmy, Thomas H. 1977. Mapping the poverty line in western Panama. Panama, MIPPE, mimeographed.

Evenson, Robert. 1984. Agricultural research and poverty in Panama. Report to the Critical Poverty Project of Panama, MIPPE, mimeographed.

———. 1985. Fertility and poverty. Report to the Critical Poverty Project of Panama, MIPPE/U.N., mimeographed.

Evenson, Robert, and M. Rosenzweig. 1977. Fertility, schooling, and the economic contribution of children in rural India. Growth Center, Yale University, mimeographed.

Goldberg, Samuel. 1984. Distribution of tax burden in Panama. Report to BID and the Ministry of Finance and Treasury, Panama, mimeographed.

Gougain, Laura. 1983. Fecundidad y participación laboral femenina in Panama. In *National fertility survey, 1975–76,* ser. D, no. 105. Santiago, Chile.

Griliches, Zvi. 1969. Capital-skill complementarity. *Review of Economics and Statistics* 51:465–68.

———. 1976. Wages of very young men. *Journal of Political Economy* 84(4): S69–85.

Heckman, James. 1976. The common structure of statistical models of truncation and censoring. *Annals of Economic and Social Measurement,* December, 492–504.

———. 1984. The labor market earnings of Panamanian males. Report to the Critical Poverty Project of Panama, MIPPE, mimeographed.

———. 1987. The labor market earnings of Panamanian males. *Journal of Human Resources* 21(4): 507–42.

ILO (International Labor Organization). 1983. La evolución de la pobreza rural en Panamá. PREALC (Programa Regional del Empleo para América Latina y el Caribe) 222, Panama, March.

Krzyzaniak, Marian, and Richard A. Musgrave. 1968. Incidence of the corporation income tax in U.S. manufacturing: Comment. *American Economic Review* 53(5): 1358–60 (part 1).

Lavados, Hugo. 1980. Cuantificación, análisis y descripción de la pobreza en Panamá. CEPAL, E/CEPAL/PROY. 1/R 40, April, mimeographed.

Lessard, Donald. 1984. Panama's International Banking Center. Report to USAID-MIPPE, Panama, September 26, mimeographed.

Lessard, Donald, and Adrian Tschoegl. 1984. Panama's International Banking Center. Report to the USAID-MIPPE, November 1, mimeographed.

Liebowitz, Arlene S. 1972. Women's allocation of time to market and non-market activities: Differences by education. Ph.D. diss., Columbia University.

McLure, Charles E. 1972. The distribution of income and tax incidence in Panama, 1969. Program of Development Studies, Discussion Paper 36, Winter, mimeographed.

———. 1974. The distribution of income and tax incidence in Panama. 1969. *Public Finance Quarterly* 2(2): 155–201.

Meade, James E. 1964. *Efficiency, equality, and the ownership of property.* London: Allen and Unwin.

———. 1976. *The just economy.* Vol. 4. *Principles of political economy.* Albany: State University of New York Press.

Mincer, J. 1958. Investments in human capital and personal income distribution. *Journal of Political Economy.* August 1958, 66(4), pp. 281–302.

———. 1974. *Schooling, experience and earnings.* New York: Columbia University Press.

Mohan, Rakesh, et al. 1980. *Measuring urban malnutrition and poverty: A case study of Bogotá and Cali, Colombia.* Washington, D.C.: World Bank.

Molina S., Sergio. 1982. La pobreza: Descripción y análisis de políticas para superarla. *Revista de la CEPAL* 18(December):93–117.

Morley, Samuel. 1984. Poverty and urban employment in Panama. Report to the Critical Poverty Project of Panama, MIPPE, mimeographed.

Musgrave, Richard A., et al. 1974. The distribution of fiscal burdens and benefits. *Public Finance Quarterly* 2(3): 259–311.

Myrdal, Gunnar. 1959. *Economic theory and underdeveloped regions.* London: Duckworth.

Panama, Caja de Seguro Social. 1982. *Estadística de seguro social, 1980–81.* Panama: Republic of Panama, Caja de Seguro, section 421.

Panama, Republic of, Controller General. 1970. *Demographic census, 1970.* Panama: Republic of Panama.

———. 1971a. *Censo agropecuario.* Panama: Republic of Panama.

———. 1971b. *Income survey, 1970.* Panama: Republic of Panama.

———. 1972. *Household expenditure survey, 1972.* Panama: Republic of Panama.

———. 1975. Encuesta especial sobre ingresos a traves de los hogares: Año 1970 (household income survey). *Estadística Panamena* 34, suppl.

———. 1979–80. *Situación Económica.* Annual.

———. 1980a. *Censos nacionales de 1980.* Vol. 1. *Annual income per median family.* Panama: Republic of Panama.

———. 1980b. *Health Bulletin.* Annual.

———. 1980c. *Situación Social: Asistencia Social.*

———. 1981. *Demographic census, 1980.* Panama: Republic of Panama.

———. 1982. *Household survey, 1982.* Panama: Republic of Panama.

———. 1983. *Population census, 1980.* Special tabulation by Critical Poverty Project, MIPPE, Panama.

———. 1984. *Household survey, 1982.* Special tabulation by Critical Poverty Project, MIPPE, Panama.

———. 1985. National socioeconomic survey, 1983. Panama, MIPPE, electronic tape.

———. Annual. *Estadística del trabajo.*

———. Annual. *Estadística panamena: Situación económica.*

———. Annual. *Panama en cifras.*

Panama, IDIAP (Instituto de Investigación Agropecuaria de Panamá). 1981. *Bulletin.*

Panama, MIDA (Ministry of Agricultural Development). 1980. Interpretación de desarrollo agropecuario, 1970–80. Mimeographed, copy with Leda Arrue.

———. 1983a. Dirección nacional de planificación sectoral. Mimeographed statistical tables.

———. 1983b. Interpretación del desarrollo agropecuario 1970–80. October, mimeographed.

Panama, Ministry of Finance and Treasury. 1984. Import tax exemptions of parastatals. Mimeographed.

———. 1984a. Special tables on tax withholdings. Typescript.

———. 1984b. Table of estimates of exemptions from property tax. Handwritten sheets.

Panama, Ministry of Health. 1976. *Contraceptive use survey.* Panama: Republic of Panama.

Panama, Ministry of Health. 1983a. Canasta basica de alimentos para Panama, 1983. Mimeographed.

————. 1983b. *National nutrition survey.* Panama: Republic of Panama.

————. 1984. Estado nutricional de la población. Panama, mimeographed.

Panama, MIPPE (Ministry of Planning and Economic Policy). 1975. *National Development Plan for 1976–80.* Panama: Republic of Panama.

————. 1977. *La radiografía de la pobreza en Panamá.* Panama: Republic of Panama.

————. 1979. *National development program for Panama: Strategy for the year 2000.* Working Paper. Panama: Republic of Panama.

————. 1980a. *Anexo: Presupuesto de inversiones publica.* Panama: Republic of Panama.

————. 1980b. *Canasta minima de alimentos para Panamá: Proyecto de investigación sobre el grado de satisfacción de necesidades basicas en el istmo estadoamericano.* Panama: Republic of Panama.

————. 1980c. *Necesidades basicas en el sector salud.* Panama: Republic of Panama.

————. 1980d. *El niño en Panamá.* Panama: Republic of Panama.

————. 1983a. *Características de la mujer Panamena en areas marginadas.* Panama: Republic of Panama.

————. 1983b. *Informe económico.*

————. 1984. *El descenso de la fecundidad segun . . . Division of Población.* Panama: Republic of Panama.

————. 1985. Canasta basica de alimentos para Panama (by Armando Villarreal). Critical Poverty Project of Panama, mimeographed.

Panama, MIPPE-U.N., Critical Poverty Project. 1983. *Methodological note for the preparation of tabulations of the socioeconomic survey, 1983.* Panama: Republic of Panama.

Panama, Social Security Department and Critical Poverty Project. 1984. Special social security merge file. Data on tape.

Parillon, C., et al. 1982a. Final report, Nutrition and Evaluation Project. Sigma One Corporation, Raleigh, N.C., mimeographed.

————. 1982b. Alimentación y nutrición en Panamá: La situación actual. Panama, Ministry of Health, mimeographed.

Parillon D., Cutberto. 1983. Estado nutricional de la población Panamena. 1983. Panama, Ministry of Health, mimeographed.

Pechman, Joseph A., and Benjamin A. Okner. 1974. *Who bears the tax burden?* Washington, D.C.: Brookings Institution.

Pindyck, Robert S. 1973. *Optimal planning for economic stabilization.* Contributions to Economic Analysis 81. Amsterdam: North-Holland/American Elsevier. (Abridged version published in Pindyck, Optimal policies for economic stabilization, *Econometrica* 41(3): 529–61.)

PREALC (Programa Regional del Empleo para América Latina y el Caribe)/ILO. 1980a. *Estrategia de necesidades basicas y empleo.* PREALC/189. Panama: Republic of Panama.

————. 1980b. Panamá: Instrumentos de incentivo al desarrollo industrial y su efecto en el empleo. Panama, mimeographed.

————. 1982. *Segmentación del mercado de trabajo.* Documento de Trabajo, PREALC/216, ILO, September.

————. 1983. *La evolución de la pobreza rural en Panamá.* Documento de Trabajo, PREALC/222, ILO, March.

Rosen, Sherwin. 1974. Hedonic prices and implicit markets: Product differentiation in pure competition. *Journal of Political Economy* 82:34–55.

————. 1985. Family structure and poverty in Panama. Report to the Critical Poverty Project, Panama, MIPPE-U.N., mimeographed.

Rosenzweig, M., and T. Paul Schultz. 1983. Estimating a household production function: Heterogeneity, the demand for health inputs and their effects on birthweight. *Journal of Political Economy* 91(5):723–46.

Rosenzweig, M., T. Paul Schultz, and K. Wolpin. 1980. Life cycle labor supply and fertility. *Journal of Political Economy* 89(6): 1059–85.

Roy, A. D. 1951. Some thoughts on the distribution of earnings. *Oxford Economic Papers* 3:135–46.

Sahota, Chander K. 1983. Theories of children's poverty: A survey. Report to the Critical Poverty Project of Panama, MIPPE, mimeographed.

Sahota, Gian S. 1971. The distribution of tax burden among different education classes in Brazil. *Economic Development and Cultural Change* 19(3):439–60.

————. 1972a. An analysis of tax burden distribution in Rio de Janeiro. *Revista Brasileira de Económia* 26(January–March):23–50.

————. 1972b. Public expenditure and income distribution in Panama. Report to the USAID–Ministry of Planning, Panama.

————. 1975. *Brazilian economic policy: Theory analysis.* New York: Praeger.

————. 1977. The distribution of the benefits of public expenditure in Panama. *Public Finance Quarterly* 5(2): 203–31.

————. 1978. Theories of personal income distribution: A survey. *Journal of Economic Literature* 16(1): 1–55.

————. 1980. The distribution of the benefits of public expenditure in Nigeria. Report to the World Bank, Washington, D.C.

Sahota, Gian S., and Carlos A. Rocca. 1980. Survey of latest developments: A general model of family income distribution, Chicago and Cambridge reconciled. *Journal of Policy Modeling* 2(2): 255–89.

————. 1985. *Income distribution: Theory, modeling, and case study of Brazil.* Ames: Iowa State University Press.

Sattinger, Michael. 1980. *Capital and the distribution of labor earnings.* Amsterdam: North-Holland.

Sen, Amartya K. 1980. *Levels of poverty: Policy and change.* Staff Working Paper 401. Washington, D.C.: World Bank.

————. 1981. *Poverty and famine.* Oxford: Oxford University Press.

Shail, Jain. 1975. *Size distribution of income: A compilation of data.* Washington, D.C.: World Bank.

Sjaastad, Larry. 1985. Poverty and unemployment policy for Panama. Report to the Critical Poverty Project of Panama, MIPPE, mimeographed.

Streeten, Paul. 1978. *Basic needs.* Washington, D.C., World Bank.

Tang, Anthony M. 1983. Critical poverty in Panama: The agricultural sector. Report to the Critical Poverty Project of Panama, MIPPE, mimeographed.

————. 1985. Critical poverty in Panama: The agricultural sector. Report to the Critical Poverty Project of Panama, MIPPE/U.N., mimeographed.

Taubman, Paul. 1975. *Sources of inequality of earnings.* Amsterdam: North-Holland.

Thurow, Lester C. 1980. *The zero-sum society.* New York: Basic Books.

Tinbergen, J. 1952. *On the theory of economic policy.* Amsterdam: North-Holland.

———. 1976. *Income distribution: Analysis and policies.* Amsterdam: North-Holland.

UNICEF. 1979. *Estudio socio-económico de la población indigena Guaymi de Panamá: A los niños Guaymies en el Año Internacional del Niño, 1979.* Geneva: UNICEF.

United States Department of Health, Education, and Welfare. 1976. The measure of poverty: A Report to Congress.

Watts, Harold W. 1975. A model of the endowment of human wealth, or Let's look at social policy through the eyes of the twenty-first century's adults. Discussion paper, Institute for Research on Poverty, University of Wisconsin—Madison.

Welch, Finis. 1970. Education in production. *Journal of Political Economy* 78(1): 35–59.

World Bank. 1984. *Annual report.* Washington, D.C.: World Bank.

World Fertility Survey. 1981. *Illustrative analysis of contraceptive sterilization and births averted in Panama.* London: World Fertility Survey.

Author Index

Subject Index

The Johns Hopkins Studies in Development

Comparative Patterns of Economic Development, 1850–1914, by Cynthia Morris and Irma Adelman

Money, Interest, and Banking in Economic Development, by Maxwell Fry

Bureaucrats and People: Grassroots Participation in Third World Development, by John Montgomery

Indirect Taxation in Developing Economies, second edition, by John Due

Agricultural Development Principles: Economic Theory and Empirical Evidence, by Robert D. Stevens and Cathy L. Jabara

New Seeds and Poor People, by Michael Lipton with Richard Longhurst

Aid and Development, by Anne O. Krueger, Constantine Michalopoulos, Vernon W. Ruttan, and others

The Cuban Economy: Measurement and Analysis of Socialist Performance, by Andrew Zimbalist and Claes Brundenius

India's Semiarid Tropics, by Thomas Walker and James Ryan

Poverty Theory and Policy: A Study of Panama, by Gian Singh Sahota